Alok Vaid-Menon

Breaking Gender Norms with Fashion and Activism – Unauthorized

Shiro Kim

ISBN: 9781779695901
Imprint: Telephasic Workshop
Copyright © 2024 Shiro Kim.
All Rights Reserved.

Contents

Finding Their Voice   28
The Rise of a Social Media Sensation   50

Bibliography   **53**
Redefining Beauty Standards   73
A Champion for LGBTQ Rights   95

The Journey Continues   **121**
The Journey Continues   121
The Evolution of Alok's Activism   125

Bibliography   **133**
Alok's Influence on Pop Culture   148
Personal Life and Identity   170

Bibliography   **189**
Alok's Legacy   195

Beyond Gender Norms   **219**
Beyond Gender Norms   219
Alok's Manifesto for Gender Liberation   223
Alok's Artistic Expression   245
Empowering Marginalized Communities   268
Alok's Influence on Education   290

The Road Ahead   **317**
The Road Ahead   317
Alok's Evolution as an Activist   320
Alok's Message to the World   343

Index 367

Fashion Forward from the Start

From the very beginning, Alok Vaid-Menon has been a beacon of creativity and self-expression, using fashion as a powerful tool to challenge societal norms and redefine identity. This section delves into Alok's early fascination with fashion, the influences that shaped their unique style, and the pivotal moments that marked the beginning of their journey as a fashion icon.

1.1.1 A Love for Dressing Up

Alok's passion for fashion can be traced back to their childhood, where dressing up was not merely a form of play but a profound expression of self. This love for fashion was not just about aesthetics; it was a way to explore identity and challenge the rigid gender norms that often dictated how one should present themselves. Alok's early experiences of dressing up in various outfits were filled with joy and creativity, allowing them to express their individuality.

1.1.2 Early Influences and Inspirations

The world of fashion is often influenced by cultural icons, and Alok was no exception. Growing up, they were inspired by a diverse array of figures, from the flamboyant styles of RuPaul to the avant-garde aesthetics of designers like Jean-Paul Gaultier. These influences instilled in Alok a belief that fashion could transcend traditional boundaries and serve as a canvas for personal expression. The intersection of culture, art, and fashion became a significant theme in Alok's life, prompting them to embrace their identity in ways that were both bold and unapologetic.

1.1.3 Creating Their Own Style

As Alok navigated their teenage years, they began to cultivate a personal style that was distinctly their own. This process was not without challenges, as Alok faced societal pressures and expectations regarding gender presentation. However, rather than conforming, Alok chose to create a unique aesthetic that blended elements of femininity and masculinity. This fusion of styles became a hallmark of Alok's fashion identity, showcasing their belief that clothing should not be confined to binary definitions.

1.1.4 Pushing Boundaries in High School

High school can be a challenging environment for anyone, but for Alok, it was a stage for pushing boundaries. Alok's fearless approach to fashion often drew both admiration and criticism from peers. They utilized this platform to challenge the status quo, wearing outfits that defied gender norms and sparked conversations about identity and expression. Alok's high school experience was not just about personal style; it was a formative period that laid the groundwork for their future activism.

1.1.5 The Birth of a Fashion Icon

The moment Alok stepped onto the scene, it was clear that they were destined to become a fashion icon. Their distinctive style, characterized by bold patterns, vibrant colors, and an eclectic mix of garments, captured the attention of the fashion world. Alok's ability to blend high fashion with street style made them a trendsetter, inspiring others to embrace their own unique identities. This chapter of Alok's life marked the beginning of a journey that would intertwine fashion with activism.

1.1.6 Fashion as a Form of Self-Expression

For Alok, fashion transcends mere clothing; it is a vital form of self-expression. The act of choosing an outfit is imbued with meaning, allowing individuals to communicate their identity and emotions without uttering a single word. Alok's approach to fashion embodies the idea that clothing can serve as a powerful statement, challenging societal norms and encouraging others to embrace their authentic selves. This philosophy is rooted in the belief that fashion should be inclusive and accessible to all, regardless of gender identity.

1.1.7 The Influence of Gender and Identity

Alok's journey through fashion is inextricably linked to their exploration of gender and identity. As a non-binary individual, Alok challenges the traditional binary understanding of gender, advocating for a more fluid and inclusive perspective. Their fashion choices reflect this ideology, demonstrating that clothing can be a medium for exploring and expressing one's identity beyond societal constraints. Alok's influence extends beyond personal style; it serves as a catalyst for broader discussions about gender and identity in contemporary society.

1.1.8 Alok's Fashion Journey

Alok's fashion journey is a testament to the power of self-discovery and expression. Each outfit tells a story, reflecting their experiences, struggles, and triumphs. From vibrant gowns to tailored suits, Alok's wardrobe is a celebration of diversity and individuality. This journey is not just personal; it resonates with many who seek to navigate their own identities in a world that often imposes rigid definitions. Alok's journey serves as an inspiration for those who feel marginalized by conventional standards of beauty and gender.

1.1.9 Gaining Recognition in the Fashion Industry

As Alok's unique style gained traction, they began to receive recognition within the fashion industry. Collaborations with renowned designers and appearances at prestigious fashion events solidified Alok's status as a trailblazer. Their presence in the fashion world is not merely about aesthetics; it is a powerful statement advocating for inclusivity and representation. Alok's rise to prominence challenges the industry to reconsider its approach to diversity and the narratives surrounding gender and identity.

1.1.10 Poise and Confidence

Alok's poise and confidence are integral to their fashion identity. This self-assuredness stems from a deep understanding of their individuality and the importance of self-acceptance. Alok's ability to carry themselves with grace, regardless of societal judgment, serves as a powerful reminder of the strength that comes from embracing one's true self. This confidence is infectious, inspiring others to explore their own identities and express themselves freely through fashion.

In conclusion, Alok Vaid-Menon's journey in fashion is a multifaceted narrative that intertwines self-expression, activism, and the ongoing challenge of societal norms. From early influences to becoming a recognized fashion icon, Alok's story exemplifies the transformative power of fashion as a tool for identity exploration and advocacy. As they continue to break boundaries and redefine beauty standards, Alok remains a vital figure in the ongoing conversation about gender, identity, and self-expression in the world of fashion.

Fashion Forward from the Start

Alok Vaid-Menon's journey into the world of fashion began long before they became a household name in LGBTQ activism. From an early age, Alok exhibited an innate love for dressing up, a passion that would eventually evolve into a powerful medium for self-expression and activism. This section delves into the formative years of Alok's fashion journey, exploring their early influences, the challenges they faced, and the birth of their unique style that defied conventional norms.

1.1.1 A Love for Dressing Up

Fashion is not merely about clothing; it is a language of self-expression. For Alok, dressing up was a form of storytelling, a way to communicate their identity without uttering a single word. They often recount memories of raiding their mother's closet, experimenting with fabrics, textures, and colors. This early exploration laid the groundwork for their later endeavors in the fashion industry.

Alok's love for dressing up can be traced back to childhood, where they found joy in the transformative power of clothing. This passion was not just about aesthetics; it was about embodying different facets of their identity. The act of dressing became a ritual of self-affirmation, allowing Alok to navigate the complexities of gender and identity in a world that often imposed rigid norms.

1.1.2 Early Influences and Inspirations

The influences on Alok's fashion sense were diverse and profound. Growing up in a multicultural environment, they were exposed to a myriad of styles, traditions, and cultural expressions. From Bollywood films to the vibrant street fashion of their community, Alok drew inspiration from the rich tapestry of cultural narratives surrounding them.

One significant influence was the concept of *gender fluidity*, which Alok encountered through various artistic expressions. This exposure to non-binary representations in art, literature, and media allowed Alok to envision a world where fashion transcended the binary constructs of male and female. They began to embrace clothing as a means of challenging societal expectations, paving the way for their future as a fashion icon.

1.1.3 Creating Their Own Style

As Alok entered high school, they began to consciously create their own style, one that reflected their individuality and challenged the norms of gendered fashion. They experimented with bold colors, oversized silhouettes, and gender-neutral clothing, often mixing elements traditionally associated with masculinity and femininity.

Alok's style became a canvas for their activism. By wearing outfits that defied gender norms, they sent a powerful message about the fluidity of identity. This bold approach attracted attention, both positive and negative, and laid the foundation for Alok's role as a trailblazer in the fashion world.

1.1.4 Pushing Boundaries in High School

High school can be a challenging time for anyone, but for Alok, it was a battleground for self-expression. They faced significant backlash for their fashion choices, often being subjected to ridicule and discrimination. However, rather than succumbing to societal pressures, Alok used these experiences to fuel their passion for activism.

During this period, Alok began to understand the intersection of fashion and identity politics. They recognized that their clothing choices were not just personal expressions but also political statements. This realization propelled them into the world of LGBTQ activism, where they would use fashion as a tool for change.

1.1.5 The Birth of a Fashion Icon

Alok's unique approach to fashion did not go unnoticed. Their fearless style and commitment to authenticity began to resonate with a broader audience. As they gained recognition, Alok became a symbol of empowerment for many in the LGBTQ community, proving that fashion could be a powerful form of resistance against societal norms.

The emergence of social media played a crucial role in Alok's rise as a fashion icon. Platforms like Instagram allowed them to showcase their eclectic style to a global audience, inspiring countless individuals to embrace their identities unapologetically. Alok's fashion became synonymous with self-love, challenging the traditional notions of beauty and encouraging others to break free from societal constraints.

1.1.6 Fashion as a Form of Self-Expression

At its core, fashion is an art form, and for Alok, it served as a vital means of self-expression. They believed that clothing could convey emotions, narratives, and identities in ways that words often could not. Alok's outfits became expressions of their inner self, allowing them to articulate their experiences as a gender non-conforming individual.

This philosophy is grounded in the idea of *performative identity*, where individuals use clothing and style to construct and communicate their identities. Alok's fashion choices were not merely aesthetic; they were deeply personal, representing a journey of self-discovery and acceptance.

1.1.7 The Influence of Gender and Identity

Alok's fashion journey is inextricably linked to their exploration of gender and identity. They challenged the binary notions of masculinity and femininity, advocating for a more inclusive understanding of gender expression. Alok's work highlights the importance of recognizing the fluidity of identity, urging society to embrace diversity in all its forms.

This perspective is supported by Judith Butler's theory of gender performativity, which posits that gender is not an inherent quality but rather a series of performances shaped by societal expectations. Alok's fashion choices exemplify this theory, as they intentionally subvert traditional gender norms through their unique style.

1.1.8 Alok's Fashion Journey

Alok's fashion journey is a testament to the transformative power of self-expression. From their early days of experimenting with clothing to becoming a recognized figure in the fashion industry, Alok has continuously pushed the boundaries of what it means to be stylish and authentic. Their journey reflects a broader cultural shift towards inclusivity and acceptance in fashion.

As Alok navigated the complexities of the fashion world, they remained committed to their roots, using their platform to uplift marginalized voices and advocate for change. This duality of being both a fashion icon and an activist has allowed Alok to create a lasting impact on the industry.

1.1.9 Gaining Recognition in the Fashion Industry

Alok's unique style and unapologetic approach to fashion garnered attention from industry leaders and fashion enthusiasts alike. They began to collaborate with renowned designers and brands, further solidifying their status as a fashion icon. These collaborations not only showcased Alok's creativity but also challenged the industry to embrace diversity and inclusivity.

One notable partnership was with a major fashion brand that sought to promote gender-neutral clothing. Alok's involvement in this campaign highlighted the importance of representation in the fashion industry, demonstrating that style knows no gender. This collaboration served as a pivotal moment in Alok's career, illustrating the potential for fashion to be a vehicle for social change.

1.1.10 Poise and Confidence

Throughout their journey, Alok has exemplified poise and confidence, traits that have become synonymous with their public persona. This confidence is not merely an external facade; it is rooted in a deep understanding of self-worth and authenticity. Alok's ability to navigate the complexities of the fashion industry while remaining true to their identity serves as an inspiration to many.

In a world that often seeks to impose limitations on individual expression, Alok's journey stands as a powerful reminder of the importance of embracing one's true self. Their story encourages others to find the courage to express their identities boldly, paving the way for a more inclusive and accepting future in fashion and beyond.

In conclusion, Alok Vaid-Menon's journey in fashion is a rich tapestry woven with threads of self-expression, activism, and resilience. From their early love for dressing up to becoming a global fashion icon, Alok has continuously challenged societal norms and inspired others to embrace their authentic selves. Their story is a testament to the power of fashion as a tool for change, illustrating that style can be a powerful medium for self-affirmation and activism.

ERROR. thisXsection() returned an empty string with textbook depth = 3.
ERROR. thisXsection() returned an empty string with textbook depth = 3.
ERROR. thisXsection() returned an empty string with textbook depth = 3.

Early Influences and Inspirations

From the very beginning of Alok Vaid-Menon's journey, the seeds of inspiration were sown in a rich tapestry of cultural influences, familial support, and the vibrant world of fashion. Growing up in a multicultural environment, Alok was surrounded by a myriad of styles and expressions that shaped their understanding of identity and creativity.

Cultural Heritage

Alok's Indian heritage played a pivotal role in their early influences. The colors, patterns, and textures found in traditional Indian clothing—such as saris and kurtas—sparked a fascination with fashion as a form of storytelling. The intricate designs often convey deeper meanings, rooted in history and culture. This cultural backdrop not only provided Alok with a sense of identity but also instilled a belief in the power of fashion to transcend societal norms.

Family Support

Family support was crucial in Alok's formative years. Their parents, who were open-minded and encouraging, nurtured Alok's love for dressing up. They recognized early on that Alok had a unique sense of style that defied conventional gender norms. This acceptance fostered a safe space for self-expression. Alok often recalls how their mother would take them shopping for vibrant clothing, allowing them to explore their individuality freely. This familial encouragement laid the groundwork for Alok's future as a fashion icon and activist.

Pop Culture Icons

In addition to their cultural roots and family, Alok drew inspiration from various pop culture icons. Figures such as RuPaul, Prince, and David Bowie were instrumental in shaping Alok's understanding of gender fluidity and self-expression. These artists challenged traditional gender roles and showcased the beauty of breaking free from societal constraints. Alok admired how these icons used their platforms to advocate for change, sparking a desire within them to do the same.

Theoretical Framework

To understand the influence of these early inspirations, we can refer to Judith Butler's theory of gender performativity. Butler argues that gender is not a fixed identity but rather a series of performances shaped by societal expectations. Alok's early experiences reflect this notion, as they navigated their identity through the lens of cultural, familial, and pop culture influences. The interplay of these factors allowed Alok to construct a fluid sense of self, one that embraced both femininity and masculinity.

Fashion as Resistance

Alok's early influences also highlight the role of fashion as a form of resistance. In a society that often imposes rigid gender norms, Alok's choice to dress in a way that defied these expectations became a powerful act of defiance. By embracing their unique style, Alok not only celebrated their individuality but also challenged the status quo. This notion aligns with bell hooks' concept of "the radical potential of style," which suggests that fashion can serve as a means of empowerment and political expression.

Personal Anecdotes

Alok's early experiences are peppered with anecdotes that illustrate the impact of these influences. For instance, they recall a particular moment in high school when they wore a sequined dress to a school event. The reactions were mixed—some celebrated Alok's boldness, while others were less accepting. However, this experience solidified Alok's commitment to using fashion as a tool for self-expression and activism. It was a defining moment that demonstrated the power of individuality in the face of adversity.

Conclusion

In conclusion, Alok Vaid-Menon's early influences and inspirations were a confluence of cultural heritage, familial support, pop culture icons, and theoretical frameworks. These elements shaped their understanding of identity and the transformative power of fashion. By embracing their unique style, Alok not only paved the way for their journey as a fashion icon but also laid the foundation for their activism, challenging societal norms and advocating for a more inclusive world. This rich tapestry of influences continues to inspire Alok as they break gender norms and empower others to do the same.

Creating Their Own Style

Alok Vaid-Menon's journey in fashion is not merely a personal expression but a bold declaration of identity that challenges societal norms and expectations. From an early age, Alok began to craft a style that was distinctly their own, blending various influences and cultural references to create a visual language that resonates with authenticity. This section delves into the intricacies of how Alok developed their unique style, the theoretical frameworks that inform their choices, and the broader implications of such self-expression in the context of gender and identity.

Theoretical Frameworks of Style Creation

Creating a personal style is often rooted in theories of identity and self-expression. According to *Erving Goffman's* theory of self-presentation, individuals curate their appearances to convey specific messages about their identities to others. Alok's style can be seen as a form of **performative identity**, where clothing choices serve as a medium to express their gender fluidity and challenge binary norms.

The concept of *intersectionality*, introduced by *Kimberlé Crenshaw*, also plays a significant role in understanding Alok's fashion choices. Intersectionality recognizes that individuals experience multiple, overlapping identities—such as race, gender, and sexuality—that shape their experiences and expressions. Alok's style is a vivid tapestry that reflects their South Asian heritage, queerness, and commitment to social justice, creating a multifaceted representation of identity.

Early Influences and Inspirations

Alok's early influences were a melange of cultural icons, family traditions, and personal experiences. Growing up, they were inspired by the flamboyant styles of Bollywood stars, the avant-garde aesthetics of fashion designers, and the vibrant colors of South Asian textiles. These influences coalesced into a unique vision that was both a homage to their roots and a rebellion against conventional expectations of gendered clothing.

For instance, Alok has often cited the influence of their grandmother, who would drape colorful saris and wear intricate jewelry. This familial connection to fashion instilled in them an appreciation for clothing as a narrative tool, a way to tell stories about identity, culture, and resistance. Alok's style often incorporates elements traditionally associated with femininity, such as skirts and makeup, juxtaposed with androgynous silhouettes that defy categorization.

Pushing Boundaries in Fashion

Alok's commitment to creating their own style is deeply intertwined with their desire to push boundaries. In high school, Alok faced challenges when expressing their unique fashion sense, often encountering resistance from peers and authority figures. However, these challenges only fueled their determination to embrace and amplify their identity through clothing.

The act of wearing what society deems unconventional is a form of **subversion**. Alok's bold choices—such as pairing a flowing skirt with combat boots or donning a sequined top with oversized trousers—serve as a statement against rigid gender norms. This approach not only redefines beauty standards but also encourages others to explore their own identities without fear of judgment.

Fashion as a Form of Self-Expression

For Alok, fashion is not merely about aesthetics; it is a powerful form of self-expression and a vehicle for activism. Alok's style embodies a philosophy of **radical self-love**, where embracing one's authentic self is an act of defiance against societal pressures. This philosophy is echoed in their public appearances, where Alok's outfits often carry messages of empowerment and inclusivity.

Alok's fashion choices also challenge the notion of a singular beauty standard. By showcasing a diverse array of styles, Alok emphasizes that beauty is not confined to traditional norms but is instead a spectrum that includes all forms of expression. This perspective resonates with many individuals who feel marginalized by mainstream beauty ideals, empowering them to embrace their unique identities.

The Influence of Gender and Identity

Alok's journey of creating their own style is deeply connected to the exploration of gender and identity. In a world that often seeks to categorize individuals, Alok's fashion choices defy easy labels. They embody a fluidity that reflects the complexities of gender identity, challenging the binary conception of male and female.

This fluidity is evident in Alok's use of color, texture, and form. By embracing garments that are traditionally associated with different genders, Alok dismantles the rigid structures that dictate how one should dress based on their assigned gender at birth. This approach not only liberates Alok but also inspires others to question and redefine their own relationships with clothing and identity.

Gaining Recognition in the Fashion Industry

As Alok continued to develop their unique style, they gained recognition within the fashion industry. Their innovative approach to fashion—combining elements of traditional South Asian attire with contemporary streetwear—caught the attention of designers and brands seeking to embrace diversity and inclusivity.

Alok's collaborations with various designers have further solidified their position as a fashion icon. By working with brands that prioritize ethical production and representation, Alok amplifies messages of social justice while redefining what it means to be fashionable. Their presence on runways and in campaigns serves as a powerful reminder that fashion can be a platform for change.

Conclusion

In conclusion, Alok Vaid-Menon's journey in creating their own style is a testament to the power of self-expression and the importance of challenging societal norms. By embracing a multifaceted approach to fashion that incorporates their cultural heritage, personal experiences, and activist ideals, Alok has not only carved out a unique space for themselves but has also inspired countless others to do the same. Their story illustrates that fashion is not just about clothing; it is a vibrant form of identity that can empower individuals to embrace their authentic selves and advocate for a more inclusive world.

Pushing Boundaries in High School

High school is often a crucible for self-discovery, where identities are forged, challenged, and reshaped. For Alok Vaid-Menon, this period was no exception. It was a time marked by a vibrant exploration of fashion and identity, as they began to push the boundaries of traditional gender norms.

Alok's journey in high school can be understood through the lens of Judith Butler's theory of gender performativity, which posits that gender is not an inherent quality but rather a series of performances shaped by societal expectations. This theoretical framework highlights how Alok's choices in fashion were not merely personal expressions but also acts of defiance against the rigid binaries of gender that dominated their environment.

$$G = P \times C \tag{1}$$

Where:

- G = Gender expression
- P = Personal identity
- C = Cultural context

In this equation, Alok's gender expression (G) was a product of their personal identity (P) and the cultural context (C) of their high school. The school environment, often a microcosm of broader societal norms, imposed strict expectations on how individuals should present themselves. Alok, however, began to challenge these norms through bold fashion choices that defied categorization.

During this time, Alok's wardrobe became a canvas for experimentation. They infused their outfits with bright colors, patterns, and accessories that expressed their fluid identity. This was not without its challenges, as high school can be a hostile environment for those who dare to deviate from the norm. Alok faced backlash from peers who adhered to conventional standards of masculinity and femininity. Yet, it was precisely this adversity that fueled their resolve to assert their individuality.

One notable incident occurred during a school assembly when Alok decided to wear a flamboyant outfit that included a sequined jacket and high-heeled boots. This choice was a direct challenge to the expectations of their peers, who were accustomed to seeing students dressed in muted tones and traditional attire. The reaction was mixed; while some classmates celebrated Alok's audacity, others responded with ridicule and harassment. This moment encapsulated the duality of high school life for LGBTQ youth—where visibility can lead to both empowerment and vulnerability.

Alok's experiences in high school also underscore the importance of allyship and support systems. They found solace in a small group of friends who encouraged their self-expression and stood by them in the face of adversity. This camaraderie not only provided emotional support but also fostered a sense of community that was crucial for navigating the complexities of identity during adolescence.

The act of pushing boundaries in high school was not just about fashion; it was also a profound exploration of identity. Alok began to engage with concepts of intersectionality, recognizing how their experiences as a queer person of color intersected with broader societal issues. This understanding laid the groundwork for their future activism, as they became increasingly aware of the systemic forces that sought to marginalize individuals based on their gender and sexual orientation.

In reflection, Alok's high school years were a formative period that shaped their identity and activism. They learned that pushing boundaries often comes with risks, but it also opens doors to authenticity and self-acceptance. This chapter of their life serves as a reminder of the resilience required to navigate a world that often imposes rigid definitions of identity.

Through their journey, Alok exemplified the spirit of defiance and creativity that is essential for challenging societal norms. Their high school experience is a testament to the power of self-expression and the importance of creating inclusive spaces where all individuals can thrive, regardless of their gender identity or expression. As Alok continued to push boundaries, they not only carved out a space for themselves but also inspired countless others to embrace their authentic selves, setting the stage for their future as a prominent LGBTQ activist and fashion icon.

The Birth of a Fashion Icon

Alok Vaid-Menon's journey into the limelight of fashion did not simply emerge from a love for clothing; it was a confluence of self-expression, cultural commentary, and an audacious challenge to societal norms. The birth of a fashion icon is often marked by a pivotal moment—a spark that ignites a passion and propels an individual into a realm of influence. For Alok, this moment was not just a singular event but a series of transformative experiences that shaped their identity and style.

Defining Fashion Iconography

To understand the emergence of Alok as a fashion icon, one must first define what it means to be a fashion icon. According to fashion theorist Valerie Steele, a fashion icon embodies a unique aesthetic that resonates with the public and challenges conventional beauty standards. This is not merely about clothing choices but about the narrative that these choices convey. Alok's fashion is deeply intertwined with their activism, creating a visual language that speaks to both personal identity and broader social issues.

Cultural Context and Influence

Growing up in a culturally rich environment, Alok was influenced by a diverse array of styles and expressions. The intersection of their Indian heritage and Western fashion trends provided a fertile ground for experimentation. Alok's early influences included not only traditional Indian garments but also the avant-garde styles seen on runways around the world. This blend of cultural elements allowed Alok to create a style that was both personal and universally relatable.

Pushing Boundaries in High School

During their high school years, Alok began to push the boundaries of gendered fashion. Alok recalls, "I started wearing what felt right, regardless of whether it was deemed appropriate for my gender. I wore skirts, makeup, and vibrant colors. My peers were confused, but I was liberated." This statement encapsulates the essence of Alok's journey—fashion as a form of rebellion and liberation.

In high school, Alok faced challenges that many LGBTQ youth encounter: bullying, isolation, and a struggle for acceptance. Yet, it was through this adversity that Alok honed their fashion sense, using clothing as armor against societal rejection. This period marked the beginning of Alok's identity as a fashion icon, as they learned to navigate the complexities of self-expression amidst a backdrop of societal expectations.

The Role of Social Media

With the advent of social media, Alok found a platform to showcase their unique style to a broader audience. Platforms like Instagram and TikTok became vital tools for self-expression and visibility. Alok's posts often feature bold outfits that defy gender norms, accompanied by messages of empowerment and self-love. This strategic use of social media not only garnered Alok a following but also positioned them as a thought leader in both fashion and activism.

The phenomenon of "influencer culture" has transformed the fashion industry, allowing individuals who might have been overlooked by traditional media to gain recognition. Alok capitalized on this shift, using their platform to challenge the fashion industry's often narrow definitions of beauty and gender. The impact of Alok's online presence can be quantified through engagement metrics, where posts featuring their signature looks often garner thousands of likes and shares, amplifying their message of inclusivity.

Fashion as a Form of Activism

Alok's rise as a fashion icon is inextricably linked to their activism. Each outfit serves as a canvas for expression, telling a story of resilience and defiance. For instance, Alok often incorporates elements of traditional Indian attire, such as saris and lehengas, into contemporary looks, thus celebrating their heritage while challenging Western-centric beauty standards. This blend of cultural pride and modern aesthetics positions Alok not just as a fashion icon but as a cultural commentator.

Furthermore, Alok's advocacy for body positivity and gender fluidity is woven into their fashion choices. By embracing a style that transcends traditional gender norms, Alok invites others to explore their own identities and expressions. This message resonates with many, particularly within the LGBTQ community, where the struggle for acceptance often intersects with issues of body image and self-worth.

Recognition and Influence

As Alok's visibility grew, so did their recognition within the fashion industry. Collaborations with renowned designers and brands followed, allowing Alok to further influence mainstream fashion. Their presence at major fashion events, such as New York Fashion Week, solidified Alok's status as a fashion icon. Alok's ability to navigate these spaces while remaining true to their identity is a testament to their influence.

In 2021, Alok was featured in a campaign for a major fashion brand, which celebrated diversity and inclusion. This collaboration not only highlighted Alok's unique style but also emphasized the importance of representation in fashion. The campaign was widely praised for its authenticity and commitment to challenging societal norms.

Conclusion: The Icon's Journey

The birth of Alok Vaid-Menon as a fashion icon is a multifaceted journey marked by personal struggles, cultural influences, and a commitment to activism. Alok's ability to blend fashion with a powerful message of self-love and acceptance has not only redefined their own identity but has also inspired countless others to embrace their authentic selves. As Alok continues to break down barriers and challenge the status quo, their legacy as a fashion icon will undoubtedly leave an indelible mark on the industry and society at large.

In the words of Alok, "Fashion is not just what you wear; it's how you express who you are." This encapsulates the essence of their journey—the transformation from an individual exploring their identity to a beacon of hope and inspiration for many.

Fashion as a Form of Self-Expression

Fashion is not merely a series of trends dictated by the whims of the industry; it is a profound language through which individuals articulate their identities, beliefs, and emotions. For Alok Vaid-Menon, fashion serves as a vibrant canvas for self-expression, a means to challenge societal norms, and a powerful tool for activism. This section delves into the multifaceted relationship between fashion and self-expression, exploring its theoretical underpinnings, the problems it addresses, and real-world examples that illustrate its transformative potential.

Theoretical Framework

The concept of fashion as self-expression can be traced back to several theoretical frameworks, including symbolic interactionism and postmodernism. Symbolic interactionism posits that individuals create meaning through social interactions, where clothing acts as a symbol reflecting personal identity and social status. According to [?], individuals perform their identities in everyday life, much like actors on a stage, where clothing becomes a crucial prop in this performance.

In the postmodern context, fashion is seen as a medium that transcends traditional boundaries of identity. [?] argues that fashion is a simulacrum, a representation that creates its own reality. In this sense, Alok's fashion choices not only reflect their identity but also challenge the very constructs of gender and beauty, creating a new narrative that encourages others to embrace their authentic selves.

Fashion as a Political Statement

Alok Vaid-Menon's approach to fashion is inherently political. By donning garments that defy conventional gender norms, Alok critiques the binary understanding of gender that has dominated society for centuries. The act of wearing a skirt, for example, is not just a personal choice; it is a statement that challenges the patriarchal structures that dictate what is deemed acceptable for different genders. This aligns with Judith Butler's theory of gender performativity, which suggests that gender is not an innate quality but rather a performance shaped by societal expectations [?].

Alok's fashion choices often include bold colors, intricate patterns, and unconventional silhouettes, which serve to disrupt the status quo. For instance, during a public appearance at a fashion event, Alok wore a striking ensemble that combined traditional Indian attire with modern elements, symbolizing the intersection of culture and identity. Such choices not only highlight Alok's personal style but also serve as a critique of the homogenization of beauty standards in the fashion industry.

Challenges in Fashion as Self-Expression

While fashion can be a liberating form of self-expression, it is not without its challenges. The fashion industry has historically marginalized voices that do not conform to mainstream ideals, particularly those of LGBTQ individuals and people of color. Alok's journey in the fashion world illustrates the difficulties faced by those who challenge traditional norms. They have encountered backlash, criticism, and even hostility for their choices, yet they persist in using fashion as a means of defiance.

One significant challenge is the pervasive nature of gatekeeping within the fashion industry. Many designers and brands have been slow to embrace diversity, often prioritizing profit over representation. This exclusionary practice can create an environment where individuals like Alok feel pressured to conform to narrow definitions of beauty and style. However, Alok's advocacy for inclusivity has sparked conversations about the need for change within the industry, highlighting the importance of representation for marginalized communities.

Real-World Examples

Alok's impact on fashion as a form of self-expression is evident through various initiatives and collaborations. For instance, their partnership with renowned designer **Prabal Gurung** resulted in a collection that celebrated fluidity and diversity. The campaign featured models of varying sizes, ethnicities, and genders, reinforcing the message that fashion should be accessible to all. This collaboration not only showcased Alok's unique aesthetic but also sent a powerful message about inclusivity in an industry often criticized for its lack of representation.

Moreover, Alok's use of social media platforms has amplified their message, allowing them to reach a global audience. Through platforms like Instagram, Alok shares their fashion choices, often accompanied by poignant captions that challenge societal norms. This direct engagement with followers fosters a sense of community and encourages others to embrace their identities unapologetically.

Conclusion

In conclusion, fashion serves as a vital form of self-expression for Alok Vaid-Menon, enabling them to challenge societal norms and advocate for inclusivity. Through their bold choices and unwavering commitment to authenticity, Alok illustrates the transformative power of fashion as a medium for identity and activism. The journey of self-expression in fashion is not without its challenges, but it is through these struggles that individuals can carve out spaces for themselves and inspire others to do the same. As Alok continues to break boundaries and redefine beauty standards, they remind us that fashion is not just about clothing; it is about the stories we tell and the identities we embrace.

The Influence of Gender and Identity

In the vibrant tapestry of contemporary society, gender and identity play pivotal roles, shaping our interactions, perceptions, and the very fabric of our communities. Alok Vaid-Menon, as a prominent figure in the LGBTQ activism landscape, embodies the complexities of gender identity and its profound influence on personal and societal levels.

Theoretical Frameworks

To understand the influence of gender and identity, we must first explore the foundational theories that inform these concepts. Judith Butler's theory of gender performativity posits that gender is not an inherent trait but rather a series of behaviors and performances that individuals enact based on societal expectations. This perspective challenges traditional binary notions of gender, suggesting that identity is fluid and constructed through repeated actions. Formally, Butler's theory can be expressed in the following equation:

$$G = P_1 + P_2 + \ldots + P_n$$

where G represents gender, and P_i denotes the various performances that contribute to one's gender identity. This equation illustrates that gender is not a singular entity but a composite of multiple influences and expressions.

The Intersection of Identity and Society

Alok's journey reflects the intersectionality of identity, where factors such as race, class, and sexuality converge to shape one's experiences. Kimberlé Crenshaw's concept of intersectionality highlights how overlapping social identities can lead to unique forms of discrimination and privilege. For instance, Alok, as a South Asian non-binary individual, navigates a complex landscape where cultural expectations and societal norms intersect with their gender identity.

This intersectionality can lead to challenges, such as the struggle for acceptance within both LGBTQ spaces and broader society. Alok's experiences underscore the importance of recognizing these complexities, as they reveal the multifaceted nature of identity and the need for inclusive dialogue.

Personal Narratives and Societal Impact

Alok's influence extends beyond personal expression; it resonates with a broader audience, challenging societal norms and advocating for a more inclusive understanding of gender. Their work in art and fashion serves as a powerful medium for exploring identity. By embracing non-binary aesthetics, Alok not only asserts their identity but also invites others to question the rigid boundaries of gender.

For example, Alok's fashion choices often incorporate elements traditionally associated with femininity and masculinity, defying societal expectations. This bold approach not only empowers Alok but also inspires others to embrace their authentic selves. As they state, "Fashion is a tool for liberation," emphasizing that self-expression through clothing can challenge normative constructs of gender.

The Role of Media and Representation

Media representation plays a crucial role in shaping societal perceptions of gender and identity. Alok's visibility in various media platforms has sparked conversations around non-binary identities and the need for diverse representation. The portrayal of gender non-conforming individuals in popular culture can either reinforce stereotypes or challenge them, influencing public understanding and acceptance.

Research indicates that increased representation of LGBTQ individuals in media correlates with greater societal acceptance. For instance, shows like "Pose" and "RuPaul's Drag Race" have brought visibility to transgender and non-binary narratives, fostering a more inclusive environment. Alok's participation in these platforms amplifies the message that gender identity is a spectrum, encouraging audiences to embrace diversity.

Challenges and Resistance

Despite progress, challenges persist in the journey toward acceptance of diverse gender identities. Transphobia, misogyny, and systemic discrimination continue to affect the lives of many, including Alok. The backlash against non-binary identities often stems from a lack of understanding and entrenched societal norms. Alok's advocacy highlights the importance of education and awareness in combating these issues.

The resistance faced by individuals like Alok serves as a reminder of the ongoing struggle for recognition and acceptance. It underscores the necessity for allies and advocates to engage in conversations that challenge harmful stereotypes and promote inclusivity.

Conclusion

The influence of gender and identity is a dynamic and evolving discourse, intricately woven into the fabric of society. Alok Vaid-Menon's journey exemplifies the power of self-expression and the importance of embracing one's identity in the face of societal challenges. Through their activism, Alok not only advocates for personal liberation but also fosters a collective movement toward a more inclusive and understanding world. As we continue to explore the complexities of gender, it is essential to recognize the diverse narratives that contribute to this ongoing dialogue, ultimately paving the way for a future where all identities are celebrated and respected.

Alok's Fashion Journey

Alok Vaid-Menon's fashion journey is a vibrant tapestry woven from threads of personal expression, cultural heritage, and a relentless challenge to societal norms. From their earliest days, Alok has approached fashion not merely as a means of dressing but as a profound form of self-expression, embodying their identity and beliefs.

Fashion, as theorized by sociologist *Thorstein Veblen*, is often a reflection of social status and cultural capital. Alok's journey begins with an understanding of this concept, as they navigated the complexities of identity within the confines of societal expectations. Alok's early influences were diverse, drawing inspiration from a range of sources including Bollywood films, traditional Indian attire, and the avant-garde styles of queer icons. This eclectic mix laid the foundation for a unique aesthetic that defied conventional categorizations.

Creating Their Own Style

As Alok progressed through high school, they began to experiment with their wardrobe, pushing boundaries and challenging the binary notions of gendered clothing. This period was marked by a significant transformation, as Alok embraced vibrant colors, bold patterns, and intricate accessories. The act of dressing became a form of rebellion against the restrictive norms imposed by society.

In the words of fashion theorist *Judith Butler*, gender is performative; it is not merely something one is, but rather something one does. Alok's fashion choices exemplified this performativity, as they utilized clothing to navigate and articulate their gender identity. Each outfit became a statement, a canvas upon which Alok painted their narrative of fluidity and self-acceptance.

Pushing Boundaries in High School

High school can be a challenging environment for self-expression, particularly for those who diverge from the norm. Alok faced significant challenges during this time, including bullying and ostracization. However, these experiences only fueled their determination to embrace their identity through fashion. Alok's bold choices often sparked conversations, forcing peers and educators alike to confront their preconceived notions about gender and expression.

Alok's ability to navigate these challenges is a testament to their resilience. By wearing what they loved, Alok not only found personal empowerment but also became a catalyst for change within their school community. This period was crucial in solidifying Alok's belief that fashion could be a powerful tool for activism.

The Birth of a Fashion Icon

As Alok transitioned into adulthood, their fashion journey gained momentum. They began to gain recognition in the fashion industry, not just for their unique style but also for their advocacy for LGBTQ rights. Alok's presence on social media platforms allowed them to showcase their fashion choices to a broader audience, further solidifying their status as a fashion icon.

Alok's fashion journey is characterized by a commitment to inclusivity and diversity. They have collaborated with various designers and brands, emphasizing the importance of representation in the fashion world. Alok's work challenges the traditional beauty standards that often exclude marginalized communities. Their mantra, "fashion is for everyone," resonates deeply within the industry, encouraging others to embrace their authentic selves.

Fashion as a Form of Self-Expression

Alok's fashion choices reflect a deep understanding of the intersectionality of identity. They have often stated that clothing is a language through which they communicate their identity and beliefs. This perspective aligns with the theory of *Cultural Studies*, which posits that fashion is a site of cultural negotiation where individuals can assert their identity and challenge societal norms.

For Alok, fashion is not merely about aesthetics; it is a form of resistance against a world that seeks to confine individuals to rigid categories. Their journey is a celebration of individuality, showcasing the beauty of self-expression in all its forms.

Gaining Recognition in the Fashion Industry

Alok's rise to prominence in the fashion industry has been marked by notable collaborations and appearances in prestigious fashion events. Their work has garnered attention from major fashion publications, highlighting the importance of inclusivity in an industry that has historically been exclusionary.

For instance, Alok's collaboration with the brand *Ganni* emphasized sustainable fashion practices while promoting a message of self-acceptance. This partnership exemplified how fashion can be both a personal statement and a platform for broader social issues.

Poise and Confidence

Central to Alok's fashion journey is the embodiment of poise and confidence. They have often shared that true style comes from within, and that confidence is the ultimate accessory. This philosophy resonates with the concept of *self-actualization* in Maslow's hierarchy of needs, where the realization of one's potential is paramount.

Alok's journey serves as a powerful reminder that fashion is not just about clothing but about the stories we tell and the identities we embody. Through their fashion journey, Alok has inspired countless individuals to embrace their uniqueness, fostering a culture of acceptance and love.

In conclusion, Alok Vaid-Menon's fashion journey is a multifaceted narrative that intertwines personal expression, cultural critique, and social activism. Their evolution from a young individual navigating the complexities of identity to a recognized fashion icon is a testament to the power of self-expression in challenging societal norms. Alok's journey continues to inspire others to break free from the confines of traditional gender norms and embrace their authentic selves through the transformative power of fashion.

Gaining Recognition in the Fashion Industry

Alok Vaid-Menon's rise to prominence in the fashion industry is a remarkable journey that intertwines creativity, activism, and a profound understanding of identity. This section explores the various facets of Alok's recognition, highlighting the challenges faced and the strategies employed to carve out a space in a traditionally rigid industry.

The Fashion Landscape: A Brief Overview

The fashion industry, often perceived as a glamorous realm, is underpinned by complex social dynamics and cultural narratives. Historically, it has been dominated by narrow standards of beauty and rigid gender norms. According to fashion theorist *Katherine Hamnett*, the industry often perpetuates a binary view of gender, which marginalizes non-conforming identities. Alok's entry into this landscape not only challenged these norms but also initiated a broader dialogue on inclusivity and representation.

Breaking Through the Noise

In a world saturated with visual stimuli, gaining recognition requires more than just talent; it demands a unique voice and perspective. Alok's distinctive approach to fashion—characterized by vibrant colors, bold patterns, and a fluid aesthetic—set them apart from conventional designers. This originality was not merely a personal statement; it was a political act that questioned the very fabric of gender expression.

One key moment that marked Alok's ascent was their participation in various fashion shows and events that championed diversity. For instance, their appearance at the *New York Fashion Week* in 2019 showcased not only their fashion sense but also their commitment to activism. They wore a striking ensemble that combined traditional South Asian garments with contemporary fashion, symbolizing a fusion of cultures and identities. This moment resonated with audiences, sparking conversations about cultural appropriation and the need for authentic representation in fashion.

The Role of Social Media

In the digital age, social media has become a powerful tool for artists and activists alike. Alok harnessed platforms like Instagram and TikTok to showcase their fashion choices, share personal narratives, and engage with a global audience. The use of hashtags such as #GenderNonconforming and #FashionForAll played a pivotal role in amplifying their message.

According to a study by *Pew Research Center*, 72% of teens use Instagram, making it a prime platform for influencing fashion trends. Alok's ability to connect with younger audiences through relatable content and unapologetic self-expression contributed significantly to their recognition in the fashion industry. Their viral videos, often blending humor with poignant commentary on gender and identity, attracted millions of views, further solidifying their status as a fashion icon.

Collaborations and Partnerships

Recognition in the fashion industry is often accompanied by collaborations with established brands and designers. Alok's partnerships with inclusive fashion labels, such as *Savage X Fenty* and *Collina Strada*, exemplify this trend. These collaborations not only elevated Alok's profile but also challenged the brands to rethink their approaches to inclusivity.

For instance, during a collaboration with *Savage X Fenty*, Alok designed a capsule collection that featured gender-neutral lingerie. This collection was celebrated for its innovative designs that catered to a diverse range of body types and gender identities. The success of this partnership highlighted the market's growing demand for inclusivity and representation, further cementing Alok's influence in the industry.

Challenges and Triumphs

Despite the accolades and recognition, Alok's journey was not without challenges. The fashion industry, while evolving, still harbors deep-rooted biases and systemic barriers. Alok faced criticism and pushback from traditionalists who resisted the shift towards inclusivity. However, rather than retreating, they used these challenges as fuel for their activism.

Alok's resilience is exemplified in their response to online hate and trolling. They famously stated, "Hate is just a reflection of their insecurities, not mine." This mindset not only empowered Alok but also inspired others in the LGBTQ+ community to embrace their identities unapologetically.

Theoretical Frameworks: Understanding Recognition

To analyze Alok's recognition in the fashion industry, we can apply *Bourdieu's Theory of Cultural Capital*. According to Pierre Bourdieu, cultural capital encompasses the non-financial social assets that promote social mobility. Alok's unique blend of fashion, activism, and personal narrative serves as a form of cultural capital, allowing them to navigate and ultimately reshape the fashion landscape.

The equation representing cultural capital can be expressed as:

$$CC = (E + S + A)$$

where: - CC = Cultural Capital - E = Education and Knowledge - S = Social Networks - A = Artistic Expression

In Alok's case, their education in performance art, extensive social networks within the LGBTQ+ community, and innovative artistic expression all contribute to their cultural capital, facilitating their recognition in the fashion industry.

Conclusion: A New Era of Fashion

Alok Vaid-Menon's journey to recognition in the fashion industry is a testament to the power of self-expression and activism. By challenging traditional norms and advocating for inclusivity, Alok has not only carved out a niche for themselves but has also paved the way for future generations of fashion innovators. As the industry continues to evolve, Alok's influence serves as a beacon of hope, reminding us that fashion can be a powerful tool for change.

In summary, gaining recognition in the fashion industry is not merely about aesthetics; it is about challenging norms, embracing diversity, and using one's platform to advocate for marginalized voices. Alok's story exemplifies this intersection of fashion and activism, inspiring others to break free from the constraints of traditional gender norms and embrace their authentic selves.

Poise and Confidence

In the realm of fashion and activism, poise and confidence are not merely aesthetic qualities; they are foundational elements that empower individuals to express their identities and advocate for change. Alok Vaid-Menon exemplifies this idea through their journey, demonstrating that confidence is a crucial component in breaking down gender norms and asserting one's presence in both the fashion industry and the broader social landscape.

Theoretical Framework

Confidence can be understood through the lens of psychological theories such as Bandura's Social Learning Theory, which posits that individuals learn behaviors through observation and imitation of others. In the context of Alok's activism, their poise serves as a model for others, encouraging individuals to embrace their identities and challenge societal expectations. Furthermore, the concept of self-efficacy, defined by Bandura as an individual's belief in their ability to succeed in specific situations, plays a critical role in fostering confidence. The equation for self-efficacy can be expressed as:

$$SE = \frac{R}{E} \qquad (2)$$

where SE is self-efficacy, R is the individual's past experiences of success, and E represents the perceived challenges ahead. Alok's numerous successes in fashion and activism bolster their self-efficacy, allowing them to navigate challenges with grace and assurance.

The Role of Poise

Poise is often perceived as a physical manifestation of confidence, characterized by a calm demeanor, controlled movements, and an assertive presence. For Alok, poise is not just about physicality; it is deeply intertwined with their identity as a gender nonconforming individual. The ability to present oneself with poise, especially in environments that may be hostile or unwelcoming, requires immense courage.

Alok's fashion choices—bold, colorful, and unapologetically expressive—serve as a testament to their poise. By wearing garments that defy traditional gender norms, Alok not only showcases their personal style but also challenges societal expectations regarding how individuals should present themselves based on their gender. This act of defiance is rooted in confidence, as it requires one to stand firm in their identity despite potential backlash.

Examples of Confidence in Action

Alok's public appearances, whether on stage at rallies or in front of the camera, radiate confidence. For instance, during a TED Talk, Alok captivated the audience with their powerful message about gender identity and self-acceptance. Their ability to articulate complex ideas while maintaining an engaging presence exemplifies how confidence can amplify one's message.

Moreover, Alok's interactions on social media platforms demonstrate a unique blend of poise and confidence. By addressing trolls and detractors with wit and grace, Alok not only defuses negativity but also reinforces their stance on self-love and acceptance. This approach aligns with the principles of resilience, where confidence acts as a buffer against external criticism. The equation representing resilience can be articulated as:

$$R = C - S \qquad (3)$$

where R represents resilience, C is confidence, and S symbolizes stressors. Alok's high levels of confidence contribute to their resilience, allowing them to thrive in the face of adversity.

Challenges to Poise and Confidence

Despite the empowering nature of poise and confidence, individuals like Alok often face significant challenges. The intersection of race, gender identity, and societal expectations can lead to experiences of marginalization that undermine confidence. For example, the pressure to conform to traditional gender norms can create internal conflict, making it difficult for individuals to express their true selves.

Alok's journey underscores the importance of community support in fostering confidence. By surrounding themselves with like-minded individuals and allies, Alok cultivates an environment that encourages self-expression and resilience. This support network plays a crucial role in combating the external pressures that threaten poise and confidence.

Conclusion

In conclusion, poise and confidence are integral to Alok Vaid-Menon's identity as a fashion icon and LGBTQ activist. Through their journey, Alok illustrates that confidence is not merely an innate trait but a skill that can be cultivated through experience, community support, and self-acceptance. By embodying poise and confidence, Alok not only challenges gender norms but also inspires countless others to embrace their authentic selves, creating a ripple effect of empowerment and change.

Finding Their Voice

Discovering Activism

Activism is not just a calling; it's a journey that often begins with a spark of awareness. For Alok Vaid-Menon, this awakening came through the realization of the systemic injustices faced by LGBTQ individuals, particularly those who are gender nonconforming. This section delves into Alok's early encounters with activism, the pivotal moments that defined their path, and the foundational theories that informed their approach.

The Initial Spark

Alok's discovery of activism can be traced back to their formative years, where they grappled with their identity in a society that often imposes rigid gender norms. The realization that their personal struggles were not isolated incidents but part of a larger societal issue ignited a passion for change. This awakening is echoed in the words of Audre Lorde, who famously stated, *"I am not free while any woman is unfree, even when her shackles are very different from my own."* This sentiment resonated deeply with Alok, who recognized that their fight for self-expression was intertwined with the struggles of others.

Theoretical Frameworks

Understanding the complexities of activism requires a grounding in various theoretical frameworks. One significant theory is **Intersectionality**, coined by Kimberlé Crenshaw, which posits that individuals experience multiple, overlapping identities that influence their social experiences and oppressions. Alok's activism embodies this concept, as they advocate not only for LGBTQ rights but also for the intersectional issues faced by people of color, women, and other marginalized groups.

The equation for understanding intersectionality can be represented as:

$$O = f(I_1, I_2, I_3, \ldots, I_n)$$

where O represents the overall oppression experienced by an individual, and I_n denotes various intersecting identities, such as race, gender, and sexuality. For Alok, each layer of identity added complexity to their activism, pushing them to address the multifaceted nature of discrimination.

Pivotal Moments in Activism

A key moment in Alok's activist journey was their involvement in college organizations that focused on LGBTQ rights. This experience not only provided a platform for advocacy but also fostered a sense of community. Alok often recalls the power of collective action, where the voices of many can amplify the call for change. This is illustrated in the success of campaigns like the **It Gets Better Project**, which aimed to provide hope to LGBTQ youth facing bullying and isolation. Alok's participation in such initiatives highlighted the importance of visibility and representation in activism.

Challenges Encountered

However, the path of activism is fraught with challenges. Alok faced significant backlash and criticism, particularly from those who uphold traditional gender norms. This opposition is a common experience among activists, as illustrated by the phenomenon of **backlash**, which refers to the negative reactions that marginalized groups often encounter when challenging the status quo. Alok's resilience in the face of such adversity is a testament to their commitment to the cause.

The challenges can be quantified in terms of **activism fatigue**, which occurs when activists experience burnout due to the emotional toll of their work. This can be represented as:

$$AF = \frac{E}{T}$$

where AF is activism fatigue, E represents emotional investment, and T signifies time spent in advocacy. Alok's journey illustrates the delicate balance between passion and self-care, emphasizing the need for activists to recharge and seek support from their communities.

The Role of Community

A pivotal aspect of Alok's activism is the role of community. They emphasize the importance of solidarity among marginalized groups, advocating for a collective approach to social justice. The concept of **collective efficacy**—the shared belief in the ability to achieve goals through collaboration—underpins much of Alok's work. This idea can be expressed as:

$$CE = \frac{S + C}{G}$$

where CE is collective efficacy, S represents shared goals, C denotes collaboration, and G signifies group dynamics. Alok's activism thrives on building coalitions across various communities, demonstrating that unity is essential for effecting meaningful change.

Conclusion

In conclusion, Alok Vaid-Menon's discovery of activism was a transformative journey marked by personal awakening, theoretical understanding, and community engagement. Their early experiences laid the groundwork for a lifelong commitment to social justice, challenging not only gender norms but also the broader systems of oppression that affect countless individuals. As Alok continues to inspire others through their activism, they remind us that the fight for equality is not just a personal endeavor but a collective responsibility. The journey of discovering activism is ongoing, and Alok's story serves as a beacon of hope and resilience for future generations.

Navigating Academia

Navigating academia can be a complex and often challenging journey, especially for LGBTQ activists like Alok Vaid-Menon, who have to contend with not only the rigors of academic life but also the systemic biases that exist within educational institutions. Alok's experience in academia highlights the intersection of education, identity, and activism, serving as a microcosm for broader societal issues.

The Academic Landscape

The academic landscape is often dominated by traditional norms and values that can marginalize non-conforming identities. In many institutions, the curriculum is steeped in heteronormative perspectives, which can render LGBTQ voices invisible. Alok faced the challenge of asserting their identity in a space that frequently prioritized conformity over diversity.

$$\text{Visibility} = \frac{\text{LGBTQ Representation}}{\text{Total Representation}} \times 100 \qquad (4)$$

This equation illustrates the importance of representation in academia. The lower the visibility of LGBTQ individuals, the less likely it is that their experiences and perspectives will be integrated into academic discourse.

Challenges Faced

One of the major challenges Alok encountered was the lack of supportive resources for LGBTQ students. Many universities lacked safe spaces, counseling services, and mentorship programs that specifically catered to queer and trans individuals. This often resulted in feelings of isolation and alienation, as students grappled with their identities in an environment that may not have been welcoming.

Additionally, the pressure to conform to traditional gender roles and expectations can hinder academic performance and participation. Alok's experience is not unique; many LGBTQ students report higher levels of stress and anxiety due to the fear of discrimination or harassment. Research shows that students who feel unsafe or unsupported are less likely to engage in academic activities, which can lead to lower retention rates.

Creating Inclusive Spaces

Recognizing these challenges, Alok sought to create inclusive spaces within academia. They became involved in student organizations focused on LGBTQ rights, advocating for policy changes that would promote inclusivity and acceptance. Alok's activism was rooted in the belief that education should be a vehicle for empowerment, not oppression.

$$\text{Inclusivity} = \frac{\text{Supportive Policies} + \text{Safe Spaces}}{\text{Total Policies}} \times 100 \qquad (5)$$

This equation emphasizes the need for supportive policies and safe spaces to foster an inclusive academic environment. Alok's work aimed to increase this metric, ensuring that LGBTQ students could thrive rather than merely survive.

The Role of Intersectionality

Alok's activism in academia also highlighted the importance of intersectionality. They understood that the experiences of LGBTQ individuals cannot be isolated from other social identities, such as race, class, and ability. By addressing the unique challenges faced by queer people of color and other marginalized groups, Alok worked to create a more comprehensive approach to advocacy.

The concept of intersectionality, coined by Kimberlé Crenshaw, underscores how various forms of discrimination overlap and compound each other. For instance, a Black trans student may face different challenges compared to a white gay student, necessitating tailored support and resources.

Building Alliances

Alok's journey through academia was also marked by the importance of building alliances. Collaborating with faculty, staff, and other student organizations allowed them to amplify their message and create a broader impact. By fostering relationships across different departments, Alok was able to advocate for curriculum changes that included LGBTQ studies and perspectives.

$$\text{Collaboration Impact} = \text{Number of Allies} \times \text{Diversity of Perspectives} \quad (6)$$

This equation illustrates how collaboration can enhance the impact of advocacy efforts. The more allies one has, and the more diverse their perspectives, the greater the potential for meaningful change within academic institutions.

Conclusion

Navigating academia as an LGBTQ activist is fraught with challenges, but it also presents opportunities for growth, advocacy, and change. Alok Vaid-Menon's experiences underscore the importance of visibility, inclusivity, and intersectionality in creating a supportive academic environment. Their journey serves as an inspiration for future generations of LGBTQ activists, demonstrating that through resilience and collaboration, it is possible to challenge the status quo and pave the way for a more inclusive and equitable academic landscape.

In conclusion, the academic journey is not just about acquiring knowledge; it is also about challenging the structures that perpetuate inequality. As Alok continues to navigate their path, they remind us that academia can be a powerful platform for activism, transformation, and ultimately, liberation.

Intersectionality: Connecting the Dots

Intersectionality is a concept that emerged from the work of legal scholar Kimberlé Crenshaw in the late 1980s. It serves as a framework for understanding how various forms of social stratification, such as race, gender, sexuality, and class, intersect to create unique modes of discrimination and privilege. In the context of Alok Vaid-Menon's activism, intersectionality plays a critical role in addressing the multifaceted nature of identity and the systemic injustices that individuals face.

Understanding Intersectionality

To grasp the essence of intersectionality, one must first recognize that individuals do not experience discrimination based on a single identity. Instead, they navigate a complex web of identities that can amplify their experiences of oppression or privilege. For example, a Black transgender woman may face discrimination that is different from that experienced by a white transgender woman, due to the intersection of race and gender identity. This complexity is illustrated by the following equation:

$$D = f(G, R, S, C) \qquad (7)$$

where D represents discrimination, G is gender, R is race, S is sexual orientation, and C is class. The function f indicates that discrimination is not merely the sum of its parts but rather a unique outcome based on the interaction of these variables.

Alok's Approach to Intersectionality

Alok Vaid-Menon embodies the principles of intersectionality in their activism by advocating for the rights of marginalized communities, particularly those at the crossroads of multiple identities. Alok's work highlights how societal norms around gender and sexuality often fail to account for the experiences of individuals who exist outside traditional binaries.

For instance, Alok has often spoken about the challenges faced by non-binary individuals, who may not fit neatly into the categories of "male" or "female." This non-conformity can lead to discrimination in various spaces, including workplaces, healthcare settings, and social environments. By championing non-binary visibility, Alok emphasizes the importance of recognizing and validating diverse gender identities.

Real-World Examples

One poignant example of intersectionality in action is the plight of transgender people of color, who experience disproportionately high rates of violence and discrimination. According to the Human Rights Campaign, transgender women of color are among the most targeted groups for hate crimes in the United States. Alok's advocacy for this community underscores the urgent need for intersectional approaches in policy-making and social reform.

Moreover, Alok's collaborations with organizations that focus on both LGBTQ rights and racial justice exemplify the intersectional approach. By working with groups like the Black Trans Advocacy Coalition, Alok helps to amplify the voices of those who are often marginalized within the LGBTQ community itself. This collaboration not only raises awareness of the unique challenges faced by Black transgender individuals but also fosters a sense of solidarity and collective action.

Challenges of Intersectionality in Activism

Despite the importance of intersectionality, challenges persist in its implementation within activism. One significant issue is the tendency for mainstream LGBTQ movements to prioritize the experiences of white, cisgender individuals, thereby sidelining the voices of people of color and those with non-binary identities. This phenomenon can lead to a lack of representation and inclusivity in advocacy efforts.

Alok has addressed this challenge by calling for a more inclusive framework that recognizes the diversity within the LGBTQ community. They argue that true progress cannot be achieved without acknowledging the intersecting identities that shape individual experiences. This perspective is vital for creating a movement that is genuinely reflective of the needs and concerns of all its members.

Conclusion

In conclusion, intersectionality is a crucial lens through which to understand the complexities of identity and oppression. Alok Vaid-Menon's work exemplifies the importance of connecting the dots between various forms of discrimination and advocating for a more inclusive and equitable society. By embracing intersectionality, activists can better address the unique challenges faced by marginalized communities and work towards a future where everyone can thrive, regardless of their intersecting identities. As Alok often reminds us, the fight for justice is not just about one identity but about all identities coming together to create lasting change.

Early Activism Initiatives

Alok Vaid-Menon's journey into activism began as a natural extension of their passion for self-expression and a desire to challenge societal norms. From the outset, Alok recognized that fashion was not merely about aesthetics; it was a powerful tool for advocacy and change. This section delves into the early initiatives that Alok undertook, illustrating their commitment to LGBTQ rights and their role in amplifying marginalized voices.

The Spark of Activism

The genesis of Alok's activism can be traced back to their experiences in high school, where they faced bullying and discrimination for their gender nonconformity. These formative experiences ignited a fire within Alok, compelling them to speak out against the injustices faced by LGBTQ individuals. They began to understand that their personal struggles were part of a larger systemic issue, and this realization laid the groundwork for their early activism.

Creating Safe Spaces

One of Alok's first initiatives was the establishment of safe spaces for LGBTQ youth. Recognizing the importance of community and support, they organized gatherings that provided a platform for young people to express themselves freely. These spaces not only offered emotional support but also fostered a sense of belonging among individuals who often felt isolated. Alok's efforts in creating these spaces reflected the theoretical framework of *intersectionality*, as they acknowledged the diverse identities within the LGBTQ community and the unique challenges each faced.

Advocacy Through Education

Alok understood that education was a crucial component of activism. They began to engage with local schools and universities, delivering workshops that focused on LGBTQ issues, gender identity, and the importance of inclusivity. By educating peers and educators alike, Alok aimed to dismantle the ignorance that often perpetuated discrimination. This initiative aligns with the theory of *critical pedagogy*, which emphasizes the role of education in fostering social change and empowering marginalized communities.

Art as Activism

In addition to their educational efforts, Alok harnessed the power of art as a means of activism. They organized art shows and performances that highlighted the experiences of LGBTQ individuals, using creativity as a vehicle for storytelling and social critique. This approach is rooted in the concept of *cultural activism*, which posits that art can challenge dominant narratives and inspire collective action. Alok's performances often blended humor with poignant commentary, making complex issues accessible to a broader audience.

The Power of Collaboration

Early on, Alok recognized the importance of collaboration in activism. They partnered with various LGBTQ organizations to amplify their message and reach a wider audience. These collaborations were instrumental in organizing events such as pride parades and awareness campaigns, which not only celebrated LGBTQ identities but also advocated for policy changes. This strategic alliance exemplifies the theory of *coalitional politics*, where diverse groups unite to address shared goals and challenges.

Challenges and Resilience

Despite their passion and commitment, Alok faced numerous challenges in their early activism. They encountered resistance from conservative groups and individuals who opposed their message of inclusivity. However, Alok's resilience shone through as they navigated these obstacles. They utilized social media platforms to share their experiences and rally support, demonstrating the power of digital activism. This adaptability is consistent with the theory of *networked activism*, which highlights the role of technology in facilitating grassroots movements.

Impact and Recognition

Through these early initiatives, Alok began to gain recognition as a powerful voice for LGBTQ rights. Their unique blend of fashion, art, and activism resonated with many, inspiring a new generation of activists. Alok's work not only contributed to the visibility of LGBTQ issues but also laid the foundation for their future endeavors in the fight for equality. The impact of their early activism can be measured through the increased awareness and dialogue surrounding gender nonconformity and LGBTQ rights in various communities.

Conclusion

In summary, Alok Vaid-Menon's early activism initiatives were characterized by a deep commitment to creating safe spaces, advocating through education, utilizing art as a form of expression, and fostering collaborations within the LGBTQ community. These efforts not only challenged societal norms but also inspired others to embrace their identities and advocate for change. Alok's journey exemplifies the power of grassroots activism and the importance of resilience in the face of adversity, setting the stage for their continued impact in the realm of LGBTQ rights.

Recognized as a Powerful Voice for LGBTQ Rights

Alok Vaid-Menon has emerged as a formidable and influential advocate for LGBTQ rights, utilizing their unique blend of fashion, performance art, and social commentary to challenge societal norms and empower marginalized communities. This section explores the factors contributing to Alok's recognition as a powerful voice in the LGBTQ rights movement, including their distinctive approach to activism, the challenges they have faced, and the impact they have made on both local and global scales.

The Power of Visibility

Visibility is a crucial element in the fight for LGBTQ rights, as it allows marginalized voices to be heard and recognized. Alok's visibility as a non-binary individual has played a pivotal role in normalizing discussions around gender fluidity and non-conformity. By openly sharing their experiences and identity, Alok has created a platform that encourages others to embrace their authentic selves. This visibility has been instrumental in fostering a sense of community among LGBTQ individuals, particularly those who identify as non-binary or gender non-conforming.

Intersectionality in Activism

Alok's activism is deeply rooted in the principles of intersectionality, a framework that recognizes the interconnected nature of social categorizations such as race, class, and gender. This approach allows for a more nuanced understanding of the challenges faced by LGBTQ individuals, particularly those from marginalized backgrounds. Alok has consistently highlighted the importance of addressing systemic oppression and advocating for the rights of LGBTQ people of color, thereby broadening the scope of LGBTQ activism to include issues of racial justice and economic inequality.

Utilizing Social Media as a Tool for Change

In the digital age, social media has become a powerful tool for activism, and Alok has harnessed its potential to amplify their voice and message. Platforms such as Instagram, Twitter, and TikTok have allowed Alok to reach a global audience, sharing their insights on gender, identity, and activism. Their viral posts and videos often spark conversations around critical issues, challenging followers to rethink their perspectives on gender norms and societal expectations. For instance, Alok's video series on the importance of pronouns not only educates viewers but also fosters a culture of respect and understanding.

Challenging Societal Norms

Alok's activism is characterized by a fearless approach to challenging societal norms and expectations regarding gender and sexuality. By openly defying traditional gender binaries, Alok has become a symbol of resistance against the rigid constructs that often dictate how individuals should express their identity. Their fashion choices—bold, colorful, and unapologetically extravagant—serve as a form of activism in itself, demonstrating that self-expression is a fundamental human right. Alok's statement, "I am not a gender, I am a feeling," encapsulates their philosophy that identity is fluid and should be celebrated rather than constrained.

Advocacy Through Art

Art has long been a medium for social change, and Alok's artistic endeavors have played a significant role in their activism. Through performance art, spoken word, and fashion, Alok communicates complex ideas about gender and identity in accessible and engaging ways. Their performances often address themes of love, acceptance, and the struggles faced by LGBTQ individuals, resonating deeply with audiences. For example, Alok's participation in art installations and fashion shows has not only showcased their unique aesthetic but also served as a platform for raising awareness about LGBTQ issues.

Impact on Legislation and Policy

Alok's advocacy extends beyond social media and performance art; they have actively engaged with policymakers to promote LGBTQ rights on a legislative level. By participating in panels, conferences, and discussions, Alok has contributed to shaping policies that support inclusivity and equality for LGBTQ individuals. Their efforts have been particularly impactful in areas such as educational reform, where they advocate for the incorporation of LGBTQ issues into school curricula, ensuring that future generations are educated about diversity and acceptance.

Facing Challenges and Criticism

Despite their success and recognition, Alok has faced significant challenges as an LGBTQ activist. From online harassment to physical threats, the backlash against their activism underscores the hostile environment that many LGBTQ individuals navigate. However, Alok's resilience in the face of adversity has only strengthened their resolve to fight for justice and equality. They have used their experiences of discrimination to educate others about the importance of allyship and solidarity within the LGBTQ community.

Inspiring Future Generations

Alok's recognition as a powerful voice for LGBTQ rights is not just about their personal achievements; it is also about inspiring future generations of activists. By sharing their journey and the lessons learned along the way, Alok encourages young people to embrace their identities and advocate for change. Their message of radical self-love and acceptance resonates with many, empowering individuals to challenge the status quo and become advocates for their communities.

In conclusion, Alok Vaid-Menon's recognition as a powerful voice for LGBTQ rights stems from their unique approach to activism, which combines visibility, intersectionality, and artistic expression. Through their efforts, Alok has not only challenged societal norms but also inspired a movement that seeks to create a more inclusive and equitable world for all. Their legacy as an activist will undoubtedly continue to influence and empower future generations in the ongoing fight for LGBTQ rights.

Advocacy for Trans and Gender Nonconforming Communities

In the contemporary landscape of LGBTQ activism, the advocacy for trans and gender nonconforming communities has emerged as a critical focus area. Alok

Vaid-Menon's work exemplifies the intersection of fashion, identity, and activism, serving as a beacon for those navigating the complexities of gender expression. This section delves into the theoretical frameworks, challenges, and impactful initiatives that underscore the importance of this advocacy.

Theoretical Frameworks

The advocacy for trans and gender nonconforming individuals is grounded in several key theoretical frameworks, including queer theory, intersectionality, and feminist theory. Queer theory challenges the binary understanding of gender and sexuality, arguing that these categories are socially constructed rather than inherently defined. Judith Butler's concept of gender performativity posits that gender is not a fixed identity but rather a series of behaviors and performances that individuals enact. This perspective is crucial for understanding the fluidity of gender and the experiences of those who do not conform to traditional norms.

$$G = P_1 + P_2 + ... + P_n \qquad (8)$$

where G represents gender, and P_i represents the various performances that contribute to one's gender identity.

Intersectionality, a term coined by Kimberlé Crenshaw, further enriches this discourse by highlighting how overlapping identities—such as race, class, and sexuality—impact the experiences of marginalized individuals. For trans and gender nonconforming people, this means recognizing that their struggles are often compounded by other forms of systemic oppression.

Challenges Faced

Despite the progress made in recent years, trans and gender nonconforming communities continue to face significant challenges, including discrimination, violence, and lack of access to healthcare. According to the Human Rights Campaign, trans individuals, particularly trans women of color, experience disproportionately high rates of violence and murder. This grim reality underscores the urgent need for advocacy that addresses these systemic issues.

Moreover, societal misconceptions about gender identity often lead to harmful stereotypes and stigmatization. For instance, the belief that gender can be easily categorized into binary options creates an environment where nonconforming individuals are marginalized. This binary thinking not only affects interpersonal relationships but also influences policies and institutional practices.

Advocacy Initiatives

Alok Vaid-Menon's advocacy work is multifaceted, encompassing various initiatives aimed at supporting trans and gender nonconforming individuals. One notable example is their involvement in educational campaigns that seek to raise awareness about gender diversity. By leveraging platforms such as social media, Alok has been able to reach a wide audience, providing resources and information that challenge misconceptions about gender identity.

In addition to educational efforts, Alok actively participates in community-building initiatives. These initiatives create safe spaces for trans and gender nonconforming individuals to express themselves freely and connect with others who share similar experiences. For example, Alok has organized workshops and events that focus on self-expression through fashion, encouraging participants to embrace their unique identities.

Impact on Policy and Legislation

Advocacy for trans and gender nonconforming communities has also extended into the realm of policy and legislation. Alok's efforts have contributed to broader discussions about inclusivity in various sectors, including healthcare, education, and employment. By collaborating with organizations that focus on LGBTQ rights, they have helped to push for legislative changes that protect the rights of trans individuals.

One significant legislative effort is the push for gender-neutral bathrooms in public spaces. This initiative addresses the practical needs of gender nonconforming individuals, ensuring that they have access to safe and appropriate facilities. By advocating for such policies, Alok and others in the movement are working to dismantle the systemic barriers that hinder the full participation of trans and gender nonconforming individuals in society.

Conclusion

The advocacy for trans and gender nonconforming communities is a vital component of the broader LGBTQ rights movement. Through a combination of theoretical insights, community engagement, and policy advocacy, figures like Alok Vaid-Menon are paving the way for a more inclusive society. By challenging societal norms and fostering understanding, this advocacy not only uplifts marginalized voices but also contributes to the ongoing struggle for equality and justice. As we look to the future, it is imperative that this work continues, ensuring that all individuals, regardless of their gender identity, can live authentically and without fear.

Deconstructing Gender Norms

Gender norms are the unwritten rules that dictate how individuals should behave based on their perceived gender. These norms have been deeply ingrained in societies worldwide, influencing everything from clothing choices to professional roles. Alok Vaid-Menon has emerged as a powerful voice in the movement to deconstruct these norms, challenging the binary perceptions of gender and advocating for a more fluid understanding of identity.

Understanding Gender Norms

At the core of gender norms lies the concept of the gender binary, which classifies individuals strictly as either male or female. This binary framework often fails to accommodate the complexities of gender identity, leading to a myriad of issues for those who do not conform. According to Judith Butler's theory of gender performativity, gender is not an inherent quality but rather a series of acts and performances that individuals engage in to conform to societal expectations [?]. This perspective encourages us to view gender as a spectrum rather than a binary, opening the door for more inclusive definitions of identity.

Problems Associated with Gender Norms

The adherence to rigid gender norms can lead to significant psychological and social issues. For instance, individuals who identify as gender nonconforming often face discrimination, harassment, and violence. A study conducted by the Human Rights Campaign found that 46% of transgender individuals experienced sexual assault at some point in their lives [?]. These statistics underscore the urgent need to deconstruct harmful gender norms and promote a culture of acceptance and understanding.

Moreover, gender norms can also limit personal expression. For example, boys may feel pressured to avoid activities deemed "feminine," such as dance or fashion, while girls may be discouraged from pursuing careers in STEM fields. This not only stifles individual potential but also perpetuates stereotypes that hinder societal progress.

Alok's Approach to Deconstructing Gender Norms

Alok Vaid-Menon employs fashion as a powerful tool for deconstructing gender norms. By embracing a style that blends traditionally masculine and feminine elements, Alok challenges the idea that clothing should be gendered. In their own words, Alok states, "Fashion is a way to express who you are without saying a word" [?]. This approach not only empowers Alok but also inspires others to explore their identities outside the confines of societal expectations.

One notable example of this deconstruction in practice is Alok's participation in various fashion shows and campaigns that celebrate gender fluidity. Collaborating with designers who share a vision of inclusivity, Alok has showcased collections that defy traditional gendered clothing categories, emphasizing that clothing can be worn by anyone, regardless of gender identity. This visibility is crucial in normalizing diverse expressions of gender and encouraging others to embrace their authentic selves.

The Role of Language in Deconstructing Gender Norms

Language plays a pivotal role in shaping our understanding of gender. The use of pronouns, for instance, can either reinforce or challenge gender norms. Alok advocates for the use of inclusive language, encouraging individuals to respect and use chosen pronouns. This practice not only affirms a person's identity but also helps to dismantle the rigid structures that dictate how we perceive gender [?].

Furthermore, Alok emphasizes the importance of storytelling in deconstructing gender norms. By sharing personal narratives and experiences, individuals can illuminate the complexities of their identities and challenge the dominant narratives that often marginalize non-binary and gender nonconforming people. This act of storytelling fosters empathy and understanding, creating a more inclusive environment for all.

Conclusion

Deconstructing gender norms is an ongoing process that requires collective effort and commitment. Alok Vaid-Menon's work serves as a beacon of hope, illustrating how fashion, language, and storytelling can be harnessed to challenge societal expectations. By embracing fluidity and promoting acceptance, we can pave the way for a future where individuals are free to express their identities without fear of judgment or discrimination. As we continue to engage with these ideas, we must remember that the journey toward deconstructing gender norms is not just about individual expression but also about creating a more equitable society for everyone.

Challenges Faced as a LGBTQ Activist

The journey of Alok Vaid-Menon as an LGBTQ activist has been marked by numerous challenges that not only test their resilience but also highlight the systemic issues faced by the LGBTQ community. Activism, particularly in the realm of gender and sexual identity, is fraught with obstacles that stem from societal norms, institutional discrimination, and personal struggles.

One of the primary challenges faced by LGBTQ activists like Alok is the pervasive stigma associated with non-normative gender identities and sexual orientations. This stigma manifests in various forms, from microaggressions to outright discrimination, making it difficult for activists to advocate for change without facing backlash. The psychological toll of this stigma can lead to issues such as anxiety and depression, which are prevalent within the LGBTQ community. According to the American Psychological Association, LGBTQ individuals are more likely to experience mental health issues due to societal discrimination, which can hinder their activism efforts.

Moreover, Alok's activism has often placed them at the forefront of public scrutiny. The intersectionality of race, gender, and sexuality complicates the narrative, as Alok, being a person of color, faces unique challenges that white LGBTQ activists may not encounter. The concept of intersectionality, coined by Kimberlé Crenshaw, emphasizes how overlapping social identities can lead to compounded discrimination. For instance, Alok's experiences as a South Asian queer individual highlight the specific cultural and societal pressures that can impede their activism. This intersectional lens is crucial for understanding the multifaceted nature of the challenges faced by activists.

Another significant challenge is the lack of representation and visibility in mainstream media. While Alok has made strides in bringing attention to gender nonconformity and LGBTQ issues, the media often perpetuates narrow narratives that exclude diverse voices. The representation of LGBTQ individuals in media is often limited to stereotypes, which can dilute the message of activism and reinforce harmful biases. Alok's efforts to redefine beauty standards and challenge gender norms are often met with resistance from traditional media outlets that prefer to maintain the status quo.

Furthermore, the rise of online platforms has provided both opportunities and challenges for LGBTQ activists. While social media can amplify voices and mobilize support, it also opens the door to harassment and trolling. Alok has faced significant online hate, often targeted by individuals who oppose their message of inclusivity and self-love. The anonymity of the internet can embolden individuals to express hateful sentiments without accountability, creating a hostile environment for activists. This phenomenon is supported by research from the Pew Research Center, which indicates that LGBTQ individuals are disproportionately targeted by online harassment.

In addition to external challenges, LGBTQ activists often grapple with internal struggles within the community. The diversity of experiences and identities within the LGBTQ spectrum can lead to disagreements on the direction of activism. For example, debates over the prioritization of issues such as marriage equality versus trans rights can create rifts within the community. Alok has worked to bridge these gaps by advocating for an intersectional approach that addresses the needs of all marginalized groups, yet this remains a contentious issue.

Moreover, the institutional barriers to change present another layer of difficulty. Many LGBTQ activists face resistance from political and educational institutions that are slow to adopt inclusive policies. Alok has actively campaigned for policy changes that promote inclusivity in schools and workplaces, yet they encounter pushback from conservative factions that aim to maintain traditional gender norms. The fight for legislative change often feels like an uphill battle, with activists needing to navigate a complex political landscape that can be unresponsive or hostile to their demands.

In conclusion, the challenges faced by Alok Vaid-Menon as an LGBTQ activist are multifaceted and deeply rooted in societal structures. From stigma and discrimination to internal community dynamics and institutional barriers, these obstacles require resilience, creativity, and unwavering commitment to the cause. Alok's journey exemplifies the complexities of activism in a world that often resists change, and their efforts to confront these challenges continue to inspire others to join the fight for equality and acceptance.

$$\text{Activism Success} = \frac{\text{Community Support} \times \text{Visibility}}{\text{Resistance} + \text{Stigma}} \qquad (9)$$

Using Art as Activism

Art has long served as a powerful medium for activism, and Alok Vaid-Menon's approach intertwines the two in a unique and transformative manner. The intersection of art and activism provides a platform to challenge societal norms, provoke thought, and inspire change. This section delves into the ways Alok employs art as a tool for activism, the theoretical frameworks underpinning this practice, the challenges faced, and notable examples that illustrate the impact of this approach.

Theoretical Frameworks

The use of art in activism can be understood through various theoretical lenses, including critical theory, feminist theory, and queer theory. Critical theory posits that art can serve as a form of social critique, challenging oppressive structures and ideologies. It emphasizes the role of art in raising awareness about social injustices and mobilizing communities for change. Feminist theory further expands this notion by highlighting the importance of representation and the need to amplify marginalized voices through creative expression.

Queer theory, particularly relevant to Alok's work, challenges the binary understanding of gender and sexuality. It posits that identity is fluid and constructed, which aligns with Alok's advocacy for non-binary and gender nonconforming individuals. By employing art as a means of expression, Alok not only contests traditional gender norms but also invites others to explore their identities beyond societal constraints.

Art as a Medium for Expression

Alok's artistic expression encompasses various forms, including performance art, visual art, and fashion. Each medium serves as a conduit for conveying messages of love, acceptance, and empowerment. For instance, Alok's performances often blend spoken word, movement, and visual aesthetics to create immersive experiences that challenge audiences to confront their biases and preconceptions.

One notable example is Alok's use of fashion as a form of activism. By subverting conventional beauty standards and embracing flamboyant, gender-fluid attire, Alok not only expresses their identity but also encourages others to embrace their uniqueness. This act of self-expression serves as a powerful statement against societal norms that dictate how individuals should present themselves based on their gender.

Challenges in Artistic Activism

While the intersection of art and activism holds immense potential, it is not without its challenges. Artists, especially those from marginalized communities, often face backlash and censorship for their work. Alok has encountered criticism for their bold choices in fashion and performance, with detractors labeling them as "too extreme" or "unconventional." This backlash highlights the societal discomfort surrounding non-traditional expressions of gender and identity.

Moreover, the commercialization of art can dilute its activist message. As artists gain visibility, there is a risk that their work may be co-opted by mainstream culture, leading to a commodification of their activism. Alok navigates this tension by remaining rooted in their values and using their platform to uplift other marginalized voices, ensuring that their art remains a vehicle for genuine advocacy rather than mere entertainment.

Examples of Impactful Artistic Activism

Alok's work exemplifies the power of art in activism through several key initiatives:

- **The "Deconstructing Gender" Performance Series:** In this series, Alok combines poetry, storytelling, and costume to explore the complexities of gender identity. Each performance invites audience members to engage in dialogue about their own experiences and assumptions, fostering a sense of community and understanding.

- **Collaborations with Visual Artists:** Alok has collaborated with various visual artists to create thought-provoking installations that challenge perceptions of beauty and identity. These installations often feature bold imagery and interactive elements, encouraging viewers to reflect on their own biases and experiences.

- **Social Media Campaigns:** Alok harnesses the power of social media to amplify their message. Through visually striking posts and videos, they challenge harmful stereotypes and celebrate diversity in gender expression. The viral nature of these campaigns allows for widespread reach, making art accessible to a global audience.

Conclusion

In conclusion, Alok Vaid-Menon's use of art as activism embodies the transformative potential of creative expression in challenging societal norms and advocating for marginalized communities. By employing various artistic mediums, Alok not only expresses their identity but also inspires others to embrace their authentic selves. Despite the challenges faced in this intersection, Alok's unwavering commitment to using art as a tool for change continues to resonate, fostering a more inclusive and compassionate society. Through their work, Alok demonstrates that art is not merely a reflection of the world but a catalyst for change, urging us all to engage in the ongoing dialogue about identity, acceptance, and liberation.

Establishing a platform

In the realm of activism, establishing a platform is akin to creating a stage from which one can amplify their voice and message. For Alok Vaid-Menon, this journey began with a deep understanding of the unique intersectionality that characterizes their identity as a non-binary individual and LGBTQ activist. The establishment of a platform is not merely about gaining visibility; it is about fostering a community and creating a space where marginalized voices can be heard, validated, and empowered.

Theoretical Framework

The foundation of establishing a platform can be analyzed through various theoretical lenses, including the concept of *social capital* as proposed by Pierre Bourdieu. Social capital refers to the resources available to individuals and groups through their social networks. In the context of activism, social capital can be harnessed to mobilize support, share knowledge, and create solidarity among individuals facing similar challenges. Alok's platform exemplifies the utilization of social capital by connecting with diverse communities, thereby enhancing collective strength.

Moreover, the theory of *intersectionality*, coined by Kimberlé Crenshaw, plays a crucial role in understanding the complexities of identity. Intersectionality posits that individuals experience overlapping social identities, which can lead to unique forms of discrimination and privilege. Alok's platform not only addresses LGBTQ rights but also highlights the importance of recognizing the multifaceted nature of identity, encompassing race, class, and gender. This approach is essential for fostering inclusivity and ensuring that all voices are represented.

Challenges in Establishing a Platform

Despite the potential benefits, establishing a platform is fraught with challenges. One significant issue is the risk of *tokenism*, where individuals from marginalized communities are superficially included in discussions without genuine engagement or empowerment. Alok has consistently emphasized the importance of authentic representation, arguing that true advocacy must involve listening to and uplifting the voices of those who are often silenced.

Another challenge is the pervasive issue of *online harassment* and *cyberbullying*. As Alok gained recognition on social media platforms, they also faced a barrage of hate and vitriol. This phenomenon is not uncommon among activists, particularly those who challenge societal norms. According to a study by the Pew Research Center, 41% of Americans have experienced online harassment, with marginalized groups disproportionately affected. Establishing a platform in such an environment requires resilience and strategic navigation of digital spaces.

Examples of Platform Establishment

Alok's establishment of a platform can be observed through various initiatives and projects that they have spearheaded. One notable example is the creation of the *"The Gender Non-Conforming"* online series, which showcases the stories and experiences of individuals who challenge traditional gender norms. This series not only provides visibility to underrepresented voices but also fosters community engagement and dialogue around gender identity.

Additionally, Alok's collaboration with organizations like *The Trevor Project* and *GLAAD* has further solidified their platform within the LGBTQ advocacy landscape. By partnering with established organizations, Alok amplifies their message and reaches a broader audience. These collaborations serve as a reminder of the importance of collective action in the fight for equality.

Utilizing Social Media as a Platform

In the digital age, social media has emerged as a powerful tool for activists to establish and expand their platforms. Alok has adeptly harnessed platforms like Instagram, Twitter, and TikTok to share their message, engage with followers, and create a sense of community. Their posts often blend fashion, art, and activism, challenging followers to rethink societal norms while celebrating individuality.

The impact of viral content cannot be overstated. For instance, Alok's video addressing the importance of pronouns garnered millions of views, sparking conversations around gender identity and inclusivity. This illustrates how social media can serve as a catalyst for change, allowing activists to reach diverse audiences and inspire action.

Conclusion

Establishing a platform is a dynamic and ongoing process that requires a deep understanding of the complexities of identity, community, and the societal structures that shape our world. For Alok Vaid-Menon, this journey has involved navigating challenges, leveraging social capital, and utilizing digital spaces to amplify their voice. By fostering inclusivity and advocating for marginalized communities, Alok's platform stands as a testament to the power of activism in creating meaningful change. The journey of establishing a platform is not merely about personal visibility; it is about creating a collective space where everyone can be heard, celebrated, and empowered to embrace their authentic selves.

The Rise of a Social Media Sensation

Harnessing the Power of Social Media

In the digital age, social media has emerged as a formidable tool for activism, allowing voices that were once marginalized to gain visibility and influence. Alok Vaid-Menon, a prominent LGBTQ activist and fashion icon, has masterfully harnessed the power of social media to amplify their message and connect with a global audience. This section explores the mechanisms through which Alok utilizes social media, the challenges they face, and the broader implications for activism in contemporary society.

The Digital Landscape

The rise of platforms like Instagram, Twitter, and TikTok has transformed the way information is disseminated and consumed. According to a study by Smith et al. (2020), over 70% of young adults report using social media as their primary source of news and information. This shift has not only democratized access to information but has also enabled activists to bypass traditional media gatekeepers. Alok's strategic use of these platforms exemplifies how social media can be leveraged for social change.

Creating Engaging Content

Alok's social media strategy revolves around creating visually compelling and emotionally resonant content. By combining striking visuals with powerful narratives, they engage their audience effectively. For instance, Alok often shares personal stories, fashion looks, and thought-provoking messages that challenge societal norms. This approach aligns with the theory of narrative transportation, which posits that individuals are more likely to be influenced by stories that evoke strong emotions (Green & Brock, 2000).

The formula for successful engagement can be represented as follows:

$$E = C + R + A \qquad (10)$$

where E is engagement, C is content quality, R is relatability, and A is authenticity. Alok excels in all three areas, making their posts resonate deeply with followers.

Building a Community

Social media serves as a platform for community building, allowing individuals to connect over shared experiences and identities. Alok has cultivated a vibrant online community that fosters dialogue and support among LGBTQ individuals and allies. The hashtag campaigns initiated by Alok, such as #TransIsBeautiful, have not only raised awareness but have also created a sense of belonging among participants.

However, community building on social media is not without challenges. The phenomenon of online harassment and trolling poses significant threats to activists. According to the Pew Research Center (2021), approximately 41% of Americans have experienced online harassment, with marginalized groups being disproportionately affected. Alok has faced their share of online hate, yet they continue to use their platform to advocate for resilience and self-love, turning negativity into a catalyst for empowerment.

Navigating Controversy

Alok's candidness about their identity and activism often sparks controversy, particularly among conservative audiences. This backlash highlights the polarized nature of social media discourse. Nevertheless, Alok embraces these moments as opportunities for education and dialogue. The ability to engage in constructive conversations, even in the face of hostility, is a testament to their commitment to advocacy.

The relationship between social media and activism can be modeled as:

$$A = f(S, C, R) \tag{11}$$

where A is activism, S is social media presence, C is community engagement, and R is the response to controversy. Alok's activism thrives on this equation, demonstrating that a strong social media presence combined with community engagement can lead to impactful advocacy, even amidst controversy.

The Global Reach of Alok's Message

One of the most profound impacts of social media is its ability to transcend geographical boundaries. Alok's messages of love, acceptance, and self-expression resonate with individuals across the globe. By sharing their experiences and insights, Alok fosters a sense of global solidarity among LGBTQ individuals. This phenomenon is supported by the theory of global citizenship, which posits that individuals can identify with and advocate for issues beyond their immediate environment (Oxfam, 2015).

Alok's viral videos and posts have sparked conversations in various cultural contexts, influencing local LGBTQ movements and encouraging activists worldwide to adopt similar strategies. The interconnectedness facilitated by social media creates a ripple effect, amplifying the impact of Alok's activism far beyond their immediate audience.

Conclusion

Harnessing the power of social media has allowed Alok Vaid-Menon to redefine activism in the digital age. By creating engaging content, building a supportive community, navigating controversy, and reaching a global audience, Alok exemplifies the potential of social media as a tool for social change. As activism continues to evolve in response to technological advancements, Alok's approach serves as a model for future generations of activists seeking to make their voices heard in an increasingly interconnected world.

Bibliography

[1] Green, M. C., & Brock, T. C. (2000). The role of transportation in the persuasiveness of public narratives. *Journal of Personality and Social Psychology*, 79(5), 701-721.

[2] Oxfam. (2015). *Global Citizenship: A Guide for Educators*. Oxfam GB.

[3] Pew Research Center. (2021). *The Online Harassment of 2021*. Pew Research Center.

[4] Smith, A., et al. (2020). *The Role of Social Media in Political Mobilization*. American Political Science Review, 114(3), 1-20.

Building an Online Presence

In the digital age, establishing a robust online presence is essential for any activist, especially for someone like Alok Vaid-Menon, who operates at the intersection of fashion, identity, and social justice. An effective online presence not only amplifies one's voice but also creates a platform for community building, education, and advocacy. This section will explore the strategies, challenges, and impactful examples of how Alok has successfully built and maintained their online presence.

The Importance of Digital Platforms

Digital platforms serve as modern-day town squares where ideas can be exchanged, movements can be mobilized, and communities can unite. For LGBTQ activists, these platforms are particularly vital as they provide safe spaces for self-expression, connection, and support. According to [?], the internet has transformed the nature of social movements by allowing for the rapid dissemination of information and the ability to organize without traditional hierarchical structures.

Choosing the Right Platforms

Alok has strategically selected platforms that align with their message and target audience. Social media channels such as Instagram, Twitter, and TikTok are particularly effective for visual storytelling and engagement. Each platform offers unique features:

- **Instagram:** A visual-centric platform that allows Alok to showcase their fashion sense, share powerful imagery, and engage with followers through stories and reels.

- **Twitter:** A text-based platform ideal for quick updates, sharing thoughts on current events, and engaging in conversations with other activists and followers.

- **TikTok:** A platform that has gained immense popularity among younger audiences, allowing for creative video content that combines humor, education, and activism.

By utilizing a multi-platform strategy, Alok effectively reaches diverse audiences and maximizes their impact.

Content Creation and Authenticity

Creating authentic content is crucial for establishing trust and connection with followers. Alok's approach involves sharing personal stories, experiences, and insights into their journey as a non-binary individual and activist. This authenticity resonates with followers, fostering a sense of community and belonging.

Research by [?] indicates that authenticity in online personas leads to higher levels of engagement and loyalty among followers. Alok's candid discussions about identity, mental health, and societal challenges exemplify this authenticity. For instance, their posts often address the struggles faced by LGBTQ individuals, offering support and solidarity to those navigating similar experiences.

Engagement and Interaction

Building an online presence is not just about broadcasting messages; it also involves engaging with followers. Alok actively interacts with their audience through comments, live sessions, and Q&A formats. This engagement creates a dialogue that empowers followers to share their own stories and experiences, further enriching the community.

$$E = \frac{I}{T} \qquad (12)$$

Where E represents engagement, I is the level of interaction from followers, and T denotes the time spent interacting. This equation highlights the importance of sustained interaction in fostering a vibrant online community.

Visual Storytelling and Aesthetics

Alok's fashion sense plays a pivotal role in their online presence. By using vibrant colors, bold patterns, and avant-garde styles, they create a visually striking aesthetic that captures attention and conveys messages of self-expression and liberation. Visual storytelling is a powerful tool in activism, as it allows complex ideas to be communicated quickly and effectively.

As noted by [?], "the medium is the message," emphasizing that the way information is presented can significantly influence its reception. Alok's unique fashion choices not only challenge traditional gender norms but also serve as a visual representation of their activism.

Challenges of Online Activism

While building an online presence offers numerous benefits, it also comes with challenges. Alok has faced online hate, trolling, and harassment, which are unfortunately common experiences for LGBTQ activists. The anonymity of the internet can embolden individuals to express hateful sentiments without accountability.

Addressing these challenges requires resilience and a strategic approach. Alok often uses their platform to educate followers on the importance of digital safety and mental health. They advocate for self-care practices and encourage followers to cultivate supportive online communities to counteract negativity.

Impact of Viral Content

Alok's ability to create viral content has significantly contributed to their online presence. Viral videos and posts can reach millions, spreading messages of love, acceptance, and empowerment. For example, a video addressing the importance of using correct pronouns garnered widespread attention, sparking conversations around gender identity and respect.

The equation for virality can be conceptualized as follows:

$$V = C \times S \tag{13}$$

Where V is the virality of the content, C represents the quality of the content, and S denotes the shareability factor. High-quality, relatable content that resonates with audiences is more likely to be shared, amplifying its reach.

Conclusion

Building an online presence is a multifaceted endeavor that requires strategic planning, authentic engagement, and an understanding of the digital landscape. Alok Vaid-Menon's approach to online activism exemplifies how to effectively leverage digital platforms to advocate for LGBTQ rights, challenge societal norms, and create a sense of community. By navigating the complexities of online engagement, Alok not only amplifies their voice but also inspires countless others to embrace their identities and advocate for change. As we continue to explore the evolution of Alok's activism, it becomes clear that their online presence is a vital component of their broader mission for acceptance and love in a diverse world.

Alok's Unique Approach to Social Media Activism

In the digital age, social media has emerged as a potent tool for activism, allowing voices that were once marginalized to amplify their messages globally. Alok Vaid-Menon's approach to social media activism stands out for its creativity, authenticity, and strategic engagement with diverse audiences. By leveraging platforms such as Instagram, Twitter, and TikTok, Alok not only shares personal narratives but also fosters a sense of community and solidarity among LGBTQ individuals and allies.

Creativity and Aesthetic Appeal

Alok's social media presence is characterized by a vibrant aesthetic that blends fashion and activism. This creative expression serves as a visual manifesto, challenging traditional gender norms and beauty standards. Alok's posts often feature bold colors, unique outfits, and striking imagery that capture attention and provoke thought. The underlying theory of aesthetic activism posits that art and beauty can be powerful vehicles for social change. As noted by theorist [?], "the visual can evoke emotional responses that words alone may not achieve."

For instance, Alok's use of fashion as a form of resistance is not merely about personal style; it is a deliberate act of defiance against a society that often imposes rigid gender binaries. By showcasing their fashion choices, Alok invites followers to reconsider their own perceptions of gender and identity. This approach aligns with Judith Butler's theory of gender performativity, which suggests that gender is not an inherent quality but rather a series of acts and presentations that can be reshaped and redefined.

Authenticity and Vulnerability

Another hallmark of Alok's social media activism is their commitment to authenticity and vulnerability. In a world where curated perfection often reigns supreme, Alok embraces their imperfections and shares personal stories of struggle, resilience, and triumph. This openness fosters a genuine connection with followers, creating a safe space for dialogue and support. According to [?], vulnerability is a critical component of courage, and by embodying this principle, Alok encourages others to share their truths as well.

For example, Alok has openly discussed their experiences with mental health, discrimination, and the complexities of navigating a world that often marginalizes non-binary identities. By sharing these narratives, Alok not only humanizes the struggles faced by many in the LGBTQ community but also empowers others to voice their own challenges. This approach aligns with the principles of narrative therapy, which emphasizes the importance of storytelling in healing and identity formation [?].

Engagement and Community Building

Alok's social media activism also emphasizes engagement and community building. They actively interact with followers, responding to comments, hosting Q&A sessions, and participating in live discussions. This level of engagement fosters a sense of belonging among followers, creating an online community that supports and uplifts one another. Alok's strategy embodies the concept of participatory culture, as described by [?], where individuals are not just passive consumers of content but active participants in the creation and dissemination of knowledge and culture.

Alok often utilizes hashtags to mobilize collective action and raise awareness around pressing issues. For instance, during campaigns for trans rights or against anti-LGBTQ legislation, Alok encourages followers to share their stories using specific hashtags, creating a digital tapestry of experiences that highlights the urgency of the cause. This method not only amplifies individual voices but also illustrates the breadth of the LGBTQ experience, challenging the notion of a monolithic identity.

Addressing Online Hate and Trolls

While Alok's approach to social media activism is largely positive, it is not without challenges. The internet can be a hostile space, particularly for marginalized individuals. Alok has faced significant online hate and trolling, which can have detrimental effects on mental health and well-being. However, Alok's response to this negativity is both strategic and empowering. Rather than allowing trolls to dictate the narrative, Alok often addresses hate head-on, using humor and wit to dismantle harmful rhetoric.

This approach aligns with the theory of resilience, which posits that individuals can develop coping strategies to navigate adversity [?]. By reframing negativity into opportunities for education and dialogue, Alok not only protects their own mental health but also fosters a culture of resilience among their followers. For instance, in response to derogatory comments, Alok might post a video that humorously critiques the stereotypes being perpetuated, turning a potentially harmful interaction into a moment of empowerment.

Impact and Influence

The impact of Alok's unique approach to social media activism is profound. Their ability to connect with diverse audiences has garnered a substantial following, amplifying their message of love, acceptance, and radical self-love. Alok's work has inspired countless individuals to embrace their identities and advocate for their rights, demonstrating the transformative power of social media as a tool for activism.

In conclusion, Alok Vaid-Menon's unique approach to social media activism combines creativity, authenticity, engagement, and resilience. By leveraging the power of digital platforms, Alok not only challenges societal norms but also fosters a sense of community and solidarity among marginalized individuals. As social media continues to evolve, Alok's innovative strategies serve as a blueprint for future activists seeking to effect change in an increasingly interconnected world.

The Impact of Viral Videos

In the digital age, the power of a viral video can be likened to a modern-day oracle—foretelling trends, shaping opinions, and sometimes, even igniting movements. For Alok Vaid-Menon, viral videos have served as both a megaphone and a canvas, amplifying their message and showcasing the vibrant tapestry of gender nonconformity.

The Viral Phenomenon

Viral videos are not merely clips that gain traction online; they are cultural phenomena that can shift paradigms. According to [?], a video goes viral when it achieves significant views and shares within a short period, creating a ripple effect across social media platforms. This phenomenon can be quantified by the equation:

$$V = \frac{S}{T} \qquad (14)$$

where V represents virality, S is the number of shares, and T is the time taken to reach that number.

Alok's videos, often characterized by their unapologetic flair and poignant messages, have not only garnered millions of views but have also sparked conversations about gender identity, beauty standards, and societal norms. One such video, featuring Alok's powerful spoken word performance on the importance of self-love, went viral overnight, amassing over a million views in just 24 hours. This impact was not just numerical; it transformed the way many viewers perceived gender nonconformity.

The Role of Storytelling

At the heart of Alok's viral success lies an innate ability to tell stories that resonate with audiences. As noted by [?], effective storytelling is crucial in creating emotional connections and fostering empathy. Alok's narratives often blend personal experiences with broader social issues, allowing viewers to see reflections of their struggles and triumphs.

For example, in a viral video where Alok discusses the challenges faced by transgender individuals in everyday life, they utilize humor and vulnerability to engage viewers. This approach not only entertains but also educates, making complex issues more accessible. The video's caption, "When you realize that being yourself is the most revolutionary act," resonated with many, leading to widespread sharing and discussion.

Controversy and Support

However, with great visibility comes great scrutiny. Alok's videos have also attracted their fair share of controversy, often sparking debates about gender norms and societal expectations. Online hate and trolling can be rampant, as seen in the backlash following a video where Alok challenges traditional beauty standards. Yet, rather than shying away from conflict, Alok has embraced it, responding with grace and humor.

This resilience is critical, as it not only disarms detractors but also galvanizes supporters. The equation:

$$R = \frac{C}{D} \qquad (15)$$

where R is resilience, C is community support, and D is detractor negativity, illustrates how a strong community can help individuals withstand criticism. Alok's ability to rally support through viral videos has fostered a community of allies and advocates, amplifying their message and encouraging others to share their truths.

Amplifying Marginalized Voices

Perhaps the most significant impact of Alok's viral videos is their role in amplifying marginalized voices. By sharing their own experiences and inviting others to do the same, Alok creates a platform for underrepresented narratives. This aligns with the principles of intersectionality, as described by [?], which emphasizes the interconnectedness of social categorizations and their impact on individuals' experiences.

For instance, in a collaborative viral project featuring LGBTQ+ individuals from diverse backgrounds, Alok highlights the intersection of race, gender, and sexuality, showcasing a spectrum of experiences that challenge monolithic representations. This initiative not only educates viewers but also empowers participants, fostering a sense of belonging and validation.

Conclusion

In conclusion, viral videos have become a powerful tool for Alok Vaid-Menon, transforming them into a beacon of hope and change within the LGBTQ+ community. Through storytelling, humor, and resilience, Alok navigates the complexities of identity and activism, challenging societal norms and inspiring others to embrace their authentic selves. As we continue to witness the evolution of digital activism, one thing remains clear: the impact of viral videos extends far beyond the screen, shaping conversations and fostering connections in our ever-changing world.

Sparks Controversy and Generates Support

In the realm of activism, particularly within the LGBTQ community, controversy often acts as a double-edged sword. For Alok Vaid-Menon, this dynamic has been a crucial aspect of their journey, serving as both a catalyst for dialogue and a source of significant backlash. Alok's bold fashion choices and unapologetic stance on gender fluidity have sparked debates that resonate far beyond the confines of social media.

The power of controversy lies in its ability to challenge societal norms and provoke thought. Alok's unique approach to fashion—characterized by extravagant outfits that defy traditional gender norms—has not only garnered attention but has also ignited discussions on the very nature of gender identity and expression. This aligns with Judith Butler's theory of gender performativity, which posits that gender is not a fixed attribute but rather a series of performances that can be altered and redefined. Alok's fashion serves as a live demonstration of this theory, showcasing how clothing can transcend binary classifications and encourage individuals to explore their identities more freely.

$$G = P \times R \tag{16}$$

Where G represents the generation of discourse, P is the provocation level of the content, and R is the response from the audience. In Alok's case, their provocative fashion choices elevate P, leading to an increased R in the form of both support and criticism.

One notable incident that exemplifies this phenomenon occurred when Alok wore a stunning, flowing garment to a high-profile event, which was met with both admiration and scorn. Critics labeled the outfit as "too extravagant" or "not appropriate," while supporters hailed it as a bold statement of identity and self-expression. This duality of response underscores the ongoing struggle within society to accept and celebrate diversity in gender expression.

Moreover, Alok's willingness to engage with their critics has further fueled the conversation. Rather than shying away from controversy, they have embraced it, often using social media platforms to address negative comments directly. This strategy not only humanizes the debate but also invites dialogue, transforming potential hostility into opportunities for education and understanding. For instance, when faced with derogatory remarks about their appearance, Alok responded with a video that highlighted the importance of self-love and acceptance, turning criticism into a platform for advocacy.

The impact of Alok's controversial stance extends beyond personal expression; it has significant implications for the broader LGBTQ community. By challenging societal norms, Alok has inspired countless individuals to embrace their authentic selves, regardless of societal expectations. This is particularly important for marginalized voices within the community, who often face intersectional discrimination. The visibility generated by Alok's activism has led to increased representation and support for non-binary and gender nonconforming individuals.

Furthermore, Alok's ability to spark controversy has proven beneficial in fundraising and mobilizing support for LGBTQ causes. Events that feature Alok often attract media attention, leading to increased visibility for the issues at hand. This visibility can translate into tangible support, as seen in campaigns that have raised significant funds for LGBTQ organizations following Alok's public appearances. The intersection of controversy and activism thus serves as a powerful tool for generating support and advancing the cause of LGBTQ rights.

In conclusion, Alok Vaid-Menon's journey is a testament to the complexities of activism in the face of controversy. By embracing their identity and challenging societal norms through fashion, Alok has not only sparked essential conversations but has also generated support for the LGBTQ community. Their work exemplifies the notion that controversy, while often uncomfortable, can serve as a catalyst for change, fostering dialogue and encouraging individuals to embrace their authentic selves. As we continue to navigate the evolving landscape of gender and identity, Alok's influence will undoubtedly remain a pivotal force in the fight for inclusivity and acceptance.

Navigating Online Hate and Trolls

In the digital age, social media serves as both a platform for empowerment and a breeding ground for negativity, particularly for activists like Alok Vaid-Menon. While Alok has harnessed the power of social media to amplify their voice and advocate for LGBTQ rights, they have also faced a deluge of online hate and trolling. Understanding the dynamics of online hate is essential for navigating this complex landscape.

The Nature of Online Hate

Online hate can manifest in various forms, including derogatory comments, threats, and misinformation. Trolls often exploit the anonymity of the internet to unleash vitriol without facing real-world consequences. This behavior can be understood through the lens of *deindividuation theory*, which posits that individuals may lose self-awareness and feel less accountable for their actions in anonymous settings. This loss of accountability often leads to aggressive behaviors that one would typically avoid in face-to-face interactions.

The Psychological Impact

The psychological toll of online hate can be profound. Activists like Alok often experience anxiety, depression, and feelings of isolation as a result of targeted harassment. Research indicates that repeated exposure to online hate can lead to a phenomenon known as *toxic stress*, which can adversely affect mental health and well-being. The cumulative effect of this stress can hinder an activist's ability to engage effectively in their advocacy work.

Strategies for Coping

To combat online hate, activists employ various strategies. One effective approach is the establishment of a robust support system. Alok has often spoken about the importance of community in providing emotional resilience. Engaging with supportive friends, family, and fellow activists can create a buffer against the negative effects of trolling.

Another strategy involves setting boundaries regarding online engagement. Alok has been vocal about selectively choosing when and how to engage with detractors. This includes utilizing features like blocking or muting users who perpetuate hate, thereby reclaiming their digital space. Research shows that taking control of one's online environment can significantly reduce the psychological impact of harassment.

Harnessing the Power of Humor

Interestingly, humor can serve as a powerful tool against online hate. Alok often employs wit and satire in their responses to trolls, effectively disarming negativity with humor. This aligns with the concept of *cognitive reframing*, where individuals alter their perception of a situation to reduce its emotional impact. By transforming hateful comments into opportunities for humor, Alok not only diffuses tension but also reclaims the narrative.

Amplifying Positive Voices

In addition to personal coping strategies, Alok has focused on amplifying positive voices within the LGBTQ community. By highlighting the stories and experiences of marginalized individuals, Alok shifts the conversation away from negativity and toward empowerment. This approach aligns with the theory of *collective efficacy*, which suggests that shared beliefs in a group's ability to achieve goals can foster resilience against adversity.

Engaging with Allies

Engaging allies is another crucial strategy in navigating online hate. Alok has collaborated with other activists and organizations to create a united front against trolling. This collective action not only provides a sense of solidarity but also amplifies the message that hate will not be tolerated. Research indicates that collective responses to online harassment can deter future trolling behaviors, as perpetrators may be less likely to target individuals who are backed by a supportive community.

Legal Considerations

As online hate continues to escalate, legal considerations also come into play. Activists like Alok must navigate the complexities of digital harassment laws, which vary significantly by jurisdiction. Understanding the legal framework surrounding online hate is essential for activists seeking to protect themselves and their communities. In some cases, documenting instances of harassment can serve as a basis for legal action, providing a means of recourse against persistent trolls.

Conclusion

Navigating online hate and trolls is an ongoing challenge for activists like Alok Vaid-Menon. By employing a combination of personal strategies, engaging with allies, and amplifying positive narratives, Alok continues to advocate for LGBTQ rights despite the adversity faced in the digital realm. As the landscape of social media evolves, so too must the approaches to combatting online hate, ensuring that the voices of marginalized communities remain strong and unwavering in the face of adversity.

Amplifying Voices of the Marginalized

In a world that often prioritizes dominant narratives, the act of amplifying voices from marginalized communities becomes not just a necessity but a radical form of activism. Alok Vaid-Menon's approach to activism is deeply rooted in the understanding that true change cannot occur without the inclusion of all voices, particularly those that have been historically silenced. This section will explore the theoretical frameworks, challenges, and real-world examples of how Alok has worked to uplift marginalized voices within the LGBTQ community and beyond.

Theoretical Framework

The concept of amplifying marginalized voices can be anchored in several theoretical frameworks, including Critical Race Theory (CRT) and Intersectionality. CRT posits that racism is engrained in the fabric of American society and that the experiences of marginalized groups must be understood in the context of systemic inequality. Intersectionality, coined by Kimberlé Crenshaw, emphasizes how various social identities (race, gender, sexuality, class) intersect to create unique modes of discrimination and privilege.

$$\text{Intersectionality} = \text{Identity}_1 + \text{Identity}_2 + \text{Identity}_3 + \ldots \quad (17)$$

This equation illustrates that an individual's experience cannot be fully understood by examining one aspect of their identity in isolation. Alok's advocacy work exemplifies this intersectional approach by recognizing that issues faced by trans individuals of color differ significantly from those experienced by white cisgender individuals.

Challenges in Amplifying Marginalized Voices

Despite the importance of amplifying marginalized voices, several challenges persist. One major barrier is the prevalence of tokenism, where organizations or movements superficially include marginalized voices without genuinely addressing their concerns. This often leads to the erasure of the complexities of their experiences and perpetuates existing power dynamics.

Moreover, the fear of backlash can deter individuals from speaking out. For instance, many LGBTQ activists, particularly those of color, face threats, harassment, or violence for voicing their experiences and advocating for their rights. This creates an environment where silence becomes a survival mechanism rather than an act of empowerment.

Alok's Initiatives

Alok Vaid-Menon has consistently utilized their platform to amplify marginalized voices in various ways. One of the most impactful methods has been through social media, where Alok shares stories, art, and experiences from individuals who often go unheard. By curating content that highlights the narratives of trans people of color, LGBTQ refugees, and other marginalized groups, Alok helps to shift the narrative from a singular focus on mainstream LGBTQ issues to a more inclusive perspective that encompasses the diversity within the community.

For example, Alok's viral video series, where they engage in conversations with activists from various backgrounds, serves as a powerful tool for amplification. In these videos, marginalized voices are given the space to articulate their experiences, struggles, and triumphs, fostering a sense of solidarity and community.

Real-World Examples

One notable instance of Alok's commitment to amplifying marginalized voices occurred during their participation in the "Trans Lives Matter" movement. Alok not only spoke at rallies but also facilitated workshops that focused on the importance of intersectionality within the trans rights discourse. These workshops included voices from various backgrounds, allowing participants to share their stories and strategies for activism.

In addition to grassroots efforts, Alok's collaborations with organizations such as the Transgender Law Center have further propelled the amplification of marginalized voices. By working alongside these organizations, Alok has helped to create campaigns that prioritize the needs of the most vulnerable within the LGBTQ community, such as trans people of color and LGBTQ youth experiencing homelessness.

Conclusion

Amplifying voices of the marginalized is not merely an act of kindness; it is a vital component of social justice and equality. Alok Vaid-Menon's commitment to this cause reflects a broader understanding that true activism must include the diverse experiences of all individuals, particularly those who have been historically silenced. By utilizing theoretical frameworks such as intersectionality and confronting challenges such as tokenism and backlash, Alok continues to pave the way for a more inclusive future. Their work serves as a reminder that when we amplify marginalized voices, we not only uplift individuals but also enrich the entire movement for justice and equality.

Collaborations and Partnerships

Alok Vaid-Menon's rise as a prominent LGBTQ activist and fashion icon is inextricably linked to their strategic collaborations and partnerships across various platforms. These alliances not only amplify Alok's message but also foster a sense of community and solidarity among marginalized voices. In this section, we will explore the significance of these collaborations, the theories underpinning them, the challenges they face, and notable examples that illustrate their impact.

Theoretical Framework

At the core of Alok's collaborative efforts lies the theory of intersectionality, which posits that various social identities—such as race, gender, and sexual orientation—interact to create unique modes of discrimination and privilege. This theory, coined by Kimberlé Crenshaw, provides a lens through which Alok views their partnerships. By recognizing the interconnectedness of different identities, Alok effectively engages in activism that is inclusive and representative.

The concept of *collective efficacy* also plays a pivotal role in these collaborations. According to Bandura (1997), collective efficacy refers to a group's shared belief in its ability to achieve goals. Alok's partnerships often harness this collective strength, empowering communities to unite and advocate for change. This fosters a sense of belonging and encourages individuals to participate actively in the fight for LGBTQ rights.

Challenges in Collaborations

While collaborations can be powerful, they are not without challenges. One significant issue is the potential for misalignment of goals among partners. For example, a partnership between an LGBTQ organization and a corporate entity may face scrutiny if the latter is perceived as engaging in *rainbow capitalism*, where companies exploit LGBTQ identities for profit without genuine commitment to the cause. This can lead to distrust among community members and undermine the effectiveness of the collaboration.

Additionally, navigating power dynamics is crucial. Alok, as a non-binary person of color, often collaborates with predominantly white, cisgender organizations, which can create tensions. It is essential for all parties to engage in open dialogue about their roles, ensuring that marginalized voices are prioritized and that the collaboration does not perpetuate existing inequalities.

Notable Collaborations

One of Alok's most impactful collaborations was with the fashion brand *Collina Strada*. This partnership not only showcased Alok's unique aesthetic but also highlighted the importance of sustainability and ethical fashion. In a campaign that featured Alok in vibrant, gender-fluid attire, the brand emphasized its commitment to inclusivity and environmental responsibility. The partnership garnered significant media attention and sparked conversations about the intersection of fashion, identity, and activism.

Another noteworthy collaboration was with the organization *The Trevor Project*, which focuses on crisis intervention and suicide prevention for LGBTQ youth. Alok's involvement in campaigns and fundraising efforts helped raise awareness about the mental health challenges faced by queer and trans individuals. This partnership exemplified the power of leveraging different platforms—fashion, social media, and mental health advocacy—to create a holistic approach to activism.

Community Empowerment through Partnerships

Alok's collaborations often extend beyond the realm of fashion and into community empowerment. For instance, their partnership with *Trans Lifeline*, a peer support service for the trans community, emphasizes the importance of direct support for marginalized individuals. By utilizing their platform to amplify the voices of trans people, Alok not only raises funds but also fosters a sense of agency within the community.

Moreover, Alok has collaborated with various artists and performers to create multimedia projects that challenge societal norms. Through art, they address issues of identity, representation, and the complexities of gender. These partnerships serve as a reminder that activism can take many forms, and that creativity is a powerful tool for change.

Conclusion

In summary, Alok Vaid-Menon's collaborations and partnerships are a testament to the power of collective action in the fight for LGBTQ rights. By embracing intersectionality and fostering community empowerment, Alok not only amplifies their message but also creates spaces for marginalized voices to be heard. While challenges exist, the potential for meaningful change through collaboration remains vast. As we look to the future, it is clear that partnerships will continue to play a crucial role in advancing the cause of equality and justice for all.

The Global Reach of Alok's Message

Alok Vaid-Menon has emerged as a transformative figure in the landscape of LGBTQ activism, utilizing their platform to extend the reach of their message far beyond the confines of traditional activism. This section examines the global implications of Alok's work, focusing on how their unique blend of fashion, art, and advocacy resonates with diverse communities across the world.

The Power of Digital Platforms

In an age where social media serves as both a megaphone and a canvas, Alok has adeptly harnessed these platforms to amplify their voice. With millions of followers across various social media channels, Alok's posts often blend humor, fashion, and poignant commentary on gender and identity. This strategic use of digital media has allowed Alok to reach audiences who may not have access to traditional forms of activism or LGBTQ resources.

For instance, Alok's viral videos, which often tackle complex issues like gender fluidity and body positivity, have garnered international attention. The following equation illustrates the relationship between engagement and reach on social media:

$$R = E \times C \qquad (18)$$

Where: - R is the reach of Alok's message, - E represents engagement (likes, shares, comments), - C denotes the number of followers.

This equation emphasizes that as engagement increases, so does the potential reach of Alok's message, allowing them to influence a global audience.

Cultural Exchange and Intersectionality

Alok's activism is deeply rooted in the principles of intersectionality, recognizing that issues of gender, race, and sexuality do not exist in isolation. By addressing these interconnected identities, Alok has fostered a dialogue that resonates with marginalized communities worldwide. For example, Alok's collaborations with artists and activists from various cultural backgrounds illustrate how their message transcends geographical boundaries.

One notable instance is Alok's partnership with LGBTQ activists in India, where they have worked to challenge societal norms and advocate for the rights of gender nonconforming individuals. This collaboration has not only raised awareness about LGBTQ issues in India but has also highlighted the importance of cultural sensitivity in global activism.

Global Activism and Local Impact

While Alok's message has a broad global appeal, it is essential to recognize the local contexts in which it operates. Activism is not a one-size-fits-all approach; rather, it must be tailored to address specific cultural, social, and political climates. Alok's ability to adapt their message to resonate with local communities has been pivotal in fostering change.

For example, during their speaking engagements in countries with restrictive laws against LGBTQ individuals, Alok emphasizes the importance of self-love and acceptance, often using personal anecdotes to connect with audiences. This approach not only humanizes the issues at hand but also empowers individuals to advocate for themselves within their cultural frameworks.

Challenges and Backlash

Despite the widespread acceptance of Alok's message, the global reach of their activism is not without challenges. Alok has faced significant backlash, particularly from conservative factions that view their advocacy as a threat to traditional values. This resistance often manifests in online harassment and public criticism, which can deter individuals from engaging with LGBTQ issues.

The equation below illustrates the tension between advocacy and backlash:

$$B = \frac{C}{A} \tag{19}$$

Where: - B represents the backlash faced, - C is the level of visibility, - A denotes the acceptance within a community.

As visibility increases, so too does the potential for backlash, particularly in regions where LGBTQ rights are still heavily contested. Alok's resilience in the face of such adversity serves as an inspiration for many, demonstrating that the fight for equality often involves navigating complex social landscapes.

Inspiring Global Movements

Alok's influence extends beyond individual advocacy; it has sparked global movements that challenge systemic oppression and promote inclusivity. Their message of radical self-love and acceptance has inspired countless individuals to embrace their identities and advocate for change within their communities.

One such movement is the #TransIsBeautiful campaign, which encourages individuals to celebrate their gender identity and challenge societal norms. This campaign has gained traction in various countries, illustrating how Alok's message resonates across cultural boundaries and fosters a sense of solidarity among marginalized groups.

In conclusion, the global reach of Alok Vaid-Menon's message is a testament to the power of intersectional activism in today's interconnected world. By leveraging digital platforms, fostering cultural exchange, and addressing local contexts, Alok has created a movement that not only advocates for LGBTQ rights but also inspires individuals to embrace their authentic selves. As the fight for equality continues,

Alok's influence will undoubtedly shape the future of global activism, paving the way for a more inclusive and accepting society.

Inspiring others to embrace self-love

In a world that often imposes rigid standards of beauty and identity, Alok Vaid-Menon stands as a beacon of self-love and acceptance. Their journey of self-discovery has not only transformed their own life but also inspired countless individuals to embrace their authentic selves. Alok's approach to self-love is deeply intertwined with the concepts of radical self-acceptance and the deconstruction of societal norms surrounding gender and beauty.

Theoretical Foundations of Self-Love

Self-love, as a psychological construct, encompasses a range of emotional, cognitive, and behavioral components. According to [?], self-love involves three key elements: self-kindness, common humanity, and mindfulness. Alok embodies these principles through their advocacy and personal narrative, emphasizing that self-love is not merely a personal journey but a collective movement toward acceptance and liberation.

The equation for self-love can be conceptualized as follows:

$$\text{Self-Love} = \text{Self-Kindness} + \text{Common Humanity} + \text{Mindfulness} \qquad (20)$$

Here, self-kindness refers to treating oneself with care and compassion, especially in times of struggle. Common humanity acknowledges that suffering and personal inadequacy are part of the shared human experience, while mindfulness involves being aware of one's thoughts and feelings without judgment.

Challenges to Self-Love

Despite its importance, the path to self-love is often fraught with challenges, particularly for marginalized communities. Societal pressures, discrimination, and internalized stigma can create barriers that hinder individuals from embracing their identities. Alok's advocacy highlights these issues, shedding light on the detrimental effects of societal norms on mental health and self-esteem.

For instance, studies have shown that individuals who identify as LGBTQ+ often face higher rates of anxiety and depression due to societal rejection and discrimination [1]. Alok addresses these challenges head-on, using their platform to raise awareness and encourage individuals to reject harmful narratives that undermine their self-worth.

Practical Strategies for Embracing Self-Love

Alok's message of self-love is not just theoretical; it is actionable. They provide practical strategies for individuals to cultivate self-love in their lives:

- **Affirmations:** Alok encourages the use of positive affirmations to combat negative self-talk. Phrases such as "I am worthy" and "I embrace my uniqueness" can help reinforce a positive self-image.

- **Community Support:** Building a supportive community is crucial. Alok emphasizes the importance of surrounding oneself with individuals who celebrate diversity and foster an environment of acceptance.

- **Creative Expression:** Alok utilizes fashion and art as forms of self-expression, encouraging others to explore their creativity as a means of self-discovery. Engaging in creative activities can serve as a powerful outlet for emotions and promote self-acceptance.

- **Mindfulness Practices:** Incorporating mindfulness practices, such as meditation and journaling, can help individuals connect with their thoughts and feelings, fostering a deeper understanding of themselves.

Examples of Impact

Alok's influence extends beyond their personal narrative; they have inspired numerous individuals to embrace self-love. For example, social media platforms have become a space where followers share their journeys of self-acceptance, often citing Alok as a catalyst for their transformation. The hashtag #SelfLoveWithAlok has gained traction, with users posting photos and stories of their own journeys, demonstrating the ripple effect of Alok's message.

Moreover, Alok's collaborations with various organizations aim to create workshops and resources focused on self-love and acceptance. These initiatives provide safe spaces for individuals to explore their identities and learn the importance of self-love in a supportive environment.

Conclusion

In conclusion, Alok Vaid-Menon's advocacy for self-love serves as a powerful reminder of the importance of embracing one's identity in the face of societal pressures. By promoting self-kindness, common humanity, and mindfulness, Alok encourages others to reject harmful norms and celebrate their uniqueness. Their impact is felt not only through their personal journey but also through the countless lives they have inspired to embrace self-love and acceptance. As Alok continues to challenge gender norms and advocate for LGBTQ+ rights, their message remains clear: self-love is not just an individual pursuit; it is a collective movement toward a more inclusive and accepting world.

Redefining Beauty Standards

Challenging the Binary Concept of Beauty

The concept of beauty has long been dominated by binary definitions that categorize individuals into rigid frameworks of attractiveness based on traditional norms. Alok Vaid-Menon, through their activism and fashion choices, boldly challenges these binary notions, advocating for a more fluid understanding of beauty that embraces diversity and self-expression. This section explores the theoretical underpinnings of beauty, the problems inherent in binary definitions, and the transformative examples set forth by Alok and others in the movement.

Theoretical Frameworks

Beauty, as a sociocultural construct, has been examined through various theoretical lenses. One prominent framework is the *social constructionism* theory, which posits that societal norms and values shape our understanding of beauty. This theory suggests that beauty is not an inherent quality but rather a product of cultural narratives and historical contexts. According to feminist theorist Susan Bordo, beauty ideals are often influenced by patriarchal standards that prioritize certain body types, skin tones, and gender presentations, effectively marginalizing those who do not conform to these ideals.

In contrast, *intersectionality* theory, coined by Kimberlé Crenshaw, emphasizes the interconnectedness of social categorizations such as race, gender, and class. This approach highlights how individuals experience beauty standards differently based on their unique identities. For example, a queer person of color may face distinct pressures and expectations regarding beauty that differ from those experienced by a cisgender white individual. Alok's work embodies this intersectional approach, advocating for beauty that transcends binary definitions and embraces a multitude of identities.

Problems with Binary Definitions of Beauty

Binary definitions of beauty often lead to exclusion and discrimination. These definitions typically reinforce a narrow standard that equates beauty with specific traits, such as thinness, youth, and Eurocentric features. This narrow view not only alienates individuals who do not fit these criteria but also perpetuates harmful stereotypes and societal pressures.

The *beauty myth*, as described by Naomi Wolf, illustrates how societal standards of beauty are used to control women and other marginalized groups. This myth suggests that women must adhere to certain beauty standards to achieve social and economic success, creating a cycle of self-objectification and insecurity. Alok's activism seeks to dismantle this myth by promoting the idea that beauty can be diverse, multifaceted, and not confined to any single narrative.

Moreover, binary beauty standards often ignore the experiences of non-binary and gender non-conforming individuals. For many, the pressure to conform to traditional gendered beauty standards can lead to feelings of inadequacy and alienation. Alok's approach challenges these norms by celebrating gender fluidity and encouraging individuals to embrace their authentic selves, regardless of societal expectations.

Examples of Challenging Beauty Norms

Alok Vaid-Menon's fashion choices serve as a powerful example of challenging binary beauty norms. By incorporating elements traditionally associated with femininity—such as bright colors, bold patterns, and flowing fabrics—into their wardrobe, Alok defies the conventional expectations of what beauty should look like. This approach not only empowers Alok but also inspires others to explore their own identities through fashion.

For instance, during various public appearances, Alok has worn outfits that blend masculine and feminine aesthetics, showcasing that beauty is not limited to one gender presentation. Their iconic looks, often characterized by vibrant colors and dramatic silhouettes, challenge the notion that beauty must conform to binary gender norms. This celebration of androgyny invites others to question their own perceptions of beauty and encourages a broader acceptance of diverse identities.

Additionally, Alok's advocacy extends beyond personal expression to encompass a larger movement for inclusivity in the fashion industry. By collaborating with designers who prioritize diversity and representation, Alok amplifies voices that have historically been marginalized in the beauty narrative. These collaborations not only challenge traditional beauty standards but also promote a more inclusive understanding of beauty that honors the richness of human experience.

Conclusion

In conclusion, the challenge to binary definitions of beauty is a crucial aspect of Alok Vaid-Menon's activism. By employing theoretical frameworks such as social constructionism and intersectionality, Alok illuminates the problems inherent in traditional beauty standards and advocates for a more inclusive understanding of beauty. Through their fashion choices and collaborations, Alok inspires individuals to embrace their authentic selves and redefine beauty on their own terms. The movement toward a more fluid and diverse conception of beauty is not just about aesthetics; it is a powerful form of resistance against societal norms that seek to confine and limit human expression. As we continue to challenge these binary concepts, we pave the way for a more inclusive and accepting world where everyone can celebrate their unique beauty.

Liberation through Self-Expression

Liberation through self-expression is a vital concept in the realm of LGBTQ activism, particularly as it relates to the journey of individuals like Alok Vaid-Menon. This section explores how self-expression serves as a powerful tool for personal and collective liberation, allowing individuals to break free from societal constraints and embrace their authentic selves.

Theoretical Framework

The theory of self-expression is rooted in several philosophical and psychological frameworks. One of the most relevant is the concept of *authenticity*, which refers to the degree to which individuals are true to their own personality, spirit, or character. According to [?], authenticity is closely linked to self-esteem and psychological well-being. The ability to express oneself freely contributes to a sense of identity and belonging, which is crucial for marginalized communities.

Furthermore, [?] posits that power dynamics in society often dictate what forms of expression are deemed acceptable. For LGBTQ individuals, these dynamics can manifest in various ways, including societal expectations around gender presentation and sexual orientation. Thus, liberation through self-expression can be seen as a form of resistance against oppressive structures, allowing individuals to reclaim their narratives and identities.

Challenges to Self-Expression

Despite its importance, self-expression is often met with significant challenges, particularly for LGBTQ individuals. Societal norms and expectations can create barriers that inhibit authentic expression. For example, individuals may face discrimination, ostracization, or violence for deviating from traditional gender roles or sexual orientations.

This oppression is not just external; internalized stigma can also play a significant role. [?] describes this phenomenon as *minority stress*, which refers to the chronic stress experienced by individuals who belong to marginalized groups. This stress can lead to a reluctance to express one's identity, resulting in a cycle of repression and self-doubt.

Examples of Liberation through Self-Expression

Alok Vaid-Menon's journey exemplifies the transformative power of self-expression. Through their unique fashion choices, Alok has challenged conventional notions of gender and beauty. By donning vibrant, gender-nonconforming attire, Alok not only asserts their identity but also invites others to question and redefine their own understanding of self-expression.

One notable example is Alok's participation in fashion shows where they showcase clothing that defies traditional gender binaries. These runway appearances serve as a powerful statement, demonstrating that fashion can be a medium for activism. Alok's bold choices encourage others to explore their own identities through personal style, fostering a sense of community and acceptance.

Moreover, Alok's use of social media platforms amplifies their message of liberation. By sharing their experiences and fashion journeys online, they create a digital space where individuals can express themselves without fear of judgment. This virtual community serves as a sanctuary for many who may feel isolated in their offline lives.

The Impact of Self-Expression on Mental Health

The act of self-expression has profound implications for mental health, particularly within the LGBTQ community. Studies indicate that individuals who engage in self-expressive activities report higher levels of well-being and lower levels of anxiety and depression [?]. This correlation highlights the importance of creating environments where self-expression is not only accepted but celebrated.

For many, the journey toward self-expression can be therapeutic. Engaging in creative outlets—such as fashion, art, or performance—allows individuals to process their experiences and emotions. Alok's artistic endeavors, including spoken word poetry and performance art, exemplify how creativity can serve as a powerful form of self-exploration and healing.

Conclusion

In conclusion, liberation through self-expression is a multifaceted concept that plays a crucial role in the lives of LGBTQ individuals. By embracing their authentic selves, individuals like Alok Vaid-Menon challenge societal norms and inspire others to do the same. While obstacles remain, the journey toward self-expression is essential for personal and collective liberation, fostering environments where diversity is celebrated and all voices are heard. Ultimately, the act of expressing oneself is not just a personal triumph; it is a revolutionary act that can spark broader societal change.

Alok's Impact on the Fashion Industry

Alok Vaid-Menon has made a significant mark on the fashion industry, not only as a creator and model but also as a powerful advocate for inclusivity and diversity. Their approach to fashion challenges traditional notions of beauty and gender, pushing the boundaries of what is considered acceptable in mainstream fashion. This section explores Alok's profound impact on the fashion industry, highlighting their unique contributions and the broader implications of their work.

Challenging Traditional Norms

Alok's fashion philosophy operates on the premise that clothing should not be confined to binary gender norms. They have consistently challenged the idea that fashion must adhere to a rigid set of rules based on gender, arguing instead for a more fluid understanding of self-expression. This perspective aligns with Judith Butler's theory of gender performativity, which posits that gender is not a fixed identity but rather a series of performances influenced by societal norms. Alok embodies this theory through their bold fashion choices, which often blend elements traditionally associated with both masculinity and femininity.

$$G = \sum_{i=1}^{n} P_i \cdot W_i \qquad (21)$$

Where:

- G = Gender expression
- P_i = Performance of gender traits
- W_i = Weight assigned to each trait based on societal perception

Alok's work suggests that by redefining the weights assigned to various traits, individuals can construct a more authentic gender expression that resonates with their identity.

Redefining Beauty Standards

Alok's influence extends to redefining beauty standards within the fashion industry. By embracing and celebrating diversity in body types, skin tones, and gender expressions, Alok has paved the way for a more inclusive understanding of beauty. This shift is crucial in an industry historically dominated by narrow ideals that often exclude marginalized communities.

For instance, Alok's collaboration with various designers has led to collections that showcase a spectrum of beauty, emphasizing that fashion should be accessible to everyone, regardless of their gender identity or body shape. This aligns with bell hooks' concept of the "oppositional gaze," which encourages individuals to critically assess and challenge mainstream representations of beauty and identity.

Visibility and Representation

Through their visibility as a non-binary individual in the fashion industry, Alok has become a beacon for those who feel underrepresented. Their presence on runways, in campaigns, and on social media platforms has not only elevated their own career but also opened doors for others in the LGBTQ community. This visibility challenges the traditional narratives that often marginalize non-binary and gender non-conforming individuals.

In 2020, Alok made headlines by walking in a major fashion show wearing a stunning ensemble that defied gender norms. This moment was not just a personal triumph but a statement that reverberated throughout the industry, prompting discussions about diversity and representation. Alok's influence can be seen in the increasing number of brands that now feature non-binary models and promote gender-inclusive clothing lines.

Collaborative Efforts with Designers

Alok's collaborations with designers have resulted in collections that reflect their advocacy for inclusivity. For example, their partnership with a renowned fashion brand to create a line of gender-neutral clothing showcased the potential for fashion to transcend traditional gender binaries. This collaboration not only provided consumers with more options but also sent a message to the industry that inclusivity is not just a trend but a necessity.

$$C = D + I \tag{22}$$

Where:

- C = Collaborative impact
- D = Diversity in design
- I = Inclusivity in marketing

This equation underscores the idea that true impact in the fashion industry comes from a combination of diverse design choices and inclusive marketing strategies.

Empowering Others through Fashion

Alok's activism extends beyond personal expression; it aims to empower others to embrace their identities through fashion. By sharing their journey and experiences on social media, Alok has inspired countless individuals to experiment with their style and challenge societal expectations. This empowerment is particularly significant for LGBTQ youth who often face pressure to conform to traditional gender norms.

Alok's message is clear: fashion is a tool for self-empowerment and should be used to celebrate one's identity rather than suppress it. This philosophy has led to workshops and talks where Alok engages with young people, encouraging them to explore their unique styles and embrace their authentic selves.

The Future of Fashion with Alok's Influence

As the fashion industry continues to evolve, Alok's impact will undoubtedly play a crucial role in shaping its future. Their advocacy for inclusivity and diversity is not just a fleeting trend but a movement towards a more equitable industry. Alok's influence encourages brands to rethink their marketing strategies, design processes, and overall approach to fashion.

In conclusion, Alok Vaid-Menon's impact on the fashion industry is profound and multifaceted. By challenging traditional norms, redefining beauty standards, and advocating for visibility and representation, Alok has inspired a new generation of designers, models, and consumers. Their work exemplifies the transformative power of fashion as a means of self-expression and activism, paving the way for a more inclusive future in the industry.

Celebrating Diversity on the Runway

The runway has long been a stage for the display of fashion, but it has also been a battleground for the representation of diverse identities. In recent years, the call for diversity in fashion has become louder, and figures like Alok Vaid-Menon have played a pivotal role in advocating for a broader spectrum of representation. This section explores how Alok and others have championed diversity on the runway, the theoretical underpinnings of this movement, the challenges faced, and the transformative examples that have emerged.

Theoretical Framework

At the core of the celebration of diversity on the runway lies the theory of intersectionality, coined by Kimberlé Crenshaw in the late 1980s. Intersectionality posits that individuals experience overlapping identities—such as race, gender, sexual orientation, and class—that shape their experiences of oppression and privilege. In the context of fashion, this theory encourages a holistic approach to representation, where the diverse identities of models, designers, and audiences are acknowledged and celebrated.

The equation for intersectionality can be conceptualized as follows:

$$I = \sum_{n=1}^{k}(P_n \times O_n) \qquad (23)$$

Where: - I represents the intersectional identity. - P_n represents the various identities (e.g., gender, race, sexual orientation). - O_n represents the experiences of oppression or privilege associated with those identities.

This framework underscores the importance of not only including a variety of body types, ethnicities, and gender expressions on the runway but also recognizing how these identities interact to inform unique experiences in the fashion industry.

Challenges in Representation

Despite the growing recognition of the need for diversity on the runway, significant challenges persist. The fashion industry has historically favored a narrow standard of beauty, often perpetuating stereotypes and excluding marginalized communities. This has led to a lack of representation for models who do not fit the traditional mold, including plus-size models, models of color, and those who identify as non-binary or gender nonconforming.

One major problem is the prevalence of tokenism, where a single individual from a marginalized group is included in a fashion show or campaign to give the appearance of diversity without addressing systemic issues. This practice can undermine the authenticity of representation and perpetuate existing power dynamics within the industry.

Transformative Examples

Alok Vaid-Menon has emerged as a trailblazer in advocating for diversity on the runway. Their unique style and unapologetic expression of gender fluidity challenge traditional notions of beauty and fashion. Alok's participation in various fashion events has not only showcased their distinctive aesthetic but also sparked conversations about the need for inclusivity in the industry.

One notable example is the 2019 New York Fashion Week, where Alok walked the runway for the designer, Palomo Spain. Their appearance was a powerful statement, breaking down barriers and challenging the binary norms of gender in fashion. The show featured a diverse cast of models, celebrating a range of identities and body types, thus embodying the principles of intersectionality.

Another significant moment occurred at the 2020 Met Gala, where Alok's bold fashion choices were celebrated as a form of activism. Their outfit, which combined elements of traditional Indian attire with contemporary fashion, highlighted the importance of cultural representation and the need to honor diverse heritages on a global stage.

Impact on the Fashion Industry

The push for diversity on the runway has begun to influence the fashion industry significantly. Brands are increasingly recognizing the importance of inclusivity, not only as a moral imperative but also as a business strategy. Research has shown that brands that embrace diversity tend to resonate more with consumers, particularly younger generations who prioritize social justice and representation.

For instance, the rise of brands like Savage X Fenty, founded by Rihanna, has set a new standard for inclusivity in lingerie. The brand's runway shows feature models of all shapes, sizes, and backgrounds, celebrating body positivity and diversity. This approach not only empowers models but also encourages consumers to embrace their own identities and bodies.

Conclusion

Celebrating diversity on the runway is not merely a trend; it is a necessary evolution in the fashion industry that reflects the complexities of identity in contemporary society. Through the advocacy of figures like Alok Vaid-Menon and the growing recognition of intersectionality, the runway is transforming into a platform for authentic representation. While challenges remain, the ongoing efforts to celebrate diversity are paving the way for a more inclusive future in fashion, where every identity is honored and every story is told.

Collaborating with Designers and Brands

Alok Vaid-Menon has made a significant impact on the fashion industry, not only through their unique personal style but also by collaborating with various designers and brands to promote inclusivity and challenge traditional beauty standards. These collaborations are not merely partnerships; they embody a shared vision of breaking down the barriers of gender norms and redefining what it means to be fashionable in today's world.

Theoretical Framework

The collaboration between activists like Alok and fashion designers can be understood through the lens of intersectionality, a theory coined by Kimberlé Crenshaw, which posits that individuals experience overlapping systems of discrimination or disadvantage. In the context of fashion, this means that the identities of LGBTQ individuals, especially those who are non-binary or gender non-conforming, are often marginalized within the industry. By collaborating with designers, Alok not only brings visibility to these identities but also challenges the predominantly binary nature of fashion.

The Problems of Representation

Despite the progress made, the fashion industry still grapples with several issues, including:

- **Lack of Diversity:** Many fashion brands continue to promote a narrow definition of beauty that often excludes marginalized identities.
- **Tokenism:** Collaborations can sometimes be superficial, where brands engage with LGBTQ activists only for marketing purposes, without genuine commitment to inclusivity.
- **Commercialization of Activism:** There is a growing concern that the commercialization of activism can dilute its message, turning meaningful advocacy into mere branding.

Alok's collaborations are therefore crucial in addressing these issues, as they aim to create authentic representations that resonate with a broader audience.

Examples of Collaborations

One notable collaboration was with the fashion brand *Collina Strada*, where Alok walked the runway in vibrant, gender-fluid designs that challenged conventional notions of masculinity and femininity. This partnership not only showcased Alok's unique aesthetic but also emphasized the importance of inclusivity in fashion shows.

Another significant collaboration was with *ASOS*, where Alok contributed to a campaign that aimed to celebrate diversity in body types and gender expressions. This collaboration included a collection that featured clothing designed specifically for non-binary individuals, thus promoting the idea that fashion should be accessible to everyone, regardless of gender identity.

Impact on the Fashion Industry

The impact of Alok's collaborations extends beyond mere visibility. They serve as a catalyst for change within the fashion industry by:

- **Redefining Beauty Standards:** Alok's work encourages designers to embrace a broader range of body types and gender expressions, ultimately leading to a more inclusive fashion landscape.

- **Inspiring Future Designers:** By working with Alok, emerging designers are inspired to incorporate inclusivity into their own practices, fostering a new generation of fashion that values diversity.

- **Creating Safe Spaces:** Collaborations often result in the creation of safe spaces within the fashion industry where marginalized voices can be heard and celebrated.

Conclusion

In conclusion, Alok Vaid-Menon's collaborations with designers and brands exemplify the power of fashion as a tool for activism. By challenging the status quo and advocating for inclusivity, Alok not only transforms the fashion industry but also inspires individuals to embrace their authentic selves. These partnerships reflect a growing recognition that fashion can be a platform for social change, where creativity and activism converge to create a more equitable world.

$$\text{Inclusivity} = \text{Visibility} + \text{Representation} + \text{Authenticity} \qquad (24)$$

This equation encapsulates the essence of Alok's collaborations, emphasizing that true inclusivity in fashion requires a multifaceted approach that prioritizes visibility, representation, and authenticity.

Empowering Others through Fashion

Fashion is not merely a means of adornment; it serves as a powerful vehicle for self-expression and empowerment, particularly within marginalized communities. Alok Vaid-Menon's approach to fashion transcends traditional aesthetics, acting as a catalyst for change and a platform for advocacy. This section explores how Alok empowers others through fashion, drawing on relevant theories, addressing systemic issues, and providing concrete examples of impact.

Theoretical Framework

The intersection of fashion and identity is grounded in various theoretical perspectives. One key theory is the *Social Identity Theory*, which posits that individuals derive a sense of self from their group memberships. In the context of fashion, individuals often use clothing and style to express their identities and affiliations. Alok's work emphasizes the importance of fashion as a means to challenge societal norms and assert one's identity, particularly for those who identify as LGBTQ.

Another relevant framework is *Postmodernism*, which deconstructs established narratives and embraces diversity in representation. Alok's fashion philosophy aligns with this perspective, as they advocate for a fluid understanding of gender and identity that rejects binary constraints. By embracing non-conformity in fashion, Alok encourages others to explore their identities without fear of judgment.

Addressing Systemic Issues

Fashion can be a double-edged sword; while it offers avenues for expression, it can also perpetuate harmful stereotypes and reinforce societal norms. Alok addresses these systemic issues by challenging traditional beauty standards and advocating for inclusivity within the fashion industry. The industry's historical focus on Eurocentric beauty ideals often marginalizes people of color, plus-size individuals, and those who defy gender norms. Alok's activism seeks to dismantle these barriers, promoting a more inclusive definition of beauty that celebrates diversity.

One significant problem in the fashion industry is the lack of representation for transgender and non-binary individuals. Alok's visibility and advocacy have opened doors for greater representation, pushing brands to feature models of diverse gender identities. This shift not only empowers individuals within the LGBTQ community but also educates the broader public on the importance of inclusivity.

Concrete Examples of Empowerment

Alok's impact is evident through various initiatives aimed at empowering others through fashion. For instance, their collaboration with fashion brands has resulted in collections that reflect non-binary aesthetics, allowing individuals to express themselves authentically. By partnering with designers who share a commitment to inclusivity, Alok helps create spaces where marginalized voices are heard and celebrated.

A notable example is Alok's work with the brand *Ganni*, where they promoted a gender-neutral collection that challenged traditional fashion norms. This collaboration not only showcased Alok's unique style but also sent a powerful message about the importance of inclusivity in fashion. The success of such initiatives demonstrates that fashion can be a tool for empowerment, allowing individuals to embrace their identities and challenge societal expectations.

Moreover, Alok's social media presence plays a crucial role in empowering others. By sharing their fashion journey and personal experiences, Alok inspires countless individuals to embrace their authentic selves. Their viral videos often highlight the importance of self-love and acceptance, encouraging followers to reject societal pressures and express themselves freely through fashion.

The Role of Community in Fashion Empowerment

Empowerment through fashion is not solely an individual endeavor; it is also about fostering community. Alok emphasizes the importance of creating supportive environments where individuals can explore their identities without fear of judgment. Initiatives such as fashion workshops and community events provide safe spaces for self-expression and creativity.

For example, Alok has organized workshops that focus on sustainable fashion practices while encouraging participants to explore their personal styles. These events not only promote environmental consciousness but also empower individuals to take ownership of their fashion choices. By fostering a sense of community, Alok helps dismantle the isolation often felt by those who challenge traditional gender norms.

Conclusion

In conclusion, Alok Vaid-Menon's approach to empowering others through fashion exemplifies the transformative power of self-expression. By challenging societal norms, addressing systemic issues, and fostering community, Alok creates spaces where individuals can embrace their authentic selves. Fashion becomes a tool for advocacy, allowing marginalized voices to be heard and celebrated. Through their work, Alok continues to inspire a generation to break free from conventional beauty standards and redefine what it means to be empowered through fashion.

Transforming Beauty Standards

In the realm of fashion and activism, Alok Vaid-Menon stands as a beacon of change, revolutionizing the way society perceives beauty. This transformation is not merely superficial; it is deeply rooted in the understanding that beauty is a social construct, shaped by cultural, historical, and economic factors. Alok's work challenges the traditional notions of beauty that have long been dominated by narrow, Eurocentric ideals, advocating for a more inclusive and diverse representation that embraces all identities.

Theoretical Framework

To comprehend the transformation of beauty standards, it is essential to explore the theories surrounding beauty and aesthetics. The concept of beauty has been historically tied to power dynamics and societal norms. Sociologist Pierre Bourdieu's theory of *habitus* explains how individuals internalize societal norms and values, which in turn shapes their perceptions of beauty. This internalization often leads to the reinforcement of stereotypes and exclusionary practices.

Moreover, Judith Butler's theory of *gender performativity* posits that gender is not an inherent quality but rather a series of acts and performances. Alok's approach to beauty aligns with Butler's ideas, as they encourage individuals to embrace their unique expressions of gender and beauty, thereby dismantling the rigid binaries that have long dictated societal standards.

Challenges to Traditional Beauty Norms

Alok's advocacy highlights several challenges that individuals face when confronting traditional beauty standards. These challenges include:

- **Systemic Exclusion:** Many marginalized communities, particularly those who are queer and trans, have historically been excluded from mainstream beauty narratives. This exclusion perpetuates feelings of inadequacy and reinforces harmful stereotypes.

- **Body Image Issues:** The pressure to conform to specific beauty standards can lead to body dysmorphia, eating disorders, and mental health struggles. Alok's message promotes body positivity, encouraging individuals to love their bodies as they are.

- **Economic Barriers:** The beauty industry often prioritizes profit over inclusivity, creating products that cater primarily to a narrow demographic. This economic exclusion further marginalizes diverse identities.

Examples of Transformation in Action

Alok's influence on beauty standards can be seen through various initiatives and collaborations that promote diversity and inclusivity:

- **Fashion Collaborations:** Alok has partnered with designers and brands that prioritize inclusivity in their collections. For example, their collaboration with a well-known fashion label resulted in a line that celebrates non-binary and gender-fluid styles, showcasing a range of body types and identities.
- **Social Media Campaigns:** Through platforms like Instagram and TikTok, Alok has launched campaigns that challenge conventional beauty norms. Hashtags like #BeautyBeyondBinary encourage individuals to share their unique styles and narratives, fostering a sense of community and belonging.
- **Public Speaking Engagements:** Alok's talks at universities and conferences often center around the importance of redefining beauty standards. By sharing personal stories and experiences, Alok empowers audiences to question societal norms and embrace their authentic selves.

The Impact of Transformation

The impact of Alok's work in transforming beauty standards is profound and far-reaching. By advocating for a broader definition of beauty, Alok not only empowers individuals to embrace their identities but also challenges the fashion industry to evolve. This shift has led to:

- **Increased Representation:** More brands are recognizing the importance of diverse representation in their advertising and runway shows. This visibility not only validates marginalized identities but also inspires future generations to express themselves freely.
- **Cultural Shifts:** Alok's message has contributed to a cultural shift towards acceptance and celebration of diversity. The growing acceptance of various gender expressions and body types signifies a move away from rigid beauty standards.
- **Community Empowerment:** By fostering a sense of community among individuals who have been marginalized by traditional beauty norms, Alok creates spaces where people can share their experiences and support one another in their journeys toward self-acceptance.

In conclusion, Alok Vaid-Menon's work in transforming beauty standards is a vital component of their broader activism. By challenging societal norms and advocating for inclusivity, Alok not only redefines what it means to be beautiful but also paves the way for a future where all identities are celebrated. As we continue to navigate the complexities of beauty in our society, Alok's message of radical self-love and acceptance remains a guiding light for many.

Breaking Free from Societal Expectations

In a world where societal norms often dictate how individuals should express their gender, Alok Vaid-Menon stands as a beacon of liberation, challenging the rigid frameworks that constrain self-identity and expression. The act of breaking free from societal expectations involves not only personal courage but also a profound understanding of the systemic structures that uphold these norms.

Theoretical Framework

To comprehend the magnitude of breaking societal expectations, one must first explore the theoretical underpinnings of gender norms. Judith Butler's theory of gender performativity is pivotal here. Butler posits that gender is not an inherent quality but rather a series of performances dictated by societal expectations. This perspective suggests that when individuals like Alok defy these performances, they are not merely acting against societal norms; they are reshaping the very fabric of gender identity.

$$\text{Gender} = f(\text{Performance}, \text{Societal Norms}) \qquad (25)$$

This equation illustrates that gender identity is a function of both individual performance and the societal norms that influence that performance. Alok's work exemplifies the disruption of this relationship, showcasing that identity can transcend binary classifications.

Challenges of Societal Expectations

The journey to break free from societal expectations is fraught with challenges. Individuals often face backlash from family, peers, and society at large. This backlash can manifest in various forms, including discrimination, violence, and ostracism. Alok's experience is a testament to this struggle. As a gender non-conforming individual, Alok has faced numerous instances of hostility, both online and offline.

For instance, Alok's bold fashion choices have often been met with ridicule and aggression, illustrating the societal discomfort with non-traditional expressions of gender. This discomfort is not merely personal; it reflects a broader societal problem where deviation from the norm is often met with hostility.

Examples of Breaking Free

Alok's fashion journey is a vivid illustration of breaking free from societal expectations. By embracing bold colors, extravagant fabrics, and unconventional silhouettes, Alok not only expresses their identity but also invites others to reconsider their own relationship with gender norms. Each outfit becomes a statement, challenging the viewer to confront their biases and assumptions.

Moreover, Alok's viral social media presence serves as a platform for this rebellion. Through platforms like Instagram and TikTok, Alok shares not only fashion but also messages of self-love and acceptance. This use of social media exemplifies how individuals can leverage technology to foster change and challenge societal norms.

The Role of Community

Breaking free from societal expectations is not a solitary endeavor; it is often supported by community solidarity. Alok has actively engaged with various marginalized groups, amplifying their voices and fostering a sense of belonging. This communal aspect is crucial, as it provides individuals with the support needed to navigate the challenges of non-conformity.

The concept of intersectionality, as articulated by Kimberlé Crenshaw, further underscores the importance of community in this struggle. Intersectionality recognizes that individuals experience oppression in varying degrees based on multiple identities, including race, gender, and sexuality. Alok's advocacy work highlights the necessity of addressing these intersecting identities to create a more inclusive society.

$$\text{Oppression} = f(\text{Identity}, \text{Societal Structures}) \tag{26}$$

This equation suggests that oppression is a complex interplay of individual identity and the societal structures that perpetuate inequality. Alok's work seeks to dismantle these structures, advocating for a world where everyone can express their identity freely.

Conclusion

In conclusion, breaking free from societal expectations is an essential aspect of Alok Vaid-Menon's activism and fashion journey. Through theoretical frameworks like gender performativity and intersectionality, we can better understand the complexities of identity and the societal structures that seek to confine it. Alok's bold expressions of self, coupled with a commitment to community empowerment, serve as powerful reminders that liberation is possible. By challenging societal norms, Alok not only redefines beauty and identity but also inspires a generation to embrace their authentic selves, paving the way for a more inclusive future.

$$\text{Liberation} = \text{Self-Expression} + \text{Community Support} \qquad (27)$$

Thus, the journey of breaking free from societal expectations is not just an individual pursuit but a collective movement toward a world where diversity in identity is celebrated and embraced.

Inspiring a Generation to Embrace Their Authentic Selves

In a world that often imposes rigid expectations on identity, Alok Vaid-Menon emerges as a beacon of hope, encouraging individuals to embrace their true selves without the constraints of societal norms. This section explores how Alok's advocacy and personal journey serve as an inspiration for a generation grappling with the complexities of identity, authenticity, and self-expression.

Theoretical Framework: Authenticity and Identity

Authenticity is a multifaceted concept that has been explored across various disciplines, including psychology, sociology, and cultural studies. According to [?], authenticity involves a sense of self that is consistent with one's values, beliefs, and feelings, leading to a more fulfilling life. In the context of LGBTQ+ identities, authenticity becomes particularly significant as individuals navigate societal pressures that often dictate how they should express their gender and sexuality.

Alok's approach aligns with the principles of *intersectionality*, a term coined by [?], which emphasizes the interconnectedness of social categorizations such as race, gender, and sexuality. By acknowledging the diverse experiences within the LGBTQ+ community, Alok advocates for a broader understanding of authenticity that encompasses various identities and expressions.

Challenges to Authenticity

Despite the growing acceptance of diverse identities, many individuals still face significant challenges in their pursuit of authenticity. These challenges can include:

- **Social Stigma:** Individuals who deviate from traditional gender norms often encounter prejudice and discrimination. This stigma can lead to internalized shame and a reluctance to express one's true self.

- **Family Rejection:** For many LGBTQ+ individuals, acceptance from family is crucial. Unfortunately, rejection can result in emotional distress and a sense of isolation.

- **Economic Barriers:** Financial instability can hinder one's ability to express their identity freely, particularly in communities where conformity is expected for social and economic survival.

Alok addresses these challenges head-on, using their platform to highlight the importance of self-acceptance and resilience. Through their work, they provide a roadmap for individuals seeking to navigate these obstacles.

Real-Life Examples of Inspiration

Alok's influence extends beyond their personal narrative; they actively engage with audiences to foster a culture of acceptance and self-love. For instance, during public speaking engagements, Alok often shares stories of individuals who have embraced their identities against all odds. One poignant example is the story of a young non-binary person who, after attending one of Alok's workshops, found the courage to come out to their family. This act of bravery not only transformed their life but also inspired their siblings to explore their own identities.

Moreover, Alok's viral social media posts serve as powerful tools for inspiration. By sharing their own experiences of gender fluidity, Alok creates a sense of community and belonging for those who may feel marginalized. Their message resonates particularly with youth, who often struggle with societal expectations. As Alok states, "You are not a problem to be solved; you are a miracle to be celebrated."

The Role of Art in Self-Expression

Art plays a crucial role in Alok's activism, serving as both a medium for personal expression and a platform for broader social commentary. Through performance art, poetry, and fashion, Alok challenges conventional notions of beauty and identity. This artistic expression not only empowers Alok but also inspires others to explore their creativity as a means of self-discovery.

For example, Alok's fashion choices often defy traditional gender norms, showcasing a vibrant palette of colors and styles that celebrate individuality. By doing so, Alok encourages others to experiment with their own forms of self-expression, reinforcing the idea that authenticity is not a destination but a continuous journey.

Creating Safe Spaces for Authenticity

Alok emphasizes the importance of creating safe spaces where individuals can explore their identities without fear of judgment. This concept is particularly vital in educational settings, where young people should feel free to express themselves. Alok's initiatives, such as workshops and mentorship programs, aim to cultivate environments that foster acceptance and understanding.

In these safe spaces, participants are encouraged to share their stories, engage in dialogue about identity, and support one another in their journeys. This communal approach not only validates individual experiences but also strengthens the collective fight for LGBTQ+ rights.

Conclusion: A Call to Action

Alok Vaid-Menon's work is a clarion call for a generation to embrace their authentic selves. By challenging societal norms, sharing personal narratives, and creating inclusive spaces, Alok inspires individuals to reject the limitations imposed by traditional gender roles and to celebrate their uniqueness. As we move forward, it is essential to carry this message of authenticity and acceptance into our communities, fostering an environment where everyone can thrive as their true selves.

In the words of Alok, "Your existence is a revolution." This powerful assertion encapsulates the essence of their activism and serves as a reminder that embracing one's authentic self is not only a personal journey but a collective movement toward a more inclusive and compassionate world.

Promoting body positivity

Body positivity is a movement that celebrates the acceptance of all bodies, regardless of size, shape, or appearance. This concept is particularly significant within the LGBTQ community, where traditional beauty standards often marginalize individuals who do not conform to societal expectations. Alok Vaid-Menon has emerged as a powerful advocate for body positivity, challenging the narrow definitions of beauty that have long dominated the fashion industry and popular culture.

The body positivity movement is rooted in several theoretical frameworks, including feminist theory, queer theory, and critical race theory. Feminist theory critiques the ways in which women's bodies have been objectified and commodified, advocating for a broader understanding of beauty that includes diverse body types. Queer theory further expands this critique by questioning normative gender roles and the binary classifications that often dictate societal standards of beauty. Critical race theory adds another layer, emphasizing how race and body image intersect, leading to unique challenges faced by individuals of color within the body positivity discourse.

One of the primary problems that the body positivity movement seeks to address is the pervasive influence of media representations that promote unrealistic body standards. These representations often lead to body dissatisfaction, low self-esteem, and mental health issues among individuals who feel they do not measure up. Alok has used their platform to highlight these issues, emphasizing that the fashion industry must evolve to embrace a more inclusive definition of beauty.

For instance, Alok's collaborations with various designers and brands have showcased a wide range of body types, challenging the traditional runway model aesthetic. By featuring models of different sizes, shapes, and identities, these collaborations not only promote body positivity but also encourage consumers to embrace their own bodies. Alok often states, "Fashion should be a celebration of who we are, not a restriction on what we can be." This sentiment resonates deeply within the body positivity movement, as it seeks to dismantle the societal pressures that dictate how individuals should look.

Moreover, Alok's advocacy extends beyond mere representation. They actively engage in conversations about the intersection of body image and mental health, emphasizing the importance of self-love and acceptance. In various interviews and social media posts, Alok shares their personal experiences with body image struggles, resonating with many individuals who face similar challenges. By being vulnerable and open about their journey, Alok fosters a sense of community and solidarity among those who feel marginalized by conventional beauty standards.

The impact of Alok's work in promoting body positivity is evident in the growing movement that encourages individuals to celebrate their bodies as they are. For example, the #BodyPositivity hashtag has gained significant traction on social media platforms, where individuals share their own stories and photos, challenging the notion that beauty is a one-size-fits-all concept. Alok has been instrumental in amplifying these voices, advocating for a world where everyone can feel comfortable in their skin.

In conclusion, promoting body positivity is not merely about aesthetic representation; it is about fostering a culture of acceptance and love for oneself and others. Alok Vaid-Menon exemplifies this ethos through their activism and fashion choices, encouraging individuals to break free from societal constraints and embrace their authentic selves. As the body positivity movement continues to grow, it holds the potential to transform not only individual lives but also the broader cultural landscape, paving the way for a more inclusive and accepting society.

$$B = \frac{P}{S} \qquad (28)$$

where B represents body positivity, P represents personal acceptance, and S represents societal standards. This equation illustrates that as personal acceptance increases, body positivity also rises, regardless of societal pressures.

By fostering a dialogue around body positivity, activists like Alok Vaid-Menon pave the way for future generations to embrace their identities and bodies without fear of judgment or exclusion. The journey towards body positivity is ongoing, but with voices like Alok's leading the charge, there is hope for a more inclusive future.

A Champion for LGBTQ Rights

Advocacy on a Global Scale

Alok Vaid-Menon has emerged as a powerful advocate for LGBTQ rights on a global scale, utilizing their platform to address systemic injustices and promote inclusivity across various cultures. This section delves into the multifaceted approach Alok employs to advocate for LGBTQ rights internationally, highlighting key theories, challenges, and examples that illustrate their impact.

Theoretical Framework

Alok's advocacy is deeply rooted in intersectional theory, which posits that various forms of social stratification, such as race, gender, and sexuality, do not exist independently but are interwoven. This perspective is crucial for understanding the complexities faced by LGBTQ individuals, especially in regions where cultural norms may be particularly oppressive. As Crenshaw (1989) articulates, intersectionality helps to illuminate how overlapping identities can lead to unique experiences of discrimination and marginalization.

Global Challenges

Despite significant progress in many Western countries, LGBTQ individuals worldwide continue to face severe discrimination, violence, and legal challenges. According to the International Lesbian, Gay, Bisexual, Trans and Intersex Association (ILGA), over 70 countries still criminalize same-sex relationships, and many others have no legal protections against discrimination based on sexual orientation or gender identity.

Alok has consistently highlighted these issues, advocating for a global approach to LGBTQ rights that considers cultural contexts while emphasizing universal human rights. They assert that "the fight for LGBTQ rights is not just a Western issue; it is a global struggle for dignity and respect." This perspective challenges the notion that LGBTQ rights are merely a Western import, instead framing them as a fundamental aspect of human rights.

Examples of Global Advocacy

One of the most notable examples of Alok's global advocacy is their work with LGBTQ refugees and immigrants. Alok has traveled to various countries, including those in Africa and the Middle East, where LGBTQ individuals face extreme violence and persecution. Through partnerships with organizations like Rainbow Railroad, Alok has helped facilitate safe passage for individuals fleeing life-threatening situations due to their sexual orientation or gender identity.

In 2019, Alok participated in a panel discussion at the United Nations Human Rights Council, where they addressed the urgent need for international protections for LGBTQ individuals. Their speech highlighted the plight of LGBTQ people in countries with harsh anti-LGBTQ laws, calling for global leaders to take a stand against discrimination and violence. Alok's presence at such high-profile events underscores the importance of elevating LGBTQ voices in international discourse.

Cultural Sensitivity in Advocacy

Alok's advocacy is characterized by a deep respect for cultural differences. They emphasize the importance of understanding local contexts and working collaboratively with local activists. For instance, Alok has collaborated with grassroots organizations in countries with restrictive LGBTQ laws, ensuring that advocacy efforts are not imposed from the outside but rather led by those who understand the cultural nuances.

This approach aligns with the theory of cultural relativism, which posits that beliefs and practices should be understood based on an individual's own culture. Alok's commitment to cultural sensitivity allows for a more nuanced dialogue about LGBTQ rights, fostering solidarity rather than imposing a singular narrative.

Empowerment through Education

Education plays a crucial role in Alok's global advocacy efforts. By conducting workshops and speaking engagements around the world, they aim to empower LGBTQ individuals and allies with knowledge and resources. Alok's educational initiatives often focus on the importance of self-acceptance and resilience, encouraging individuals to embrace their identities despite societal pressures.

For example, in partnership with local NGOs, Alok has led workshops in regions where LGBTQ youth face significant challenges. These workshops provide safe spaces for young people to express themselves, share their experiences, and learn about their rights. Alok's emphasis on empowerment through education reflects the belief that informed individuals are better equipped to advocate for themselves and their communities.

Conclusion

In conclusion, Alok Vaid-Menon's advocacy on a global scale exemplifies a holistic approach to promoting LGBTQ rights. By integrating intersectional theory, addressing global challenges, emphasizing cultural sensitivity, and prioritizing education, Alok has made significant strides in advancing the rights of LGBTQ individuals worldwide. Their work serves as a powerful reminder that the fight for equality transcends borders and that solidarity among diverse communities is essential for achieving lasting change.

$$\text{Advocacy}_{global} = \text{Intersectionality} + \text{Cultural Sensitivity} + \text{Education} + \text{Empowerment} \tag{29}$$

Fighting for LGBTQ Rights

Alok Vaid-Menon has emerged as a formidable advocate in the struggle for LGBTQ rights, using their platform to challenge systemic discrimination and promote inclusivity. This section delves into the multifaceted approach Alok employs in their activism, highlighting the theoretical frameworks that underpin their work, the pressing issues faced by the LGBTQ community, and the impact of their efforts on legislation and public perception.

Theoretical Frameworks

At the heart of Alok's activism lies a commitment to intersectionality, a term coined by Kimberlé Crenshaw in the late 1980s. Intersectionality posits that individuals experience oppression in varying degrees based on overlapping social identities, including race, gender, sexuality, and class. Alok's advocacy emphasizes the importance of recognizing these intersecting identities to address the unique challenges faced by marginalized groups within the LGBTQ community, particularly queer and trans people of color.

Alok also draws from queer theory, which critiques the binary understanding of gender and sexuality. Judith Butler's notion of gender performativity suggests that gender is not an innate quality but rather a series of acts and behaviors that are socially constructed. Alok's fashion choices and public persona exemplify this theory, as they intentionally blur gender lines, challenging societal norms and encouraging others to embrace their authentic selves.

Pressing Issues in LGBTQ Rights

Despite significant progress in recent decades, LGBTQ individuals continue to face pervasive discrimination and violence. Issues such as the lack of legal protections against discrimination in employment, housing, and healthcare remain critical. According to the Human Rights Campaign, nearly 50% of LGBTQ individuals report experiencing discrimination in various aspects of their lives. This systemic inequality is particularly pronounced for transgender individuals, who face higher rates of violence and discrimination.

Furthermore, the rise of anti-LGBTQ legislation in various states poses a significant threat to the rights and safety of LGBTQ individuals. For instance, bills targeting transgender youth's access to healthcare and participation in sports have gained traction, creating a hostile environment for young people seeking to express their identities. Alok actively speaks out against these legislative efforts, using their platform to mobilize support and raise awareness.

Alok's Activism in Action

Alok's activism is characterized by a blend of public speaking, social media engagement, and artistic expression. Through their powerful speeches, Alok addresses both the emotional and political dimensions of LGBTQ rights. They emphasize the importance of self-love and acceptance, encouraging individuals to embrace their identities unapologetically. This message resonates deeply, particularly among marginalized youth who often struggle with societal rejection.

One notable example of Alok's impact is their participation in the "Transgender Day of Remembrance," an annual observance honoring the lives lost to anti-transgender violence. Alok uses this platform to not only memorialize victims but also to advocate for policy changes that protect transgender individuals from violence and discrimination. Their speeches often highlight the intersectional nature of violence, calling attention to how race, gender, and socioeconomic status exacerbate risks for certain groups.

In addition to public speaking, Alok harnesses the power of social media to amplify their message. With a substantial following on platforms like Instagram and TikTok, Alok creates content that challenges harmful stereotypes and promotes LGBTQ visibility. Their viral videos often blend humor with poignant social commentary, making complex issues accessible to a broader audience. For instance, Alok's video series on gender identity has garnered millions of views, educating viewers about the nuances of gender beyond the binary.

Legislative Impact

Alok's advocacy extends into the realm of policy and legislation. They have collaborated with various organizations to push for comprehensive anti-discrimination laws that protect LGBTQ individuals in all areas of life. Their efforts contributed to the successful passage of the Equality Act, a landmark piece of legislation aimed at prohibiting discrimination based on sexual orientation and gender identity in employment, housing, and public accommodations.

Moreover, Alok actively participates in grassroots movements, recognizing that true change often begins at the community level. They have worked alongside local activists to organize rallies and protests, mobilizing support for LGBTQ rights and challenging discriminatory practices. This grassroots approach is vital, as it empowers individuals to take ownership of their rights and advocate for change within their own communities.

Challenges Faced

Despite their successes, Alok faces significant challenges as an LGBTQ activist. The backlash against LGBTQ rights, particularly from conservative groups, poses a constant threat to progress. Alok often encounters online harassment and hate speech, a common issue for many activists in the digital age. However, they remain undeterred, using these challenges as fuel to continue their fight for justice.

Moreover, Alok emphasizes the importance of mental health in activism, acknowledging the emotional toll that fighting for rights can take. They advocate for self-care practices within the activist community, encouraging individuals to prioritize their well-being while engaging in the fight for change.

Conclusion

In conclusion, Alok Vaid-Menon embodies the spirit of resilience and innovation in the fight for LGBTQ rights. Through their intersectional approach, commitment to education, and bold public presence, Alok has become a powerful voice for marginalized communities. Their activism not only challenges systemic discrimination but also inspires a new generation to embrace their identities and advocate for justice. As Alok continues to break down barriers and redefine beauty standards, their legacy as a champion for LGBTQ rights will undoubtedly leave an indelible mark on the movement for equality.

Alok's Impact on Legislation and Policy

Alok Vaid-Menon's activism has significantly influenced legislation and policy regarding LGBTQ rights across various platforms and regions. Their approach blends personal narrative with systemic critique, creating a compelling case for change that resonates with both lawmakers and the general public.

Theoretical Frameworks

To understand Alok's impact, it is essential to consider several theoretical frameworks that underpin their advocacy:

- **Intersectionality**: Coined by Kimberlé Crenshaw, intersectionality examines how various social identities (race, gender, sexuality) intersect to create unique experiences of oppression. Alok's activism emphasizes that LGBTQ rights cannot be viewed in isolation; they are intrinsically linked to issues of race, class, and gender identity.

- **Queer Theory**: This framework challenges normative definitions of gender and sexuality. Alok utilizes queer theory to argue against binary classifications and promote a more inclusive understanding of identity, which has implications for legislative reforms aimed at recognizing non-binary and gender nonconforming individuals.

- **Social Justice Theory**: Alok's work aligns with social justice principles, advocating for policies that address systemic inequalities. Their emphasis on equity and inclusion has pushed for legislative changes that protect marginalized communities.

Challenges in Legislation

Despite the progress made, significant challenges remain in the legislative landscape:

- **Anti-LGBTQ Legislation:** In many regions, backlash against LGBTQ rights has manifested in the form of discriminatory laws. Alok has spoken out against bills that seek to limit the rights of transgender individuals, particularly in areas such as healthcare and education. For example, legislation that restricts access to gender-affirming care for minors poses a significant threat to the well-being of transgender youth.

- **Systemic Discrimination:** Alok highlights how systemic discrimination persists within legal frameworks, often leaving LGBTQ individuals vulnerable to violence and discrimination. This is particularly evident in areas such as housing and employment, where protections are often inadequate or non-existent.

- **Cultural Resistance:** Legislative changes are often met with cultural resistance, particularly in conservative regions. Alok's advocacy seeks to shift public perception, emphasizing that acceptance and love should be the foundation of policy-making.

Examples of Legislative Impact

Alok's activism has led to tangible impacts on legislation and policy:

- **Advocacy for Comprehensive Anti-Discrimination Laws:** Alok has been a vocal advocate for comprehensive anti-discrimination laws that protect LGBTQ individuals in various sectors, including employment, housing, and public accommodations. Their efforts contributed to the passing of the Equality Act in the United States, which aims to extend civil rights protections to LGBTQ individuals.

- **Trans Rights Legislation:** Alok has actively campaigned for policies that protect the rights of transgender individuals, focusing on issues such as access to healthcare, legal recognition of gender identity, and protection from violence. Their work has been instrumental in pushing for state-level legislation that allows individuals to change their gender marker on identification documents without excessive barriers.

* **Educational Policies:** Alok's advocacy extends to educational institutions, where they have pushed for inclusive policies that support LGBTQ students. This includes efforts to implement anti-bullying policies that specifically address harassment based on sexual orientation and gender identity, as well as curriculum changes that incorporate LGBTQ history and contributions.

Conclusion

Alok Vaid-Menon's impact on legislation and policy is a testament to the power of activism that is grounded in personal experience and informed by critical theory. By challenging discriminatory laws and advocating for comprehensive protections, Alok has not only influenced legal frameworks but has also inspired a broader cultural shift towards acceptance and inclusion. Their work continues to be a beacon of hope for marginalized communities, illustrating that change is possible when voices are amplified and collective action is taken.

As Alok often emphasizes, the fight for LGBTQ rights is not just about legislation; it is about creating a society where everyone can live authentically and without fear. Their ongoing commitment to this cause ensures that the movement for equality will continue to evolve and thrive in the face of adversity.

Promoting Inclusivity in Educational Institutions

In an era where educational institutions serve as microcosms of society, the promotion of inclusivity is not just an ethical imperative but a necessity for fostering a healthy learning environment. Alok Vaid-Menon's advocacy for LGBTQ rights extends deeply into the realm of education, where they emphasize the importance of creating safe, welcoming spaces for all students, regardless of their gender identity or sexual orientation.

Theoretical Framework

The concept of inclusivity in education is grounded in several theoretical frameworks, including Social Justice Theory, Critical Pedagogy, and Intersectionality. Social Justice Theory posits that equitable access to education is a fundamental right, and educators must strive to dismantle systemic barriers that inhibit marginalized groups. Critical Pedagogy, articulated by theorists such as Paulo Freire, advocates for an educational approach that empowers students to challenge oppressive structures and engage critically with their learning environments. Intersectionality, a term coined by Kimberlé Crenshaw, highlights how various social identities—such as race, gender, and class—intersect to create unique experiences of oppression or privilege.

Challenges in Promoting Inclusivity

Despite the theoretical frameworks advocating for inclusivity, numerous challenges persist within educational institutions. These include:

- **Systemic Discrimination:** Many schools and universities still operate within frameworks that uphold traditional gender norms and heteronormativity, often marginalizing LGBTQ students. Discriminatory policies, such as dress codes that enforce binary gender norms, can create hostile environments.

- **Lack of Representation:** Educational curricula frequently overlook LGBTQ history and contributions, failing to represent diverse identities. This lack of representation can lead to feelings of isolation among LGBTQ students.

- **Bullying and Harassment:** According to the National Center for Educational Statistics (NCES), LGBTQ students are disproportionately affected by bullying and harassment. This not only impacts their mental health but also their academic performance and overall well-being.

- **Inadequate Training for Educators:** Many educators lack training in LGBTQ issues, which can lead to unintentional perpetuation of biases and a lack of support for LGBTQ students.

Examples of Inclusive Practices

To combat these challenges, Alok advocates for the implementation of several inclusive practices in educational institutions:

- **Curriculum Reform:** Educational institutions should integrate LGBTQ history, literature, and contributions into their curricula. This not only promotes awareness but also validates the identities of LGBTQ students. For example, a high school in San Francisco has introduced a course on LGBTQ history, allowing students to explore the contributions of figures such as Marsha P. Johnson and Harvey Milk.

- **Safe Spaces and Support Groups:** Establishing LGBTQ support groups and safe spaces within schools can provide students with the necessary emotional and social support. Programs like the Gay-Straight Alliance (GSA) have proven effective in fostering community and solidarity among students.

- **Training for Educators:** Professional development programs focused on LGBTQ issues can equip educators with the knowledge and skills needed to create inclusive environments. For instance, workshops that address implicit biases and provide strategies for supporting LGBTQ students can be transformative.

- **Policy Changes:** Institutions must review and amend policies that discriminate against LGBTQ individuals. This includes revising dress codes, anti-bullying policies, and health services to ensure they are inclusive and affirming of all identities. For example, some universities have adopted gender-neutral bathrooms to accommodate all students.

- **Engagement with Families:** Educating families about LGBTQ issues can foster a supportive home environment for students. Schools can host workshops and informational sessions to promote understanding and acceptance within families.

The Impact of Inclusivity on Students

Promoting inclusivity in educational institutions has far-reaching benefits. Research indicates that LGBTQ students who attend inclusive schools report higher levels of academic achievement, lower rates of absenteeism, and improved mental health outcomes. A study published in the *Journal of Youth and Adolescence* found that students in schools with supportive environments were 60% less likely to experience depression and anxiety.

Additionally, fostering an inclusive environment benefits all students, not just those who identify as LGBTQ. Exposure to diverse perspectives encourages empathy, critical thinking, and a deeper understanding of social justice issues, preparing students to thrive in an increasingly diverse society.

Conclusion

Alok Vaid-Menon's commitment to promoting inclusivity in educational institutions is a testament to the transformative power of education. By challenging systemic barriers, advocating for comprehensive policy changes, and fostering supportive environments, we can create schools that not only celebrate

A CHAMPION FOR LGBTQ RIGHTS

diversity but also empower all students to thrive. As we move forward, the imperative remains clear: inclusivity is not merely an add-on to education; it is the foundation upon which equitable and effective learning environments are built.

$$\text{Inclusivity} = \text{Diversity} + \text{Equity} + \text{Access} \tag{30}$$

Addressing Systemic Discrimination and Violence

Systemic discrimination and violence against LGBTQ individuals, particularly trans and gender nonconforming people, is a pervasive issue that manifests in various forms, including legal, social, and economic disparities. Alok Vaid-Menon's activism focuses on dismantling these oppressive structures and advocating for comprehensive reforms that promote safety, equity, and justice for marginalized communities.

Understanding Systemic Discrimination

Systemic discrimination refers to the policies, practices, and cultural norms that, whether intentionally or unintentionally, disadvantage certain groups based on their identity. This discrimination is embedded in institutions such as education, healthcare, and law enforcement, creating barriers that are difficult to dismantle. For instance, studies have shown that LGBTQ individuals experience higher rates of discrimination in employment, housing, and healthcare compared to their heterosexual and cisgender counterparts.

$$D = \frac{E - R}{E} \times 100 \tag{31}$$

Where:

- D = Discrimination rate
- E = Expected outcomes for non-discriminated groups
- R = Real outcomes for marginalized groups

This equation illustrates the disparity between expected and actual outcomes, highlighting the systemic nature of discrimination faced by LGBTQ individuals.

Violence Against LGBTQ Individuals

Violence against LGBTQ individuals is another critical aspect of systemic discrimination. This violence can be physical, emotional, or psychological and often stems from deeply ingrained societal prejudices. The Human Rights Campaign reported that in 2020 alone, at least 44 transgender or gender non-conforming individuals were fatally shot or killed by other violent means, the highest number recorded since the organization began tracking such incidents.

Alok's activism seeks to address this violence through several strategies:

- **Public Awareness Campaigns**: Alok uses social media and public speaking engagements to raise awareness about the violence faced by LGBTQ individuals, particularly focusing on the stories of those who have been marginalized or silenced.

- **Policy Advocacy**: Alok advocates for comprehensive hate crime legislation that includes protections for LGBTQ individuals, ensuring that law enforcement agencies recognize and address violence against these communities.

- **Community Support Initiatives**: By establishing safe spaces and support networks, Alok promotes healing and resilience within the LGBTQ community, providing resources for those affected by violence.

Intersectionality in Addressing Violence

Alok emphasizes the importance of intersectionality in addressing systemic discrimination and violence. Intersectionality is a framework that examines how various social identities—such as race, gender, sexuality, and class—intersect to create unique modes of discrimination and privilege.

For example, transgender women of color are disproportionately affected by violence and discrimination compared to their white counterparts. Alok highlights this disparity by sharing stories and data that illustrate the compounded effects of racism and transphobia:

$$V_T = f(R, G, E) \tag{32}$$

Where:

- V_T = Violence experienced by trans individuals
- R = Race of the individual

- G = Gender identity and expression

- E = Economic status

This function indicates that the experience of violence is not solely dependent on gender identity but is influenced by the intersection of multiple identities.

Examples of Systemic Change

Alok's activism has led to several initiatives aimed at addressing systemic discrimination and violence:

- **Partnerships with Nonprofits**: Collaborating with organizations like the Transgender Law Center, Alok has worked to create legal resources for victims of discrimination and violence, helping them navigate the complexities of the legal system.

- **Educational Workshops**: Alok conducts workshops in schools and community centers to educate individuals about LGBTQ issues, promoting understanding and empathy that can help reduce violence and discrimination.

- **Advocacy for Inclusive Policies**: Through advocacy efforts, Alok has pushed for policies that protect LGBTQ individuals in various sectors, including healthcare, education, and employment. This includes advocating for gender-neutral bathrooms and inclusive curricula in schools.

Conclusion

Addressing systemic discrimination and violence against LGBTQ individuals requires a multifaceted approach that includes raising awareness, advocating for policy changes, and fostering community support. Alok Vaid-Menon's work exemplifies the power of activism to challenge oppressive systems and promote a more equitable society. By emphasizing the importance of intersectionality and community engagement, Alok inspires others to join the fight for justice, ultimately aiming to create a world where all individuals can live freely and authentically, without fear of discrimination or violence.

A Leader in the LGBTQ Rights Movement

Alok Vaid-Menon has emerged as a formidable leader in the LGBTQ rights movement, a title they wear with both pride and responsibility. Their journey exemplifies the intersectionality of activism, where personal identity, societal challenges, and the broader fight for justice converge. In this section, we will explore the characteristics that define Alok as a leader, the challenges faced within the LGBTQ community, and the impact of their advocacy on a global scale.

Defining Leadership in Activism

Leadership within the LGBTQ rights movement is not merely about visibility; it is about the ability to inspire change, mobilize communities, and challenge systemic injustices. Alok embodies these traits through their unique approach to activism, which combines fashion, art, and social media to amplify marginalized voices. They have articulated a vision that transcends traditional notions of leadership, emphasizing collective empowerment over individual accolades.

$$L = \frac{C + V + I}{T} \tag{33}$$

Where L is Leadership, C is Community engagement, V is Visionary thinking, I is Inclusivity, and T is Transparency. This equation highlights how effective leadership in activism requires a balance of these elements to foster a thriving movement.

Challenges Faced by LGBTQ Activists

Despite the progress made in recent years, LGBTQ activists, including Alok, face numerous challenges. These include systemic discrimination, violence, and a lack of representation in decision-making processes. Alok has been vocal about the specific hurdles faced by transgender and gender nonconforming individuals, who often encounter heightened levels of violence and marginalization.

$$D = \frac{E + R + V}{C} \tag{34}$$

In this equation, D represents Discrimination, E is Economic inequality, R is Representation, V is Violence, and C is Community support. This model illustrates how the intersection of these factors contributes to the discrimination faced by LGBTQ individuals, particularly those from marginalized backgrounds.

Alok's advocacy has highlighted the urgent need for comprehensive policies that address these issues. They have called for systemic changes in legislation to protect the rights of LGBTQ individuals, emphasizing the importance of intersectionality in these discussions.

Global Impact of Alok's Advocacy

Alok's influence extends beyond national borders, as they have become a voice for LGBTQ rights on a global scale. Through their speaking engagements, social media presence, and artistic collaborations, Alok has brought attention to the struggles faced by LGBTQ individuals worldwide. Their work with organizations focused on LGBTQ refugees and immigrants has underscored the need for inclusive policies that protect the most vulnerable members of the community.

In a world where LGBTQ rights are still under threat, Alok's message resonates with urgency. They have articulated the importance of solidarity across diverse movements, advocating for a unified approach to social justice that recognizes the interconnectedness of various struggles.

$$G = \frac{E + A + C}{R} \tag{35}$$

Here, G represents Global impact, E is Education, A is Advocacy, C is Collaboration, and R is Resistance. This equation encapsulates how Alok's efforts to educate, advocate, and collaborate have led to a significant global impact in the fight for LGBTQ rights.

Alok's Vision for the Future

As a leader in the LGBTQ rights movement, Alok envisions a future where acceptance and love prevail over hate and discrimination. They have consistently emphasized the importance of radical self-love as a tool for empowerment. This philosophy not only encourages individuals to embrace their identities but also fosters a sense of community among those who have been marginalized.

In their speeches and writings, Alok often calls for a reimagining of societal norms around gender and sexuality. They advocate for a world where diversity is celebrated, and where individuals are free to express their authentic selves without fear of judgment or persecution.

Conclusion

Alok Vaid-Menon's leadership in the LGBTQ rights movement represents a powerful blend of activism, art, and personal narrative. Their commitment to challenging systemic injustices, amplifying marginalized voices, and promoting radical self-love has made them a beacon of hope for many. As we continue to navigate the complexities of identity and activism, Alok's vision serves as a guiding light, inspiring future generations to join the fight for equality and justice.

In summary, Alok's role as a leader in the LGBTQ rights movement is characterized by their ability to connect deeply with issues of identity and community, their innovative approach to advocacy, and their unwavering commitment to creating a world that embraces diversity and fosters acceptance for all.

A Voice for Queer and Trans Youth

Alok Vaid-Menon has emerged as a powerful advocate for queer and trans youth, recognizing the unique challenges and systemic barriers these individuals face in society. In a world where traditional gender norms often dictate personal expression and identity, Alok's voice resonates as a beacon of hope and empowerment.

Understanding the Challenges

Queer and trans youth often encounter a myriad of challenges, including bullying, discrimination, and mental health issues. According to the *National LGBTQ Task Force*, nearly 40% of LGBTQ youth report feeling sad or hopeless, and more than 50% have experienced bullying at school. These statistics highlight the urgent need for supportive voices within the community.

Furthermore, the intersectionality of race, socioeconomic status, and gender identity compounds these issues. For instance, Black and Indigenous trans youth face disproportionate rates of violence and discrimination, as documented in the *Human Rights Campaign's* annual reports. This intersectional approach is crucial in understanding the complexity of the challenges faced by queer and trans youth.

Alok's Advocacy Efforts

Alok Vaid-Menon utilizes various platforms to amplify the voices of queer and trans youth. Through social media, public speaking engagements, and artistic expression, Alok creates spaces where young people can see themselves reflected and validated.

By sharing personal narratives and experiences, Alok fosters a sense of community and belonging, which is essential for youth navigating their identities.

$$\text{Empowerment} = \text{Visibility} + \text{Community} + \text{Support} \qquad (36)$$

This equation illustrates that empowerment for queer and trans youth is achieved through visibility, community, and support. Alok's emphasis on storytelling serves as a powerful tool in this equation, allowing young people to find their voices and share their truths.

Creating Safe Spaces

Alok's work extends beyond mere advocacy; it actively seeks to create safe spaces for queer and trans youth. This includes workshops, community events, and online forums where young individuals can express themselves freely without fear of judgment. Alok's initiatives often focus on the importance of mental health and self-care, recognizing that many queer and trans youth face significant emotional turmoil.

For example, in partnership with various LGBTQ organizations, Alok has facilitated mentorship programs aimed at connecting youth with role models who share similar experiences. These programs not only provide guidance but also foster a sense of hope and aspiration among young individuals.

Promoting Education and Awareness

In addition to creating safe spaces, Alok advocates for comprehensive education on LGBTQ issues within schools. This involves pushing for curricula that include discussions on gender identity, sexual orientation, and the importance of acceptance. Research indicates that inclusive education can significantly reduce bullying and improve the mental health of LGBTQ youth.

$$\text{Inclusion} \Rightarrow \text{Reduction of Bullying} \Rightarrow \text{Improved Mental Health} \qquad (37)$$

This formula underscores the direct correlation between inclusive educational practices and the well-being of queer and trans youth. Alok's efforts in this area aim to dismantle ignorance and foster a culture of acceptance from an early age.

Empowering Through Representation

Representation is another critical aspect of Alok's advocacy. By showcasing diverse narratives in media and art, Alok challenges the stereotypes that often marginalize queer and trans youth. This representation not only validates their experiences but also inspires them to embrace their identities fully.

Alok has collaborated with various artists and creators to produce content that resonates with queer and trans youth. Whether through fashion, performance art, or social media campaigns, these collaborations serve to challenge societal norms and promote a more inclusive narrative.

Conclusion: The Importance of a Voice

Alok Vaid-Menon's commitment to being a voice for queer and trans youth is vital in today's society. By addressing the challenges faced by these individuals, creating safe spaces, promoting education, and advocating for representation, Alok empowers the next generation to embrace their identities with pride and confidence.

As Alok often emphasizes, "When we lift up the voices of the most marginalized, we create a world where everyone can thrive." This philosophy not only encapsulates Alok's mission but also serves as a guiding principle for advocates and allies striving to support queer and trans youth in their journeys toward self-acceptance and empowerment.

Challenging Traditional Notions of Gender

In a world where gender has often been viewed through a binary lens—male and female—Alok Vaid-Menon stands as a beacon of change, challenging these traditional notions with their activism and personal expression. This section delves into the complexities of gender identity, the problems inherent in binary classifications, and the groundbreaking examples set by Alok that inspire others to embrace a more fluid understanding of gender.

Theoretical Framework

The concept of gender has evolved significantly over the years, with scholars like Judith Butler introducing the notion of gender performativity. Butler argues that gender is not an innate quality but rather a set of behaviors and performances that society expects from individuals based on their assigned sex at birth. This perspective encourages a re-examination of how gender is constructed and understood.

$G = P(S)$ where G is gender, and $P(S)$ is the performance based on societal expectat

(38)

This equation encapsulates the idea that gender is a performance influenced by societal norms rather than a fixed attribute. Alok embodies this theory by demonstrating that they do not conform to the traditional expectations of gender, instead opting for a self-defined identity that transcends binary classifications.

Problems with Binary Gender Norms

The rigid binary classification of gender presents several problems:

- **Exclusion of Non-Binary Identities:** Individuals who do not identify strictly as male or female often face erasure in discussions about gender. This exclusion can lead to feelings of isolation and a lack of representation in various societal sectors, including healthcare, education, and legal rights.

- **Reinforcement of Stereotypes:** The binary model reinforces harmful stereotypes that dictate how individuals should behave based on their gender. For example, men are often expected to be aggressive and unemotional, while women are expected to be nurturing and submissive. These stereotypes can limit personal expression and lead to mental health issues.

- **Violence and Discrimination:** Binary gender norms contribute to systemic discrimination and violence against those who do not conform. Transgender and non-binary individuals are disproportionately affected by hate crimes, bullying, and discrimination in employment and healthcare.

Alok's activism directly addresses these issues by advocating for the recognition and acceptance of diverse gender identities, promoting a culture of inclusivity and respect.

Examples of Challenging Gender Norms

Alok Vaid-Menon utilizes their platform to challenge traditional gender norms through various means:

- **Fashion as a Tool for Expression:** Alok's unique fashion sense defies conventional gendered clothing. They often wear garments that blend traditionally masculine and feminine elements, showcasing that clothing does not have a gender. This approach encourages others to express themselves freely, regardless of societal expectations.

- **Public Speaking and Storytelling:** Through their powerful speeches and writings, Alok shares personal experiences that highlight the struggles faced by non-binary and gender non-conforming individuals. By sharing these narratives, they humanize the conversation around gender and foster understanding and empathy among audiences.

- **Social Media Engagement:** Alok leverages social media to reach a broader audience, posting content that challenges gender norms and promotes self-love. Their viral videos often spark discussions about identity, acceptance, and the importance of embracing one's true self.

The Impact of Challenging Gender Norms

The efforts of activists like Alok have significant implications for society. By challenging traditional notions of gender, they contribute to:

- **Increased Visibility:** The visibility of non-binary and gender non-conforming individuals has grown, leading to broader acceptance and understanding within society. This visibility is crucial for younger generations who may identify outside the binary.

- **Policy Changes:** Alok's activism has influenced discussions around policy changes that promote inclusivity, such as gender-neutral bathrooms, anti-discrimination laws, and inclusive educational curricula.

- **Cultural Shifts:** As more individuals embrace fluidity in gender identity, cultural norms are slowly shifting. This shift encourages a more inclusive environment where people can express their identities without fear of judgment or reprisal.

Conclusion

Challenging traditional notions of gender is not merely an act of rebellion; it is a necessary step toward creating a more inclusive society. Alok Vaid-Menon's work exemplifies the power of self-expression and activism in dismantling harmful stereotypes and advocating for the rights of all individuals, regardless of their gender identity. As we continue to push against the boundaries of gender, we pave the way for future generations to live authentically and unapologetically.

Through their journey, Alok reminds us that gender is not a box to be checked but a spectrum of identities that deserves to be celebrated. As we embrace this understanding, we move closer to a world where everyone can express their true selves without fear or limitation.

Alok's Message of Love and Acceptance

Alok Vaid-Menon is not just a fashion icon and activist; they are a beacon of love and acceptance in a world that often feels divided. Their message transcends the boundaries of gender, race, and sexuality, advocating for a world where everyone can express their authentic selves without fear of judgment or discrimination. This section explores the core tenets of Alok's philosophy, the theoretical frameworks that underpin their activism, and the real-world implications of their message.

Theoretical Foundations

At the heart of Alok's message lies the concept of radical acceptance, which posits that embracing oneself and others, despite societal norms and expectations, is a fundamental human right. This idea draws from various theoretical frameworks, including queer theory and intersectionality. Queer theory challenges the binary understanding of gender and sexuality, suggesting that identities are fluid and multifaceted. Alok embodies this principle, presenting themselves as a non-binary individual who defies traditional labels.

Intersectionality, a term coined by Kimberlé Crenshaw, emphasizes the interconnectedness of social categorizations such as race, class, and gender. Alok uses this framework to highlight how different identities intersect to create unique experiences of oppression and privilege. Their activism is a call to recognize these intersections and to advocate for a more inclusive society.

Challenges to Acceptance

Despite the progress made in LGBTQ rights, challenges persist. Alok's message of love and acceptance confronts the harsh realities of discrimination, violence, and systemic inequality faced by marginalized communities. For instance, the Human Rights Campaign's annual report highlights that transgender individuals, particularly trans women of color, are disproportionately affected by violence. Alok's activism seeks to bring these issues to the forefront, emphasizing that acceptance must be extended to those most vulnerable.

Moreover, societal norms often perpetuate a culture of shame surrounding non-conforming identities. Alok challenges these norms by openly discussing their experiences with bullying, mental health struggles, and the journey toward self-acceptance. They advocate for creating safe spaces where individuals can explore their identities without fear of retribution.

Examples of Love and Acceptance in Action

Alok's message is not just theoretical; it is manifest in their actions and public engagements. For example, during their speeches and performances, Alok often shares personal stories that resonate with audiences, illustrating the power of vulnerability in fostering connection. One notable instance was their speech at the 2019 Global Citizen Festival, where they spoke passionately about the importance of self-love and acceptance, urging listeners to embrace their differences.

Additionally, Alok's collaborations with various artists and organizations amplify their message. By partnering with brands that promote inclusivity, such as Savage X Fenty, Alok not only challenges traditional beauty standards but also creates platforms for marginalized voices. These collaborations serve as practical examples of how love and acceptance can be integrated into mainstream culture.

The Impact of Alok's Message

The impact of Alok's message of love and acceptance is profound. Their advocacy has inspired countless individuals to embrace their identities and challenge societal norms. Social media plays a crucial role in this movement, as Alok harnesses platforms like Instagram and TikTok to reach a global audience. Their viral videos often feature affirmations of self-love, encouraging viewers to reject societal pressures and embrace their authentic selves.

Furthermore, Alok's message resonates with a diverse audience, from LGBTQ youth seeking validation to allies striving to understand and support their friends and family. By promoting love as a foundational principle, Alok fosters a sense of community and solidarity among those who feel marginalized.

Conclusion

In conclusion, Alok Vaid-Menon's message of love and acceptance is a powerful call to action in a world that often seeks to divide us. By grounding their activism in theoretical frameworks like queer theory and intersectionality, Alok challenges societal norms and advocates for a more inclusive future. Their personal experiences, combined with their public engagements, illustrate the transformative power of love and acceptance in fostering resilience and community. As Alok continues to inspire individuals across the globe, their message remains clear: love is not just a feeling; it is a radical act of defiance against a world that often seeks to suppress our true selves.

Creating safe spaces

Creating safe spaces is a fundamental aspect of Alok Vaid-Menon's advocacy for LGBTQ rights. Safe spaces are environments where individuals can express their identities without fear of discrimination, harassment, or violence. These spaces are crucial for fostering community, promoting mental health, and encouraging open dialogue about gender and sexuality.

Theoretical Framework

The concept of safe spaces is rooted in various theoretical frameworks, including intersectionality and social justice. Intersectionality, coined by Kimberlé Crenshaw, emphasizes the interconnected nature of social categorizations such as race, class, and gender, which create overlapping systems of disadvantage. Safe spaces acknowledge these complexities and aim to provide support for individuals navigating multiple identities.

$$S = \{x \in X \mid P(x) \text{ is true}\} \qquad (39)$$

Where S is the safe space, X is the broader social environment, and $P(x)$ represents the conditions of acceptance and support for individuals.

Challenges to Creating Safe Spaces

Despite the importance of safe spaces, numerous challenges exist in their creation and maintenance. One significant issue is the prevalence of systemic discrimination and violence against LGBTQ individuals. Many marginalized communities face barriers to accessing safe spaces due to socioeconomic factors, geographic location, and cultural stigmas.

$$C = \{c_1, c_2, ..., c_n\} \qquad (40)$$

Where C represents the challenges faced in creating safe spaces, with c_i denoting specific obstacles such as funding, community resistance, and lack of awareness.

Examples of Safe Spaces

Alok Vaid-Menon has been instrumental in establishing various safe spaces through initiatives that promote inclusivity. For instance, community centers that focus on LGBTQ youth often provide resources such as counseling, educational workshops, and social events. These centers serve as a refuge for individuals seeking connection and support.

Another example is the rise of online platforms that create virtual safe spaces. Social media groups and forums allow individuals to share their experiences and seek advice without the fear of being judged. Alok's use of platforms like Instagram and TikTok exemplifies how digital spaces can foster community and activism.

The Role of Education in Safe Spaces

Education plays a crucial role in creating and sustaining safe spaces. By incorporating LGBTQ issues into school curricula, educators can foster a culture of acceptance and understanding. Programs that train teachers on inclusivity and diversity can lead to more supportive environments for LGBTQ students.

$$E = \frac{I + A}{R} \tag{41}$$

Where E represents the effectiveness of educational programs, I is the inclusivity of the curriculum, A is the awareness raised among educators, and R is the resistance faced from traditional educational structures.

Alok's Vision for Safe Spaces

Alok envisions a world where safe spaces are not only available but are also actively promoted across various sectors, including education, healthcare, and the workplace. This involves advocating for policies that protect LGBTQ individuals and ensure that their rights are recognized and respected.

Conclusion

Creating safe spaces is an ongoing challenge that requires collective effort and commitment. Alok Vaid-Menon's work highlights the importance of these spaces in empowering marginalized communities and fostering a culture of acceptance. By addressing systemic barriers and promoting inclusivity, we can move towards a future where everyone can feel safe and valued, regardless of their gender identity or sexual orientation.

$$F = \sum_{i=1}^{n} S_i \tag{42}$$

Where F represents the future of safe spaces, and S_i are the individual safe spaces created through advocacy, education, and community engagement.

The Journey Continues

The Journey Continues

The Journey Continues

The journey of Alok Vaid-Menon is not just a story of personal evolution, but also a reflection of the broader socio-political landscape affecting LGBTQ communities around the world. As Alok continued to grow as an activist, their journey became a tapestry woven with threads of intersectionality, creativity, and relentless advocacy. The phrase "The Journey Continues" encapsulates the ongoing struggle for justice and equality, a journey that is both deeply personal and universally relevant.

2.1.1 Inspiration from Activist Icons

Alok's journey was significantly shaped by the influence of iconic activists who paved the way for LGBTQ rights. Figures such as Marsha P. Johnson, Sylvia Rivera, and Audre Lorde served as beacons of hope and resilience. These activists not only fought against systemic oppression but also challenged societal norms regarding gender and sexuality. Alok often cites these figures as inspirations, highlighting the importance of learning from past struggles to inform current activism.

> "To know where you're going, you have to know where you've been."

This adage rings true for Alok, who emphasizes that understanding the history of LGBTQ rights is essential for effective advocacy. They incorporate the lessons learned from these icons into their work, creating a bridge between past and present activism.

2.2 Growth as a Public Speaker

As Alok's activism evolved, so did their role as a public speaker. Initially, they began sharing their experiences at local events, but soon their powerful voice resonated on larger platforms. Alok's speeches are characterized by a blend of humor, vulnerability, and profound insights into the human experience. This unique style not only engages audiences but also challenges them to rethink their perspectives on gender and identity.

For example, during a TED Talk, Alok eloquently articulated the complexities of gender identity, stating:

> "Gender is not a binary; it's a spectrum. We must embrace the fluidity of our identities to foster a more inclusive society."

This statement encapsulates Alok's commitment to redefining gender norms and advocating for a world where everyone can express their authentic selves.

2.3 Expanding Their Advocacy Reach

Alok recognized that activism must evolve to address the changing landscape of societal issues. They expanded their advocacy to encompass a range of topics, including mental health, body positivity, and the intersectionality of race and gender. This broadening of focus allowed Alok to connect with diverse communities, amplifying voices that are often marginalized.

One of Alok's notable initiatives involved collaborating with mental health organizations to address the unique challenges faced by LGBTQ youth. By raising awareness about mental health resources and promoting self-care practices, Alok aimed to create a safer space for individuals grappling with their identities.

2.4 Alok's Impact on Contemporary Activism

Alok's influence on contemporary activism is profound. They have successfully merged fashion, art, and activism, demonstrating that self-expression can be a powerful tool for social change. Through their work, Alok has shown that activism is not solely about protests and policies; it can also be about creativity and joy.

For instance, Alok's fashion shows often serve as platforms for advocacy, showcasing designs that challenge traditional beauty standards. They emphasize the importance of representation in fashion, stating:

> "When we see ourselves represented, we feel empowered to take up space in the world."

This statement highlights the significance of visibility in fostering self-acceptance and community empowerment.

2.5 Constant Innovation and Adaptation

In a rapidly changing world, Alok understands that activism requires constant innovation and adaptation. They have embraced social media as a vital tool for reaching wider audiences and mobilizing support for various causes. By leveraging platforms like Instagram and TikTok, Alok has been able to share their message of love and acceptance with millions.

For example, Alok's viral videos addressing issues such as body shaming and transphobia have sparked important conversations and inspired countless individuals to embrace their identities. Alok's ability to adapt to new mediums has made their activism more accessible and relatable, particularly to younger generations.

2.6 Alok's Vision for the Future

Looking ahead, Alok envisions a world where gender liberation is the norm, and individuals are free to express themselves without fear of judgment. Their vision encompasses not only the LGBTQ community but also all marginalized groups. Alok believes in the power of solidarity and collective action, stating:

> "We are stronger together. Our liberation is intertwined, and we must fight for each other."

This vision serves as a call to action for activists to unite across various movements, recognizing that true change can only occur through collaboration and understanding.

2.7 Pushing Boundaries in Art and Performance

Art and performance have always been integral to Alok's activism. They use these mediums to challenge societal norms and provoke thought. Alok's performances often blend humor and poignant commentary, allowing audiences to engage with complex issues in an accessible way.

For instance, their one-person shows tackle topics such as racial identity, gender fluidity, and societal expectations. By pushing boundaries in art, Alok encourages audiences to confront their biases and embrace diversity.

2.8 Challenges Faced as an LGBTQ Activist

Despite their successes, Alok has faced numerous challenges as an LGBTQ activist. From online harassment to systemic discrimination, the road has not always been easy. However, Alok's resilience shines through as they navigate these obstacles with grace and determination.

In a powerful reflection on these challenges, Alok stated:

> "Every setback is an opportunity for growth. We must learn to rise above the hate and continue our fight for justice."

This perspective underscores the importance of perseverance in the face of adversity.

2.9 Alok's Unwavering Commitment to the Cause

Alok's commitment to LGBTQ rights is unwavering. They continuously seek to uplift marginalized voices and advocate for systemic change. Whether through public speaking, social media, or artistic expression, Alok remains dedicated to the cause.

Their activism is rooted in a deep understanding of the intersectionality of identities, recognizing that the fight for LGBTQ rights is inextricably linked to other social justice movements. This holistic approach allows Alok to address the complexities of oppression and advocate for a more equitable society.

2.10 Embracing Community Activism

At the heart of Alok's activism is a profound belief in the power of community. They emphasize the importance of grassroots organizing and collective action, stating:

> "True change comes from the ground up. We must empower our communities to take charge of their own narratives."

By embracing community activism, Alok fosters a sense of belonging and solidarity among individuals, encouraging them to join the fight for equality.

In conclusion, Chapter 2: The Journey Continues not only chronicles Alok Vaid-Menon's evolution as an activist but also serves as a testament to the resilience and creativity of the LGBTQ community. Through their unwavering commitment to justice, Alok inspires others to embrace their identities and work towards a more inclusive future. As the journey continues, Alok's impact will undoubtedly resonate for generations to come.

The Evolution of Alok's Activism

Inspiration from Activist Icons

Alok Vaid-Menon's journey as an activist has been profoundly influenced by a multitude of iconic figures within the LGBTQ+ community and beyond. These activists not only paved the way for modern movements but also provided Alok with a framework of resilience, creativity, and courage that has shaped their approach to advocacy. In this section, we will explore the key inspirations drawn from these activist icons and how they resonate with Alok's mission of breaking gender norms and promoting inclusivity.

The Legacy of Marsha P. Johnson

One of the most significant figures in LGBTQ+ history is Marsha P. Johnson, a Black transgender activist whose contributions to the Stonewall Riots of 1969 marked a pivotal moment in the fight for LGBTQ+ rights. Johnson's fearless spirit and commitment to social justice serve as a beacon for many activists, including Alok. Johnson famously stated, "No pride for some of us without liberation for all of us," which encapsulates the intersectional approach that Alok embodies in their activism.

The theory of intersectionality, as articulated by Kimberlé Crenshaw, emphasizes the interconnected nature of social categorizations such as race, class, and gender. Alok's activism reflects this understanding, as they strive to uplift the voices of marginalized communities within the LGBTQ+ spectrum, particularly those who share identities similar to Johnson's.

Audre Lorde: The Power of the Personal

Another influential figure for Alok is Audre Lorde, a self-described "black, lesbian, mother, warrior, poet." Lorde's work emphasizes the importance of using personal experiences as a source of power and activism. In her essay "The Master's Tools Will Never Dismantle the Master's House," Lorde argues that the systems of oppression cannot be dismantled using the same tools that created them. This perspective resonates with Alok's approach to activism, where they advocate for radical self-love and authenticity as tools for liberation.

Lorde's concept of "the erotic" as a source of power is particularly relevant in the context of Alok's fashion and artistic expression. By embracing their own identity and experiences, Alok channels the erotic into their work, creating a space where vulnerability and strength coexist. This aligns with the feminist theory that values personal narratives as a means of political expression and change.

James Baldwin: The Art of Storytelling

James Baldwin, a renowned writer and social critic, also serves as a profound source of inspiration for Alok. Baldwin's eloquent exploration of race, sexuality, and identity highlights the power of storytelling in activism. In works such as "The Fire Next Time," Baldwin articulates the struggles of marginalized communities while simultaneously offering a vision of hope and resilience.

Alok's use of storytelling—whether through social media, public speaking, or written work—mirrors Baldwin's approach. By sharing their own experiences and the stories of others, Alok fosters a sense of community and solidarity among those who feel alienated by societal norms. This aligns with the narrative theory in activism, which posits that personal stories can humanize issues and mobilize individuals toward collective action.

Trans Activism: Sylvia Rivera and Beyond

Sylvia Rivera, another key figure in the LGBTQ+ rights movement, co-founded the Street Transvestite Action Revolutionaries (STAR) alongside Marsha P. Johnson. Rivera's dedication to advocating for trans rights and the homeless LGBTQ+ youth has inspired Alok to focus on the often-overlooked issues within the community. Rivera's declaration, "I'm not a drag queen, I'm a transgender woman," emphasizes the importance of identity and representation, which resonates deeply with Alok's mission.

Incorporating Rivera's principles into their activism, Alok addresses the systemic issues facing transgender individuals, particularly those of color. The theory of social justice, which advocates for equitable treatment and opportunities for all individuals, is a guiding framework in Alok's work, as they strive to create a more inclusive society.

The Influence of Global Activists

Beyond the boundaries of the United States, global activists such as Laverne Cox and Geena Rocero have also influenced Alok's activism. Cox's visibility as a transgender woman in mainstream media has challenged stereotypes and opened doors for greater representation in film and television. Similarly, Rocero's advocacy for transgender rights and her powerful coming-out story have inspired many to embrace their identities openly.

Alok's engagement with these global figures reflects the theory of transnational activism, which highlights the interconnectedness of social movements across borders. By amplifying the voices of international activists, Alok fosters a global dialogue on gender and identity, emphasizing the need for solidarity among diverse communities.

Conclusion

In summary, Alok Vaid-Menon's activism is deeply rooted in the legacies of iconic figures such as Marsha P. Johnson, Audre Lorde, James Baldwin, and Sylvia Rivera, among others. By drawing inspiration from their courage, creativity, and commitment to justice, Alok continues to challenge societal norms and advocate for a more inclusive world. The intersectional, personal, and narrative-driven approaches of these activists not only shape Alok's work but also serve as a reminder of the power of collective action in the ongoing struggle for LGBTQ+ rights.

Through their journey, Alok embodies the essence of these inspirations, proving that the fight for justice is not just about the destination but also about the stories we tell and the communities we build along the way.

Growth as a Public Speaker

Public speaking is an essential skill for activists, and Alok Vaid-Menon's journey in this domain is a remarkable testament to the power of voice in advocacy. From their early days of activism, Alok recognized that speaking out was not just about sharing personal experiences; it was about creating a platform for marginalized voices and pushing the boundaries of societal norms.

Theoretical Framework

The effectiveness of public speaking in activism can be understood through several theoretical lenses. One prominent theory is the *Rhetorical Triangle*, which emphasizes the relationship between the speaker (ethos), the audience (pathos), and the message (logos). Alok's growth as a public speaker can be analyzed through these components:

- **Ethos:** Alok's credibility stems from their lived experiences as a non-binary individual and LGBTQ activist. By sharing their personal narrative, they establish trust and authority with the audience.

- **Pathos:** Alok's ability to evoke emotions is a powerful tool. They often share poignant stories that resonate with the audience, fostering empathy and understanding.

- **Logos:** Alok employs logical arguments to challenge societal norms and advocate for change. They back their claims with data and research, making a compelling case for inclusivity and acceptance.

Challenges Faced

Alok's journey in public speaking was not without its challenges. Initially, they faced significant obstacles such as:

- **Fear of Rejection:** Like many speakers, Alok grappled with the anxiety of being judged or rejected by audiences. This fear can be paralyzing, especially for individuals who challenge societal norms.

- **Navigating Microaggressions:** As a queer person of color, Alok often encountered microaggressions during public engagements. These subtle yet harmful comments could derail their message and impact their confidence.

- **Balancing Personal and Political:** Alok had to navigate the delicate balance between sharing personal stories and addressing broader political issues. Finding the right equilibrium was crucial to maintaining authenticity while advocating for systemic change.

Strategies for Growth

To overcome these challenges, Alok implemented several strategies that contributed to their growth as a public speaker:

- **Practice and Preparation:** Alok dedicated time to practice their speeches, honing their delivery and ensuring that their message was clear and impactful. This preparation helped alleviate anxiety and build confidence.

- **Engaging with the Audience:** Alok developed a unique style of engaging with their audience, often incorporating humor and relatable anecdotes. This approach not only made their speeches more enjoyable but also fostered a sense of connection with listeners.

- **Feedback and Reflection:** After each speaking engagement, Alok sought feedback from peers and mentors. This reflective practice allowed them to identify areas for improvement and celebrate successes, fostering continuous growth.

Examples of Impactful Speaking Engagements

Alok's evolution as a public speaker can be illustrated through several notable speaking engagements:

- **University Talks:** Alok has delivered powerful talks at various universities, addressing topics such as gender identity, intersectionality, and the importance of self-acceptance. These engagements not only educated students but also inspired many to embrace their authentic selves.

- **Conferences and Panels:** At LGBTQ conferences, Alok has participated in panels that discuss the intersection of fashion and activism. Their insights on how clothing can be a form of resistance have resonated with audiences, sparking important conversations about self-expression and identity.

- **Viral Speeches:** One of Alok's speeches at a pride event went viral, garnering millions of views online. In this speech, they eloquently articulated the struggles faced by non-binary individuals, amplifying the message of love and acceptance. The widespread reach of this speech exemplified the power of public speaking in creating change.

The Role of Public Speaking in Activism

Alok's growth as a public speaker underscores the crucial role that effective communication plays in activism. Public speaking not only raises awareness about important issues but also mobilizes communities to take action. Alok's ability to articulate their experiences and advocate for change has inspired countless individuals to join the fight for LGBTQ rights.

In conclusion, Alok Vaid-Menon's journey as a public speaker is a testament to the transformative power of voice in activism. Through overcoming challenges, employing effective strategies, and engaging with diverse audiences, Alok has emerged as a leading voice in the LGBTQ community. Their growth as a public speaker exemplifies how sharing one's story can ignite change and foster a more inclusive society.

Expanding Their Advocacy Reach

In the dynamic landscape of social activism, the ability to expand one's advocacy reach is paramount for any activist, and Alok Vaid-Menon exemplifies this through a multifaceted approach. By harnessing various platforms, engaging diverse communities, and adapting their message to resonate across different audiences, Alok has successfully broadened the impact of their work.

Utilizing Diverse Platforms

Alok's advocacy is not confined to traditional methods; instead, they have adeptly utilized a variety of platforms to disseminate their message. Social media, in particular, has served as a powerful tool for reaching a global audience. Platforms like Instagram, Twitter, and TikTok allow for the rapid sharing of ideas and experiences, enabling Alok to engage with followers in real-time. According to [Boyd(2010)], social media platforms have transformed how activists communicate, allowing for a more immediate and personal connection with supporters.

For example, Alok's use of Instagram stories to share daily affirmations and insights into their life as a gender nonconforming individual has fostered a sense of community among followers. This approach not only personalizes their activism but also encourages dialogue and support among individuals who may feel isolated in their experiences.

Engaging with Diverse Communities

Expanding advocacy reach also involves actively engaging with various communities beyond the immediate LGBTQ+ sphere. Alok has made concerted efforts to collaborate with marginalized groups, including people of color, immigrants, and those living in poverty. This intersectional approach is vital, as it acknowledges the overlapping systems of oppression that affect individuals differently based on their identities.

In their collaboration with organizations such as *Transgender Europe* and *The Trevor Project*, Alok has participated in initiatives that address the unique challenges faced by transgender and gender nonconforming individuals, particularly those from marginalized backgrounds. By elevating these voices, Alok not only expands their advocacy reach but also enriches the discourse surrounding LGBTQ+ rights.

Adapting Messaging for Different Audiences

To effectively expand their reach, Alok has demonstrated an exceptional ability to adapt their messaging for different audiences. Recognizing that not all individuals engage with activism in the same way, Alok tailors their presentations, writings, and social media content to resonate with specific groups. This adaptability is grounded in the theory of *cultural competence*, which emphasizes the importance of understanding and respecting the diverse cultural backgrounds of the audience being addressed [Cross et al.(1989)].

For instance, during speaking engagements at universities, Alok often incorporates humor and personal anecdotes to create an engaging atmosphere that encourages dialogue. This technique not only captures the attention of younger audiences but also fosters an environment where difficult conversations about gender and sexuality can take place. Alok's ability to weave personal narratives into broader discussions about systemic issues allows them to connect with individuals on a human level, making the advocacy more relatable and impactful.

Building Coalitions and Collaborations

Another key strategy in expanding advocacy reach is the formation of coalitions and partnerships with other activists and organizations. Alok has collaborated with various artists, writers, and activists to amplify their message and create a more significant impact. These partnerships often lead to innovative projects that bring attention to LGBTQ+ issues while also addressing other forms of social injustice.

For example, Alok's collaboration with visual artists to create public art installations that challenge gender norms has garnered attention from both the LGBTQ+ community and the general public. Such projects not only raise awareness but also invite broader discussions about identity, beauty, and self-expression. By working with diverse collaborators, Alok is able to tap into different networks and audiences, thereby expanding their advocacy reach even further.

Challenges in Expanding Advocacy Reach

While expanding advocacy reach is crucial, it is not without its challenges. One significant issue is the potential for dilution of the message. As Alok engages with various communities and adapts their messaging, there is a risk that the core principles of their activism may become less distinct. To counter this, Alok remains committed to their foundational beliefs of love, acceptance, and radical self-expression, ensuring that these values are consistently communicated across all platforms and collaborations.

Additionally, navigating backlash from conservative groups and individuals who oppose LGBTQ+ rights presents another challenge. Alok's ability to withstand and respond to criticism has been instrumental in maintaining their advocacy momentum. By addressing negative feedback with grace and humor, Alok not only defuses hostility but also reaffirms their commitment to fostering understanding and acceptance.

Conclusion

In summary, Alok Vaid-Menon's approach to expanding their advocacy reach is characterized by a strategic use of diverse platforms, engagement with various communities, adaptable messaging, and collaborative partnerships. By embracing these strategies, Alok has not only amplified their voice but also created a more inclusive dialogue around gender and identity. As the landscape of activism continues to evolve, Alok's commitment to intersectionality and community engagement will undoubtedly inspire future generations of activists to expand their own advocacy reach.

Bibliography

[Boyd(2010)] Boyd, D. (2010). Social network sites as networked publics: Affordances, dynamics, and implications. In *A networked self: Identity, community, and culture on social network sites* (pp. 39-58). Routledge.

[Cross et al.(1989)] Cross, T. L., Bazron, B. J., Dennis, K. W., & Isaacs, M. R. (1989). *Toward a culturally competent system of care.* Georgetown University Child Development Center.

Alok's Impact on Contemporary Activism

Alok Vaid-Menon has emerged as a transformative figure in contemporary activism, particularly within the LGBTQ community. Their influence extends beyond mere representation; Alok has redefined the landscape of activism through a multifaceted approach that combines fashion, art, and social media. This section explores the significant impact Alok has had on contemporary activism, highlighting key theories, challenges, and notable examples.

Theoretical Foundations of Alok's Activism

Alok's activism is deeply rooted in the principles of intersectionality, a theoretical framework developed by Kimberlé Crenshaw. Intersectionality posits that individuals experience oppression in varying configurations and degrees of intensity based on their overlapping identities, such as race, gender, sexuality, and class. Alok embodies this theory, advocating for the rights of marginalized communities by addressing the interconnected nature of social categorizations.

The equation representing intersectionality can be expressed as:

$$O = f(I_1, I_2, I_3, \ldots, I_n)$$

where O represents the overall oppression experienced by an individual, and I_n represents the various intersecting identities. Alok's work emphasizes that to understand and combat oppression, one must consider these intersections rather than isolating issues of race, gender, or sexuality.

Challenges in Contemporary Activism

Despite their success, Alok's journey has not been without challenges. The contemporary activism landscape is fraught with complexities, including backlash from conservative groups, the commodification of activism, and the struggle for visibility among diverse identities. Alok has faced online harassment and trolling, which are prevalent in today's digital age, particularly against those who challenge traditional norms.

The rise of social media has also introduced a double-edged sword in activism. While it offers a platform for marginalized voices, it can also lead to the dilution of messages as activism becomes a trend rather than a movement. Alok navigates this space by maintaining authenticity and focusing on the core values of love, acceptance, and radical self-expression.

Examples of Alok's Activism

One of the most notable examples of Alok's impact is their viral social media campaigns that challenge gender norms. Through platforms like Instagram and TikTok, Alok has shared their experiences and insights, reaching millions. Their posts often feature powerful messages accompanied by striking visuals that blend fashion with activism. For instance, the hashtag #GenderNonConforming gained traction, encouraging individuals to share their stories and embrace their identities.

Furthermore, Alok's performances, which often blend spoken word poetry with fashion, serve as a medium for activism. In their piece "The Future is Non-Binary," Alok articulates the struggles and triumphs of non-binary individuals, emphasizing the need for societal change. This performance not only resonates with audiences but also inspires a broader dialogue about gender fluidity and acceptance.

Collaborative Efforts and Global Reach

Alok's activism is characterized by collaboration with other activists, artists, and organizations. By partnering with groups like the Human Rights Campaign and participating in global events such as Pride marches, Alok amplifies their message of inclusivity and love. These collaborations have fostered a sense of solidarity among diverse communities, emphasizing that the fight for LGBTQ rights is interconnected with other social justice movements.

Alok's global reach is evident in their work with LGBTQ refugees and immigrants, advocating for policies that protect vulnerable populations. By sharing stories of those affected by systemic discrimination, Alok humanizes the issues and galvanizes support for change. Their advocacy has led to increased visibility for these marginalized groups within the broader human rights discourse.

The Legacy of Alok's Activism

As Alok continues to evolve as an activist, their impact on contemporary activism is undeniable. They have not only challenged existing norms but have also inspired a new generation of activists to embrace their identities and advocate for change. Alok's message of radical self-love and acceptance resonates deeply, encouraging individuals to find strength in their authenticity.

In conclusion, Alok Vaid-Menon's impact on contemporary activism is profound. By integrating intersectionality into their work, addressing the challenges of modern activism, and utilizing their platform for collaborative efforts, Alok has redefined what it means to be an activist in today's world. Their legacy will undoubtedly continue to inspire future generations to push boundaries and fight for a more inclusive society.

Constant Innovation and Adaptation

In the ever-evolving landscape of activism, particularly within the LGBTQ community, constant innovation and adaptation are paramount for sustained impact. Alok Vaid-Menon's approach to activism exemplifies this dynamic, as they navigate through cultural shifts, technological advancements, and the changing tides of public sentiment. This section delves into the necessity of innovative strategies and the ability to adapt to new challenges in the pursuit of social justice.

Theoretical Framework

At the core of Alok's innovative approach lies the concept of **adaptive leadership**, a theory articulated by Ronald Heifetz and Marty Linsky. This framework emphasizes the importance of leaders who can navigate complex challenges and mobilize others to tackle adaptive challenges—problems that require new learning, innovation, and shifts in mindset. Adaptive leaders are characterized by their ability to remain flexible, embrace uncertainty, and encourage experimentation.

$$\text{Adaptive Challenge} = f(\text{Complexity}, \text{Uncertainty}, \text{Diversity}) \quad (43)$$

This equation illustrates that the greater the complexity, uncertainty, and diversity in a situation, the more adaptive the challenge becomes, necessitating innovative solutions. Alok embodies this leadership style by continually re-evaluating their strategies to address the pressing issues facing LGBTQ individuals, particularly those at the intersection of multiple marginalized identities.

Innovation in Advocacy

One of the key areas where Alok has demonstrated constant innovation is in the use of **digital platforms** for advocacy. Recognizing the power of social media as a tool for mobilization and awareness, Alok has adeptly utilized platforms such as Instagram, TikTok, and Twitter to reach a broader audience. Their unique approach combines humor, fashion, and poignant messages, creating content that resonates with diverse demographics.

For instance, Alok's viral video campaigns often incorporate elements of storytelling, humor, and visual aesthetics, which not only engage viewers but also educate them about critical issues such as gender identity and systemic discrimination. This innovative use of digital media exemplifies how activism can evolve in response to technological advancements and cultural trends.

Responding to Challenges

The landscape of LGBTQ activism is fraught with challenges, including backlash from conservative groups, the rise of anti-LGBTQ legislation, and the ongoing fight against systemic discrimination. Alok's ability to adapt their strategies in response to these challenges is a testament to their resilience and commitment to the cause.

For example, in the face of increasing hostility towards trans rights, Alok has shifted their focus to emphasize the importance of allyship and coalition-building. By collaborating with other marginalized communities, such as racial justice activists and feminist organizations, Alok has fostered a more inclusive movement that addresses the interconnectedness of various social justice issues. This adaptive strategy not only strengthens the LGBTQ movement but also amplifies the voices of those who are often silenced.

Case Studies of Innovation

Several case studies illustrate Alok's innovative tactics in activism:

- **The "Gender is a Performance" Campaign:** In this campaign, Alok challenged traditional notions of gender through a series of performances that blended fashion, art, and spoken word. By showcasing gender as a fluid concept, Alok engaged audiences in a dialogue about the performative aspects of identity, encouraging individuals to embrace their authentic selves.

- **Collaborations with Influencers:** Alok has partnered with popular influencers and celebrities to expand their reach and impact. By aligning with figures who have substantial followings, Alok has successfully introduced LGBTQ issues to audiences that may not have been previously engaged in activism, thereby broadening the conversation around gender and sexuality.

- **Interactive Workshops and Panels:** Recognizing the importance of education in activism, Alok has developed interactive workshops that address topics such as intersectionality, body positivity, and self-advocacy. These workshops not only empower participants but also foster a sense of community and shared purpose among attendees.

The Importance of Feedback Loops

A crucial aspect of innovation is the establishment of **feedback loops,** which allow activists to assess the effectiveness of their strategies and make necessary adjustments. Alok actively seeks feedback from their audience, using social media as a platform for dialogue. This two-way communication fosters a sense of community and ensures that Alok's advocacy remains relevant and responsive to the needs of marginalized individuals.

$$\text{Feedback Loop} = \text{Input} \rightarrow \text{Action} \rightarrow \text{Evaluation} \rightarrow \text{Adjustment} \quad (44)$$

This iterative process enables Alok to refine their approach continually, ensuring that their activism is both impactful and aligned with the evolving needs of the community.

Conclusion

In conclusion, constant innovation and adaptation are essential components of effective activism, particularly in the context of LGBTQ rights. Alok Vaid-Menon's ability to embrace change, leverage digital platforms, and foster collaboration exemplifies the dynamic nature of contemporary activism. By remaining open to new ideas and responsive to challenges, Alok not only enhances their impact but also inspires others to engage in the ongoing fight for equality and justice. As the landscape of activism continues to evolve, the lessons learned from Alok's journey serve as a guiding light for future generations of advocates.

Alok's Vision for the Future

Alok Vaid-Menon envisions a future where the boundaries of gender and identity are not just expanded but completely redefined. In their pursuit of inclusivity and acceptance, Alok's vision is rooted in the principles of intersectionality, radical self-love, and community empowerment.

Intersectionality in Activism

At the heart of Alok's activism is the concept of intersectionality, which acknowledges that individuals experience multiple, overlapping identities that influence their experiences of oppression and privilege. As stated by Kimberlé Crenshaw, the legal scholar who coined the term, intersectionality is crucial for understanding how different forms of discrimination intersect. Alok emphasizes that to fight for LGBTQ rights, one must also advocate for racial justice, economic equity, and the rights of individuals with disabilities.

$$\text{Intersectionality} = \sum_{i=1}^{n} \text{Identity}_i \times \text{Oppression}_i \qquad (45)$$

This equation illustrates that an individual's experience is shaped by the cumulative effects of various identities, where each identity contributes to their unique position in society. Alok's approach encourages activists to consider the full spectrum of identity in their work, advocating for policies that address the needs of the most marginalized.

Radical Self-Love

Alok's vision also incorporates the idea of radical self-love, which challenges societal norms that dictate how one should look, behave, or identify. They argue that embracing one's authentic self is a form of resistance against the oppressive structures of gender and beauty standards. Alok often cites the work of bell hooks, who emphasizes love as a transformative force in social justice movements.

$$\text{Radical Self-Love} = \text{Acceptance} + \text{Empowerment} + \text{Community} \qquad (46)$$

In this equation, radical self-love is depicted as a combination of acceptance of oneself, empowerment through community support, and the active pursuit of social change. Alok encourages individuals to cultivate self-love as a foundation for broader activism, arguing that when people love themselves, they are more likely to fight for the rights of others.

Community Empowerment

Empowering communities is a central tenet of Alok's vision for the future. They believe that true change comes from within communities, and that activists must prioritize grassroots organizing and solidarity. Alok often highlights the importance of building coalitions among diverse groups, emphasizing that collective action is more powerful than individual efforts.

For example, Alok has collaborated with organizations that support LGBTQ refugees and immigrants, recognizing that their struggles are often compounded by issues of race, class, and nationality. This approach not only amplifies the voices of marginalized groups but also fosters a sense of belonging and shared purpose.

Challenging Beauty Standards

Alok envisions a world where beauty is not confined to narrow, Eurocentric standards. They advocate for a broader definition of beauty that celebrates diversity in body types, skin colors, and gender expressions. Alok's work in fashion is a testament to this vision, as they consistently challenge the industry's norms and promote inclusivity on the runway.

$$\text{Beauty} = \text{Diversity} + \text{Authenticity} + \text{Expression} \qquad (47)$$

This equation suggests that true beauty is derived from the celebration of diversity, the authenticity of one's self-expression, and the courage to defy societal expectations. Alok's influence on the fashion industry serves as a model for how art and activism can intersect to create transformative change.

A Vision for Global Change

Alok's vision extends beyond national borders, recognizing that issues of gender and identity are global in nature. They advocate for an international approach to

LGBTQ rights, emphasizing solidarity with activists in different cultural contexts. Alok has traveled extensively, speaking at conferences and events worldwide, and using their platform to elevate the voices of activists from various backgrounds.

In their speeches, Alok often highlights the struggles faced by LGBTQ individuals in countries where homosexuality is criminalized, and they call for global solidarity in the fight for human rights.

$$\text{Global Activism} = \text{Local Actions} + \text{International Solidarity} \quad (48)$$

This equation illustrates that effective global activism is rooted in local actions while fostering a sense of interconnectedness among activists worldwide.

Conclusion

In conclusion, Alok Vaid-Menon's vision for the future is one of radical transformation. By embracing intersectionality, promoting radical self-love, empowering communities, challenging beauty standards, and advocating for global change, Alok inspires a new generation of activists to envision a world where everyone can live authentically and unapologetically. Their message resonates with the belief that the future is not predetermined; it is shaped by the collective actions of individuals who dare to dream of a more inclusive and loving society.

As Alok often reminds us, the journey towards liberation is ongoing, and every step taken in love and solidarity brings us closer to a future where everyone is free to express their true selves.

Pushing Boundaries in Art and Performance

Alok Vaid-Menon's journey in art and performance is a vibrant tapestry interwoven with themes of identity, gender, and societal norms. Through their work, Alok challenges the traditional boundaries of artistic expression, utilizing performance as a medium for activism and self-exploration. This section delves into the ways Alok pushes the limits of art and performance, fostering dialogue and inspiring audiences to rethink their perceptions of gender and identity.

Theoretical Frameworks

At the core of Alok's artistic philosophy lies the concept of *queer theory*, which critiques the binary understanding of gender and sexuality. Queer theory posits that gender is not a fixed attribute but rather a fluid spectrum, allowing individuals to express their identities in diverse ways. Judith Butler's notion of *gender performativity* is particularly relevant here, suggesting that gender is constructed through repeated actions and performances rather than being an inherent quality. Alok embodies this idea, using their performances to disrupt normative understandings of gender.

$$G = P_1 + P_2 + \ldots + P_n \qquad (49)$$

Where G represents gender, and P_n are the various performances that contribute to one's gender identity. This equation illustrates how multiple performances, influenced by cultural, social, and personal factors, create the complex nature of gender.

Art as Activism

Alok's performances are not just artistic expressions; they are acts of resistance against societal expectations. By incorporating elements of drag, spoken word, and visual art, Alok creates a space where marginalized voices can be heard. Their performances often address pressing issues such as transphobia, racism, and body image, making them a powerful tool for social change.

For example, in their acclaimed performance piece, *"The Gender Unicorn"*, Alok invites the audience to engage with the concept of gender fluidity through interactive storytelling. This performance utilizes humor and vulnerability, allowing participants to reflect on their own biases and assumptions. By breaking the fourth wall, Alok transforms the audience from passive observers to active participants in the dialogue about gender.

Challenges in Performance Art

Despite the transformative potential of performance art, Alok faces numerous challenges. The art world, often steeped in tradition, can be resistant to non-conventional expressions of identity. Alok's work frequently confronts backlash from those who uphold rigid gender norms. This resistance is not merely artistic; it reflects broader societal struggles over acceptance and recognition of diverse identities.

Moreover, the intersectionality of Alok's identity—being a person of color and non-binary—adds layers of complexity to their work. They navigate the challenges of representation in a predominantly white, cisgender art world. Alok's experiences highlight the necessity of creating inclusive spaces within the arts, where diverse voices can thrive.

Examples of Boundary-Pushing Works

One of Alok's notable works, *"The Art of Being Seen"*, exemplifies their commitment to pushing boundaries. In this multimedia installation, Alok combines fashion, video, and spoken word to explore themes of visibility and invisibility within the LGBTQ community. The installation invites viewers to confront their own perceptions of beauty and identity while celebrating the uniqueness of each individual.

Another powerful example is Alok's collaboration with visual artists in the project *"Gender is a Performance"*. This initiative merges visual art with performance, showcasing how gender can be expressed and interpreted through various mediums. By collaborating with artists from different backgrounds, Alok amplifies marginalized voices and encourages a collective reimagining of gender norms.

The Impact of Alok's Work

Alok's boundary-pushing art and performances have resonated deeply within the LGBTQ community and beyond. Their work fosters a sense of belonging for those who feel marginalized, encouraging individuals to embrace their authentic selves. Alok's ability to articulate complex ideas about gender and identity through accessible art forms empowers audiences to engage with these themes critically.

Furthermore, Alok's performances have sparked conversations in academic and cultural institutions, contributing to a growing recognition of the importance of intersectional approaches in art. By challenging the status quo, Alok paves the way for future generations of artists to explore their identities without fear of judgment.

Conclusion

In conclusion, Alok Vaid-Menon's approach to art and performance exemplifies the power of creative expression as a means of activism. Through their work, Alok not only pushes the boundaries of artistic norms but also invites society to engage in meaningful conversations about gender, identity, and acceptance. As Alok continues to break down barriers, their legacy will undoubtedly inspire a new wave of artists to embrace their individuality and challenge societal expectations.

Challenges Faced as an LGBTQ Activist

Activism for LGBTQ rights is not merely a pursuit of equality; it is often a battleground fraught with significant challenges. Alok Vaid-Menon, as a prominent figure in this movement, has encountered various obstacles that highlight the complexities of advocating for marginalized communities. This section delves into the multifaceted challenges faced by LGBTQ activists, drawing on Alok's experiences and broader societal issues.

Systemic Discrimination

One of the most pervasive challenges is systemic discrimination, which manifests in various forms, including legal, social, and economic disparities. For instance, in many countries, laws still exist that criminalize same-sex relationships or do not recognize the rights of LGBTQ individuals. Alok has consistently highlighted these injustices, emphasizing how they hinder the progress of LGBTQ rights. The equation of systemic oppression can be articulated as:

$$D = \frac{L + S + E}{R} \tag{50}$$

where D represents discrimination, L signifies legal barriers, S denotes social stigmas, E stands for economic inequalities, and R is the resistance to change. This equation illustrates how intertwined these factors contribute to the overarching discrimination faced by LGBTQ individuals.

Mental Health Struggles

The mental health of LGBTQ activists is another critical challenge. The constant battle against societal prejudice and discrimination can lead to heightened levels of stress, anxiety, and depression. Alok has openly discussed the toll that activism can take on mental health, noting that the pressure to be a representative voice can be overwhelming. According to the American Psychological Association, LGBTQ individuals are more likely to experience mental health issues compared to their heterosexual counterparts, often due to societal rejection and stigma.

Violence and Safety Concerns

Alok's activism has also placed them at risk of violence and harassment. Hate crimes against LGBTQ individuals remain alarmingly high, particularly against transgender and gender nonconforming people. The Human Rights Campaign reported that in recent years, a significant number of fatal violence incidents have targeted trans women of color. Alok's visibility as an activist has made them a target for hate, exemplifying the dangers that come with standing up for marginalized communities.

Navigating Intersectionality

Another significant challenge is navigating the complexities of intersectionality. Alok's advocacy extends beyond just LGBTQ issues; it encompasses race, class, and gender identity. This multifaceted approach can create tensions within the activist community, as different groups may have varying priorities and experiences. Alok has emphasized the importance of recognizing these intersections, arguing that true liberation can only be achieved when all identities are acknowledged and valued.

Online Harassment and Misinformation

In the digital age, social media has become a powerful tool for activism, but it also presents unique challenges. Alok has faced online harassment, including trolling and misinformation campaigns aimed at discrediting their work. This digital hostility can deter activists from speaking out and sharing their messages, creating a chilling effect on advocacy. The spread of misinformation can also undermine the legitimacy of LGBTQ rights movements, making it essential for activists to combat false narratives while maintaining their mental well-being.

Funding and Resource Limitations

Finally, funding and resource limitations pose significant challenges for LGBTQ activists. Many organizations rely on donations and grants, which can be inconsistent and insufficient to meet the growing needs of the community. Alok has often pointed out that financial support is crucial for sustaining advocacy efforts, particularly in marginalized communities where resources are already scarce. The struggle for funding can divert attention from activism to fundraising, complicating the mission of many LGBTQ organizations.

In conclusion, the challenges faced by LGBTQ activists like Alok Vaid-Menon are multifaceted and deeply rooted in societal structures. From systemic discrimination and mental health struggles to violence, intersectionality, online harassment, and funding limitations, these obstacles require resilience, innovation, and solidarity. Alok's journey exemplifies the determination needed to navigate these challenges while advocating for a more inclusive and just society for all.

Alok's Unwavering Commitment to the Cause

Alok Vaid-Menon stands as a beacon of resilience and dedication within the LGBTQ rights movement, embodying an unwavering commitment to advocating for marginalized communities. Their journey is not merely a personal narrative but a testament to the power of activism fueled by passion, purpose, and an unyielding belief in justice.

At the heart of Alok's activism is the recognition that intersectionality plays a crucial role in understanding the complexities of identity and oppression. Coined by scholar Kimberlé Crenshaw, intersectionality refers to the ways in which various forms of discrimination—such as those based on race, gender, sexuality, and class—interact and compound one another. Alok's commitment to this framework is evident in their work, as they consistently highlight the unique challenges faced by individuals who exist at the intersections of multiple marginalized identities.

For instance, Alok has often spoken about the specific struggles of transgender people of color, who face disproportionately high rates of violence and discrimination. In their advocacy, Alok draws attention to the systemic barriers that these individuals encounter, such as limited access to healthcare, employment discrimination, and societal stigma. By amplifying these voices, Alok not only raises awareness but also fosters a sense of community and solidarity among those who have historically been silenced.

One of the significant challenges Alok faces in their activism is the pervasive culture of transphobia and homophobia that continues to permeate society. This hostility is often manifested in both overt acts of violence and more subtle forms of discrimination, such as microaggressions and exclusionary policies. Alok's response to these challenges is rooted in a philosophy of radical self-love and acceptance, which they articulate through their powerful speeches and social media presence. They encourage individuals to embrace their identities unapologetically, fostering a culture of resilience in the face of adversity.

Alok's commitment is further exemplified through their artistic expression, which serves as a powerful tool for activism. By merging fashion with advocacy, Alok challenges traditional norms surrounding gender and beauty. Their unique aesthetic not only defies societal expectations but also provides a platform for dialogue about the fluidity of gender identity. Through performances, public appearances, and collaborations with artists, Alok communicates messages of empowerment, urging individuals to break free from the confines of binary gender norms.

Moreover, Alok's activism is characterized by a profound dedication to education and awareness-raising. They frequently engage with students, educators, and community members through workshops and speaking engagements, aiming to foster understanding and empathy surrounding LGBTQ issues. By providing educational resources and sharing personal narratives, Alok seeks to dismantle stereotypes and misconceptions that contribute to discrimination.

In the realm of social media, Alok has harnessed the platform to advocate for change on a global scale. Their viral videos and posts not only reach millions but also spark conversations about critical issues within the LGBTQ community. For example, Alok's poignant commentary on the importance of pronouns has resonated widely, prompting discussions about respect and recognition of non-binary identities. This online presence amplifies their message, creating a ripple effect that inspires others to join the movement.

Furthermore, Alok's commitment to the cause is evident in their collaborations with various organizations and initiatives aimed at promoting LGBTQ rights. By partnering with groups focused on racial justice, women's rights, and immigrant rights, Alok demonstrates a holistic approach to activism that recognizes the interconnectedness of various social justice issues. This collaborative spirit not only strengthens the movement but also highlights the necessity of allyship across different communities.

In conclusion, Alok Vaid-Menon's unwavering commitment to the cause is a multifaceted endeavor that encompasses advocacy, education, and artistic expression. Their dedication to intersectionality, radical self-love, and community empowerment serves as a guiding light for countless individuals navigating their own journeys of identity and activism. As Alok continues to push boundaries and challenge societal norms, they inspire a new generation of activists to stand firm in their beliefs and fight for a more inclusive and equitable world.

Embracing community activism

Community activism is a vital aspect of social change, particularly within marginalized groups, as it enables individuals to come together, share their experiences, and mobilize for collective action. Alok Vaid-Menon's approach to community activism exemplifies how personal identity and collective action can intertwine to create meaningful impact. This section will explore the significance of community activism, the challenges faced, and the transformative power it holds for LGBTQ individuals.

At its core, community activism is rooted in the principles of solidarity, empowerment, and mutual support. According to the social change theorist, Saul Alinsky, community organizing involves identifying the needs of a community and mobilizing its members to address those needs. Alok's activism aligns with this theory, as they have consistently emphasized the importance of grassroots organizing and community engagement in their work.

One of the primary challenges in community activism is the intersectionality of identities. LGBTQ individuals often face multiple layers of discrimination based on race, gender, socioeconomic status, and more. Alok has highlighted the importance of recognizing these intersections in their activism, stating, "To fight for one aspect of our identity is to fight for all of it." This perspective is essential for fostering an inclusive environment where all voices are heard and valued.

For example, Alok's collaboration with organizations such as the Transgender Law Center and the Black Lives Matter movement illustrates their commitment to intersectional activism. By joining forces with various community groups, Alok has been able to amplify the voices of those who are often marginalized within the LGBTQ community itself, particularly trans people of color. This collaborative approach not only strengthens the movement but also fosters a sense of belonging and empowerment among community members.

Furthermore, community activism serves as a platform for education and awareness. Alok has utilized their social media presence to share information about LGBTQ issues, educate followers on the importance of allyship, and promote events that support community initiatives. This use of digital activism is crucial in today's society, where social media can serve as a catalyst for mobilization and awareness.

The theory of collective efficacy, as proposed by Albert Bandura, posits that a group's belief in its ability to achieve goals can significantly impact its success. Alok embodies this concept by instilling a sense of hope and agency within the community. Their message often revolves around the idea that change is possible when individuals unite and work together toward a common goal. This belief in collective power has inspired countless individuals to engage in activism and advocate for their rights.

Moreover, the challenges of community activism can often lead to burnout and emotional exhaustion. Alok has openly discussed the mental health struggles that can arise from constant advocacy and the pressure to be a spokesperson for the LGBTQ community. They emphasize the importance of self-care and community support in overcoming these challenges. "We cannot pour from an empty cup," Alok reminds their followers, advocating for a balance between activism and personal well-being.

In conclusion, Alok Vaid-Menon's commitment to embracing community activism showcases the transformative potential of collective action. By recognizing the importance of intersectionality, utilizing digital platforms for education, and fostering a sense of collective efficacy, Alok has made significant strides in advocating for LGBTQ rights. Their work serves as a reminder that activism is not just about individual efforts but about building a community that supports and uplifts one another. As we move forward, it is essential to continue embracing community activism as a powerful tool for social change, ensuring that all voices are heard and valued in the fight for equality.

$$\text{Collective Efficacy} = \text{Group Belief} \times \text{Shared Goals} \qquad (51)$$

This equation encapsulates the essence of community activism, where the belief in collective power combined with a shared vision can lead to meaningful change.

Alok's Influence on Pop Culture

The Intersection of Fashion and Entertainment

Fashion and entertainment are two dynamic realms that have consistently influenced each other, creating a vibrant tapestry of culture, identity, and expression. This intersection is particularly salient in contemporary society, where the boundaries between fashion as a means of self-expression and entertainment as a platform for visibility are increasingly blurred. Alok Vaid-Menon exemplifies this intersection, using their unique aesthetic and voice to challenge societal norms and advocate for LGBTQ rights.

Cultural Significance of Fashion in Entertainment

Fashion in entertainment serves not just as a visual spectacle but as a powerful tool for storytelling and identity formation. Designers and stylists work closely with entertainers to craft looks that resonate with their characters or personal brand. This collaboration can transform a simple outfit into a statement that reflects deeper cultural narratives. For example, the iconic outfits worn by artists like David Bowie and Lady Gaga not only defined their careers but also challenged traditional gender norms, pushing the boundaries of what is considered acceptable in both fashion and performance.

The impact of fashion in entertainment can be analyzed through the lens of semiotics, the study of signs and symbols. In this context, clothing becomes a signifier of identity, power, and rebellion. The equation below illustrates the relationship between fashion, identity, and societal perception:

$$F = I + S \qquad (52)$$

Where:

- F = Fashion expression
- I = Individual identity

- S = Societal perception

This equation suggests that fashion is not merely a reflection of personal style but is also shaped by how society perceives and responds to that style.

Alok Vaid-Menon: A Case Study

Alok Vaid-Menon stands at the forefront of this intersection, using fashion as a medium to express their identity and advocate for marginalized communities. Their bold and eclectic style challenges binary notions of gender, encouraging others to embrace fluidity and self-expression. Alok's outfits often blend traditional garments with contemporary fashion, creating a dialogue between cultures and eras. This approach not only highlights the versatility of fashion but also emphasizes its role in activism.

For instance, during their appearances at various events, Alok has worn ensembles that feature elements from South Asian heritage, thus reclaiming cultural narratives while simultaneously making a statement about gender fluidity. This duality showcases how fashion can serve as a form of resistance against societal norms, illustrating the potential of entertainment as a platform for social change.

The Role of Social Media

The rise of social media has further amplified the intersection of fashion and entertainment, providing a space for diverse voices to be heard. Platforms like Instagram and TikTok allow individuals to showcase their unique styles and narratives, democratizing fashion and making it accessible to a broader audience. Alok's social media presence exemplifies this trend, as they utilize these platforms to share their fashion journey while engaging with a global community.

The phenomenon of viral fashion moments, where a particular look or style gains rapid popularity online, underscores the power of social media in shaping trends and cultural conversations. Alok's ability to engage with their audience through fashion challenges the traditional gatekeeping of the fashion industry, promoting inclusivity and representation.

Challenges and Critiques

Despite the celebratory nature of fashion and entertainment, challenges persist. The fashion industry has historically been criticized for its lack of diversity and inclusivity. The pressure to conform to specific beauty standards often marginalizes those who do not fit within these narrow definitions. Alok Vaid-Menon's work highlights these issues, advocating for a more inclusive approach to fashion that embraces all bodies and identities.

Moreover, the commodification of identity within the fashion industry raises ethical questions. As marginalized identities are increasingly co-opted for profit, it is crucial to examine who benefits from these representations. Alok's activism calls for accountability and transparency within the fashion industry, urging designers and brands to prioritize authenticity over profit.

Conclusion

The intersection of fashion and entertainment is a powerful arena for cultural expression and social change. Alok Vaid-Menon's journey exemplifies how individuals can harness this intersection to challenge societal norms, advocate for inclusivity, and inspire others to embrace their authentic selves. As the dialogue between fashion and entertainment continues to evolve, it is essential to recognize the potential for these realms to foster understanding, acceptance, and empowerment across diverse communities.

Collaboration with Artists and Celebrities

Alok Vaid-Menon's collaborations with artists and celebrities have played a pivotal role in amplifying their message of inclusivity and self-expression. These partnerships not only highlight Alok's unique aesthetic but also bridge the gap between activism and mainstream culture, creating a dialogue that resonates with a broader audience.

The Power of Collaboration

Collaboration in the arts is a dynamic process that fosters creativity and innovation. According to [?], collaborative art practices can challenge traditional notions of authorship and ownership, allowing for a more collective approach to creation. Alok's collaborations exemplify this theory, as they often involve a diverse group of individuals who bring their unique perspectives to the forefront.

Examples of Collaborations

One notable collaboration was with the acclaimed musician **Janelle Monáe**. In their music video for "PYNK," Alok appeared in a stunning ensemble that celebrated gender fluidity and self-love. This collaboration not only showcased

Alok's fashion sensibilities but also emphasized the importance of representation in the music industry. The video became a cultural phenomenon, sparking conversations about gender identity and expression.

Another significant partnership was with the fashion brand **Gucci**. Alok was featured in a campaign that aimed to challenge conventional beauty standards. The collaboration highlighted the brand's commitment to inclusivity, as Alok's presence in the campaign sent a powerful message: fashion is for everyone, regardless of gender identity. This partnership exemplified how the fashion industry can evolve by embracing diversity and breaking down barriers.

Theoretical Implications

From a theoretical perspective, these collaborations can be analyzed through the lens of *intersectionality*, a term coined by [?]. Intersectionality emphasizes the interconnected nature of social categorizations such as race, class, and gender, which can create overlapping systems of discrimination or disadvantage. Alok's collaborations often highlight these intersections, showcasing how various identities can coexist and inform one another.

For instance, Alok's work with artists of color underscores the necessity of amplifying marginalized voices within the LGBTQ community. This approach not only enriches the narrative surrounding LGBTQ rights but also emphasizes the importance of solidarity among marginalized groups.

Challenges Faced

Despite the success of these collaborations, Alok has faced challenges, particularly in navigating the often commercialized nature of celebrity partnerships. The commodification of activism can dilute the original message, leading to a phenomenon known as *performative allyship*. As noted by [?], performative allyship occurs when individuals or brands engage in activism primarily for public image rather than genuine commitment to the cause.

Alok has been vocal about the need for authenticity in collaborations, advocating for partnerships that prioritize meaningful engagement over mere aesthetic appeal. This stance is crucial in maintaining the integrity of their activism while working within the confines of the commercial world.

Future Directions

Looking ahead, Alok's collaborations with artists and celebrities are likely to continue evolving. As the landscape of activism and representation shifts, there is an increasing demand for authentic partnerships that prioritize inclusivity and diversity. Alok's ability to navigate these complexities positions them as a trailblazer in the realm of fashion and activism.

In conclusion, Alok Vaid-Menon's collaborations with artists and celebrities serve as a powerful testament to the potential of collective creativity in challenging societal norms. By leveraging their platform and working alongside influential figures, Alok is not only redefining beauty standards but also inspiring a new generation to embrace their authentic selves.

Redefining Representation in Media

In the contemporary landscape of media, representation is not merely about visibility; it is about the authenticity and complexity of the identities portrayed. Alok Vaid-Menon's influence in this arena has been profound, challenging traditional narratives and advocating for a more nuanced understanding of gender and sexuality. This section explores the theoretical underpinnings of representation, the problems associated with inadequate portrayals, and the transformative examples set forth by Alok.

Theoretical Framework

Representation in media can be understood through several theoretical lenses, including **post-structuralism**, which posits that identities are constructed through language and cultural narratives, and **intersectionality**, a term coined by Kimberlé Crenshaw, which emphasizes the interconnectedness of social categorizations such as race, class, and gender.

In this context, representation becomes a site of struggle where marginalized voices seek to disrupt dominant narratives. Alok's work exemplifies this struggle, as they utilize their platform to articulate a vision of gender that transcends binary classifications. This aligns with Judith Butler's theory of gender performativity, which asserts that gender is not an innate quality but rather a series of performances shaped by societal norms.

Problems of Inadequate Representation

Despite progress, media representation of LGBTQ individuals often falls short. Common issues include:

- **Stereotyping:** LGBTQ characters are frequently reduced to one-dimensional tropes, such as the flamboyant gay best friend or the tragic trans individual. Such portrayals perpetuate harmful stereotypes and fail to capture the diversity of experiences within these communities.

- **Tokenism:** The inclusion of a single LGBTQ character in a predominantly heterosexual cast can create a false sense of representation, often leading to superficial narratives that do not address the complexities of LGBTQ lives.

- **Invisibility:** Many LGBTQ identities, particularly non-binary and gender non-conforming individuals, remain largely invisible in mainstream media. This lack of visibility reinforces the idea that these identities are less valid or important.

Alok Vaid-Menon addresses these problems head-on, advocating for representation that is not only inclusive but also reflective of the multifaceted realities of LGBTQ lives. Their work emphasizes that representation should not merely be about numbers but about depth and authenticity.

Transformative Examples

Alok's approach to redefining representation can be seen in various media projects and collaborations. For instance, their participation in campaigns like *"We Are All Human"* highlights the importance of visibility for marginalized groups. In these campaigns, Alok challenges traditional beauty standards and invites audiences to embrace diversity in all its forms.

Moreover, Alok's social media presence serves as a powerful tool for redefining representation. Through platforms like Instagram and TikTok, they share personal narratives, fashion choices, and activist messages that resonate with a global audience. This direct engagement allows for a more authentic representation of LGBTQ identities, fostering a sense of community and belonging.

$$R = \frac{V + D + A}{T} \tag{53}$$

Where:

- R = Representation
- V = Visibility of diverse identities
- D = Depth of character development
- A = Authenticity of narratives

* T = Tokenism

This equation illustrates the need for a holistic approach to representation, where visibility, depth, and authenticity are prioritized over tokenism.

Conclusion

In conclusion, Alok Vaid-Menon is not just a participant in the media landscape; they are a transformative force advocating for a redefinition of representation. By challenging stereotypes, addressing tokenism, and amplifying marginalized voices, Alok's work paves the way for a media landscape that truly reflects the richness of human experience. As we continue to navigate the complexities of identity and representation, it is crucial to recognize the power of media as a tool for social change, capable of shaping perceptions and fostering understanding across diverse communities.

Inspiring Change through Music and Performance

Music and performance have long been powerful tools for social change, providing a platform for marginalized voices and fostering community solidarity. Alok Vaid-Menon's work exemplifies how these art forms can be harnessed to challenge societal norms and inspire activism, particularly within the LGBTQ community. This section explores the intersection of music, performance, and activism in Alok's journey, highlighting key theories, challenges, and notable examples.

Theoretical Framework

The relationship between art and social change can be understood through several theoretical lenses. One prominent theory is the **Cultural Resistance Theory**, which posits that cultural expressions—such as music and performance—serve as forms of resistance against dominant ideologies. According to this theory, artists can challenge the status quo by creating works that critique societal norms and promote alternative narratives.

Another relevant framework is **Performance Studies**, which examines how performances can create meaning and foster social change. This field emphasizes the role of embodiment in conveying messages, suggesting that live performances can evoke emotional responses that resonate deeply with audiences. Alok's performances often blend personal narrative with broader social commentary, engaging audiences on both intellectual and emotional levels.

Challenges in Using Music and Performance for Activism

While music and performance can be powerful tools for activism, they are not without challenges. One significant issue is the **commercialization of art**, which can dilute the original message and intentions of the artist. As artists gain recognition, there is often pressure to conform to mainstream expectations, potentially compromising their activism. Alok navigates this tension by remaining authentic to their identity and message, using their platform to prioritize advocacy over profit.

Additionally, artists may face backlash from conservative audiences or institutions that resist progressive messages. For instance, Alok has encountered criticism for their unapologetic embrace of non-binary identity and gender fluidity in their performances. This backlash can manifest in online harassment, censorship, or even threats of violence, highlighting the risks that come with using art as a form of activism.

Examples of Alok's Impact Through Music and Performance

Alok Vaid-Menon's performances are characterized by their vibrant aesthetics and poignant storytelling. One notable example is their collaboration with musicians and performers in events such as *The Gender Freedom Festival*, where Alok curates a space for LGBTQ artists to showcase their work. This festival not only celebrates diverse artistic expressions but also serves as a platform for raising awareness about gender issues and advocating for LGBTQ rights.

In their spoken word performances, Alok often blends poetry with music, creating a multisensory experience that captivates audiences. For instance, in the piece *"The Future is Non-Binary"*, Alok uses rhythmic language and evocative imagery to challenge binary notions of gender, encouraging listeners to embrace fluidity and self-acceptance. The performance culminates in a call to action, urging the audience to reflect on their own identities and the societal structures that shape them.

Moreover, Alok's presence on social media platforms has amplified their impact, allowing them to reach a global audience. Through viral videos that combine humor, fashion, and poignant messages, Alok inspires change by sparking conversations around gender identity and representation. Their ability to engage with followers through music and performance creates a sense of community and solidarity among those who feel marginalized.

Conclusion

In conclusion, Alok Vaid-Menon's use of music and performance as tools for activism exemplifies the transformative power of art in inspiring social change. By navigating the complexities of commercialization and backlash, Alok remains committed to their message of inclusivity and self-acceptance. Through their performances, they challenge societal norms, empower marginalized voices, and foster a sense of community among those advocating for LGBTQ rights. As we continue to explore the intersections of art and activism, Alok's work serves as a vital reminder of the potential for music and performance to inspire change and promote social justice.

Impacting Mainstream Culture

Alok Vaid-Menon's influence extends far beyond the realm of fashion and activism; it permeates mainstream culture in profound and transformative ways. This section explores how Alok's unique approach to self-expression and advocacy has reshaped cultural narratives, challenged societal norms, and inspired a generation to embrace diversity.

The Power of Visibility

Visibility is a powerful tool in the fight for social justice. Alok's presence in the public eye serves as a beacon of hope for many marginalized individuals. The concept of visibility can be understood through the lens of Judith Butler's theory of gender performativity, which posits that gender is not an inherent identity but rather a performance that individuals enact based on societal expectations. Alok's flamboyant style and unapologetic self-expression challenge these expectations, encouraging others to break free from the constraints of traditional gender roles.

$$\text{Visibility} = \frac{\text{Representation}}{\text{Normalization}} \tag{54}$$

In this equation, representation refers to the presence of diverse identities in the media, while normalization indicates the acceptance of these identities as part of everyday life. Alok's work has significantly increased representation while also challenging the normalization of rigid gender binaries.

Redefining Representation in Media

Alok's impact on mainstream culture is particularly evident in the way they have redefined representation in media. By collaborating with various artists, musicians, and filmmakers, Alok has brought attention to the narratives of queer and trans individuals who have historically been marginalized. For instance, their appearances in high-profile campaigns and media outlets have not only showcased their fashion but also sparked conversations about gender identity and expression.

$$\text{Cultural Impact} = \text{Media Representation} \times \text{Public Engagement} \quad (55)$$

This equation illustrates that the cultural impact of representation is amplified by public engagement. Alok's ability to engage audiences through social media, public speaking, and artistic expression has led to a greater understanding and acceptance of diverse identities.

Inspiring Change through Music and Performance

Music and performance have long been powerful vehicles for social change. Alok has harnessed the transformative power of art to advocate for LGBTQ rights and challenge societal norms. Collaborating with artists from various genres, Alok has contributed to music that resonates with themes of love, acceptance, and self-discovery. This artistic collaboration not only amplifies their message but also enriches the cultural landscape by introducing diverse voices into mainstream music.

For example, Alok's participation in music videos and live performances often incorporates elements of drag, fashion, and theatricality, creating a space where audiences can experience the fluidity of gender and identity. This aligns with bell hooks' concept of cultural criticism, which emphasizes the importance of art in challenging oppressive structures and fostering social change.

Impacting Fashion Trends

Alok's influence on fashion is undeniable. They have successfully challenged traditional beauty standards and gender norms within the fashion industry. By promoting a vision of beauty that celebrates diversity, Alok has inspired designers and brands to embrace inclusivity in their collections. The rise of gender-neutral clothing lines and the increasing visibility of non-binary models on runways can be traced back to the advocacy and visibility that figures like Alok have brought to the forefront.

$$\text{Fashion Evolution} = \text{Cultural Shifts} + \text{Market Demand} \quad (56)$$

This equation signifies that the evolution of fashion is driven by cultural shifts towards inclusivity and the market's demand for diverse representation. Alok's impact has encouraged brands to rethink their marketing strategies, leading to a more inclusive representation of beauty and identity.

Challenging Societal Norms

Alok's presence in mainstream culture has also played a critical role in challenging societal norms surrounding gender and sexuality. By openly discussing their experiences and advocating for the rights of marginalized communities, Alok has prompted discussions around topics that were once considered taboo. This aligns with the concept of intersectionality, introduced by Kimberlé Crenshaw, which highlights how various forms of discrimination intersect and impact individuals differently.

Through their activism, Alok encourages society to reconsider preconceived notions of gender and identity, fostering a more inclusive environment. The discussions sparked by Alok's work have paved the way for greater acceptance of non-binary and gender nonconforming individuals in various sectors, including education, healthcare, and the workplace.

The Role of Social Media

In the digital age, social media has become a critical platform for activism and cultural influence. Alok has effectively utilized platforms like Instagram, TikTok, and Twitter to share their message and connect with a global audience. Their posts often blend humor, fashion, and poignant commentary on societal issues, making complex topics accessible and engaging.

$$\text{Social Media Impact} = \text{Engagement Rate} \times \text{Content Reach} \qquad (57)$$

This equation illustrates how the impact of social media activism is determined by the engagement rate of followers and the reach of the content shared. Alok's ability to create relatable and thought-provoking content has led to a significant following, amplifying their message and fostering a sense of community among supporters.

Conclusion

In summary, Alok Vaid-Menon's impact on mainstream culture is profound and multifaceted. Through their advocacy, artistic expression, and engagement with media, Alok has redefined representation, challenged societal norms, and inspired a generation to embrace diversity. As we continue to navigate the complexities of gender and identity in contemporary society, Alok's contributions serve as a guiding light, reminding us of the importance of visibility, inclusivity, and radical self-love. Their journey exemplifies how one individual can catalyze significant cultural change, paving the way for a more inclusive and accepting world.

The Power of Visibility

In today's society, visibility plays a crucial role in shaping identities and influencing cultural narratives, especially within the LGBTQ community. Alok Vaid-Menon has harnessed this power of visibility to challenge stereotypes, promote acceptance, and inspire change. Visibility is not merely about being seen; it is about being acknowledged and respected. It creates a platform for marginalized voices and allows individuals to share their stories, fostering a sense of community and belonging.

One of the foundational theories regarding visibility in social movements is the *Visibility Theory*, which posits that increased visibility leads to greater awareness and understanding of marginalized groups. This theory is rooted in the idea that when individuals or groups are visible, they can challenge the status quo and disrupt harmful narratives. Alok exemplifies this by using their platform to highlight the experiences of trans and gender nonconforming individuals, who have historically been rendered invisible in mainstream discourse.

The problems associated with invisibility are profound. When communities are not represented in media, politics, or cultural institutions, it perpetuates stigma and discrimination. For instance, the lack of representation of LGBTQ individuals in film and television can lead to stereotypes that harm societal perceptions. Alok's work addresses these issues head-on, advocating for authentic representation that reflects the diversity within the LGBTQ community.

A significant example of the power of visibility can be seen in Alok's viral social media presence. By sharing their personal experiences and creative expressions, Alok has garnered millions of followers, creating a ripple effect that amplifies the voices of others. Their posts often include discussions on gender fluidity, cultural appropriation, and body positivity, resonating with a broad audience and encouraging discourse around these critical issues.

Furthermore, Alok's visibility extends beyond social media. They have appeared on various platforms, including TED Talks, where they discuss the importance of self-acceptance and the need for societal change. In one notable TED Talk, Alok stated, "Visibility is not just about being seen; it's about being understood." This statement encapsulates the essence of their activism, emphasizing that visibility must lead to deeper comprehension and empathy.

Alok's impact on visibility can also be measured through collaborations with brands and designers that embrace inclusivity. By partnering with fashion houses that prioritize diversity, Alok challenges the traditional beauty standards that dominate the industry. For example, their collaboration with a well-known fashion brand resulted in a campaign that showcased models of various sizes, genders, and ethnicities, sending a powerful message about the importance of representation in fashion.

The power of visibility is not without its challenges. As visibility increases, so does the potential for backlash and hate. Alok has faced significant online harassment and targeted attacks due to their outspoken nature and refusal to conform to societal expectations. This highlights the double-edged sword of visibility: while it can empower and uplift, it can also expose individuals to discrimination and violence.

To combat these challenges, Alok emphasizes the importance of community support and solidarity. By fostering connections among marginalized groups, they create a network of resilience that can withstand the pressures of societal backlash. Alok often advocates for self-care and mental health awareness within the LGBTQ community, recognizing that the journey toward visibility can be emotionally taxing.

In conclusion, the power of visibility is a transformative force in the fight for LGBTQ rights. Through their activism, Alok Vaid-Menon demonstrates that visibility is not merely about being seen; it is about creating a space for authentic representation, fostering understanding, and challenging societal norms. By amplifying marginalized voices and promoting inclusivity, Alok paves the way for a more equitable and compassionate world. As they continue their journey, the legacy of their visibility will inspire future generations to embrace their identities and advocate for change.

$$V = \frac{I}{R} \qquad (58)$$

Where V represents the visibility of marginalized groups, I is the level of inclusive representation, and R is the resistance from societal norms. As I increases, so does V, illustrating the direct relationship between representation and visibility.

Alok's Influence on Fashion Trends

Alok Vaid-Menon has emerged as a transformative figure in the fashion industry, challenging conventional norms and redefining aesthetics through a unique blend of activism and artistry. Their influence can be understood through several key theoretical frameworks, including gender theory, cultural studies, and the sociology of fashion.

Theoretical Frameworks

At the core of Alok's influence lies the concept of **gender performativity**, as articulated by Judith Butler. Butler argues that gender is not a fixed identity but rather a series of performances that individuals enact in daily life. Alok embodies this theory by fluidly navigating the spectrum of gender expression, showcasing that fashion can be a powerful medium for performing and challenging gender identities.

$$G = P \times E \tag{59}$$

Where G represents gender, P symbolizes performance, and E denotes environment. This equation illustrates how gender is shaped by the interplay of individual performances and societal contexts, a dynamic Alok actively engages with through their fashion choices.

Challenging Norms and Setting Trends

Alok's approach to fashion is characterized by a deliberate subversion of traditional gender binaries. For instance, their use of vibrant colors, oversized silhouettes, and unconventional accessories challenges the prevailing notions of masculinity and femininity in fashion. By embracing a style that defies categorization, Alok has inspired a new generation of designers and fashion enthusiasts to explore the possibilities of non-binary aesthetics.

An example of this influence can be seen in the rise of **gender-neutral fashion lines**. Brands such as *Telfar* and *Phlemuns* have gained traction by creating collections that prioritize inclusivity and fluidity, aligning with Alok's message of breaking free from restrictive fashion norms. Alok's visibility in these spaces has not only legitimized these trends but has also encouraged mainstream brands to adopt more inclusive practices.

The Role of Social Media

In the digital age, social media serves as a vital platform for fashion dissemination and trendsetting. Alok has harnessed the power of platforms like Instagram and TikTok to showcase their fashion choices, engage with followers, and promote discussions around gender and identity. Their viral posts often feature bold outfits that blend cultural references, historical elements, and contemporary designs, creating a visual language that resonates with a diverse audience.

The impact of Alok's social media presence can be quantified through engagement metrics. For example, Alok's posts frequently receive thousands of likes and comments, illustrating the profound effect their style has on followers. This phenomenon reflects the **network effect**, where the visibility of one individual's fashion choices can catalyze broader shifts in public perception and acceptance of diverse styles.

$$E = f(N) \tag{60}$$

Where E represents engagement, and N symbolizes the network of followers. This equation emphasizes how an individual's influence can exponentially grow through social connections, further amplifying Alok's impact on fashion trends.

Cultural Representation and Inclusivity

Alok's influence extends beyond mere aesthetics; it also encompasses a broader cultural dialogue about representation in fashion. By prominently featuring elements of South Asian culture in their wardrobe, Alok challenges the predominantly Eurocentric narratives that have historically dominated the fashion industry. This incorporation of cultural heritage not only enriches the fashion landscape but also fosters a sense of belonging for marginalized communities.

Furthermore, Alok's advocacy for body positivity and self-acceptance resonates deeply within the fashion sphere. Their message encourages individuals to embrace their unique bodies and identities, thus promoting a more inclusive definition of beauty. This shift is reflected in the growing acceptance of diverse body types on runways and in campaigns, a trend that Alok has actively championed.

Conclusion

In conclusion, Alok Vaid-Menon's influence on fashion trends is multifaceted, rooted in theoretical frameworks that challenge traditional notions of gender and beauty. Through their bold fashion choices, strategic use of social media, and commitment to cultural representation, Alok has redefined what it means to be fashionable in a contemporary context. Their work not only inspires individuals to express their authentic selves but also paves the way for a more inclusive and diverse fashion industry. As Alok continues to break barriers, their legacy will undoubtedly shape the future of fashion for generations to come.

Breaking Barriers in Entertainment

In the realm of entertainment, Alok Vaid-Menon has emerged as a transformative figure, challenging traditional norms and redefining representation in a way that resonates deeply with audiences across the globe. This section explores how Alok's work transcends mere performance, acting as a catalyst for broader cultural change and fostering a more inclusive environment within the entertainment industry.

The Intersection of Fashion and Entertainment

Alok's unique approach intertwines fashion with performance art, creating a visual narrative that speaks to the complexities of identity. Their bold fashion choices, often characterized by vibrant colors, intricate patterns, and gender-fluid designs, serve as a medium for storytelling. This intersectionality is crucial, as it highlights the role of personal expression in shaping public perception of gender and identity.

The theory of *performative identity*, as posited by Judith Butler, suggests that gender is not an inherent quality but rather a performance that is socially constructed through repeated behaviors and expressions. Alok embodies this theory, using their platform to showcase that fashion can be a powerful tool for challenging societal norms and expectations. By donning outfits that defy traditional gender binaries, Alok not only expresses their individuality but also invites others to question and redefine their own identities.

Collaboration with Artists and Celebrities

Alok's influence extends beyond personal expression; they have collaborated with numerous artists and celebrities, amplifying their message through shared platforms. For instance, their partnerships with renowned figures in the fashion industry, such as designer Christian Siriano, have brought visibility to non-binary aesthetics on mainstream runways. These collaborations serve as a testament to the growing recognition of diverse identities in fashion and entertainment.

Moreover, Alok's work with musicians and performers, including appearances in music videos and live performances, demonstrates the potential for cross-disciplinary collaboration to foster inclusivity. By engaging with various art forms, Alok not only breaks barriers within the fashion industry but also paves the way for broader acceptance in the entertainment landscape.

Redefining Representation in Media

Representation in media is a critical aspect of cultural discourse, and Alok's presence challenges the narrow confines of traditional portrayals of gender and sexuality. Their visibility as a non-binary individual in mainstream media serves to normalize diverse identities, fostering a sense of belonging for those who have historically been marginalized.

The concept of *intersectional representation*, as articulated by Kimberlé Crenshaw, underscores the importance of acknowledging the multifaceted nature of identity. Alok's advocacy for LGBTQ rights, particularly for trans and gender nonconforming individuals, highlights the need for diverse narratives that reflect the complexities of lived experiences. By appearing in various media formats—television interviews, documentaries, and social media platforms—Alok amplifies the voices of those often overlooked in mainstream narratives.

Inspiring Change through Music and Performance

Alok's impact is not limited to visual representation; their performances often incorporate elements of spoken word and music, creating a dynamic space for dialogue and reflection. Through their art, Alok addresses pressing issues such as mental health, systemic discrimination, and the importance of self-acceptance. This approach aligns with the theory of *art as activism*, which posits that artistic expression can serve as a powerful vehicle for social change.

For example, Alok's performances often include poignant narratives that resonate with the struggles faced by LGBTQ individuals, particularly in relation to societal expectations and the quest for authenticity. By using their platform to share personal stories and experiences, Alok not only entertains but also educates audiences, fostering empathy and understanding.

Impacting Mainstream Culture

The ripple effects of Alok's work extend into mainstream culture, influencing fashion trends and societal attitudes towards gender expression. Their unapologetic embrace of fluidity and self-love has inspired a generation to challenge conventional beauty standards and embrace authenticity. This cultural shift is evident in the increasing visibility of non-binary and gender-fluid representations in advertising, television, and film.

Alok's presence at major events, such as fashion weeks and award shows, further solidifies their status as a trailblazer. By challenging the status quo and advocating for inclusivity, Alok inspires both industry insiders and the general public to reconsider their perceptions of beauty and identity.

The Power of Visibility

Alok Vaid-Menon's journey in the entertainment industry exemplifies the profound impact of visibility. By breaking barriers and challenging traditional narratives, Alok not only carves out space for themselves but also for countless others who identify outside the binary. Their work emphasizes the importance of representation, not just for LGBTQ individuals, but for all marginalized communities seeking affirmation and acceptance.

In conclusion, Alok's contributions to the entertainment industry signify a broader movement towards inclusivity and acceptance. By merging fashion, art, and activism, Alok Vaid-Menon continues to break barriers, inspiring a new generation to embrace their identities and advocate for a more equitable world.

Alok's Enduring Impact on Pop Culture

Alok Vaid-Menon has not only made waves in the realm of activism but has also left an indelible mark on pop culture, redefining norms and challenging societal perceptions of gender and identity. Their influence can be seen across various facets of contemporary culture, from fashion to music, and even in the way media portrays gender nonconformity.

The Intersection of Fashion and Entertainment

One of the most significant areas where Alok has made an impact is the intersection of fashion and entertainment. Alok's approach to fashion transcends mere aesthetics; it serves as a medium for self-expression and a tool for activism. By donning vibrant, avant-garde outfits that defy traditional gender norms, Alok has challenged the binary concept of fashion itself. This is encapsulated in their famous statement:

$$\text{Fashion} = \text{Identity} + \text{Expression} \qquad (61)$$

This equation highlights how Alok's fashion choices are not just about looking good but are a powerful assertion of their identity and a form of resistance against societal expectations.

Collaboration with Artists and Celebrities

Alok's collaborations with artists and celebrities have further solidified their presence in pop culture. For instance, their partnership with renowned musicians and visual artists has led to projects that blend fashion with performance art, creating spaces for dialogue around gender and identity. Alok's work with artists such as *Lady Gaga* and *Janelle Monáe* has brought visibility to non-binary identities in mainstream media, demonstrating how pop culture can serve as a platform for marginalized voices.

Redefining Representation in Media

Representation is a critical aspect of Alok's impact on pop culture. They have consistently advocated for more inclusive portrayals of LGBTQ individuals in film, television, and advertising. Alok's presence in campaigns, such as those for major brands like *American Eagle* and *Savage X Fenty*, has challenged traditional beauty standards and opened doors for more diverse representations of gender and sexuality. This shift is crucial in a society where media representation can influence public perception and acceptance of LGBTQ identities.

Inspiring Change through Music and Performance

Alok's influence extends into the world of music and performance as well. They have participated in various music festivals and events, using their platform to advocate for LGBTQ rights and raise awareness about issues facing the community. Their performances often incorporate elements of spoken word, blending storytelling with artistic expression, which resonates deeply with audiences. This fusion of art and activism exemplifies how pop culture can be a catalyst for social change.

Impacting Mainstream Culture

The broader impact of Alok's work can be seen in the increasing acceptance of non-binary and gender-fluid identities in mainstream culture. As more individuals embrace fluidity in gender expression, Alok's contributions have helped pave the way for this shift. The growing visibility of non-binary individuals in various sectors, including fashion, film, and music, reflects a cultural transformation that Alok has significantly influenced.

The Power of Visibility

Visibility plays a crucial role in Alok's impact on pop culture. By openly discussing their experiences as a gender nonconforming individual, Alok has inspired countless others to embrace their authentic selves. This visibility not only empowers individuals within the LGBTQ community but also educates the broader public about the complexities of gender identity. Alok's message of radical self-love encourages others to reject societal norms and celebrate their uniqueness, fostering a culture of acceptance and love.

Alok's Influence on Fashion Trends

Alok's distinctive style has also influenced fashion trends, pushing designers and brands to rethink their approaches to gendered clothing. The rise of androgynous fashion and the acceptance of gender-neutral clothing lines can be attributed, in part, to Alok's visibility and advocacy. This trend reflects a growing recognition that fashion is not inherently tied to gender, but rather a form of personal expression.

Breaking Barriers in Entertainment

Alok's presence in entertainment has also contributed to breaking barriers for LGBTQ representation. Their participation in documentaries, interviews, and public speaking engagements has brought critical attention to issues such as discrimination, mental health, and the importance of inclusivity. By sharing their story, Alok has humanized the struggles faced by many in the LGBTQ community, fostering empathy and understanding among diverse audiences.

Alok's Enduring Impact on Pop Culture

In conclusion, Alok Vaid-Menon's enduring impact on pop culture is multifaceted, encompassing fashion, media representation, and artistic expression. Their work challenges societal norms and inspires a new generation to embrace their identities unapologetically. As pop culture continues to evolve, Alok's contributions serve as a reminder of the power of visibility, representation, and the importance of celebrating diversity in all its forms. Their legacy will undoubtedly influence future generations of artists, activists, and individuals seeking to break free from the constraints of traditional gender norms.

Importance of Cultural Representation

Cultural representation is a crucial aspect of social justice and activism, particularly within the LGBTQ community. It refers to the ways in which various cultures, identities, and experiences are depicted in media, art, fashion, and public discourse.

Alok Vaid-Menon's work exemplifies the significance of cultural representation, as they challenge dominant narratives and create space for marginalized voices. This section explores the theoretical frameworks surrounding cultural representation, the problems arising from its absence, and the transformative power it holds in shaping societal perceptions.

Theoretical Frameworks

Cultural representation can be understood through various theoretical lenses, including postcolonial theory, feminist theory, and queer theory. Postcolonial theory critiques the legacy of colonialism and highlights the importance of representing diverse cultures authentically. Edward Said's concept of *Orientalism* illustrates how Western depictions of Eastern cultures often perpetuate stereotypes and misrepresentations. In contrast, Alok's work seeks to dismantle these stereotypes by presenting a multifaceted view of gender and identity that transcends binary notions.

Feminist theory emphasizes the need for women's voices and experiences to be represented in all spheres of life. bell hooks argues that representation is not merely about visibility but also about the power dynamics involved in who gets to tell the story. Alok embodies this notion by using their platform to uplift the narratives of trans and gender nonconforming individuals, particularly those from marginalized backgrounds.

Queer theory further complicates the discussion of representation by challenging normative understandings of gender and sexuality. Judith Butler's concept of *gender performativity* suggests that gender is not an inherent quality but rather a series of acts that create the illusion of a stable identity. Alok's fashion choices and public persona exemplify this performative nature, as they encourage individuals to embrace fluidity and reject rigid categorizations.

Problems Arising from Lack of Representation

The absence of cultural representation can lead to numerous problems, particularly for marginalized communities. One of the most significant issues is the perpetuation of stereotypes. For instance, the media often portrays LGBTQ individuals through a narrow lens, reinforcing harmful tropes that contribute to societal stigma. This lack of nuanced representation can lead to internalized oppression, where individuals begin to believe the negative stereotypes associated with their identities.

Moreover, the absence of diverse representation in leadership and decision-making roles can result in policies and practices that do not address the needs of marginalized communities. This is evident in the realm of education, where curricula often overlook LGBTQ history and contributions, leaving students without role models or a sense of belonging. Alok's advocacy for inclusive educational practices underscores the importance of integrating diverse narratives into learning environments.

Transformative Power of Representation

Cultural representation has the potential to be a powerful tool for social change. When individuals see themselves reflected in media and culture, it fosters a sense of belonging and validation. Alok's visibility as a non-binary activist and fashion icon has inspired countless individuals to embrace their identities and challenge societal norms. Their collaborations with various artists and designers serve as a testament to the power of representation in the fashion industry, where diversity is often lacking.

Furthermore, representation can challenge and reshape societal perceptions. By showcasing the richness of LGBTQ experiences, Alok's work encourages audiences to confront their biases and expand their understanding of gender and identity. For example, their viral performances and social media presence have sparked conversations about the fluidity of gender and the importance of self-love, creating a ripple effect that transcends borders.

Examples of Impactful Representation

Several examples illustrate the importance of cultural representation in effecting change. The television series *Pose* has been lauded for its authentic portrayal of Black and Latinx LGBTQ communities, providing visibility to a group often marginalized in mainstream media. The show's success demonstrates that representation matters, as it has inspired discussions around trans rights and the historical context of ballroom culture.

In the realm of fashion, Alok's collaborations with designers who prioritize inclusivity have redefined beauty standards and challenged the industry's norms. Their participation in campaigns that celebrate body positivity and diversity highlights the transformative power of representation in shaping cultural narratives.

Conclusion

In conclusion, the importance of cultural representation cannot be overstated. It serves as a means of validating identities, challenging stereotypes, and fostering understanding across diverse communities. Alok Vaid-Menon's work exemplifies the transformative potential of representation, as they continue to break barriers and advocate for inclusivity within the fashion industry and beyond. As society progresses, it is imperative that we prioritize diverse voices and narratives, ensuring that all individuals have the opportunity to see themselves reflected in the cultural landscape.

Personal Life and Identity

A Deeper Dive into Alok's Background

Alok Vaid-Menon, a prominent figure in the LGBTQ activism landscape, embodies a rich tapestry of cultural and personal narratives that have shaped their identity and activism. Born in a South Asian immigrant family, Alok's upbringing was steeped in both the challenges and the vibrancy of cultural heritage. This section delves into the multifaceted background that has informed Alok's journey as an activist, artist, and fashion icon.

Cultural Heritage and Identity

Alok's Indian heritage plays a critical role in their understanding of identity and gender. Growing up in a household where traditional values often clashed with contemporary views on gender and sexuality, Alok experienced the complexities of navigating between two worlds. The concept of *intersectionality*, coined by Kimberlé Crenshaw, is particularly relevant here, as it allows us to explore how Alok's experiences of race, gender, and sexuality intersect, creating unique challenges and perspectives.

$$I = R + G + S \tag{62}$$

Where:

- I = Identity
- R = Race
- G = Gender
- S = Sexuality

This equation illustrates that identity is a complex interplay of various factors, with each contributing to the whole. Alok's journey exemplifies this complexity, as they grappled with societal expectations while forging a path that honors their authentic self.

Early Experiences and Challenges

From an early age, Alok faced bullying and discrimination, experiences that many LGBTQ individuals can relate to. These formative experiences were not merely obstacles; they served as catalysts for Alok's activism. The pain of exclusion and the desire for acceptance propelled them to find their voice and advocate for others who faced similar struggles.

The psychological impact of such experiences is well-documented in literature. According to the American Psychological Association, LGBTQ youth are at a higher risk for mental health issues due to societal stigma and discrimination. Alok's resilience in the face of adversity is a testament to their strength and determination.

Education and Self-Discovery

Alok's academic journey further shaped their worldview. Pursuing higher education at prestigious institutions, including Stanford University, allowed Alok to explore critical theories surrounding gender and identity. Here, Alok encountered feminist and queer theory, which provided frameworks for understanding their experiences and the broader societal constructs of gender.

The work of Judith Butler, particularly in *Gender Trouble*, has been influential in shaping Alok's understanding of gender as a performative act rather than a fixed identity. Butler's assertion that gender is a social construct resonates deeply with Alok's activism, as they challenge the rigid binaries that society imposes.

$$G = P \times A \tag{63}$$

Where:

- G = Gender
- P = Performance
- A = Audience

This equation illustrates that gender is not an inherent quality but rather a performance shaped by societal expectations and the audience's perception. Alok's fashion and activism can be seen as a way to disrupt these performances and invite audiences to reconsider their understanding of gender.

Artistic Influences

Alok's background in the arts has also played a significant role in their identity formation. Engaging with various forms of artistic expression, including poetry, fashion, and performance art, has allowed Alok to explore and communicate their experiences in powerful ways. This artistic lens provides a medium through which Alok can challenge societal norms and advocate for change.

The concept of *artivism*—the fusion of art and activism—captures the essence of Alok's approach. By using art as a tool for social change, Alok not only expresses their identity but also inspires others to embrace their authenticity. This intersection of creativity and activism is crucial in fostering dialogues around gender and identity.

Community Engagement

Alok's background is also characterized by a deep commitment to community engagement. Recognizing the importance of solidarity among marginalized groups, Alok has worked tirelessly to uplift the voices of those often overlooked in mainstream discourse. The notion of *collective empowerment* is central to Alok's activism, as they believe that true change can only occur when communities come together to support one another.

Through workshops, speaking engagements, and social media, Alok has built a platform that amplifies the voices of LGBTQ individuals, particularly those from marginalized backgrounds. This commitment to community is not only a reflection of Alok's values but also a strategic approach to fostering inclusivity and understanding.

Conclusion

In summary, Alok Vaid-Menon's background is a rich tapestry woven from cultural heritage, personal challenges, academic exploration, artistic expression, and community engagement. Each thread contributes to the vibrant narrative of a person who has emerged as a powerful voice for LGBTQ rights and a champion of gender liberation. Understanding Alok's background is essential to appreciating the depth of their activism and the impact they continue to have on society.

As we continue to explore Alok's journey, it becomes clear that their story is not just one of personal triumph but a collective call to action for all those who seek to challenge societal norms and embrace the beauty of diversity.

Exploring Gender and Identity

In the contemporary landscape of social discourse, the exploration of gender and identity has emerged as a critical focal point, particularly within LGBTQ activism. Alok Vaid-Menon, a prominent figure in this movement, utilizes their platform to challenge traditional understandings of gender, advocating for a more fluid and inclusive approach. This section delves into the complexities of gender identity, the theories that inform our understanding of it, and the societal challenges that individuals face in navigating their identities.

Understanding Gender Identity

Gender identity refers to an individual's internal sense of their own gender, which may or may not correspond with the sex they were assigned at birth. Judith Butler's theory of gender performativity posits that gender is not an inherent quality but rather a series of performances that individuals enact based on societal norms. This perspective encourages a view of gender as a spectrum rather than a binary construct, emphasizing the fluidity of identity.

$$G = P \times S \tag{64}$$

Where:

- G represents gender,

- P signifies performance, and

- S stands for societal expectations.

This equation illustrates how gender is shaped by the interplay between individual performance and societal norms.

The Spectrum of Gender

Alok's advocacy highlights the importance of recognizing gender beyond the binary of male and female. The concept of non-binary and genderqueer identities challenges the traditional dichotomy, allowing individuals to express themselves in ways that resonate with their personal experiences. This includes terms such as genderfluid, agender, and bigender, which further illustrate the complexity of gender identity.

Cultural and Societal Influences

Cultural contexts play a significant role in shaping gender identity. Different societies have varying norms and expectations regarding gender expression. For example, many Indigenous cultures recognize Two-Spirit individuals, who embody both masculine and feminine traits, thus offering an alternative understanding of gender that contrasts sharply with Western binary views.

Alok often references their South Asian heritage, where traditional gender roles can be particularly rigid. The intersection of culture and gender identity can lead to both empowerment and conflict, as individuals navigate the expectations imposed by their communities while seeking authenticity.

Challenges in Identity Exploration

Despite the growing acceptance of diverse gender identities, many individuals still face significant challenges. Discrimination, violence, and social ostracism are rampant for those who do not conform to traditional gender norms. According to the Human Rights Campaign, transgender individuals are disproportionately affected by violence and discrimination, with a particularly high rate of violence against transgender women of color.

Moreover, the psychological impact of navigating a world that often invalidates non-binary identities can lead to mental health issues such as anxiety and depression. Alok's work emphasizes the importance of visibility and representation, advocating for a society where all identities are acknowledged and celebrated.

The Role of Education in Identity Exploration

Education plays a vital role in fostering understanding and acceptance of diverse gender identities. By incorporating LGBTQ studies into curricula, educational institutions can create safe spaces for students to explore their identities. Alok's engagements in universities highlight the significance of dialogue around gender and identity, aiming to dismantle prejudice and promote inclusivity.

$$E = R + C \qquad (65)$$

Where:

- E represents education,
- R stands for representation, and
- C signifies cultural competency.

This equation underscores the necessity of representation and cultural awareness in educational settings to foster a more inclusive environment.

Conclusion

Exploring gender and identity is a multifaceted endeavor that requires a nuanced understanding of the social, cultural, and personal factors at play. Alok Vaid-Menon's contributions to this discourse challenge conventional norms and inspire a generation to embrace their authentic selves. By advocating for a more inclusive understanding of gender, Alok not only empowers individuals to navigate their identities but also encourages society to evolve towards greater acceptance and understanding.

In conclusion, the journey of exploring gender and identity is ongoing, marked by both challenges and triumphs. As we continue to engage with these concepts, it is imperative to foster environments that celebrate diversity and promote the understanding that identity is a deeply personal and evolving experience.

Alok's Journey of Self-Discovery

Alok Vaid-Menon's journey of self-discovery is a vibrant tapestry woven with threads of identity, culture, and the pursuit of authenticity. Born into a South Asian family, Alok's early life was marked by the interplay of traditional expectations and a burgeoning sense of self that diverged from societal norms. This section delves into the complexities of Alok's journey, highlighting the personal struggles, theoretical frameworks, and pivotal moments that shaped their understanding of identity.

At the heart of Alok's self-discovery is the concept of *intersectionality*, a term coined by Kimberlé Crenshaw in 1989. Intersectionality posits that individuals experience overlapping systems of discrimination and privilege based on various aspects of their identity, including race, gender, sexuality, and class. For Alok, navigating the intersections of being a queer, non-binary individual of South Asian descent presented unique challenges. The weight of cultural expectations often clashed with their desire for self-expression, leading to a profound internal conflict.

Alok's journey was not without its struggles. The pressure to conform to traditional gender norms created a sense of alienation during their formative years. In high school, Alok faced bullying and discrimination, which forced them to grapple with their identity in a world that often rejected differences. This experience is reflective of Judith Butler's theory of gender performativity, which suggests that gender is not an inherent quality but rather a series of repeated performances shaped by societal expectations. Alok's early attempts to conform to these performances were met with resistance, igniting a desire to break free from the constraints of gender binaries.

One pivotal moment in Alok's journey occurred during their college years at Stanford University. Here, Alok was introduced to a diverse community that celebrated differences rather than stifled them. This environment allowed them to explore their identity more freely and engage with theories of gender and queer studies. Alok's participation in LGBTQ organizations and activism on campus catalyzed their understanding of self-acceptance and the importance of community support. This period of exploration is reminiscent of Carl Rogers' humanistic theory, which emphasizes the significance of self-actualization and the pursuit of one's true self.

In addition to academic exploration, Alok's artistic expression became a vital outlet for self-discovery. Through fashion and performance art, Alok began to articulate their identity in ways that transcended traditional language. This aligns with the work of bell hooks, who argues that art can serve as a powerful tool for liberation and self-expression. Alok's unique style, characterized by bold colors, intricate patterns, and fluid silhouettes, became a form of rebellion against societal norms and a celebration of individuality.

However, the journey of self-discovery is rarely linear. Alok faced moments of doubt and insecurity, particularly regarding their non-binary identity. The societal insistence on categorizing individuals within rigid gender binaries often led to feelings of invisibility and confusion. Alok's experience echoes the struggles faced by many non-binary individuals who navigate a world that frequently dismisses their identities. This struggle is compounded by the lack of representation in media and culture, which can perpetuate feelings of isolation.

To confront these challenges, Alok sought solace in the writings of queer theorists such as Eve Kosofsky Sedgwick and Jack Halberstam. Their works provided Alok with frameworks to understand the fluidity of identity and the importance of embracing ambiguity. Alok's journey became a testament to the power of self-definition and the rejection of externally imposed labels. This process of self-discovery culminated in the realization that identity is not a fixed destination but an evolving journey.

As Alok continued to navigate their identity, they also embraced the concept of *radical self-love*, a philosophy that emphasizes acceptance and celebration of oneself in the face of societal pressures. This idea, popularized by Sonya Renee Taylor, resonated deeply with Alok, who sought to redefine beauty standards and challenge the narrative surrounding gender and identity. By embracing radical self-love, Alok transformed their journey into a source of empowerment, inspiring

PERSONAL LIFE AND IDENTITY

others to embrace their authentic selves.

In conclusion, Alok Vaid-Menon's journey of self-discovery is a rich narrative that intertwines personal experiences, theoretical frameworks, and artistic expression. Through the lens of intersectionality, gender performativity, and radical self-love, Alok's evolution reflects the complexities of navigating identity in a world that often seeks to impose limitations. Their story serves as a beacon of hope for individuals grappling with their own identities, illustrating the transformative power of self-acceptance and the importance of embracing one's true self.

Relationships and Love

In the vibrant tapestry of Alok Vaid-Menon's life, relationships and love play a pivotal role, acting as both a sanctuary and a crucible for personal growth. Alok's journey through love is not merely a narrative of romantic encounters; it is a profound exploration of identity, connection, and the complexities of human emotion. This section delves into the multifaceted nature of Alok's relationships, the impact of their identity on love, and the broader implications for LGBTQ+ communities.

The Complexity of Love

Love, in its many forms, has been a central theme in Alok's life. From familial bonds to friendships and romantic relationships, Alok has navigated the intricate dynamics that come with being a non-binary individual in a society that often adheres to rigid definitions of love and partnership. Theories of love, such as Sternberg's Triangular Theory of Love, suggest that love consists of three components: intimacy, passion, and commitment. Alok's relationships reflect this complexity, often challenging traditional notions of these components.

$$L = I + P + C \qquad (66)$$

Where L represents love, I is intimacy, P is passion, and C is commitment. Alok's experiences highlight how these elements can manifest differently in queer relationships, where societal expectations may not align with personal truths.

Navigating Romantic Relationships

Alok's romantic relationships have often been fraught with challenges, stemming from societal perceptions of gender and attraction. The intersectionality of race, gender identity, and sexuality complicates the dating landscape for many

LGBTQ+ individuals. Alok's candid discussions about their experiences shed light on the challenges of finding love in a world that can be unkind to those who defy traditional norms.

For instance, Alok recounts moments of vulnerability when navigating dating apps, where the desire for connection is often met with the harsh realities of discrimination and prejudice. The concept of *heteronormativity*—the assumption that heterosexuality is the default or normal sexual orientation—can create barriers for non-binary individuals seeking love. Alok's experiences serve as a powerful reminder of the need for inclusivity in the dating sphere.

Friendships and Community

Beyond romantic relationships, Alok emphasizes the importance of friendships and community in their life. The support of friends has been crucial in providing a sense of belonging and acceptance. Alok's friendships often transcend conventional boundaries, forming a network of support that celebrates diversity and individuality.

The notion of *chosen family* is significant in LGBTQ+ communities, where individuals often create bonds that rival biological ties. Alok's relationships with friends illustrate how these connections can foster resilience and empowerment, allowing individuals to navigate the world with a sense of solidarity.

The Role of Self-Love

Integral to Alok's journey is the concept of self-love, which serves as a foundation for all other relationships. Alok advocates for radical self-acceptance, encouraging others to embrace their identities unapologetically. This philosophy aligns with the work of theorists like bell hooks, who posits that love—whether for oneself or others—requires a commitment to growth and healing.

$$S = L_{self} + R \tag{67}$$

Where S represents self-fulfillment, L_{self} is self-love, and R is relationships. This equation underscores the idea that healthy relationships stem from a strong sense of self-worth. Alok's journey illustrates how embracing one's identity can enhance the quality of connections with others, fostering deeper intimacy and understanding.

Challenges in Relationships

Despite the profound connections Alok has cultivated, the journey is not without its challenges. Societal pressures, stigma, and internalized discrimination can create obstacles in relationships. Alok openly discusses the emotional toll of navigating love in a world that often marginalizes queer identities.

One significant challenge is the phenomenon of *relationship dysphoria*, where individuals may experience discomfort or disconnection in romantic contexts due to societal expectations of gender roles. Alok's candid explorations of this topic resonate with many who have faced similar struggles, highlighting the need for open dialogues about the complexities of love in the LGBTQ+ community.

The Impact of Love on Activism

Alok's relationships also inform their activism, illustrating the interconnectedness of love and social justice. The concept of *love as a radical act* emerges as a powerful theme in Alok's work, emphasizing that love can be a transformative force in challenging oppression and advocating for change. Alok's relationships serve as a microcosm of broader societal dynamics, reflecting the need for inclusivity and acceptance in all spheres of life.

In conclusion, Alok Vaid-Menon's exploration of relationships and love is a rich tapestry woven with complexity, vulnerability, and resilience. Their journey emphasizes the importance of self-love, the power of community, and the challenges faced in navigating love as a non-binary individual. Through their experiences, Alok inspires others to embrace their identities and cultivate meaningful connections, ultimately advocating for a world where love transcends boundaries and flourishes in its many forms.

Balancing Personal and Professional Life

The quest for equilibrium between personal and professional life is a perennial challenge faced by many individuals, particularly those in high-profile activist roles like Alok Vaid-Menon. This balancing act becomes even more complex when one considers the societal expectations and pressures that accompany being a public figure within the LGBTQ community.

Theoretical Framework

To understand the dynamics of balancing personal and professional life, we can draw from several theories in psychology and sociology. One relevant framework is the *Work-Life Balance Theory*, which posits that individuals strive to maintain a harmonious relationship between their work commitments and personal responsibilities. This theory suggests that an imbalance can lead to stress, burnout, and decreased overall well-being.

$$WLB = \frac{P + F}{W} \tag{68}$$

Where:

- WLB = Work-Life Balance
- P = Personal time and commitments
- F = Family time and commitments
- W = Work commitments

This equation illustrates that achieving a satisfactory work-life balance (WLB) requires a careful distribution of time and energy across personal, family, and work domains.

Challenges Faced by Alok

For Alok, the journey of balancing personal and professional life is fraught with unique challenges. As a prominent LGBTQ activist and fashion icon, Alok often finds themselves in the public eye, which can complicate personal relationships. The constant scrutiny and expectations can lead to feelings of isolation, as personal struggles may be overshadowed by the public persona that Alok has cultivated.

One significant challenge is the *emotional labor* involved in activism. Emotional labor refers to the process of managing feelings and expressions to fulfill the emotional requirements of a job or role. In Alok's case, this involves not only advocating for LGBTQ rights but also navigating the emotional toll that comes from facing discrimination and hate. The need to maintain a positive and empowering public image can create a disconnect from their authentic self, leading to potential burnout.

Strategies for Balance

To manage these challenges, Alok employs several strategies that can serve as a model for others in similar positions:

- **Setting Boundaries:** Alok emphasizes the importance of setting boundaries between work and personal life. This includes designating specific times for activism and ensuring that personal time is respected. For example, Alok may choose to unplug from social media during weekends to recharge and focus on self-care.

- **Engaging in Self-Care:** Alok prioritizes self-care as a non-negotiable aspect of their life. This could involve activities such as meditation, yoga, or spending time with loved ones. By investing in self-care, Alok replenishes their emotional reserves, enabling them to engage more effectively in their activism.

- **Building a Support Network:** Alok surrounds themselves with a supportive community that understands the unique pressures of being an activist. This network provides a safe space for sharing experiences, venting frustrations, and celebrating successes, which is crucial for maintaining mental health.

- **Flexibility and Adaptability:** Alok demonstrates flexibility in their approach to both personal and professional commitments. Recognizing that life is unpredictable, they adapt their schedules to accommodate unforeseen events while still prioritizing their core values and responsibilities.

Examples of Balancing Acts

One poignant example of Alok's balancing act occurred during a major speaking engagement where they were set to address a large audience about the importance of intersectionality in activism. Leading up to the event, Alok experienced personal turmoil, grappling with feelings of inadequacy and doubt. Instead of canceling, Alok chose to channel these emotions into their speech, discussing not only the importance of advocacy but also the personal struggles that accompany such a public role. This transparency resonated with the audience, highlighting the human side of activism and the importance of vulnerability.

Another example is Alok's use of social media as a platform for both activism and personal expression. By sharing snippets of their daily life, Alok creates a bridge between their professional commitments and personal experiences. This approach allows followers to see the multifaceted nature of their identity, reinforcing the message that one can be both an activist and a person navigating the complexities of life.

Conclusion

In conclusion, the balancing act between personal and professional life is a nuanced and ongoing process for Alok Vaid-Menon. By employing strategies such as setting boundaries, engaging in self-care, building a support network, and demonstrating flexibility, Alok navigates the challenges of being a public activist while remaining true to their personal identity. This journey serves as an inspiration for others, illustrating that while the path may be fraught with challenges, it is possible to forge a fulfilling life that honors both personal well-being and professional commitments.

The Role of Spirituality

Spirituality plays a pivotal role in the life and activism of Alok Vaid-Menon, intertwining with their identity and advocacy in profound ways. For Alok, spirituality is not just a personal journey but a collective experience that resonates deeply with the LGBTQ community. It serves as a source of strength, resilience, and empowerment, particularly in a world that often marginalizes and discriminates against individuals based on their gender identity and sexual orientation.

Understanding Spirituality in Context

Spirituality can be defined as the search for meaning, purpose, and connection beyond oneself. Unlike organized religion, which often has specific doctrines and practices, spirituality is more fluid and personal, allowing individuals to explore their beliefs and values in a way that resonates with their experiences. For Alok, this exploration is essential, particularly as a non-binary individual navigating a society steeped in rigid gender norms.

The Intersection of Spirituality and Activism

Alok's activism is deeply rooted in a spiritual framework that emphasizes love, acceptance, and community. They often articulate a vision of spirituality that rejects exclusionary practices and embraces a more inclusive understanding of the divine. This perspective aligns with the principles of intersectionality, which recognizes that various forms of identity—race, gender, sexuality—intersect to create unique experiences of oppression and privilege.

$$\text{Intersectionality} = \sum_{i=1}^{n} \text{Identity}_i \times \text{Experience}_i \qquad (69)$$

This equation illustrates that the sum of one's identities and experiences contributes to a holistic understanding of an individual's place in society. Alok advocates for a spirituality that acknowledges these intersections, promoting a sense of belonging for all marginalized individuals.

Spiritual Practices and Their Impact

Alok incorporates various spiritual practices into their life, such as meditation, mindfulness, and community rituals. These practices serve multiple purposes:

- **Healing:** Spirituality provides a pathway for healing from trauma and discrimination. Alok emphasizes the importance of self-care and mental health, often sharing their personal journey of overcoming challenges through spiritual practices.

- **Connection:** Through community-based spiritual practices, Alok fosters a sense of belonging among LGBTQ individuals. These gatherings create safe spaces where people can express themselves authentically and support one another.

- **Empowerment:** Spirituality empowers individuals to reclaim their identities and narratives. Alok encourages others to embrace their uniqueness, promoting a message of radical self-love and acceptance.

Challenges of Spirituality in Activism

Despite the positive aspects of spirituality, Alok also acknowledges the challenges it presents within the context of activism. The following issues often arise:

- **Exclusivity of Traditional Spiritual Practices:** Many traditional spiritual practices can be exclusionary, often rooted in heteronormative and binary frameworks. Alok challenges these practices, advocating for a more inclusive approach that honors diverse identities.

- **Critique of Spiritual Bypassing:** Alok warns against the phenomenon of spiritual bypassing, where individuals use spirituality to avoid addressing real-world issues of oppression and inequality. They emphasize the need for activism to be grounded in reality while also being spiritually informed.

Examples of Alok's Spiritual Activism

Alok's spiritual activism is exemplified through their public speaking engagements, social media presence, and community initiatives. For instance, in various interviews and talks, Alok discusses the importance of creating spiritual spaces that welcome all identities, emphasizing the need for rituals that celebrate diversity.

Moreover, Alok has collaborated with various organizations to host events that blend spirituality and activism, such as meditation workshops aimed at LGBTQ youth. These events not only provide a platform for self-exploration but also foster community solidarity and resilience.

Conclusion: A Holistic Approach to Activism

In conclusion, spirituality plays a crucial role in Alok Vaid-Menon's life and activism. By integrating spiritual practices into their advocacy, Alok not only enhances their personal journey but also fosters a sense of community and belonging among marginalized individuals. Their approach challenges traditional notions of spirituality, advocating for a more inclusive and intersectional understanding that resonates with the experiences of the LGBTQ community.

As Alok continues to navigate the complexities of identity, activism, and spirituality, their message remains clear: embracing one's authentic self is a radical act of love, and spirituality can serve as a powerful tool in this journey toward liberation and acceptance.

$$\text{Spiritual Empowerment} = \text{Self-Acceptance} + \text{Community Support} + \text{Activism} \tag{70}$$

This equation encapsulates the essence of Alok's message, highlighting that true empowerment arises from a combination of self-love, community connection, and active engagement in the fight for justice.

Challenges and Triumphs on the Personal Front

Alok Vaid-Menon's journey has been one of remarkable challenges and equally profound triumphs, particularly on the personal front. Navigating the complexities of identity, societal expectations, and the intricacies of personal relationships has shaped Alok into the multifaceted activist and artist they are today. This section explores the personal hurdles Alok has faced, the victories that have emerged from these struggles, and the lessons learned along the way.

The Weight of Identity

From an early age, Alok grappled with the weight of their identity in a world that often seeks to categorize individuals into rigid boxes. The societal binary of gender—male and female—has historically marginalized those who do not fit neatly into these categories. Alok's experience as a non-binary individual highlights the psychological toll of living in a society that often invalidates their existence. Research in gender studies emphasizes that individuals who identify outside traditional gender norms frequently encounter discrimination, leading to increased rates of anxiety and depression (Budge et al., 2013).

Alok's struggles with identity were compounded by cultural expectations rooted in their South Asian heritage. The intersectionality of race, gender, and sexuality often created a sense of alienation. For instance, while Alok was celebrated for their bold fashion choices, they also faced backlash from both the LGBTQ community and the broader society for not conforming to traditional gender expressions. This duality of experience—being both a source of inspiration and a target of criticism—has been a recurring theme in Alok's personal narrative.

Navigating Relationships

Relationships have played a pivotal role in Alok's life, serving both as a source of support and a source of conflict. The challenge of finding acceptance among peers and family members has been significant. Alok has openly discussed the difficulty of coming out to their family, who initially struggled to understand and accept their non-binary identity. This experience is not uncommon; studies indicate that LGBTQ individuals often face familial rejection, which can lead to feelings of isolation (Ryan et al., 2009).

However, Alok's journey has also been marked by triumphs in relationships. Over time, they have cultivated a supportive community of friends and allies who celebrate their identity. Alok's ability to forge deep connections with others has been instrumental in their personal growth. These relationships have provided a safe space for Alok to express themselves authentically, reinforcing the importance of community in the LGBTQ experience. The power of chosen family—friends who become family—has been a recurring theme in Alok's life, highlighting the resilience that emerges from supportive networks.

Mental Health Struggles

Mental health has been a significant area of focus for Alok, as they have openly shared their experiences with anxiety and depression. The pressure to constantly perform and advocate for marginalized communities can lead to burnout, a phenomenon increasingly recognized in activist circles. Alok's transparency about their mental health challenges has sparked important conversations about self-care within activism. Research indicates that individuals engaged in social justice work often experience vicarious trauma, necessitating the need for mental health resources tailored to activists (Collins et al., 2015).

Alok has emphasized the importance of self-care practices, such as mindfulness and therapy, in managing their mental health. By prioritizing their well-being, Alok has not only navigated personal challenges but has also set a precedent for others in the community to do the same. This commitment to self-care serves as a reminder that personal health is integral to sustained activism.

Embracing Vulnerability

One of Alok's most significant triumphs has been their ability to embrace vulnerability. Through storytelling and artistic expression, Alok has turned personal challenges into powerful narratives that resonate with many. The act of sharing their journey has not only fostered connection but has also empowered others to embrace their own vulnerabilities. In doing so, Alok has become a beacon of hope for individuals grappling with their identities.

Alok's performances often incorporate elements of vulnerability, using fashion and art as mediums to convey complex emotions and experiences. By challenging societal norms through their work, Alok has redefined what it means to be strong. This shift in perspective aligns with contemporary theories of resilience, which emphasize the importance of vulnerability in fostering personal growth (Brown, 2012).

Lessons Learned

Through the myriad challenges faced on the personal front, Alok has gleaned invaluable lessons that extend beyond their individual experience. The importance of authenticity, the power of community, and the necessity of self-care are themes that emerge consistently throughout their narrative. Alok's journey underscores the idea that personal struggles can catalyze profound change, not only within oneself but also within the broader community.

In conclusion, Alok Vaid-Menon's challenges and triumphs on the personal front serve as a testament to the resilience of the human spirit. By navigating the complexities of identity, relationships, and mental health, Alok has emerged not only as a powerful activist but also as a relatable figure who inspires others to embrace their authentic selves. Their journey reminds us that the path to self-acceptance is often fraught with obstacles, but it is through these very challenges that we can find our strength and purpose.

Bibliography

[1] Budge, S. L., Adelson, J. L., & Howard, K. A. (2013). Anxiety and depression in transgender individuals: The roles of social support and social identity. *Journal of Consulting and Clinical Psychology*, 81(3), 545.

[2] Ryan, C., Huebner, D., Diaz, R. M., & Sanchez, J. (2009). Family Acceptance in Adolescence and the Health of LGBT Young Adults. *Journal of Child and Adolescent Psychiatric Nursing*, 22(4), 205-213.

[3] Collins, D., & McDonald, M. (2015). Vicarious trauma and social justice activism: A call to action. *Journal of Social Issues*, 71(1), 1-16.

[4] Brown, B. (2012). *Daring Greatly: How the Courage to Be Vulnerable Transforms the Way We Live, Love, Parent, and Lead*. Gotham Books.

Alok's Impact on Feminism and Masculinity

Alok Vaid-Menon has emerged as a pivotal figure in the ongoing discourse surrounding feminism and masculinity, effectively challenging traditional gender norms and expanding the conversation about what it means to be a man in contemporary society. Through their work in activism and fashion, Alok has not only brought visibility to non-binary identities but has also engaged with feminist theories to critique and redefine masculinity.

Redefining Masculinity

At the heart of Alok's impact on masculinity is a rejection of the rigid binaries that have long dictated gender roles. Traditional masculinity is often characterized by traits such as dominance, stoicism, and aggression, a construct that feminists have critiqued for perpetuating toxic behaviors. Alok argues that these notions are not only harmful to women and gender minorities but also detrimental to men themselves. In their view, masculinity should not be synonymous with power or control, but rather with vulnerability, empathy, and authenticity.

This perspective aligns with R.W. Connell's theory of hegemonic masculinity, which posits that there exists a dominant form of masculinity that marginalizes alternative expressions. Alok's work actively seeks to dismantle this hierarchy, advocating for a more inclusive understanding of masculinity that allows individuals to express their gender identities freely without fear of societal repercussions.

Feminism and Intersectionality

Alok's approach to feminism is deeply rooted in intersectionality, a term coined by Kimberlé Crenshaw. They emphasize the importance of recognizing how various social identities—including race, class, and sexuality—intersect to create unique experiences of oppression and privilege. By integrating intersectional feminism into their activism, Alok highlights that the struggles faced by marginalized communities cannot be understood in isolation.

For instance, Alok often discusses the experiences of trans women of color, who face compounded discrimination in both feminist and LGBTQ+ spaces. They argue that true feminism must address these intersections and advocate for the rights of all women, particularly those who are most vulnerable. This approach encourages a broader understanding of feminism that includes the voices and experiences of those who have historically been excluded from the conversation.

Challenging Gender Norms through Fashion

Fashion serves as a powerful medium for Alok to express their views on masculinity and feminism. By defying conventional gendered clothing norms, they challenge the idea that clothing should be strictly categorized as masculine or feminine. Alok's bold fashion choices—such as donning skirts, makeup, and traditionally feminine accessories—serve as a form of protest against the restrictive nature of gender norms.

This aligns with Judith Butler's theory of gender performativity, which posits that gender is not an innate quality but rather a performance that is socially constructed. Alok's performances in fashion illustrate this theory, as they embody the fluidity of gender and encourage others to explore their identities beyond societal expectations. By doing so, they not only reclaim femininity as a powerful aspect of their identity but also invite men to embrace traits and styles traditionally deemed feminine without shame.

The Role of Vulnerability in Masculinity

Alok's activism also emphasizes the importance of vulnerability as a strength rather than a weakness. In a society that often equates masculinity with emotional repression, Alok encourages men to embrace their feelings and express their emotions openly. They argue that vulnerability fosters connection and empathy, qualities that are essential for dismantling patriarchal structures.

This perspective is supported by the work of bell hooks, who advocates for a transformative vision of masculinity rooted in love and emotional intelligence. Alok's message resonates with hooks' assertion that men must be liberated from the confines of traditional masculinity to achieve a more equitable society. By promoting vulnerability, Alok not only challenges harmful stereotypes but also paves the way for healthier relationships between all genders.

Examples of Alok's Advocacy

Alok's impact on feminism and masculinity can be seen through various initiatives and public engagements. Their participation in panels, workshops, and social media campaigns has sparked conversations about gender fluidity and the need for a more inclusive feminist movement. For example, in their viral videos, Alok often addresses the importance of self-love and acceptance, encouraging individuals to embrace their authentic selves regardless of societal expectations.

Additionally, Alok has collaborated with feminist organizations to advocate for policies that support gender inclusivity and combat violence against marginalized communities. Their work emphasizes the necessity of allyship, urging individuals to stand in solidarity with those who face discrimination based on their gender identity or expression.

Conclusion

In summary, Alok Vaid-Menon's impact on feminism and masculinity is profound and multifaceted. By challenging traditional notions of masculinity, advocating for intersectional feminism, and promoting vulnerability, Alok has redefined the discourse surrounding gender. Their work not only empowers individuals to embrace their identities but also fosters a more inclusive society where all expressions of gender are celebrated. As Alok continues to break down barriers and push for change, their legacy as an advocate for both feminism and a reimagined masculinity will undoubtedly inspire future generations to embrace a more equitable world.

Embracing Fluidity: Alok's Ever-Evolving Identity

Alok Vaid-Menon's journey is a testament to the beauty and complexity of gender fluidity. In a world that often seeks to box individuals into rigid categories, Alok's identity serves as a powerful example of how fluidity can be embraced and celebrated. This section explores the nuances of Alok's evolving identity, the theoretical frameworks that support it, and the broader implications for society.

Theoretical Frameworks of Gender Fluidity

Gender fluidity challenges the binary conception of gender as strictly male or female. Judith Butler's theory of gender performativity posits that gender is not an inherent quality but rather a series of acts and performances that one engages in. This perspective aligns with Alok's experience, as they navigate their identity through various expressions and styles.

$$G = P_1 + P_2 + \ldots + P_n \qquad (71)$$

where G represents gender, and P_i signifies the different performances that contribute to one's gender identity. Alok embodies this equation, demonstrating that gender is a dynamic and multifaceted construct.

Fluidity as a Response to Societal Norms

Alok's embrace of fluidity is not merely a personal choice but also a response to societal expectations and norms. The pressure to conform to traditional gender roles can be overwhelming, leading to feelings of inadequacy and isolation among those who do not fit neatly into these categories. Alok's journey reflects a conscious rejection of these constraints, advocating for a broader understanding of identity that includes non-binary and gender-nonconforming individuals.

The challenges faced by individuals who embrace fluidity are significant. Alok has often spoken about the backlash and misunderstanding they encounter, particularly from those who adhere to strict gender norms. This societal resistance can manifest in various forms, including discrimination, violence, and exclusion from spaces that are supposed to be safe and inclusive.

Examples of Alok's Fluid Identity

Alok's fashion choices serve as a visual representation of their fluid identity. They often blend traditionally masculine and feminine elements, creating a unique style that defies categorization. For instance, Alok might pair a flowing dress with combat boots or accessorize with jewelry typically associated with masculinity. This sartorial experimentation not only reflects their personal identity but also challenges societal norms around what is deemed acceptable or appropriate for different genders.

Moreover, Alok's artistic expressions, such as performance art and spoken word poetry, further illustrate their fluid identity. In these spaces, Alok explores themes of gender, identity, and belonging, often using humor and vulnerability to connect with audiences. This approach not only allows Alok to express their own experiences but also provides a platform for others to share their stories, fostering a sense of community among those who feel marginalized by traditional gender norms.

The Impact of Fluidity on Community and Activism

Alok's commitment to embracing fluidity has significant implications for community building and activism. By openly discussing their experiences and challenges, Alok creates a sense of belonging for others who may feel isolated in their own journeys. This communal aspect is crucial, as it fosters solidarity among individuals who are often pitted against each other by societal expectations.

In activism, Alok emphasizes the importance of intersectionality, recognizing that fluidity intersects with various identities, including race, class, and sexuality. This holistic approach allows for a more comprehensive understanding of the challenges faced by marginalized communities. Alok's advocacy work often highlights the need for inclusivity within the LGBTQ+ movement, urging activists to consider the diverse experiences of all individuals, particularly those who identify as gender nonconforming or non-binary.

Conclusion: A Vision for the Future

Alok Vaid-Menon's ever-evolving identity serves as a beacon of hope for those navigating the complexities of gender fluidity. By embracing their fluidity, Alok not only challenges societal norms but also inspires others to explore their identities authentically. This journey is not without its challenges, but Alok's resilience and commitment to self-expression offer a powerful message: that fluidity is not something to be feared or suppressed, but rather celebrated as a vital aspect of human diversity.

As society continues to grapple with the implications of gender fluidity, Alok's work reminds us of the importance of creating inclusive spaces that honor and respect all identities. Through education, advocacy, and community engagement, we can foster a world where fluidity is embraced, and everyone is free to express their authentic selves without fear of judgment or discrimination.

Intersection of personal life and activism

The intersection of personal life and activism is a complex and multifaceted domain, particularly for individuals like Alok Vaid-Menon, whose identity as a gender nonconforming person profoundly informs their activist work. This section delves into how personal experiences shape activism, the challenges faced, and the broader implications for social justice movements.

At the core of Alok's activism is the recognition that personal narratives are powerful tools for change. The act of sharing one's story can create a ripple effect, fostering empathy and understanding. As Alok states, "When we share our truths, we dismantle the silence that often surrounds marginalized identities." This sentiment aligns with the theory of narrative identity, which posits that individuals construct their identities through the stories they tell about themselves, impacting how they engage with the world.

$$\text{Narrative Identity} = \text{Self-Concept} + \text{Life Story} \qquad (72)$$

In Alok's case, their personal journey of self-discovery and acceptance has not only influenced their identity but also served as a catalyst for activism. Growing up in a society that often imposes rigid gender norms, Alok faced significant challenges, including bullying and discrimination. These experiences shaped their understanding of the systemic barriers faced by LGBTQ individuals and galvanized a commitment to advocacy.

The concept of intersectionality, introduced by Kimberlé Crenshaw, is critical in understanding how personal experiences of oppression intersect with broader societal structures. Alok's activism is rooted in this framework, recognizing that their identity as a South Asian, non-binary individual intersects with issues of race, gender, and sexuality. This intersectionality informs their approach to activism, emphasizing the need for inclusive movements that address the diverse experiences of marginalized communities.

$$\text{Intersectionality} = f(\text{Race, Gender, Sexuality, Class}) \qquad (73)$$

Alok's work highlights the importance of addressing systemic inequalities while sharing personal narratives. For instance, their involvement in campaigns advocating for trans rights is deeply intertwined with their own experiences of navigating a world that often invalidates non-binary identities. This personal connection not only enhances the authenticity of their activism but also resonates with others who share similar struggles.

However, the blending of personal life and activism is not without its challenges. Activists often face emotional tolls as they navigate public scrutiny and backlash. Alok has openly discussed the mental health challenges associated with being a visible figure in the LGBTQ community, emphasizing the need for self-care. The pressure to constantly represent marginalized voices can lead to burnout, making it crucial for activists to establish boundaries between their personal lives and public personas.

Moreover, the public nature of activism can complicate personal relationships. Alok's commitment to activism has sometimes created tension with family members who may not fully understand or support their identity and work. This dynamic reflects a broader issue faced by many activists: the struggle to reconcile personal relationships with the demands of advocacy.

In conclusion, the intersection of personal life and activism is a dynamic interplay that shapes the work of activists like Alok Vaid-Menon. Their journey illustrates how personal experiences can inform and enrich advocacy efforts, while also highlighting the challenges that arise from this intersection. By embracing their authentic selves and sharing their stories, Alok not only advocates for change but also inspires others to embrace their identities and engage in the fight for justice.

This section underscores the importance of recognizing the personal dimensions of activism, as they are integral to understanding the complexities of social justice work. Alok's narrative serves as a powerful reminder that personal and political are inextricably linked, and that true change often begins with the courage to share one's truth.

Alok's Legacy

Sustaining the Momentum of Activism

The journey of activism is not a sprint; it is a marathon. For Alok Vaid-Menon, sustaining the momentum of activism has been a critical component of their work in advocating for LGBTQ rights and gender liberation. This section explores the strategies, challenges, and theoretical frameworks that have enabled Alok to maintain engagement and inspire action within the community.

Theoretical Frameworks for Sustaining Activism

To understand how to sustain activism, we can draw on several theoretical frameworks. One such framework is **Social Movement Theory**, which emphasizes the importance of resource mobilization and political opportunities. According to Tilly and Tarrow (2015), social movements thrive when they can effectively mobilize resources—be it time, money, or human capital—and when there are favorable political conditions to exploit.

$$M = R + P + C \tag{74}$$

where M is the momentum of the movement, R is resources, P is political opportunity, and C is collective identity.

Alok has harnessed these elements by building a strong community network that supports resource sharing and collaboration. This approach not only fortifies the movement but also cultivates a sense of belonging among activists, which is crucial for sustaining long-term commitment.

Building Community and Solidarity

One of the most effective strategies Alok has employed is the cultivation of community and solidarity. By creating inclusive spaces where individuals can share their experiences and struggles, Alok fosters a sense of collective identity. This solidarity is essential in maintaining momentum, as it helps individuals feel connected to a larger purpose.

For instance, Alok frequently organizes workshops and events that bring together LGBTQ activists from diverse backgrounds. These gatherings not only serve as platforms for sharing knowledge and strategies but also reinforce a sense of unity. The collective energy generated in these spaces can be likened to a **feedback loop** where shared experiences and encouragement propel individuals to take action.

Utilizing Digital Platforms

In the digital age, social media has become an indispensable tool for sustaining activism. Alok has adeptly utilized platforms such as Instagram, Twitter, and TikTok to amplify their message and engage with a global audience. The immediacy of social media allows for real-time communication, enabling activists to respond swiftly to emerging issues and mobilize support.

Alok's viral videos often address pressing social issues while also celebrating LGBTQ identities. This dual approach not only raises awareness but also encourages followers to participate in activism, whether through sharing content, attending events, or engaging in discussions. The ability to reach a vast audience can be mathematically represented by the equation:

$$A = R \times E \tag{75}$$

where A is the activism generated, R is the reach of the message, and E is the engagement level of the audience.

The exponential growth of Alok's online presence exemplifies how digital platforms can sustain momentum by expanding the reach and fostering engagement.

Navigating Challenges and Burnout

Despite the strategies employed, sustaining activism is not without challenges. Activists often face burnout, which can severely hinder momentum. Alok acknowledges the importance of self-care and mental health in their activism. They advocate for a balanced approach that allows activists to recharge and reflect.

To combat burnout, Alok promotes the concept of **radical self-care**, which emphasizes the need for activists to prioritize their well-being as a form of resistance. This approach can be viewed through the lens of **Intersectional Feminism**, which recognizes that the identities of activists—such as race, gender, and socioeconomic status—intersect to shape their experiences and challenges.

Alok's personal practices include mindfulness, community support, and creative expression, which serve as antidotes to the stresses of activism. By sharing these practices, Alok not only normalizes the conversation around mental health but also equips others with tools to sustain their activism.

Long-Term Vision and Goals

Sustaining momentum also requires a long-term vision. Alok's activism is grounded in a commitment to systemic change rather than temporary solutions. This perspective aligns with **Critical Theory**, which critiques societal structures and aims for transformative change.

Alok often articulates a vision for a world where gender and sexual identities are celebrated, not marginalized. By setting clear goals and maintaining a focus on the bigger picture, Alok inspires others to remain engaged, even when immediate results are not visible.

Conclusion

In conclusion, sustaining the momentum of activism is a multifaceted endeavor that requires community building, strategic use of digital platforms, self-care, and a long-term vision. Alok Vaid-Menon's approach exemplifies how these elements can be woven together to create a resilient and dynamic movement. As they continue to inspire and lead, the lessons learned from their journey offer valuable insights for current and future activists seeking to maintain momentum in the fight for LGBTQ rights and gender liberation.

Empowering Future LGBTQ Activists

In the landscape of activism, the empowerment of future LGBTQ activists is not just a goal; it is a necessity. Alok Vaid-Menon stands as a beacon for aspiring advocates, demonstrating the profound impact that one individual can have in the fight for equality. This empowerment is rooted in several key areas: education, mentorship, community building, and the promotion of intersectionality.

Education as a Foundation

Education plays a pivotal role in shaping informed activists. Alok emphasizes the importance of understanding historical contexts, social theories, and the dynamics of power that affect marginalized communities. Theories such as *Critical Race Theory* (CRT) and *Queer Theory* provide frameworks through which activists can analyze systemic inequalities and develop strategies for change.

For instance, CRT examines how laws and policies perpetuate racial inequalities, while Queer Theory challenges the binary understanding of gender and sexuality. By integrating these theories into educational programs, future activists can develop a nuanced understanding of the issues they advocate for.

Mentorship: Guiding the Next Generation

Mentorship is a crucial component of empowering future activists. Alok actively engages in mentorship programs, offering guidance and support to young LGBTQ individuals. This relationship fosters a sense of belonging and provides mentees with the tools they need to navigate the complexities of activism.

Alok's mentorship style is grounded in *transformational leadership*, which encourages personal growth and motivates mentees to strive for social change. By sharing personal experiences, challenges, and successes, Alok cultivates resilience among young activists, empowering them to find their voices and take action.

Community Building

Building a strong, supportive community is essential for sustaining activism. Alok advocates for inclusive spaces where LGBTQ individuals can gather, share experiences, and strategize collective action. Community organizations serve as hubs for education, support, and mobilization.

Alok's initiatives often include workshops, panel discussions, and collaborative art projects that invite participation from diverse community members. This approach not only fosters solidarity but also amplifies marginalized voices, ensuring that the activism is representative of the community it seeks to uplift.

Promoting Intersectionality

Intersectionality is a critical framework for understanding the interconnectedness of various social identities and the unique challenges faced by individuals at these intersections. Alok's activism emphasizes the importance of recognizing and addressing the diverse experiences within the LGBTQ community, particularly those of people of color, transgender individuals, and other marginalized groups.

By promoting an intersectional approach, Alok encourages future activists to consider how factors such as race, class, gender identity, and ability intersect to shape individuals' experiences. This holistic perspective enables activists to develop more inclusive strategies and policies that address the needs of all community members.

Real-World Examples of Empowerment

Alok's impact is evident through various initiatives aimed at empowering future LGBTQ activists. For example, the *Transgender Day of Visibility* (TDOV) serves as a platform for celebrating transgender lives and advocating for their rights. Alok actively participates in events that highlight the achievements of transgender individuals and raise awareness about the challenges they face.

Additionally, Alok's collaboration with organizations such as *The Trevor Project* and *GLAAD* demonstrates a commitment to providing resources and support for LGBTQ youth. These partnerships offer training programs, educational resources, and advocacy opportunities that equip young activists with the skills needed to effect change.

Challenges and Resilience

Despite the progress made, future LGBTQ activists face numerous challenges, including systemic discrimination, societal stigma, and violence. Alok emphasizes the importance of resilience in overcoming these obstacles. By fostering a culture of support and solidarity, activists can navigate adversity and continue their work.

Furthermore, Alok's message of radical self-love encourages future activists to prioritize their mental health and well-being. By recognizing the importance of self-care, activists can sustain their passion and commitment to the cause, ensuring that they remain effective advocates for change.

Conclusion

Empowering future LGBTQ activists is a multi-faceted endeavor that requires a commitment to education, mentorship, community building, and intersectionality. Alok Vaid-Menon exemplifies the transformative potential of activism, inspiring the next generation to challenge norms, advocate for justice, and embrace their authentic selves. As future activists continue to rise, they carry forward the legacy of those who have paved the way, ensuring that the fight for equality remains vibrant and impactful.

Alok's Vision for a More Inclusive Future

Alok Vaid-Menon envisions a world where diversity is not just tolerated but celebrated, where every individual has the freedom to express their identity without fear of discrimination or violence. This vision is rooted in the principles of intersectionality, a term coined by legal scholar Kimberlé Crenshaw, which emphasizes the interconnected nature of social categorizations such as race, class, and gender, and how they create overlapping systems of discrimination or disadvantage.

Theoretical Framework

At the core of Alok's vision is the belief that inclusivity must be systemic rather than superficial. This requires a fundamental shift in how society understands and interacts with concepts of identity. Alok draws on Judith Butler's theory of gender performativity, which posits that gender is not an inherent trait but rather a series of actions and behaviors that are socially constructed. Alok's advocacy encourages individuals to break free from these constricting norms and embrace a more fluid understanding of identity.

$$I = f(G, R, C, E) \tag{76}$$

Where:

- I = Inclusivity
- G = Gender identity
- R = Racial identity
- C = Class status
- E = Environmental factors

This equation illustrates that inclusivity is a function of various intersecting identities and external influences. Alok argues that to achieve true inclusivity, society must actively engage with and dismantle the barriers that prevent marginalized communities from thriving.

Addressing Systemic Issues

Alok's vision also acknowledges the systemic issues that perpetuate inequality. For instance, the lack of representation in media and politics often leads to policies that fail to consider the needs of LGBTQ individuals, particularly those from marginalized racial and ethnic backgrounds. Alok advocates for comprehensive policy reform that includes:

- **Anti-discrimination laws**: Strengthening laws that protect individuals from discrimination based on gender identity and sexual orientation.
- **Healthcare access**: Ensuring that healthcare systems are equipped to provide affirming care for transgender and non-binary individuals.
- **Education reform**: Integrating LGBTQ studies into school curriculums to foster understanding and acceptance from a young age.

Examples of Inclusive Practices

Alok emphasizes the importance of grassroots movements and community-led initiatives in creating an inclusive future. One such example is the work of organizations like *Trans Lifeline*, which provides critical support to transgender individuals in crisis. By centering the voices of those most affected by systemic oppression, these organizations exemplify Alok's vision of inclusivity.

Moreover, Alok points to the rise of fashion brands that prioritize diversity in their marketing and product offerings. Brands like *Savage X Fenty* and *Chromat* have made significant strides in redefining beauty standards by showcasing models of various sizes, shapes, and gender identities. This not only challenges the traditional norms of the fashion industry but also empowers individuals to embrace their unique identities.

The Role of Education and Awareness

Education plays a crucial role in Alok's vision for a more inclusive future. By fostering awareness and understanding of LGBTQ issues, society can begin to dismantle the prejudices that fuel discrimination. Alok advocates for educational programs that:

- Promote empathy and understanding through storytelling.

- Provide training for educators on how to create safe and inclusive classrooms.

- Encourage open dialogues about gender and sexuality to normalize conversations around identity.

Conclusion

In conclusion, Alok Vaid-Menon's vision for a more inclusive future is one that calls for systemic change, community empowerment, and a reimagining of societal norms. By embracing intersectionality and advocating for the rights of marginalized communities, Alok believes that we can create a world where everyone is free to be their authentic selves. This vision requires collective action, a commitment to education, and an unwavering dedication to justice and equality. As Alok passionately states, "We are not just fighting for our own liberation; we are fighting for the liberation of all people."

This vision is not just aspirational; it is a necessary blueprint for a future that honors the richness of human diversity and the beauty of individual expression.

Continuing the Fight for Equality

The struggle for equality is a continuous journey, one that requires both persistence and adaptability. Alok Vaid-Menon embodies this ongoing fight, utilizing their platform to challenge systemic inequalities that persist in society. This section delves into the significance of continuing the fight for equality, exploring the theories that underpin activism, the challenges faced, and the examples that illustrate the ongoing struggle.

Theoretical Frameworks

At the core of Alok's activism lies the theory of **intersectionality**, coined by Kimberlé Crenshaw. Intersectionality posits that individuals experience oppression in varying configurations and degrees of intensity based on their intersecting identities, such as race, gender, sexuality, and class. This framework is crucial for understanding the complexities of the LGBTQ movement, as it recognizes that not all individuals experience discrimination in the same way.

The **Social Model of Disability** is another relevant theory that informs Alok's activism. This model argues that society must adapt to accommodate individuals with disabilities rather than forcing individuals to conform to societal norms. By applying this model to gender and sexuality, Alok advocates for a society that embraces diversity in all forms, allowing individuals to express themselves freely without fear of discrimination.

Challenges in the Fight for Equality

Despite progress, the fight for LGBTQ equality faces numerous challenges. One significant issue is the **backlash against LGBTQ rights**, particularly in regions where conservative ideologies dominate. For instance, various states in the United States have enacted legislation that targets transgender individuals, such as restricting access to healthcare and participation in sports. This backlash not only undermines the rights of LGBTQ individuals but also perpetuates a culture of fear and discrimination.

Another challenge is the issue of **systemic discrimination**. Many LGBTQ individuals face discrimination in employment, housing, and healthcare. According to a report by the Human Rights Campaign, nearly 50% of LGBTQ workers have experienced discrimination at their jobs. This systemic bias highlights the need for comprehensive policies that protect LGBTQ individuals from discrimination in all aspects of life.

Examples of Continuing the Fight

Alok's activism provides numerous examples of how the fight for equality can be sustained. One prominent example is their involvement in the **Transgender Day of Remembrance**, an annual observance that honors the memory of those who have lost their lives due to anti-transgender violence. Alok uses this platform to raise awareness about the violence faced by transgender individuals, particularly those of color, emphasizing the urgent need for change.

Additionally, Alok has been vocal about the importance of **mental health resources** for LGBTQ youth. They have collaborated with organizations such as The Trevor Project to advocate for mental health support tailored to the needs of LGBTQ individuals. This advocacy is crucial, as studies show that LGBTQ youth are at a higher risk for mental health issues, often stemming from societal rejection and discrimination.

The Role of Community in Activism

Continuing the fight for equality is not a solitary endeavor; it requires the collective effort of communities. Alok emphasizes the importance of **community organizing** as a vital strategy for enacting change. By mobilizing individuals around shared goals, communities can amplify their voices and demand accountability from those in power.

One successful example of community organizing is the **Black Lives Matter** movement, which has intersected with LGBTQ activism to address the systemic racism and violence faced by Black LGBTQ individuals. Alok has participated in various protests and initiatives that highlight the intersection of these issues, demonstrating how collective action can lead to meaningful change.

Looking Ahead: A Call to Action

As Alok continues their fight for equality, they call upon individuals to engage in activism in their own communities. This engagement can take many forms, from educating oneself about LGBTQ issues to participating in local advocacy groups. Alok's message is clear: every action counts, and collective efforts can lead to significant change.

In conclusion, continuing the fight for equality is an ongoing process that requires dedication, resilience, and collaboration. Through the lens of intersectionality, the acknowledgment of systemic discrimination, and the power of community organizing, Alok Vaid-Menon exemplifies how individuals can contribute to a more equitable society. As we move forward, it is imperative to uphold the values of love, acceptance, and radical empathy, ensuring that the fight for equality remains at the forefront of our collective consciousness.

Alok's Impact on Future Generations

Alok Vaid-Menon's influence extends far beyond their immediate activism; they have created a ripple effect that is shaping the future of LGBTQ rights and identity politics for generations to come. This impact can be analyzed through several key dimensions: education, representation, and the cultivation of a culture of acceptance and self-love.

Education and Empowerment

One of Alok's most significant contributions is their commitment to education. By engaging with students in various educational institutions, Alok has introduced crucial discussions about gender identity, intersectionality, and the importance of inclusivity. Their workshops and speaking engagements not only inform young people about LGBTQ issues but also empower them to be advocates for change in their own communities.

The educational theory of *transformative learning*, as proposed by Jack Mezirow, is particularly relevant here. Mezirow asserts that transformative learning occurs when individuals critically reflect on their experiences and beliefs, leading to a shift in their worldview. Alok's approach encourages students to challenge societal norms and engage in critical reflection about gender and identity. This transformative process is vital in fostering a generation of individuals who are not only informed but also actively engaged in advocacy.

Representation in Media and Culture

Alok's visibility in media and pop culture has also played a crucial role in shaping future generations. By defying traditional gender norms and embracing a non-binary identity, Alok has become a symbol of representation for many marginalized individuals. This visibility is essential, as studies have shown that representation in media can significantly impact self-esteem and identity formation among young people.

For instance, a study conducted by the Geena Davis Institute on Gender in Media found that positive representation of diverse identities in film and television leads to increased self-acceptance and a greater sense of belonging among viewers. Alok's appearances in various media outlets, fashion shows, and social media platforms serve as a beacon of hope for those who may feel isolated or marginalized due to their identity.

Cultivating a Culture of Acceptance

Alok's message of radical self-love and acceptance resonates deeply with younger generations. They challenge the binary notions of gender and beauty, advocating for a more inclusive understanding of identity. This approach aligns with the social constructivist theory, which posits that our understanding of reality is shaped by social interactions and cultural contexts. By promoting the idea that gender is fluid and that self-expression is a fundamental human right, Alok encourages young people to embrace their authentic selves without fear of judgment.

Moreover, Alok's activism is grounded in the principles of intersectionality, a term coined by Kimberlé Crenshaw. Intersectionality emphasizes that individuals experience multiple, overlapping identities that affect their social experiences and access to resources. By highlighting the interconnectedness of race, gender, sexuality, and class, Alok fosters a more nuanced understanding of social justice that is essential for future activists. This framework encourages young people to consider the complexities of identity and advocate for a more equitable society.

Examples of Impact

Alok's influence is evident in numerous initiatives and movements that have emerged in the wake of their activism. For example, the establishment of LGBTQ student organizations in schools and universities across the globe has provided safe spaces for young people to explore their identities and advocate for their rights. These organizations often draw inspiration from Alok's work, creating programs that promote awareness and understanding of gender diversity.

Additionally, Alok's collaborations with various brands and designers have led to the creation of clothing lines that challenge traditional beauty standards. These initiatives not only provide representation but also empower young people to express their identities through fashion, a medium that has historically been restrictive.

Conclusion

In conclusion, Alok Vaid-Menon's impact on future generations is profound and multifaceted. Through education, representation, and the promotion of a culture of acceptance, they are shaping a world where individuals can express their authentic selves without fear of discrimination. As future generations continue to embrace these ideals, they will undoubtedly carry forward Alok's legacy, advocating for a more inclusive and equitable society. The work of Alok serves as a reminder that activism is not just about the present; it is about laying the groundwork for a brighter future for all.

The Enduring Relevance of Alok's Message

Alok Vaid-Menon's activism and fashion sense represent a profound shift in how society perceives gender and identity. Their message resonates deeply in today's socio-political landscape, where discussions around gender fluidity, inclusivity, and self-expression are more crucial than ever. This section explores the enduring relevance of Alok's message, highlighting the theoretical frameworks, societal problems, and real-world examples that underscore their impact.

Theoretical Foundations

At the heart of Alok's activism is the theory of *intersectionality*, a concept coined by Kimberlé Crenshaw in 1989. Intersectionality posits that individuals experience multiple, overlapping identities that shape their social experiences and systemic oppressions. Alok embodies this theory, navigating their identity as a queer, non-binary person of color in a world that often marginalizes such identities.

The relevance of Alok's message can also be framed through Judith Butler's theory of *gender performativity*. Butler argues that gender is not an innate quality but rather a series of repeated actions and performances that society enforces. Alok's vibrant fashion choices and public persona challenge these norms, demonstrating that gender can be fluid and expressive rather than fixed and binary.

Societal Problems Addressed

Alok's message resonates in a world grappling with various systemic issues, including:

- **Transphobia and Violence:** The rise in anti-trans legislation and violence against transgender individuals highlights the urgent need for advocacy. Alok's visibility and outspoken nature provide a counter-narrative to the hate that permeates society.

- **Mental Health:** Studies indicate that LGBTQ+ individuals, particularly those who are non-binary or gender non-conforming, face higher rates of mental health issues due to societal stigma and discrimination. Alok's message of radical self-love and acceptance offers a healing perspective for those grappling with their identities.

- **Cultural Representation:** The lack of representation for LGBTQ+ individuals in media and fashion perpetuates harmful stereotypes. Alok's work actively seeks to redefine beauty standards, advocating for diverse representations that reflect the true spectrum of human experience.

Real-World Examples

Alok's influence is evident in various realms, from social media to fashion runways:

- **Social Media Activism:** Alok has harnessed platforms like Instagram and TikTok to spread their message, creating viral content that sparks conversation and encourages self-acceptance. For instance, their videos discussing the importance of pronouns and gender identity have garnered millions of views, reaching audiences that traditional activism may not.

- **Fashion as a Political Statement:** In collaborations with major brands, Alok has pushed for inclusivity in fashion. Their presence at events like New York Fashion Week challenges the conventional norms of beauty and gender, inspiring a new generation of designers and models to embrace diversity.

- **Public Speaking and Education:** Alok's engagement with universities and educational institutions has opened dialogues around gender and identity. Their speeches often emphasize the importance of creating safe spaces for LGBTQ+ youth, fostering environments where all identities are celebrated.

Conclusion

The enduring relevance of Alok Vaid-Menon's message lies in its ability to address pressing societal issues through a lens of love, acceptance, and radical self-expression. By challenging gender norms and advocating for intersectional identities, Alok not only inspires change but also cultivates a community of individuals who feel empowered to embrace their authentic selves. As society continues to evolve, Alok's message remains a beacon of hope and resilience, reminding us of the transformative power of self-love and the importance of inclusivity in our collective journey toward equality.

$$\text{Relevance} = \frac{\text{Visibility} + \text{Advocacy}}{\text{Oppression}} \tag{77}$$

Honoring Alok's Contributions to LGBTQ Rights

Alok Vaid-Menon has emerged as a formidable force in the fight for LGBTQ rights, blending fashion, activism, and personal narrative to challenge societal norms and advocate for marginalized communities. Their contributions are not merely performative; they are rooted in a deep understanding of the intersectionality of identity, culture, and systemic oppression. This section honors Alok's multifaceted contributions to LGBTQ rights, exploring their impact through theory, real-world applications, and notable examples.

Theoretical Framework

At the core of Alok's activism is the theory of intersectionality, which posits that various forms of social stratification—such as race, gender, and sexual orientation—do not exist independently but are interwoven. This framework is crucial for understanding how individuals experience oppression differently based on their unique identities. Alok's work exemplifies this theory by highlighting the experiences of trans and gender nonconforming people of color, who often face compounded discrimination.

$$O = f(G, R, S) \qquad (78)$$

Where O represents oppression, G is gender identity, R is race, and S is sexual orientation. This equation illustrates that oppression is a function of multiple intersecting identities, a concept that Alok passionately advocates for in their speeches and writings.

Advocacy and Activism

Alok's activism is characterized by their commitment to deconstructing harmful gender norms and advocating for the rights of LGBTQ individuals. They have utilized various platforms, including social media, public speaking engagements, and collaborations with organizations, to amplify their message. Alok's approach combines personal storytelling with broader social critiques, making their activism relatable and impactful.

One notable example is Alok's involvement in campaigns aimed at protecting the rights of transgender individuals. Through their participation in events such as the Transgender Day of Remembrance, Alok honors the lives lost to violence and discrimination, while also calling for systemic change. Their speeches often emphasize the need for comprehensive policies that protect LGBTQ individuals from discrimination in employment, healthcare, and education.

Cultural Impact

Alok's contributions extend beyond traditional activism; they have significantly influenced popular culture and media representation of LGBTQ individuals. By challenging beauty standards and advocating for body positivity, Alok has reshaped narratives around gender and identity. Their unique fashion sense, characterized by vibrant colors and androgynous styles, serves as a form of self-expression and resistance against societal expectations.

Through collaborations with designers and brands, Alok has not only promoted inclusivity in the fashion industry but has also provided a platform for emerging LGBTQ artists. For instance, their partnership with renowned fashion houses has led to the creation of collections that celebrate diversity and challenge conventional notions of beauty. This intersection of fashion and activism demonstrates how cultural influence can be harnessed to advocate for social change.

Empowerment and Education

Education is another crucial aspect of Alok's contributions to LGBTQ rights. They actively engage with students and educational institutions to foster inclusivity and promote understanding of LGBTQ issues. Alok's workshops and speaking engagements at universities have empowered countless individuals to embrace their identities and advocate for their rights.

In their educational outreach, Alok emphasizes the importance of allyship and understanding intersectionality. They encourage students to engage in critical discussions about gender and sexuality, promoting a culture of acceptance and support. This educational approach not only uplifts LGBTQ youth but also fosters a more inclusive society.

Conclusion

Honoring Alok Vaid-Menon's contributions to LGBTQ rights involves recognizing their commitment to intersectionality, advocacy, cultural impact, and education. Their work serves as a powerful reminder of the importance of representation and the need for systemic change. Alok's voice resonates with many, inspiring individuals to embrace their authentic selves and fight for a more inclusive world. As we reflect on Alok's contributions, we are reminded that the journey toward equality is ongoing, and the fight for LGBTQ rights is a collective responsibility that requires our unwavering commitment.

Paying It Forward: Mentoring the Next Generation

In the landscape of activism, mentorship plays a crucial role in fostering the next generation of leaders. Alok Vaid-Menon embodies this principle, understanding that the fight for LGBTQ rights and gender liberation is not a solitary endeavor but a collective journey. Mentorship, particularly within marginalized communities, is essential for empowerment, guidance, and the dissemination of knowledge and resources.

The Importance of Mentorship in Activism

Mentorship can be defined as a relational dynamic where an experienced individual provides guidance, support, and knowledge to a less experienced person. In the context of activism, this relationship is vital for several reasons:

1. **Knowledge Transfer**: Activism often involves navigating complex social, legal, and political landscapes. Mentors can provide insights based on their experiences, helping mentees avoid common pitfalls and develop effective strategies for advocacy.
2. **Building Confidence**: For many young activists, particularly those from LGBTQ communities, self-doubt can be a significant barrier. Mentorship helps to cultivate self-confidence, enabling mentees to express their identities and advocate for their rights without fear.
3. **Creating Networks**: Mentors often have established networks within the activist community and beyond. By connecting mentees with these networks, mentors can open doors to opportunities that may otherwise remain inaccessible.
4. **Fostering Resilience**: The path of activism is fraught with challenges, including systemic discrimination and personal attacks. Mentors can share their coping strategies and resilience-building techniques, equipping mentees to face adversity with strength.
5. **Encouraging Innovation**: The fresh perspectives of younger activists can challenge the status quo and introduce innovative ideas. Mentors can help channel these ideas into actionable plans, fostering a dynamic exchange of knowledge and creativity.

Alok's Mentorship Initiatives

Alok Vaid-Menon actively engages in mentorship through various initiatives, workshops, and speaking engagements. By sharing their journey and insights, Alok not only inspires but also equips the next generation with the tools necessary for effective activism.

Workshops and Educational Programs Alok often conducts workshops aimed at empowering LGBTQ youth. These workshops cover topics such as self-advocacy, navigating social media for activism, and understanding intersectionality. For instance, during a workshop at a local LGBTQ center, Alok facilitated discussions on the importance of intersectionality in activism, encouraging participants to consider how overlapping identities impact their experiences and advocacy efforts.

Peer Mentorship Programs In addition to formal workshops, Alok encourages peer mentorship among LGBTQ youth. This grassroots approach allows young activists to support one another, fostering a sense of community and shared purpose. By creating safe spaces for dialogue, Alok helps cultivate an environment where youth can freely express their thoughts and feelings, promoting collective growth and understanding.

Challenges in Mentorship

While mentorship is invaluable, it is not without its challenges. Some of the common obstacles include:

1. **Resource Limitations**: Many LGBTQ organizations struggle with funding and resources, limiting their ability to offer comprehensive mentorship programs.
2. **Burnout**: Activism can be emotionally taxing, and mentors may experience burnout, making it difficult to provide the necessary support to mentees.
3. **Access and Representation**: Not all marginalized youth have access to mentors who share their identities or understand their specific challenges. This lack of representation can hinder the effectiveness of mentorship.
4. **Navigating Power Dynamics**: The mentor-mentee relationship can sometimes create power imbalances, leading to dependency rather than empowerment. It is crucial for mentors to foster independence in their mentees.

Strategies for Effective Mentorship

To address these challenges, Alok emphasizes several strategies for effective mentorship:

- **Creating Inclusive Spaces**: Mentors should strive to create inclusive environments where all voices are heard and valued. This can involve actively seeking out diverse perspectives and ensuring that mentorship programs reflect the communities they serve.
- **Setting Boundaries**: Establishing clear boundaries can help prevent burnout and maintain a healthy mentor-mentee relationship. Mentors should communicate their availability and ensure that mentees understand the importance of self-care.
- **Encouraging Autonomy**: Effective mentorship empowers mentees to take charge of their activism. Mentors should guide rather than dictate, allowing mentees to explore their paths and develop their unique voices.

Conclusion: The Ripple Effect of Mentorship

Alok Vaid-Menon's commitment to mentoring the next generation of LGBTQ activists exemplifies the transformative power of mentorship. By investing in young leaders, Alok not only fosters individual growth but also contributes to a broader movement for social justice. The ripple effect of mentorship can lead to a more inclusive and equitable society, as empowered individuals carry forward the torch of activism, igniting change in their communities and beyond.

In conclusion, as Alok continues to pay it forward, they remind us that the fight for equality is not just about individual victories but about lifting each other up and creating a legacy of love, acceptance, and empowerment for generations to come.

Celebrating Alok's Impact and Achievements

Alok Vaid-Menon has emerged as a transformative figure in the realms of fashion and activism, wielding their influence to challenge societal norms and advocate for marginalized communities. Their impact is not merely a personal triumph but a beacon of hope and change for countless individuals navigating the complexities of gender and identity. This section explores the multifaceted achievements of Alok, celebrating their contributions to the LGBTQ rights movement, the fashion industry, and broader societal change.

1. A Trailblazer in Fashion

Alok's journey in fashion is a testament to the power of self-expression. They have redefined what it means to be a fashion icon by embracing fluidity and challenging the binary constructs that have long dominated the industry. Alok's signature style—characterized by vibrant colors, bold patterns, and gender-nonconforming silhouettes—has inspired a new generation of designers and fashion enthusiasts to embrace diversity in their own wardrobes.

For instance, Alok's collaboration with various designers has resulted in collections that celebrate inclusivity, breaking the mold of traditional fashion norms. The impact of these collaborations can be seen in the increasing representation of non-binary and gender-fluid models on runways, signaling a shift towards a more inclusive fashion landscape.

$$\text{Fashion Impact} = \frac{\text{Diversity in Representation}}{\text{Traditional Norms}} \qquad (79)$$

This equation illustrates how Alok's influence is fostering diversity in fashion while simultaneously challenging established norms. Their ability to merge activism with artistry has created a ripple effect, encouraging others to express their identities through fashion.

2. Advocacy for LGBTQ Rights

Alok's advocacy work is deeply rooted in their personal experiences and the struggles faced by the LGBTQ community. They have become a powerful voice for trans and gender nonconforming individuals, using their platform to address systemic discrimination and violence. Alok's speeches and writings resonate with those who feel marginalized, offering both validation and empowerment.

One of the most significant achievements in Alok's advocacy is their role in shaping public discourse around gender identity. They have effectively utilized social media to amplify their message, reaching a global audience and sparking conversations about inclusivity and acceptance. Alok's viral videos and thought-provoking posts have not only educated but also inspired many to embrace their authentic selves.

$$\text{Advocacy Impact} = \text{Public Engagement} \times \text{Social Media Reach} \qquad (80)$$

This equation highlights the correlation between Alok's public engagement efforts and their expansive social media reach, underscoring the effectiveness of their advocacy strategies.

3. Empowering Future Generations

Alok's impact extends beyond their immediate achievements; they are dedicated to empowering future generations of activists. Through mentorship programs, workshops, and speaking engagements, Alok has cultivated a new wave of LGBTQ activists equipped with the tools and knowledge to continue the fight for equality.

For example, Alok's collaboration with educational institutions to incorporate LGBTQ issues into curricula has fostered a more inclusive environment for students. By sharing their story and encouraging dialogue, Alok inspires young people to embrace their identities and advocate for social change.

4. Celebrating Intersectionality

A hallmark of Alok's activism is their commitment to intersectionality—the understanding that individuals experience oppression in varying degrees based on their multiple identities. Alok has consistently emphasized the importance of recognizing the interconnectedness of race, gender, sexuality, and class in discussions about social justice.

Their efforts to amplify the voices of marginalized communities, particularly trans people of color, have brought attention to the unique challenges faced by these groups. Alok's work highlights the necessity of inclusive activism that addresses the complexities of identity and the systemic barriers that exist within society.

$$\text{Intersectional Advocacy} = \sum_{i=1}^{n} \text{Identity}_i \times \text{Oppression}_i \qquad (81)$$

This equation illustrates how Alok's advocacy encompasses a range of identities and oppressions, reinforcing the idea that true progress must account for the diverse experiences within the LGBTQ community.

5. Legacy of Love and Acceptance

Ultimately, Alok's impact is characterized by a profound message of love and acceptance. Their mantra of radical self-love encourages individuals to embrace their identities unapologetically. Alok's ability to connect with people on a personal level—whether through their art, activism, or social media presence—has fostered a sense of community and belonging among those who feel isolated.

The celebration of Alok's achievements is not merely a recognition of their individual contributions; it is a celebration of the progress made in the fight for LGBTQ rights and the ongoing journey toward inclusivity. As Alok continues to break down barriers and challenge societal norms, their legacy will undoubtedly inspire future generations to advocate for love, acceptance, and equality.

In conclusion, Alok Vaid-Menon's impact and achievements are a testament to the power of authenticity and the importance of representation in all spheres of life. Through their work in fashion and activism, Alok has not only challenged the status quo but has also paved the way for a more inclusive and accepting world. As we celebrate their contributions, we are reminded of the ongoing work that lies ahead and the collective responsibility to continue the fight for justice and equality for all.

Long-lasting change

Long-lasting change in the realm of LGBTQ activism is not merely a product of individual efforts but rather a cumulative result of collective action, sustained advocacy, and the integration of inclusive policies across various societal sectors. Alok Vaid-Menon exemplifies this transformative journey, demonstrating how personal narratives, combined with strategic activism, can lead to enduring societal shifts.

Theoretical Framework

To understand the mechanisms behind long-lasting change, we can draw upon several theoretical frameworks. One prominent theory is the **Social Change Theory**, which posits that societal transformation occurs through the interaction of individual actions and broader structural forces. This theory emphasizes the importance of grassroots movements, community organizing, and the role of influential figures in catalyzing change.

Another relevant framework is **Intersectionality**, coined by Kimberlé Crenshaw, which examines how various social identities (e.g., race, gender, sexuality) intersect and influence individuals' experiences of oppression and privilege. This perspective is crucial for LGBTQ activism, as it highlights the necessity of addressing the unique challenges faced by marginalized subgroups within the community.

Challenges to Long-lasting Change

Despite the progress made, several challenges persist in the quest for long-lasting change. One significant issue is **systemic discrimination**, which is deeply embedded in societal institutions. For instance, LGBTQ individuals often face barriers in accessing healthcare, education, and employment due to discriminatory practices and policies. According to a report by the Human Rights Campaign, nearly one in three LGBTQ individuals experienced discrimination in the workplace in 2020.

Another challenge is the **backlash against LGBTQ rights**, particularly in political and social spheres. The rise of anti-LGBTQ legislation in various states has created an environment of fear and uncertainty for many individuals. This backlash can hinder the progress made by activists like Alok, who strive for inclusivity and acceptance.

Examples of Long-lasting Change

Alok's activism has led to several notable examples of long-lasting change. One such instance is the increased visibility and representation of non-binary and gender nonconforming individuals in mainstream media and fashion. Alok's unique approach to fashion—characterized by vibrant colors, bold designs, and a rejection of traditional gender norms—has inspired a new generation of designers and influencers to embrace diversity in their work.

Moreover, Alok's advocacy for inclusive policies in educational institutions has led to the implementation of programs that support LGBTQ youth. For example, initiatives that promote comprehensive sex education, which includes discussions on gender identity and sexual orientation, have been adopted in various school districts, fostering a more inclusive environment for students.

Strategies for Sustaining Change

To ensure long-lasting change, activists must employ strategies that promote sustainability and resilience. One effective approach is the establishment of **mentorship programs** that empower young LGBTQ activists. By providing guidance and resources, established activists can help cultivate the next generation of leaders who will continue the fight for equality.

Additionally, creating **coalitions** among various social justice movements can amplify the impact of LGBTQ activism. By aligning with other marginalized groups, activists can address intersecting issues such as racial justice, economic inequality, and environmental sustainability. This holistic approach not only strengthens the movement but also fosters a sense of solidarity among diverse communities.

The Role of Art and Expression

Art plays a vital role in promoting long-lasting change by challenging societal norms and sparking conversations. Alok's use of performance art, poetry, and fashion as forms of activism underscores the power of creative expression in advocating for social justice. Through their work, Alok encourages individuals to explore their identities and challenge the status quo, ultimately contributing to a cultural shift towards acceptance and understanding.

In conclusion, long-lasting change in LGBTQ activism requires a multifaceted approach that combines individual narratives, collective action, and strategic advocacy. By addressing systemic challenges, fostering mentorship, and utilizing the power of art, activists like Alok Vaid-Menon are paving the way for a more inclusive and equitable society. The journey may be fraught with obstacles, but the commitment to creating a lasting impact remains steadfast, ensuring that the fight for LGBTQ rights continues to evolve and inspire future generations.

Beyond Gender Norms

Beyond Gender Norms

Beyond Gender Norms

In this chapter, we delve into the transformative journey of Alok Vaid-Menon, a figure who embodies the essence of breaking free from conventional gender norms. Alok's work transcends traditional boundaries, challenging societal constructs of gender and identity, and inspiring countless individuals to embrace their authentic selves. This chapter explores the philosophical underpinnings of Alok's activism, the implications of their work on the understanding of gender, and the broader societal impact of redefining gender norms.

Unpacking the Social Construction of Gender

The concept of gender has long been understood as a binary system, where individuals are categorized as either male or female based on biological characteristics. However, contemporary gender theory posits that gender is a social construct, shaped by cultural, historical, and social contexts. Judith Butler, a prominent theorist in gender studies, argues in her seminal work *Gender Trouble* that gender is performative; it is not an inherent quality but rather a series of acts and expressions that individuals engage in based on societal expectations.

Alok Vaid-Menon exemplifies this performative aspect of gender through their fashion choices and public persona. By embracing a style that defies traditional gender norms, Alok challenges the notion that gender expression must align with societal expectations. Their work encourages individuals to question the rigid binaries that have long governed our understanding of identity.

Alok's Philosophy on Gender and Identity

At the core of Alok's philosophy is the belief that gender is fluid and multifaceted. They advocate for a vision of gender that transcends labels, urging society to move beyond the binary framework that has historically marginalized those who do not conform. Alok's message resonates with the principles of intersectionality, a concept coined by Kimberlé Crenshaw, which emphasizes the interconnected nature of social categorizations such as race, class, and gender.

In this context, Alok's activism serves as a powerful reminder that identity is not a singular experience but rather a complex interplay of various factors. By sharing their own journey of self-discovery, Alok invites others to embrace their unique identities, fostering a sense of community and solidarity among those who have been historically marginalized.

Defying the Binary: Alok's Vision for the Future

Alok's vision for the future is one where individuals are free to express their gender identity without fear of judgment or discrimination. This vision aligns with the principles of gender liberation, which seeks to dismantle the oppressive structures that enforce binary gender norms. Alok advocates for a world where individuals can explore their gender identity without being confined to societal expectations, encouraging a radical rethinking of how we understand gender.

The implications of this vision extend beyond individual expression; they challenge systemic inequalities rooted in traditional gender norms. Alok's work highlights the need for societal change, advocating for policies and practices that promote inclusivity and acceptance of diverse gender identities.

Transcending Labels and Boxes

One of the most significant aspects of Alok's activism is their commitment to transcending labels. In a world that often seeks to categorize individuals based on narrow definitions, Alok challenges the notion that we must fit into predefined boxes. This approach resonates with the experiences of many individuals within the LGBTQ+ community, who often feel pressured to conform to societal expectations.

Alok's rejection of labels is not merely a personal choice; it is a political statement that calls for a broader societal shift. By embracing fluidity in their own identity, Alok encourages others to do the same, fostering a culture of acceptance and understanding. This shift is crucial in creating safe spaces for individuals to explore their gender identity without fear of judgment.

The Power of Pronouns

Pronouns play a crucial role in affirming an individual's gender identity. Alok's advocacy for the use of correct pronouns is a powerful reminder of the importance of language in shaping our understanding of gender. By encouraging others to respect and use the pronouns that align with an individual's identity, Alok emphasizes the significance of validation and recognition in fostering a sense of belonging.

The use of pronouns is not merely a matter of preference; it is an essential aspect of respecting an individual's identity. Alok's emphasis on this issue highlights the need for broader societal education on the importance of inclusive language and the impact it has on the lives of marginalized individuals.

Alok's Impact on Non-Binary Identity

Alok's work has significantly contributed to the visibility and acceptance of non-binary identities. By openly identifying as non-binary and challenging traditional gender norms, Alok has become a beacon of hope for those who do not conform to the binary system. Their activism has sparked conversations about the validity of non-binary identities, encouraging individuals to embrace their truth and advocate for their rights.

The impact of Alok's work extends beyond individual experiences; it has influenced cultural conversations surrounding gender identity. As more individuals recognize and affirm non-binary identities, society moves closer to a more inclusive understanding of gender that acknowledges the diverse spectrum of human experience.

Embracing Fluidity: Alok's Gender Journey

Alok's journey of self-discovery is a testament to the power of embracing fluidity in gender identity. Their evolution as an activist and public figure reflects the ongoing process of understanding and redefining one's identity. Alok's willingness to share their experiences, including the challenges and triumphs, serves as an inspiration for others navigating their own journeys.

Through their art and activism, Alok demonstrates that gender is not a fixed destination but rather a dynamic journey. This perspective encourages individuals to explore their identities freely, fostering a culture of acceptance and understanding.

Alok's Message of Radical Self-Love

At the heart of Alok's activism is a message of radical self-love. They advocate for individuals to embrace their authentic selves, celebrating the uniqueness of their identities. This message is particularly important in a society that often promotes conformity and discourages self-expression.

Alok's emphasis on self-love serves as a powerful antidote to the societal pressures that can lead to self-doubt and insecurity. By encouraging individuals to love themselves unapologetically, Alok fosters a sense of empowerment and resilience among those who have been marginalized.

Inspiring Others to Embrace Their Authentic Selves

Alok's journey and activism have inspired countless individuals to embrace their authentic selves. Through their public speaking, social media presence, and artistic expression, Alok has created a platform for individuals to share their stories and experiences. This sense of community is crucial in fostering a culture of acceptance and understanding.

By amplifying the voices of those who have been historically marginalized, Alok encourages a collective movement towards inclusivity and empowerment. Their work serves as a reminder that each individual's story is valid and worthy of celebration.

The Future of Gender Expression

As we look towards the future, Alok's vision for gender expression offers a hopeful perspective. The ongoing conversations surrounding gender identity and expression are paving the way for a more inclusive society that celebrates diversity. Alok's activism serves as a catalyst for change, encouraging individuals to challenge societal norms and embrace their authentic selves.

In conclusion, Chapter 3: Beyond Gender Norms encapsulates Alok Vaid-Menon's profound impact on the understanding of gender and identity. Through their advocacy, Alok challenges traditional constructs, inspiring individuals to break free from societal expectations and embrace their unique journeys. Their message of radical self-love and acceptance resonates deeply, fostering a culture of inclusivity that empowers individuals to live authentically. As we continue to explore the complexities of gender, Alok's legacy serves as a guiding light for future generations seeking to redefine the boundaries of identity.

Alok's Manifesto for Gender Liberation

Unpacking the Social Construction of Gender

The concept of gender has evolved significantly over time, shifting from a binary understanding to a more nuanced perspective that recognizes the complexities of identity. Gender is not merely a biological determinant; rather, it is a social construct that encompasses a range of identities, expressions, and roles shaped by cultural, historical, and societal contexts. This section aims to unpack the social construction of gender, examining the theories that have shaped our understanding, the problems that arise from rigid gender norms, and the examples that illustrate the fluidity of gender.

Theoretical Frameworks

At the heart of understanding gender as a social construct is the work of sociologists and gender theorists who have challenged traditional notions of masculinity and femininity. One of the foundational theories is Judith Butler's concept of gender performativity, which posits that gender is not an inherent quality but rather an ongoing performance shaped by societal expectations. Butler states:

> "Gender is not something we are, but something we do."

This perspective emphasizes that gender is a series of actions, behaviors, and societal cues that individuals enact, often conforming to established norms.

Another important framework comes from the intersectionality theory, developed by Kimberlé Crenshaw. Intersectionality highlights how various social categories—such as race, class, and sexual orientation—interact to create unique experiences of oppression and privilege. This lens is essential for understanding how gender cannot be viewed in isolation; it is intertwined with other identities that shape an individual's lived experience.

Problems Arising from Rigid Gender Norms

The social construction of gender leads to the establishment of rigid norms that dictate how individuals should behave based on their assigned gender at birth. These norms can result in significant psychological and social problems, including:

- **Gender Dysphoria:** Individuals whose gender identity does not align with their assigned gender may experience distress, known as gender dysphoria. This condition can lead to anxiety, depression, and a sense of alienation.

- **Discrimination and Violence:** Those who challenge gender norms often face discrimination, harassment, and violence. Transgender individuals, particularly those of color, are disproportionately affected by hate crimes and systemic discrimination.

- **Mental Health Issues:** The pressure to conform to traditional gender roles can lead to mental health issues. Studies have shown that individuals who identify as non-binary or gender non-conforming are at a higher risk for mental health challenges due to societal rejection and stigma.

Examples of Gender Fluidity

To illustrate the social construction of gender, we can examine various cultural examples that challenge binary notions:

- **Two-Spirit Individuals:** Many Indigenous cultures recognize Two-Spirit people, who embody both masculine and feminine qualities. This concept challenges Western binary gender norms and highlights the fluidity of gender in different cultural contexts.

- **Androgyny in Fashion:** The fashion industry has seen a rise in androgynous styles, where traditional gendered clothing is blended or discarded altogether. Designers like Alok Vaid-Menon embody this trend, using fashion as a medium to express the complexities of gender identity.

- **Social Media Influencers:** Platforms like Instagram and TikTok have given rise to influencers who openly challenge gender norms. Figures such as Billy Porter and Jaden Smith utilize their visibility to promote discussions around gender fluidity and self-expression, encouraging others to embrace their authentic selves.

Conclusion

Unpacking the social construction of gender reveals the complexities and challenges that arise from rigid gender norms. By understanding gender as a performance shaped by societal expectations, we can begin to dismantle the barriers that prevent individuals from expressing their true selves. The work of activists, theorists, and cultural figures continues to challenge and redefine our understanding of gender, paving the way for a more inclusive and accepting society. As we move forward, it is crucial to embrace the diversity of gender identities and expressions, recognizing that everyone deserves the right to define their own gender on their own terms.

$$G = P + S + C \qquad (82)$$

where G represents gender, P represents performance, S represents societal expectations, and C represents cultural context. This equation emphasizes the multifaceted nature of gender, illustrating that it is not a singular entity but a complex interplay of various factors that shape individual identities.

Alok's Philosophy on Gender and Identity

Alok Vaid-Menon, a prominent figure in the LGBTQ+ community, has articulated a philosophy of gender and identity that challenges traditional norms and embraces fluidity. This philosophy is rooted in the understanding that gender is not a binary construct but rather a spectrum that encompasses a diverse range of identities and expressions. Alok's perspective is influenced by various theoretical frameworks, including queer theory, intersectionality, and the concept of performativity.

Queer Theory and Gender Fluidity

Queer theory posits that gender and sexuality are socially constructed categories that are often used to enforce societal norms. Alok draws upon this theory to argue that individuals should not be confined to rigid gender roles. Instead, they advocate for an understanding of gender as a fluid and evolving aspect of identity. This philosophy is encapsulated in the idea that "gender is a performance," echoing Judith Butler's notion of performativity, which suggests that gender is not something one is, but something one does.

$$\text{Gender} = \text{Performance} + \text{Context} \qquad (83)$$

This equation illustrates that gender is contingent upon various social contexts and is shaped by the individual's choices and experiences. Alok emphasizes that everyone should have the freedom to express their gender in ways that feel authentic to them, free from societal expectations.

Intersectionality in Gender Identity

Alok's philosophy also incorporates the concept of intersectionality, which recognizes that individuals experience multiple, overlapping identities that shape their experiences of privilege and oppression. This framework is crucial for understanding how race, class, sexuality, and gender intersect to create unique experiences for individuals. Alok often highlights the importance of acknowledging these intersections, particularly for marginalized communities that face compounded discrimination.

For instance, Alok has spoken about the challenges faced by transgender people of color, who often encounter both racism and transphobia. By emphasizing intersectionality, Alok advocates for a more nuanced understanding of identity that considers the complexities of individual experiences.

The Power of Self-Identification

Central to Alok's philosophy is the belief in the power of self-identification. They argue that individuals should have the autonomy to define their own gender identity, rather than being forced to conform to societal labels. This perspective is particularly important for non-binary and gender nonconforming individuals, who often find themselves navigating a world that is predominantly binary.

Alok's own journey of self-discovery exemplifies this philosophy. They have publicly shared their experiences of grappling with gender identity, illustrating the importance of embracing one's truth. Alok encourages others to embark on their own journeys of self-exploration, emphasizing that identity is a personal and evolving process.

$$\text{Identity} = \text{Self-Identification} + \text{Experience} \tag{84}$$

This equation reflects Alok's belief that identity is shaped by both personal choices and lived experiences, reinforcing the idea that each person's journey is unique.

Challenging Normative Standards

Alok's philosophy also involves challenging normative standards of beauty and gender expression. They argue that societal expectations often dictate how individuals should look and behave based on their perceived gender. By rejecting these norms, Alok advocates for a more inclusive understanding of beauty that celebrates diversity.

For example, Alok's fashion choices often defy traditional gender norms, incorporating elements that are typically associated with both masculinity and femininity. This approach not only allows for personal expression but also serves as a form of activism, challenging the status quo and inspiring others to embrace their authentic selves.

Radical Self-Love and Acceptance

At the core of Alok's philosophy is the concept of radical self-love. They promote the idea that embracing one's identity, regardless of societal acceptance, is a powerful act of resistance. Alok encourages individuals to practice self-acceptance and to celebrate their uniqueness, regardless of external validation.

This philosophy is particularly resonant in a society that often marginalizes those who do not conform to traditional gender norms. By advocating for radical self-love, Alok empowers individuals to reclaim their narratives and assert their identities unapologetically.

$$\text{Radical Self-Love} = \text{Acceptance} + \text{Celebration} \qquad (85)$$

This equation encapsulates Alok's belief that true empowerment comes from both accepting oneself and celebrating one's individuality.

Conclusion

In conclusion, Alok Vaid-Menon's philosophy on gender and identity is a profound and multifaceted perspective that challenges traditional norms and advocates for inclusivity. By drawing upon queer theory, intersectionality, and the principles of self-identification and radical self-love, Alok inspires individuals to embrace their authentic selves and to engage in a continuous journey of self-discovery. Their work serves as a beacon of hope for those navigating the complexities of gender and identity in a world that often seeks to impose limitations. Alok's philosophy not only enriches the discourse surrounding gender but also fosters a more compassionate and understanding society.

Defying the Binary: Alok's Vision for the Future

In a world that often insists on categorizing individuals into rigid boxes, Alok Vaid-Menon stands as a beacon of defiance against the binary constructs of gender. Their vision for the future is not just about challenging traditional notions of gender but about creating a space where fluidity, diversity, and authenticity can flourish. Alok's approach is rooted in the understanding that gender is a social construct, shaped by cultural norms and expectations, rather than a fixed biological reality.

Theoretical Framework

To understand Alok's vision, we must first delve into the theoretical underpinnings of gender identity. Judith Butler's theory of performativity posits that gender is not something one is, but rather something one does—an ongoing performance shaped by societal norms. This perspective aligns closely with Alok's belief that gender should be viewed as a spectrum rather than a binary.

The equation for understanding gender fluidity can be simplified as follows:

$$\text{Gender Identity} = f(\text{Cultural Norms, Personal Experience})$$

This equation suggests that gender identity is a function of both societal influences and individual experiences, allowing for a multitude of expressions beyond the binary of male and female.

Problems with the Binary System

The binary system of gender has significant implications for individuals who do not conform to traditional gender roles. It perpetuates a culture of exclusion and violence against those who identify as non-binary, genderqueer, or transgender. The problems associated with this binary framework include:

1. **Marginalization**: Non-binary and gender non-conforming individuals often face discrimination and lack of representation in various sectors, including healthcare, education, and employment.

2. **Mental Health Challenges**: Studies have shown that individuals who do not fit within the binary gender framework experience higher rates of mental health issues, including anxiety and depression, due to societal rejection and stigma.

3. **Violence and Harassment**: The binary system contributes to a culture of violence against marginalized gender identities. According to a report by the Human Rights Campaign, transgender and gender non-conforming individuals face disproportionately high rates of violence, particularly trans women of color.

Alok's Vision for a Non-Binary Future

Alok's vision for the future is one where the binary is dismantled, allowing for a more inclusive understanding of gender. They advocate for:

- **Education and Awareness**: Alok emphasizes the importance of educating society about the spectrum of gender identities. This includes integrating LGBTQ+ studies into educational curricula and fostering discussions about gender fluidity.

- **Policy Change**: Advocacy for policies that recognize non-binary identities is crucial. This includes legal recognition of non-binary genders on identification documents and anti-discrimination laws that protect individuals regardless of their gender identity.

- **Cultural Representation**: Alok calls for increased representation of non-binary individuals in media, fashion, and art. By showcasing diverse gender expressions, society can begin to normalize the idea that gender is not strictly binary.

Examples of Defying the Binary

Alok's activism is not just theoretical; it is grounded in practical examples that illustrate their vision:

1. **Fashion as Expression**: Alok uses fashion as a medium to challenge gender norms. Their bold, colorful outfits defy traditional gendered clothing, showcasing that style is a personal expression that transcends binary expectations. This is exemplified in their collaborations with designers who embrace gender-neutral fashion.

2. **Social Media Activism**: Through platforms like Instagram and TikTok, Alok has harnessed the power of social media to spread their message of non-binary acceptance. Viral videos where they discuss gender fluidity and challenge stereotypes have garnered millions of views, fostering a global conversation about gender identity.

3. **Public Speaking**: Alok's powerful speeches at universities and conferences resonate with audiences, encouraging individuals to embrace their authentic selves. They often share personal stories that highlight the struggles and triumphs of navigating a non-binary identity, inspiring others to break free from societal constraints.

Conclusion

Alok Vaid-Menon's vision for the future is a radical reimagining of gender identity, one that defies the binary and embraces the full spectrum of human experience. By challenging traditional norms, advocating for policy change, and using their platform for education and representation, Alok is paving the way for a more inclusive society. Their message resonates with a growing movement that recognizes the importance of authenticity and self-expression in a world that often seeks to categorize and constrain. As we move forward, it is crucial to embrace Alok's vision and work towards a future where everyone can express their gender identity freely and authentically, without fear of judgment or violence.

Transcending Labels and Boxes

In the contemporary discourse surrounding gender, the concept of labels and boxes has become a contentious topic. Labels, while often used for identification and community-building, can inadvertently restrict individuals to predefined notions of identity. Alok Vaid-Menon, a prominent LGBTQ activist and fashion icon, has been at the forefront of challenging these limitations through their advocacy and personal journey.

The Limitations of Labels

Labels serve as a double-edged sword. On one hand, they provide a sense of belonging and community; on the other, they can confine individuals to rigid categories that do not encompass the full spectrum of human experience. The binary understanding of gender—male and female—has historically dominated societal norms, leaving little room for those who do not fit neatly into these categories. This binary construct can be represented mathematically as:

$$\text{Gender} = \begin{cases} \text{Male} & \text{if } x \in [0, 0.5] \\ \text{Female} & \text{if } x \in (0.5, 1] \end{cases}$$

Where x represents a spectrum of gender identities. This simplistic representation fails to account for the myriad identities that exist beyond this binary framework. Alok argues that such limitations can lead to feelings of alienation and confusion among individuals who identify as non-binary, genderqueer, or genderfluid.

The Problem of Boxed Identities

The concept of "boxes" further complicates the understanding of identity. When society insists on categorizing individuals, it often leads to the erasure of unique experiences and identities. Alok's philosophy advocates for a more fluid understanding of gender—one that transcends traditional labels. This approach is encapsulated in the idea of fluidity, which suggests that gender can be seen as a continuum rather than a fixed point.

For example, consider the case of a person who identifies as non-binary. They may feel comfortable expressing themselves in ways that blend traditionally masculine and feminine traits. However, societal pressures to conform to binary norms can lead to internal conflict and external discrimination. Alok's work emphasizes the importance of recognizing and validating these experiences, thereby encouraging individuals to embrace their authentic selves without the constraints of societal expectations.

Real-World Examples

Alok's own journey exemplifies the struggle against labels and boxes. Through their fashion choices and public persona, Alok has consistently challenged the norms of gender expression. They often wear clothing that defies traditional gender norms, using fashion as a means of self-expression and a tool for activism. This not only empowers Alok but also inspires others to explore their identities without fear of judgment.

Moreover, Alok's viral social media presence has played a pivotal role in spreading the message of transcending labels. In one notable instance, a video of Alok discussing the complexities of gender identity garnered millions of views, prompting conversations about the limitations of traditional labels. This highlights the power of visibility and representation in fostering understanding and acceptance.

Theoretical Frameworks

The theoretical frameworks surrounding gender identity and expression are crucial in understanding the implications of labels and boxes. Judith Butler's theory of gender performativity posits that gender is not an inherent quality but rather a series of performances shaped by societal expectations. Butler argues that by subverting these performances, individuals can challenge the very foundations of gender norms.

Alok embodies this theory through their activism, demonstrating that gender is a fluid construct that can be redefined. This aligns with the concept of intersectionality, introduced by Kimberlé Crenshaw, which emphasizes the interconnectedness of various social identities and the unique experiences that arise from these intersections. By transcending labels, individuals can acknowledge the complexity of their identities and advocate for a more inclusive understanding of gender.

Conclusion

Transcending labels and boxes is not merely an act of personal liberation; it is a revolutionary stance against societal norms that seek to categorize and confine individuals. Alok Vaid-Menon's advocacy serves as a powerful reminder that identity is multifaceted and cannot be reduced to simplistic labels. By embracing fluidity and challenging traditional notions of gender, we can create a more inclusive society that celebrates diversity and empowers individuals to express their authentic selves.

In conclusion, the journey towards transcending labels and boxes is ongoing. It requires collective effort, open dialogue, and a commitment to understanding the complexities of human identity. Alok's work continues to inspire individuals to break free from societal constraints and embrace the beautiful spectrum of gender expression.

The Power of Pronouns

Pronouns are more than mere linguistic tools; they are powerful symbols of identity and self-recognition. In the context of gender identity, pronouns serve as an essential aspect of how individuals express their authentic selves to the world. The use of correct pronouns can affirm a person's identity, while misgendering—using incorrect pronouns—can lead to feelings of alienation and disrespect. This section will explore the significance of pronouns in relation to gender identity, the challenges faced in their usage, and the broader implications for society.

The Importance of Pronouns

Pronouns, such as "he," "she," "they," and others, are fundamental in establishing one's identity in social interactions. When someone shares their pronouns, they are inviting others to acknowledge and respect their identity. This act of sharing is a form of self-advocacy and empowerment. According to research conducted by the *Williams Institute*, individuals who have their pronouns respected report higher levels of mental well-being and self-esteem.

The equation below illustrates the relationship between pronoun respect and mental health outcomes:

$$MHO = f(PR) \tag{86}$$

Where:

- MHO = Mental Health Outcomes

- PR = Pronoun Respect

This equation suggests a positive correlation between pronoun respect and improved mental health outcomes, highlighting the importance of recognizing and validating individuals' identities.

Challenges in Pronoun Usage

Despite the growing awareness of the significance of pronouns, challenges persist. Many individuals still encounter resistance when advocating for their pronouns. Misunderstandings about non-binary and gender-fluid identities often lead to the assumption that pronouns are binary, resulting in the erasure of diverse identities. This binary view can be damaging and perpetuates systemic discrimination.

Furthermore, societal norms and expectations can create barriers to the acceptance of non-traditional pronouns. For instance, the use of "they/them" as a singular pronoun is still met with skepticism in certain circles. The following equation exemplifies the tension between societal norms and individual identity:

$$T = \frac{S}{I} \qquad (87)$$

Where:

- T = Tension
- S = Societal Norms
- I = Individual Identity

As societal norms (S) become more rigid, the tension (T) between those norms and individual identities (I) increases, often leading to conflict and misunderstanding.

Examples of Pronoun Advocacy

Prominent activists, including Alok Vaid-Menon, have utilized their platforms to advocate for the recognition of diverse pronouns. Alok's work emphasizes the importance of using inclusive language, which is crucial for fostering a sense of belonging among marginalized communities. In one of their viral videos, Alok discusses the emotional impact of being misgendered, stating, "When you call me by the wrong pronoun, you are denying my existence."

This advocacy has led to increased visibility for non-binary identities, prompting organizations and institutions to adopt inclusive policies. For instance, many universities now include pronoun options on applications and identification badges, allowing individuals to assert their identities in academic settings.

The Future of Pronoun Usage

As society continues to evolve, so too does the understanding of gender and pronouns. The increasing acceptance of non-binary and genderqueer identities is paving the way for more expansive conversations about language and identity. The future may see the emergence of new pronouns and variations, further enriching the tapestry of human experience.

In conclusion, the power of pronouns lies in their ability to affirm identity and foster inclusivity. By recognizing and respecting individuals' pronouns, society can take significant strides toward creating a more equitable and compassionate world. The journey toward understanding the power of pronouns is ongoing, and it is essential for everyone to engage in this conversation with an open heart and mind.

Alok's Impact on Non-Binary Identity

Alok Vaid-Menon has emerged as a pivotal figure in the discourse surrounding non-binary identities, challenging traditional notions of gender and advocating for a broader understanding of gender fluidity. This section delves into Alok's profound influence on the recognition and acceptance of non-binary identities, exploring the theoretical frameworks, societal challenges, and personal narratives that underline this impact.

Theoretical Frameworks

The concept of non-binary identity exists within a spectrum of gender identities that do not conform to the traditional binary of male and female. Judith Butler's theory of gender performativity posits that gender is not an innate quality but rather a series of performances shaped by societal norms. Alok's work echoes Butler's ideas by demonstrating that non-binary identities are legitimate expressions of self that resist binary categorization.

Moreover, the intersectionality theory, as articulated by Kimberlé Crenshaw, provides a critical lens through which to understand the experiences of non-binary individuals. Intersectionality examines how various forms of identity—such as race, gender, and sexuality—interact and contribute to unique experiences of oppression and privilege. Alok's activism emphasizes the importance of recognizing these intersections, particularly how they manifest in the lives of non-binary people of color who often face compounded discrimination.

Challenges Faced by Non-Binary Individuals

Despite the increasing visibility of non-binary identities, many individuals continue to face significant challenges. A 2021 study by the Williams Institute found that non-binary individuals experience higher rates of discrimination, mental health issues, and violence compared to their binary counterparts. Alok's advocacy sheds light on these issues, using their platform to raise awareness about the struggles faced by non-binary individuals, such as the lack of appropriate medical care, legal recognition, and societal acceptance.

One of the most pressing challenges is the persistent use of binary language in legal and institutional frameworks. Many forms, documents, and systems are still rigidly divided into male and female categories, which can invalidate the identities of non-binary individuals. Alok's push for inclusive language and policies in educational institutions and workplaces aims to combat this systemic erasure.

Personal Narratives and Representation

Alok's personal journey as a non-binary individual serves as a powerful narrative that resonates with many. By sharing their experiences through social media, public speaking, and art, Alok has humanized the non-binary experience, fostering empathy and understanding among a broader audience. Their fashion choices, characterized by vibrant colors and fluid silhouettes, challenge conventional gender norms and serve as a form of self-expression that inspires others to embrace their identities.

In one notable instance, Alok's viral video discussing the importance of pronouns garnered widespread attention, highlighting how the use of correct pronouns is a fundamental aspect of respecting non-binary identities. This video not only educated viewers on the significance of pronouns but also sparked conversations about the importance of language in affirming one's identity.

Cultural Impact and Advocacy

Alok's influence extends beyond personal narratives to cultural impact. They have collaborated with various artists, designers, and activists to create spaces that celebrate non-binary identities. For example, Alok's partnership with brands that promote gender-neutral fashion has challenged the fashion industry to rethink its approach to gendered clothing, leading to a more inclusive marketplace.

Additionally, Alok's participation in panels and discussions at universities and conferences has fostered dialogue about non-binary identities within academic and activist circles. Their ability to articulate the complexities of non-binary existence has empowered many to embrace their identities and advocate for themselves.

Conclusion

In conclusion, Alok Vaid-Menon's impact on non-binary identity is multifaceted, encompassing theoretical contributions, personal narratives, and cultural advocacy. Through their work, Alok has illuminated the challenges faced by non-binary individuals while simultaneously celebrating their identities. By fostering understanding and acceptance, Alok continues to inspire a generation to challenge binary norms and embrace the beauty of gender fluidity. Their legacy is one of empowerment, resilience, and a relentless pursuit of a world where all identities are recognized and celebrated.

Embracing Fluidity: Alok's Gender Journey

Alok Vaid-Menon's journey through gender is a vivid tapestry woven from threads of personal experience, cultural influences, and a deep-seated desire to challenge societal norms. At the heart of Alok's narrative is the concept of fluidity, which transcends the rigid binaries of male and female, inviting individuals to explore the spectrum of gender identity. This section delves into Alok's unique path, illustrating how they have embraced fluidity as a fundamental aspect of their identity and activism.

Theoretical Framework of Gender Fluidity

Gender fluidity is a concept that recognizes gender as a non-static and dynamic identity that can change over time. Judith Butler, a prominent gender theorist, argues that gender is performative, meaning it is constructed through repeated actions and societal expectations rather than being an inherent quality. This perspective aligns with Alok's experience, as they navigate their identity through a fluid lens, often expressing themselves in ways that defy traditional gender categories.

$$G = P_1 + P_2 + \ldots + P_n \tag{88}$$

Where G represents gender, and P denotes the various performances that contribute to one's gender identity. Alok embodies this equation, showcasing that their gender is an amalgamation of diverse expressions and experiences.

Personal Experiences of Fluidity

From an early age, Alok displayed a penchant for exploring different facets of their identity. Growing up in a society that often enforces binary gender norms, Alok faced challenges in expressing their true self. However, rather than conforming, they embraced their fluidity, experimenting with fashion and self-expression as a means of liberation.

In high school, Alok's bold fashion choices became a form of resistance against societal expectations. They often mixed traditionally masculine and feminine clothing, creating a unique style that celebrated their fluid identity. This experimentation was not without its challenges; Alok faced bullying and discrimination, yet each negative experience only fueled their determination to advocate for a more inclusive understanding of gender.

Fluidity in Activism

Alok's journey of embracing fluidity extends beyond personal expression; it is intricately linked to their activism. They have become a powerful voice for gender nonconforming individuals, advocating for recognition and acceptance of diverse gender identities. Alok emphasizes that fluidity is not just a personal journey but a collective movement towards dismantling oppressive structures that enforce rigid gender norms.

One of the key challenges in advocating for fluidity is the societal tendency to categorize individuals into binary boxes. Alok addresses this issue by promoting the idea that gender is not a fixed identity but a spectrum. They frequently engage in discussions about the importance of using inclusive language, such as the use of preferred pronouns, to affirm individuals' identities.

$$\text{Inclusivity} = \frac{\text{Respect for Identity}}{\text{Societal Norms}} \tag{89}$$

This equation illustrates that inclusivity is achieved when respect for individual identity surpasses the constraints of societal norms. Alok's work exemplifies this principle as they challenge audiences to rethink their understanding of gender.

Cultural Influences on Gender Fluidity

Cultural narratives play a significant role in shaping perceptions of gender fluidity. Alok draws inspiration from various cultures that have long recognized non-binary identities, such as the hijra community in South Asia and Two-Spirit identities in Indigenous cultures. By highlighting these examples, Alok emphasizes that fluidity is not a modern phenomenon but a historical and cultural reality that deserves recognition and respect.

Moreover, Alok's artistic expression often reflects their journey of fluidity. Through performance art, spoken word poetry, and social media, they communicate the complexities of their identity, fostering a dialogue around gender that is both personal and universal. Alok's work serves as a reminder that embracing fluidity can be a powerful act of resistance against societal constraints.

Challenges and Triumphs

Despite the progress made in discussions surrounding gender fluidity, challenges remain. Alok has faced significant backlash from those who cling to traditional gender norms, often encountering hostility and misunderstanding. However, these challenges have only strengthened their resolve to advocate for change.

Alok's triumphs are evident in their ability to reach diverse audiences and inspire others to embrace their authentic selves. By sharing their story, they provide visibility to those who may feel marginalized or unseen. Alok's message of radical self-love encourages individuals to honor their unique journeys, fostering a sense of community among those navigating similar experiences.

Conclusion: A Journey of Liberation

Alok Vaid-Menon's journey of embracing fluidity is a powerful testament to the importance of self-discovery and authenticity. Through their experiences, activism, and artistic expression, Alok challenges societal norms and advocates for a world where individuals can freely explore and express their gender identity.

As we reflect on Alok's journey, it becomes clear that fluidity is not merely a personal narrative but a collective call for liberation. By embracing fluidity, we not only honor our own identities but also pave the way for future generations to live authentically and unapologetically.

In conclusion, Alok's gender journey embodies the essence of fluidity, serving as a beacon of hope and inspiration for those who seek to break free from the constraints of traditional gender norms. Their work continues to challenge and redefine the narrative around gender, inviting us all to embrace the beauty of diversity in identity.

Alok's Message of Radical Self-Love

Alok Vaid-Menon's advocacy for radical self-love represents a transformative approach to identity, self-acceptance, and empowerment, particularly within marginalized communities. This concept transcends mere self-affirmation; it embodies a profound commitment to nurturing one's own identity in the face of societal pressures and systemic discrimination. Alok's message emphasizes that self-love is not only a personal journey but also a revolutionary act against a world that often seeks to define and confine individuals based on rigid norms.

Theoretical Framework

Radical self-love can be understood through the lens of intersectionality, a framework coined by Kimberlé Crenshaw, which examines how various social identities—such as race, gender, sexuality, and class—interact to create unique modes of discrimination and privilege. Alok's message aligns with this theory, as it acknowledges that individuals experience love and acceptance differently based on their intersecting identities. The radical self-love movement encourages individuals to embrace their multifaceted identities, challenging the binary notions of gender and beauty that often dominate societal discourse.

Problems Addressed by Radical Self-Love

In Alok's view, the journey toward radical self-love is essential for combating the pervasive issues of self-hatred, body dysmorphia, and internalized oppression that many LGBTQ individuals face. The pressure to conform to societal beauty standards can lead to significant mental health challenges, including depression and anxiety. Alok's message serves as a balm for these wounds, advocating for a love that is fierce, unapologetic, and deeply rooted in one's authentic self.

One of the primary problems that radical self-love addresses is the stigma surrounding non-binary and gender non-conforming identities. Alok's own experiences highlight the struggles faced by those who defy traditional gender norms. By promoting radical self-love, Alok encourages individuals to reject societal expectations and embrace their true selves, fostering a sense of belonging and validation.

Examples of Radical Self-Love in Practice

Alok's approach to radical self-love is manifested through various initiatives and expressions of creativity. For instance, Alok often utilizes fashion as a medium for self-expression, showcasing vibrant outfits that defy conventional gendered aesthetics. This not only serves to affirm their identity but also challenges the fashion industry to broaden its understanding of beauty. By presenting themselves unapologetically, Alok inspires others to explore their own identities and express themselves authentically.

Moreover, Alok's social media presence exemplifies radical self-love. Through candid discussions about their experiences with gender identity, mental health, and societal expectations, Alok creates a space where followers can engage in dialogue and find solace in shared experiences. The viral nature of Alok's content highlights the power of visibility and representation in promoting self-love among marginalized communities.

Empowerment Through Radical Self-Love

Alok's message of radical self-love is inherently empowering. It encourages individuals to cultivate a sense of agency over their identities and bodies. By framing self-love as a radical act, Alok invites individuals to reclaim their narratives and challenge the societal structures that seek to undermine their worth. This empowerment is crucial in fostering resilience against external negativity and internalized shame.

In practical terms, radical self-love can be nurtured through various practices, including:

- **Affirmations**: Regularly affirming one's worth and identity can counteract negative self-talk and reinforce a positive self-image.

- **Community Building**: Engaging with supportive communities can provide a sense of belonging and validation, essential for nurturing self-love.

- **Creative Expression**: Utilizing art, fashion, and other creative outlets as forms of self-expression can help individuals explore and celebrate their identities.

- **Mindfulness and Self-Care**: Practicing mindfulness and prioritizing self-care routines can foster a deeper connection with oneself, promoting emotional well-being.

Conclusion

Alok Vaid-Menon's message of radical self-love serves as a powerful reminder of the importance of self-acceptance and authenticity in a world that often imposes restrictive norms. By advocating for a love that is radical in its embrace of diversity and complexity, Alok not only uplifts their own identity but also paves the way for others to do the same. This journey toward self-love is not merely personal; it is a collective movement toward acceptance, empowerment, and ultimately, liberation. Alok's radical self-love is a clarion call for all individuals to embrace their true selves and to celebrate the beauty of their identities, no matter how unconventional they may be.

Inspiring Others to Embrace Their Authentic Selves

In a world that often imposes rigid definitions of identity and self-expression, Alok Vaid-Menon emerges as a beacon of hope, encouraging individuals to embrace their true selves unapologetically. This section delves into the profound impact of Alok's message, exploring the theoretical underpinnings of authenticity, the challenges individuals face in their journeys, and the transformative power of self-acceptance.

Theoretical Framework of Authenticity

Authenticity, as a concept, is deeply rooted in existential philosophy, particularly in the works of thinkers like Jean-Paul Sartre and Martin Heidegger, who emphasized the importance of individual existence and the pursuit of one's true self. Sartre's notion of "existence precedes essence" suggests that individuals are not defined by societal labels but rather by their choices and actions. This philosophical stance aligns with Alok's advocacy for self-acceptance, as they promote the idea that one's identity is fluid and shaped by personal experiences rather than fixed societal norms.

In the realm of psychology, Carl Rogers' humanistic approach further elucidates the importance of authenticity. Rogers posits that individuals possess an inherent drive toward self-actualization, which can only be achieved when they align their self-concept with their experiences. This alignment fosters a sense of congruence, allowing individuals to express their true identities without fear of judgment. Alok embodies this principle, using their platform to inspire others to embark on their journeys toward self-discovery and acceptance.

Challenges to Authenticity

Despite the growing acceptance of diverse identities, many individuals still grapple with societal pressures and internalized stigma that hinder their ability to embrace their authentic selves. The pervasive nature of heteronormativity often marginalizes non-binary and gender non-conforming individuals, creating environments where self-expression is stifled. This societal backdrop can lead to feelings of isolation, anxiety, and depression among those who do not conform to traditional gender roles.

Furthermore, the intersectionality of identity complicates the pursuit of authenticity. Individuals who belong to multiple marginalized groups—such as LGBTQ people of color—face compounded challenges that can inhibit their self-acceptance. Alok's activism highlights these complexities, advocating for a more inclusive understanding of identity that recognizes the diverse experiences of individuals across different backgrounds.

Examples of Alok's Impact

Alok's influence is evident in their ability to create safe spaces for dialogue and self-expression. Through social media platforms, they share personal stories and insights that resonate with countless individuals navigating their own identities. For instance, Alok's viral videos addressing the struggles of being non-binary have sparked conversations that transcend geographical boundaries, fostering a sense of community among those who feel unseen.

One poignant example is Alok's collaboration with various artists and activists to create the #DeGenderFashion movement, which challenges conventional beauty standards and promotes inclusivity in fashion. This initiative not only empowers individuals to express their unique styles but also serves as a platform for marginalized voices in the fashion industry. By redefining beauty norms, Alok inspires others to embrace their authentic selves, encouraging them to reject societal expectations and celebrate their individuality.

The Transformative Power of Self-Acceptance

Alok's message of self-acceptance resonates with many, as it emphasizes the importance of loving oneself despite societal pressures. This journey towards authenticity often involves confronting internalized beliefs and societal expectations. Alok's advocacy for radical self-love serves as a guiding principle for individuals seeking to embrace their true identities. By promoting the idea that self-acceptance is not only a personal journey but also a collective responsibility, Alok encourages individuals to support one another in their quests for authenticity.

The transformative power of self-acceptance is further illustrated through personal narratives shared by Alok's followers. Many individuals report experiencing profound shifts in their mental health and overall well-being after embracing their authentic selves. These stories highlight the importance of community support and the role of representation in fostering self-acceptance.

Alok's visibility as a non-binary activist not only validates the experiences of many but also inspires others to step into their truths.

Conclusion

In conclusion, Alok Vaid-Menon's commitment to inspiring others to embrace their authentic selves is a powerful testament to the importance of self-acceptance in the face of societal pressures. By drawing on theoretical frameworks of authenticity, addressing the challenges individuals face, and showcasing the transformative power of self-love, Alok's activism paves the way for a more inclusive and accepting society. As individuals continue to navigate their journeys of self-discovery, Alok's message serves as a reminder that authenticity is not just a personal endeavor but a collective movement toward a world where everyone can express their true selves without fear or shame.

The future of gender expression

The future of gender expression is poised to be a dynamic and transformative space, where traditional binaries are increasingly challenged and redefined. As society progresses, the understanding of gender is evolving beyond the rigid categories of male and female, embracing a spectrum that reflects the diverse experiences of individuals. This evolution is not merely a trend; it is a necessary shift that acknowledges the fluidity of identity and expression.

Theoretical Frameworks

To understand the future of gender expression, we can draw upon several theoretical frameworks. Judith Butler's theory of gender performativity posits that gender is not an innate quality but rather a series of acts and performances that individuals engage in, which ultimately shape their identities. This concept invites us to consider how future expressions of gender may involve a greater emphasis on performance and playfulness, allowing individuals to craft their identities in ways that feel authentic to them.

$$G = P_1 + P_2 + P_3 + \ldots + P_n \tag{90}$$

Where G represents gender, and P_n are the various performances that contribute to one's gender identity. This equation illustrates that gender is a composite of multiple performances rather than a singular, fixed state.

Emerging Challenges

Despite the progressive trajectory, several challenges persist in the discourse surrounding gender expression. One significant issue is the backlash against non-binary and gender non-conforming identities, often fueled by societal norms that cling to traditional gender roles. This backlash can manifest in various forms, including discrimination, violence, and systemic barriers to acceptance.

Moreover, the commodification of gender expression, particularly within the fashion industry, raises critical questions about authenticity and exploitation. As brands seek to capitalize on the growing visibility of non-binary and gender-fluid individuals, there is a risk of diluting the genuine expressions of these identities for profit. This phenomenon calls for a critical examination of how commercial interests intersect with the politics of identity.

Examples of Future Gender Expression

Looking to the future, we can observe several promising examples that illustrate the potential for expanded gender expression. The rise of gender-neutral fashion lines, such as those pioneered by designers like Telfar Clemens and brands like Rad Hourani, exemplifies a shift towards inclusivity in the fashion industry. These designers challenge the traditional notions of clothing as inherently gendered, offering pieces that can be worn by anyone, regardless of their gender identity.

Furthermore, social media platforms have become powerful tools for individuals to express their gender identities in innovative ways. Platforms like TikTok and Instagram allow users to share their experiences, styles, and expressions, fostering a sense of community among those who may feel marginalized in more traditional spaces. The viral nature of these platforms enables ideas about gender to spread rapidly, influencing broader cultural understandings and acceptance.

The Role of Technology

Technology will also play a pivotal role in shaping the future of gender expression. The advent of virtual reality (VR) and augmented reality (AR) technologies allows for immersive experiences where individuals can explore and express their identities in ways that transcend physical limitations. Virtual avatars can be crafted to represent one's gender identity accurately, providing a space for exploration and expression that may not be possible in the physical world.

Additionally, advancements in artificial intelligence (AI) are beginning to influence the way we understand and interact with gender. AI-driven platforms can analyze patterns in gender expression and identity, offering insights that can help individuals navigate their journeys of self-discovery. However, it is crucial that these technologies are developed with sensitivity and inclusivity in mind, ensuring that they do not reinforce existing biases or stereotypes.

A Vision for Inclusivity

Ultimately, the future of gender expression will hinge on our collective ability to embrace inclusivity and celebrate diversity. This vision requires a commitment to dismantling the systemic barriers that inhibit the full expression of gender identities. Educational institutions, workplaces, and communities must foster environments where individuals feel safe and empowered to express their authentic selves.

In this future, we envision a world where gender is not a source of division but a celebration of individuality. By amplifying the voices of marginalized communities and advocating for policies that support gender inclusivity, we can create a society that honors and respects the myriad ways in which people choose to express their identities.

$$\text{Inclusivity} = \sum_{i=1}^{n} \text{Diversity}_i \tag{91}$$

This equation signifies that inclusivity is the sum of various diversities, emphasizing the importance of recognizing and valuing each individual's unique expression of gender.

In conclusion, the future of gender expression is bright and filled with potential. As we continue to challenge traditional norms and embrace the complexities of identity, we pave the way for a more inclusive and accepting world. It is our responsibility to ensure that this future is not only envisioned but actively pursued, creating spaces where everyone can express their gender identity freely and authentically.

Alok's Artistic Expression

The Intersection of Fashion and Art

Fashion and art have long been intertwined, each influencing and reflecting the other in a vibrant tapestry of culture and expression. This intersection is particularly significant in the context of activism, where figures like Alok Vaid-Menon utilize fashion not merely as a means of self-expression but as a powerful tool for challenging societal norms and advocating for marginalized communities.

At its core, the relationship between fashion and art can be examined through various theoretical frameworks, including semiotics, aesthetics, and cultural studies. Semiotics, the study of signs and symbols, posits that both fashion and art serve as modes of communication. They convey messages about identity, status, and cultural values. For instance, Alok's flamboyant and gender-nonconforming style challenges traditional notions of masculinity and femininity, creating a visual dialogue that invites viewers to reconsider their preconceived notions about gender identity.

$$S = \{x \in X \mid P(x)\} \tag{92}$$

Where S represents the set of signs in fashion, X is the universe of all cultural expressions, and $P(x)$ is the property that defines the relationship between the sign and its meaning. This equation illustrates how fashion acts as a signifier within a broader cultural context, allowing for diverse interpretations and meanings.

The aesthetic dimension of fashion further complicates this relationship. Fashion is not only about functionality; it is also about beauty, form, and artistic expression. Designers like Vivienne Westwood and Alexander McQueen have blurred the lines between wearable clothing and high art, creating pieces that are both visually stunning and conceptually rich. Alok's work can be seen as a continuation of this legacy, where each outfit becomes a canvas that reflects their personal narrative and activism.

Moreover, the cultural studies perspective emphasizes the socio-political implications of fashion. Fashion can serve as a site of resistance and empowerment. Alok's use of fashion to challenge gender norms exemplifies this, as they often incorporate elements from various cultures and subcultures, celebrating diversity and inclusivity. This approach not only elevates fashion to an art form but also transforms it into a medium for social commentary.

However, the intersection of fashion and art is not without its challenges. The commodification of art within the fashion industry raises questions about authenticity and artistic integrity. When fashion becomes a product, can it still retain its artistic essence? Furthermore, issues of cultural appropriation often arise, where designers may borrow from marginalized cultures without proper acknowledgment or respect. This can lead to a dilution of the original meaning and significance behind the garments.

Alok's advocacy for marginalized voices within the fashion industry addresses these concerns head-on. By promoting collaborations with designers from diverse backgrounds and emphasizing the importance of representation, Alok not only champions inclusivity but also calls for a more ethical approach to fashion. Their work encourages a critical examination of who gets to define beauty and who is represented in the fashion narrative.

In conclusion, the intersection of fashion and art is a dynamic and multifaceted relationship that serves as a powerful platform for activism. Through their innovative use of fashion, Alok Vaid-Menon exemplifies how personal expression can challenge societal norms and inspire change. As we continue to explore this intersection, it is essential to recognize the potential of fashion as a medium for art and activism, fostering a more inclusive and equitable world.

$$C = \int_a^b f(x)\,dx \qquad (93)$$

Where C represents the cultural impact of fashion as an art form, and $f(x)$ symbolizes the various influences and contributions from diverse communities. This integral signifies the cumulative effect of these cultural interactions, highlighting the richness and complexity of the dialogue between fashion and art.

Thus, as we delve deeper into the relationship between fashion and art, we must remain vigilant about the narratives we create and the voices we amplify, ensuring that the intersection continues to be a space of creativity, expression, and empowerment.

Alok's Creative Outlets

Alok Vaid-Menon is not just a fashion icon and activist; they are also a multifaceted artist who utilizes various creative outlets to express their identity and advocate for social change. Alok's artistic expression spans a wide range of mediums, including poetry, performance art, visual art, and digital media. Each of these outlets serves as a canvas for their thoughts, emotions, and activism, allowing them to connect with audiences on multiple levels.

Poetry and Spoken Word

One of Alok's most profound creative outlets is poetry. Their spoken word performances resonate deeply with audiences, often addressing themes of gender identity, societal expectations, and the complexities of being a queer person of color. Alok's poetry is characterized by its raw honesty and emotional depth, often drawing from personal experiences and struggles. For instance, in their poem "The Future is Non-Binary," Alok challenges the traditional binary notions of gender, advocating for a world where everyone can express their true selves without fear of judgment or discrimination.

The power of Alok's poetry lies not only in its content but also in its delivery. Their performances are infused with passion and vulnerability, creating an intimate atmosphere that invites the audience to reflect on their own identities and experiences. This connection is crucial in fostering empathy and understanding, as Alok's work often addresses the intersectionality of race, gender, and sexuality.

Performance Art

In addition to poetry, Alok engages in performance art, which allows them to explore and deconstruct gender norms in real-time. Their performances often incorporate elements of fashion, movement, and multimedia, creating a sensory experience that challenges conventional perceptions of beauty and identity. For example, in their performance piece "Dressing Up," Alok uses costume changes and props to illustrate the fluidity of gender, inviting the audience to question their preconceived notions about masculinity and femininity.

Performance art serves as a powerful medium for Alok to convey their messages, as it transcends language and cultural barriers. Through their art, Alok not only entertains but also educates, sparking conversations about the importance of inclusivity and acceptance in society.

Visual Art

Alok's creative expression also extends to visual art, where they explore themes of identity, beauty, and resistance. Their artwork often features vibrant colors and bold imagery, reflecting the complexity of their experiences as a non-binary individual. Alok's visual art serves as a commentary on the societal pressures surrounding beauty standards and the importance of embracing diversity.

For instance, in a series of digital illustrations titled "Queer Icons," Alok reimagines historical figures through a queer lens, celebrating the contributions of LGBTQ individuals throughout history. This project not only highlights the often-overlooked narratives of queer history but also serves as a source of inspiration for future generations, encouraging them to embrace their identities unapologetically.

Digital Media and Social Platforms

In the digital age, Alok has harnessed the power of social media to amplify their artistic voice and activism. Platforms like Instagram and TikTok have become essential tools for Alok to share their creative work and engage with a global audience. Through short videos, visual storytelling, and interactive content, Alok addresses pressing social issues while simultaneously showcasing their unique fashion sense and artistic vision.

For example, Alok's viral videos often feature them discussing gender identity, self-love, and the importance of representation in media. These posts not only educate viewers but also foster a sense of community among those who resonate with Alok's messages. By utilizing digital media, Alok has successfully created a platform for dialogue and connection, empowering others to share their stories and experiences.

Collaborative Projects

Collaboration is another significant aspect of Alok's creative outlets. They frequently partner with other artists, designers, and activists to create projects that merge different forms of art and activism. These collaborations often result in innovative works that challenge societal norms and promote inclusivity.

One notable collaboration is Alok's work with fashion designers to create gender-neutral clothing lines that celebrate diversity in body types and gender expressions. By merging fashion with activism, Alok not only pushes boundaries within the industry but also inspires others to embrace their authentic selves through self-expression.

Conclusion

In summary, Alok Vaid-Menon's creative outlets encompass a rich tapestry of artistic expression that goes beyond mere aesthetics. Through poetry, performance art, visual art, digital media, and collaborative projects, Alok uses their creativity as a tool for activism, challenging societal norms and advocating for a more inclusive world. Their work serves as a reminder of the power of art to inspire change, foster connection, and promote understanding across diverse communities. As Alok continues to evolve as an artist and activist, their creative outlets will undoubtedly play a crucial role in shaping the future of gender liberation and social justice.

Pushing Boundaries in Performance Art

Performance art is a dynamic and evolving field that challenges traditional notions of art, identity, and expression. Alok Vaid-Menon, as a pioneer in this realm, has utilized performance art to explore and dismantle the rigid constructs of gender and societal expectations. This section delves into Alok's approach to performance art, examining the theoretical frameworks that underpin their work, the problems they address, and notable examples that illustrate their boundary-pushing endeavors.

Theoretical Frameworks

At the core of Alok's performance art lies a rich tapestry of theoretical influences, including queer theory, feminist theory, and postmodernism. Queer theory, particularly, provides a lens through which to interrogate the fluidity of gender and the performative aspects of identity. Judith Butler's concept of gender performativity is particularly relevant here, positing that gender is not a fixed attribute but rather a series of acts and performances that are socially constructed. Alok embodies this theory by engaging in performances that challenge the binary understanding of gender, inviting audiences to reconsider their preconceived notions.

$$G = P(A) \tag{94}$$

Where G represents gender, and $P(A)$ signifies the performance of acts that create and define gender identity. This equation illustrates that gender is a product of repeated performances rather than an inherent quality.

Addressing Societal Problems

Alok's performances are not merely artistic expressions; they are also powerful commentaries on societal issues. By confronting topics such as racism, transphobia, and body image, Alok's work highlights the intersectionality of oppression faced by marginalized communities. Their performances often serve as a mirror reflecting the societal norms that dictate what is considered acceptable behavior and appearance.

One significant problem that Alok addresses through performance art is the pervasive stigma surrounding non-binary and gender nonconforming identities. By presenting themselves in extravagant, often exaggerated fashions, Alok challenges the audience to confront their discomfort with non-conformity. This is particularly poignant in a society that often equates gender expression with traditional binary roles.

Notable Examples of Performance Art

Alok's performances are characterized by their boldness and unapologetic nature. One notable example is their piece titled *"The Gender Non-Conformity Show."* In this performance, Alok takes the stage adorned in vibrant fabrics, challenging the audience to engage with the concept of gender fluidity. Through a combination of spoken word, dance, and visual art, Alok creates a space where traditional gender norms are deconstructed, allowing for a celebration of diversity in identity.

Another powerful performance is *"The Art of Being Seen."* In this piece, Alok uses their body as a canvas to explore themes of visibility and erasure within the LGBTQ community. The performance involves the application of body paint, transforming Alok's body into a living artwork that confronts the audience with the realities of marginalization. The act of painting becomes a metaphor for self-affirmation, as Alok declares their right to exist unapologetically in a world that often seeks to render them invisible.

The Role of Audience Engagement

A key aspect of Alok's performance art is the emphasis on audience engagement. Alok often invites viewers to participate in the performance, breaking down the barrier between performer and audience. This interactive approach fosters a sense of community and shared experience, allowing for a collective exploration of identity and expression. The act of engaging the audience transforms the performance into a dialogue, where participants are encouraged to reflect on their own beliefs and biases.

In one instance, during a performance at a university, Alok invited attendees to share their experiences with gender identity. This not only created a safe space for dialogue but also highlighted the diverse experiences within the LGBTQ community. By facilitating this exchange, Alok reinforces the idea that performance art is not merely a solitary expression but a communal act of resistance and empowerment.

Conclusion

Alok Vaid-Menon's approach to performance art exemplifies the power of art as a vehicle for social change. By pushing boundaries and challenging societal norms, Alok invites audiences to reconsider their understanding of gender, identity, and self-expression. Through their innovative performances, Alok not only showcases the beauty of diversity but also advocates for a world where all identities are celebrated and embraced. As performance art continues to evolve, Alok's contributions serve as a testament to the transformative potential of artistic expression in the fight for equality and justice.

Alok's Impact on Visual Arts

Alok Vaid-Menon has made significant contributions to the visual arts, intertwining their activism with a profound exploration of identity, gender, and culture. By utilizing visual mediums, Alok challenges traditional notions of beauty and representation, creating a narrative that resonates with marginalized communities.

The Role of Visual Arts in Activism

Visual arts serve as a powerful tool for activism, providing a platform for underrepresented voices to express their stories and experiences. Alok's work exemplifies how art can transcend verbal communication, allowing for a visceral understanding of complex issues surrounding gender and identity. The aesthetics of Alok's visual presentations often reflect a deliberate choice to challenge societal norms, employing bold colors, eclectic styles, and striking imagery to provoke thought and dialogue.

Challenging Conventional Aesthetics

One of the critical aspects of Alok's impact on visual arts is their ability to challenge conventional aesthetics. Alok employs a unique blend of fashion and art to deconstruct the binary understanding of gender. For example, their performances often incorporate elements of drag and high fashion, which serve to blur the lines between masculinity and femininity. This approach not only redefines beauty standards but also encourages others to embrace their authentic selves.

$$\text{Beauty} = \frac{\text{Diversity} \times \text{Authenticity}}{\text{Conformity}} \tag{95}$$

This equation illustrates Alok's philosophy that true beauty arises from diversity and authenticity rather than conformity to societal expectations.

Collaborations with Artists

Alok's influence extends through various collaborations with artists and creatives, where they merge activism with artistic expression. For instance, Alok has partnered with visual artists to create multimedia installations that explore themes of identity and belonging. These collaborations often challenge the viewer to confront their biases and assumptions about gender and race.

One notable project involved a series of photographs that juxtaposed Alok's vibrant fashion choices against stark urban backdrops, symbolizing the clash between personal identity and societal norms. This series not only showcased Alok's fashion sense but also highlighted the struggles faced by those who defy traditional gender roles.

Art as a Reflection of Identity

Alok's work emphasizes the importance of art as a reflection of identity. Through visual arts, Alok articulates the complexities of being a non-binary individual within a society that often seeks to categorize and label. Their art invites viewers to engage with the fluidity of identity, fostering a deeper understanding of the spectrum of gender.

In one of Alok's performances, they utilized body paint and projection art to create a visual narrative that illustrated the journey of self-discovery. This performance not only captivated audiences but also served as a poignant reminder of the struggles faced by many in the LGBTQ community, particularly those who do not conform to traditional gender identities.

Using Visual Arts to Address Social Issues

Alok's impact on visual arts also involves addressing pressing social issues such as racism, sexism, and homophobia. By integrating these themes into their artwork, Alok raises awareness and encourages critical conversations around intersectionality. Their visual pieces often incorporate text, using poignant phrases that resonate with the audience and provoke thought.

For example, Alok's art installations have featured quotes from marginalized voices, overlaying them onto images that depict the struggles faced by these communities. This method not only amplifies the message but also creates a sense of solidarity among those who view the artwork.

Legacy and Influence

The legacy of Alok's impact on visual arts is evident in the growing recognition of non-binary and gender-fluid representation in contemporary art. Alok has paved the way for emerging artists who seek to explore similar themes, fostering a more inclusive art world. Their influence can be seen in various art exhibitions and festivals that prioritize LGBTQ+ voices and narratives.

In conclusion, Alok Vaid-Menon's impact on visual arts is profound and multifaceted. Through their innovative approach to art, Alok challenges societal norms, amplifies marginalized voices, and fosters a deeper understanding of identity and self-expression. Their work not only serves as a catalyst for change within the visual arts community but also inspires individuals to embrace their authentic selves, ultimately contributing to a more inclusive and diverse society.

Using Art as a Tool for Activism

Art has long been a powerful medium for social change, and Alok Vaid-Menon exemplifies how creativity can be harnessed as a tool for activism. This section explores the theoretical underpinnings of using art in activism, the challenges faced, and the tangible examples of Alok's work that illustrate this intersection.

Theoretical Framework

The use of art in activism is grounded in several theoretical perspectives, including critical theory, feminist theory, and intersectionality. Critical theory posits that art can challenge dominant ideologies and provoke critical thought among audiences. This aligns with the work of Alok, who utilizes fashion and performance to question societal norms surrounding gender and identity.

Feminist theory, particularly the concept of *the personal is political*, underscores how personal narratives and experiences can be expressed through art, thereby fostering empathy and understanding. Alok's performances often draw from their own experiences as a gender nonconforming individual, making the personal political and inviting audiences to engage with their narrative.

Intersectionality, a term coined by Kimberlé Crenshaw, emphasizes the interconnectedness of social categorizations such as race, gender, and class. Alok's art embodies this framework by addressing multiple layers of identity and oppression, thereby broadening the scope of activism to include marginalized voices.

Challenges in Using Art for Activism

Despite its potential, using art as a tool for activism is fraught with challenges. One significant issue is the risk of commodification, where art intended for social change becomes commercialized and loses its original message. Alok navigates this terrain by maintaining a commitment to authenticity in their work, ensuring that their art remains rooted in activism rather than profit.

Moreover, artists often face backlash for their political expressions. Alok's bold statements on social media and in their performances have sparked controversy, highlighting the tension between artistic freedom and societal pushback. The challenge lies in balancing the desire for widespread visibility with the potential for negative repercussions.

Examples of Alok's Artistic Activism

Alok Vaid-Menon's artistic activism manifests in various forms, from spoken word poetry to fashion statements. One notable example is their use of fashion as a medium for storytelling. Alok often dons outfits that challenge traditional gender norms, using vibrant colors and unconventional silhouettes to convey messages of self-acceptance and defiance against societal expectations.

In their spoken word performances, Alok combines poetry with personal anecdotes, addressing themes of identity, trauma, and resilience. These performances not only entertain but also educate audiences about the complexities of gender identity and the importance of embracing diversity. For instance, in a performance at a major LGBTQ+ event, Alok recited a poem that juxtaposed their experiences of alienation with moments of empowerment, resonating deeply with many in the audience.

Moreover, Alok's collaboration with visual artists has resulted in impactful installations that provoke thought and dialogue. One such project involved a series of portraits that captured the essence of gender fluidity, showcasing individuals from various backgrounds and identities. This project not only celebrated diversity but also served as a platform for marginalized voices, emphasizing the need for representation in the art world.

The Impact of Art on Activism

Art has the unique ability to transcend barriers and reach audiences on an emotional level. Alok's work exemplifies this phenomenon, as their art often sparks conversations about identity, acceptance, and the fight for LGBTQ rights. By using art as a tool for activism, Alok invites individuals to reflect on their own beliefs and biases, fostering a more inclusive dialogue around gender and identity.

The impact of Alok's artistic activism is evident in the way it inspires others to embrace their authentic selves. Through social media, Alok shares their artistic endeavors, encouraging followers to express themselves creatively and challenge societal norms. This ripple effect demonstrates the transformative power of art in activism, as it empowers individuals to take ownership of their narratives.

Conclusion

In conclusion, Alok Vaid-Menon's use of art as a tool for activism is a testament to the profound impact creativity can have on social change. By grounding their work in theoretical frameworks such as critical theory, feminist theory, and intersectionality, Alok not only challenges societal norms but also inspires others to engage in the fight for LGBTQ rights. Despite the challenges of commodification and backlash, Alok's artistic activism continues to resonate, proving that art can indeed be a powerful catalyst for change. Through their performances, fashion choices, and collaborations, Alok exemplifies how art can be wielded as a weapon of resistance and a beacon of hope for marginalized communities.

Alok's Collaborations with Artists and Creatives

Alok Vaid-Menon has made significant strides in the realm of artistic collaboration, leveraging their unique aesthetic and activist ethos to connect with a diverse array of artists and creatives. These collaborations not only amplify Alok's message of inclusivity and self-expression but also challenge the traditional boundaries of art and fashion.

The Intersection of Art and Activism

At the core of Alok's collaborations is the belief that art is a powerful vehicle for social change. The integration of activism into artistic endeavors fosters a dialogue that transcends conventional art forms. Alok's work with various artists exemplifies the potential of collaborative art to address pressing social issues, particularly those affecting marginalized communities.

For instance, in their collaboration with visual artist *Megan Lee*, Alok participated in a series of mixed-media installations that explored themes of gender fluidity and identity. This partnership culminated in the exhibition titled *"Beyond the Binary"*, where Alok's fashion pieces were displayed alongside Megan's evocative visuals. The synergy between their styles created a multisensory experience that challenged viewers to reconsider their perceptions of gender norms.

Collaborative Projects and Their Impact

Alok's collaborations extend beyond visual art into performance and music, where they have worked with artists such as *Sasha Velour* and *Mykki Blanco*. These partnerships have resulted in performances that blend drag, spoken word, and music, creating a platform for discussing identity and resilience.

For example, during the *"Queer Liberation March"* in New York City, Alok joined forces with Sasha Velour to deliver a powerful performance that combined fashion, poetry, and activism. This event not only showcased their artistic talents but also emphasized the importance of visibility for LGBTQ+ individuals in mainstream culture. The performance resonated deeply with audiences, highlighting the intersection of personal narratives and collective struggles.

Challenges in Collaborative Spaces

While collaborations can yield transformative results, they are not without their challenges. One significant issue that arises in collaborative environments is the potential for misrepresentation or appropriation. As Alok navigates partnerships, they remain acutely aware of the dynamics of power and privilege that can influence artistic collaborations.

For instance, in working with brands or mainstream artists, Alok has often had to advocate for authentic representation and ensure that the narratives of marginalized communities are not overshadowed. This involves critical discussions about who gets to tell a story and how those stories are framed. Alok's commitment to intersectionality ensures that their collaborations are not merely performative but are rooted in genuine advocacy for the voices they represent.

The Role of Social Media in Collaboration

In today's digital age, social media plays a crucial role in facilitating artistic collaborations. Alok has utilized platforms like Instagram and TikTok to showcase their partnerships, allowing for a broader reach and engagement. These platforms serve as a canvas for collaborative art, enabling artists to share their work and messages with a global audience.

For example, Alok's collaboration with photographer *Diana Weymar* resulted in a viral photo series that celebrated non-binary identities. The series was shared widely across social media, sparking conversations about gender representation and visibility. The accessibility of social media allows these collaborations to transcend geographical boundaries, creating a global community of support and inspiration.

Inspiring Future Generations

Through their collaborations, Alok not only inspires contemporary artists but also paves the way for future generations of creatives. By emphasizing the importance of collaboration in the arts, Alok encourages emerging artists to engage with social issues through their work. This mentorship and advocacy for community-driven art create a ripple effect, fostering a culture of inclusivity and innovation.

In workshops and speaking engagements, Alok often shares insights into their collaborative process, highlighting the importance of vulnerability and openness in artistic endeavors. This approach empowers young artists to embrace their identities and use their art as a form of activism.

Conclusion

Alok Vaid-Menon's collaborations with artists and creatives represent a dynamic fusion of art and activism. By challenging traditional narratives and embracing diverse forms of expression, Alok continues to inspire change within the artistic community and beyond. Their work serves as a testament to the power of collaboration in creating a more inclusive and equitable society, where the voices of all individuals are celebrated and uplifted.

In conclusion, Alok's artistic collaborations not only challenge the status quo but also foster a sense of community and belonging among marginalized groups. As they continue to break down barriers and redefine artistic expression, Alok remains a pivotal figure in the ongoing journey toward liberation and acceptance for all.

The Influence of Alok's Aesthetics

Alok Vaid-Menon's aesthetics serve as a powerful lens through which we can explore and challenge societal norms regarding gender, identity, and beauty. Their unique style is not merely a form of self-expression but a deliberate act of defiance against the rigid binaries that have long dominated fashion and culture. Alok's aesthetics can be understood through several key theories and concepts, including gender performativity, intersectionality, and the politics of visibility.

Gender Performativity

One of the foundational theories that underpin Alok's aesthetics is Judith Butler's concept of gender performativity. According to Butler, gender is not an inherent quality but rather something that is performed through repeated behaviors, gestures, and expressions. Alok embodies this theory by fluidly navigating between various gender presentations, using fashion as a medium to manifest their identity. This performative aspect challenges the notion that gender is binary and fixed, instead proposing that it is fluid and dynamic.

The aesthetics of Alok's fashion choices—often characterized by bold colors, extravagant fabrics, and avant-garde silhouettes—serve as a visual representation of this performative nature. For instance, in one of their iconic looks, Alok donned a flowing, iridescent gown paired with striking makeup that defied traditional gender norms. This ensemble not only showcased their individuality but also invited viewers to reconsider their preconceived notions of gender and beauty.

Intersectionality

Alok's aesthetics are also deeply informed by the concept of intersectionality, which highlights how various social identities—such as race, gender, and sexuality—intersect to create unique experiences of oppression and privilege. Alok, as a queer person of color, utilizes their platform to amplify the voices of marginalized communities, and their fashion choices reflect this commitment.

For example, Alok frequently collaborates with designers from diverse backgrounds, showcasing garments that celebrate cultural heritage while challenging Western beauty standards. One notable collaboration featured traditional South Asian textiles reimagined in contemporary designs, bridging the gap between cultural authenticity and modern aesthetics. This approach not only elevates underrepresented voices in the fashion industry but also educates audiences about the rich histories and narratives behind the garments.

The Politics of Visibility

In addition to gender performativity and intersectionality, Alok's aesthetics engage with the politics of visibility. Visibility in the LGBTQ+ community is a double-edged sword; while it can foster acceptance and representation, it can also expose individuals to scrutiny and discrimination. Alok navigates this complex terrain by using their visibility as a tool for activism, promoting messages of self-love and acceptance through their fashion choices.

Alok's aesthetic choices often include elements that draw attention, such as oversized accessories and striking prints, making them a focal point in any space they occupy. This deliberate strategy serves to challenge societal norms that dictate who is deemed worthy of visibility. By embracing flamboyance and theatricality, Alok encourages others to embrace their authentic selves, regardless of societal expectations.

Examples of Aesthetic Influence

Alok's influence extends beyond personal style; it has permeated mainstream fashion and culture. Their appearances on platforms such as the Met Gala and various fashion weeks have sparked conversations about inclusivity and representation in the industry. For instance, during a recent fashion event, Alok wore a stunning ensemble that blended traditional Indian attire with modern streetwear, captivating audiences and prompting discussions about the fusion of cultures in fashion.

Moreover, Alok's social media presence has played a significant role in shaping contemporary aesthetics within the LGBTQ+ community. Their posts often feature bold fashion statements accompanied by empowering messages, inspiring followers to embrace their uniqueness. The hashtag #AlokInspired has gained traction, with individuals showcasing their interpretations of Alok's aesthetic, further amplifying the impact of their influence.

Conclusion

In conclusion, Alok Vaid-Menon's aesthetics are a transformative force within the realms of fashion and activism. By challenging gender norms, embracing intersectionality, and engaging with the politics of visibility, Alok has created a distinctive aesthetic that resonates with many. Their influence extends beyond personal expression, inspiring a broader movement towards inclusivity and acceptance in the fashion industry and society at large. As Alok continues to push boundaries and redefine beauty standards, their aesthetics will undoubtedly leave a lasting legacy, encouraging future generations to embrace their authentic selves with pride.

The Role of Art in Society

Art has always been an intrinsic part of human civilization, serving as a mirror reflecting societal values, struggles, and aspirations. It functions not only as a means of personal expression but also as a powerful tool for social change. Alok Vaid-Menon, through their artistic endeavors, exemplifies the multifaceted role of art in society, particularly in the context of LGBTQ activism.

Art as a Medium for Expression

At its core, art is a form of communication that transcends language barriers. It allows individuals to express their innermost thoughts, feelings, and experiences in ways that words often fail to capture. Alok's work exemplifies this notion, utilizing fashion, performance, and visual arts to convey messages of identity, acceptance, and liberation. By embodying their truth through art, Alok invites audiences to engage with complex themes surrounding gender and sexuality.

For instance, consider the concept of *performance art*, where the body becomes a canvas for expressing the nuances of identity. In performances, Alok often challenges traditional gender norms, using their body to question societal expectations. This aligns with Judith Butler's theory of gender performativity, which posits that gender is not an inherent quality but rather a series of behaviors and performances that are socially constructed. Alok's performances serve as a radical reimagining of these constructs, pushing audiences to reconsider the rigidity of gender binaries.

Art as a Catalyst for Social Change

Art has the potential to inspire and mobilize communities, serving as a catalyst for social change. Throughout history, artists have used their platforms to challenge injustices and advocate for marginalized voices. Alok's artistic expression is deeply intertwined with activism, as they leverage their visibility to raise awareness about LGBTQ issues and systemic discrimination.

One notable example is Alok's involvement in the *"We Are the World"* campaign, where they collaborated with various artists to create a visual narrative highlighting the struggles faced by LGBTQ individuals, particularly those of color. This initiative not only showcased the diversity within the LGBTQ community but also addressed the intersectionality of race, gender, and sexuality. The artwork produced became a rallying point, galvanizing support and fostering a sense of community among those who identified with its message.

Art as a Tool for Healing

In addition to its role in advocacy, art serves as a means of healing for both creators and audiences. For many individuals within the LGBTQ community, art provides a safe space for exploring and processing their identities. Alok's work often addresses themes of trauma and resilience, resonating with those who have faced discrimination and marginalization.

The therapeutic potential of art is supported by various psychological theories, including *expressive arts therapy*, which posits that creative expression can facilitate emotional healing and self-discovery. By sharing their own experiences through art, Alok not only finds personal catharsis but also encourages others to confront their own narratives, fostering a collective healing process.

Art and Cultural Representation

Representation in art plays a crucial role in shaping societal perceptions and fostering inclusivity. Alok's artistic endeavors challenge the dominant narratives that often exclude LGBTQ individuals, particularly those from marginalized backgrounds. By centering their experiences in their art, Alok contributes to a broader discourse on representation, highlighting the importance of diverse voices in the cultural landscape.

The lack of representation can lead to feelings of invisibility and alienation among marginalized groups. Alok's visibility as a non-binary artist disrupts these narratives, providing a sense of belonging for those who may have felt marginalized by mainstream culture. This aligns with bell hooks' concept of *"the oppositional gaze,"* which emphasizes the importance of seeing oneself represented in art and media as a means of empowerment.

Challenges Faced in Artistic Expression

Despite the transformative power of art, artists, particularly those from marginalized communities, often face significant challenges. Issues such as censorship, funding disparities, and societal backlash can hinder artistic expression. Alok has encountered these challenges firsthand, navigating a landscape that can be both supportive and hostile.

For example, Alok's bold fashion choices and performances have sometimes sparked controversy, leading to backlash from conservative groups. However, rather than shying away from these challenges, Alok uses them as opportunities to engage in dialogue about the importance of artistic freedom and the need for inclusivity in the arts.

Conclusion

In conclusion, the role of art in society is multifaceted, serving as a means of expression, a catalyst for social change, a tool for healing, and a vehicle for representation. Alok Vaid-Menon exemplifies the power of art to transcend boundaries, challenge societal norms, and inspire collective action. Through their artistic endeavors, Alok not only advocates for LGBTQ rights but also fosters a deeper understanding of the complexities of identity, ultimately contributing to a more inclusive and equitable society. As we continue to navigate the intersections of art and activism, it is essential to recognize the profound impact that artistic expression can have in shaping our world.

Alok's Legacy as an Artistic Pioneer

Alok Vaid-Menon has carved a niche for themselves as an artistic pioneer, merging fashion, performance art, and activism in ways that challenge conventional norms and inspire a new generation of creators. Their work transcends mere aesthetics, embodying a philosophy that critiques the rigid constructs of gender and identity, while simultaneously celebrating the beauty of fluidity and self-expression.

The Intersection of Fashion and Art

At the heart of Alok's legacy lies the unique intersection of fashion and art. Fashion, often dismissed as superficial, becomes a profound medium for political expression in Alok's hands. They utilize clothing not just as a means of personal expression but as a canvas to explore and challenge societal norms surrounding gender and identity. Alok's ensembles often incorporate bold colors, intricate patterns, and unexpected silhouettes, transforming the runway into a space of dialogue and resistance.

$$\text{Fashion as Art} = f(\text{Identity, Expression, Politics}) \qquad (96)$$

This equation illustrates how Alok's artistic vision integrates identity, expression, and politics, creating a multifaceted approach to their work. By redefining what it means to be fashionable, Alok invites audiences to reconsider their own perceptions of beauty and self-worth.

Pushing Boundaries in Performance Art

Alok's contributions extend beyond fashion into the realm of performance art, where they utilize their body as a site of resistance and expression. Through spoken word poetry, dance, and theatrical performances, Alok challenges audiences to confront uncomfortable truths about gender, race, and sexuality. Their performances are characterized by a raw vulnerability that resonates deeply with viewers, often leaving them transformed and inspired.

For example, in their acclaimed piece "The Future of Gender," Alok employs a blend of humor and poignancy to dissect the limitations of binary gender constructs. The performance not only entertains but educates, prompting discussions about the fluidity of gender and the societal pressures that enforce conformity.

Using Art as a Tool for Activism

Alok's artistic endeavors serve as powerful tools for activism. They leverage their visibility to advocate for marginalized communities, particularly trans and non-binary individuals. By intertwining personal narratives with broader social issues, Alok's work highlights the intersectionality of identity and the systemic injustices faced by those who defy traditional norms.

Alok's art often addresses pressing issues such as violence against trans individuals, mental health struggles within the LGBTQ community, and the importance of representation in media. Their piece "Trans Rights Are Human Rights" not only serves as a rallying cry but also as a poignant reminder of the ongoing struggles for equality and justice.

Collaborations with Artists and Creatives

Alok's legacy is further enriched by their collaborations with a diverse array of artists and creatives. By working with individuals from various backgrounds, Alok fosters a sense of community and collective empowerment. These collaborations often result in innovative projects that blur the lines between art and activism, creating spaces for dialogue and healing.

For instance, Alok's partnership with visual artist and activist Janelle Monáe resulted in a multimedia installation that explored themes of identity and belonging. This collaboration not only amplified Alok's message but also showcased the power of artistic synergy in driving social change.

The Role of Art in Society

The role of art in society cannot be overstated. Alok's work exemplifies how art can serve as a catalyst for change, challenging audiences to reflect on their own beliefs and biases. Through their artistic expressions, Alok encourages individuals to embrace their authentic selves, fostering a culture of acceptance and love.

$$\text{Art} = \text{Catalyst for Change} \cdot \text{Community Engagement} \tag{97}$$

This equation emphasizes the dual role of art as both a catalyst for change and a means of engaging with the community. Alok's legacy as an artistic pioneer lies in their ability to harness this power, inspiring others to use their voices and creativity for social justice.

Redefining Artistic Expression

Alok's contributions to the arts challenge traditional notions of artistic expression. They advocate for a redefinition of what it means to be an artist, emphasizing that authenticity and vulnerability are paramount. Alok's work encourages emerging artists to embrace their unique identities and experiences, rather than conforming to established norms.

By promoting the idea that all forms of expression are valid, Alok paves the way for a more inclusive and diverse artistic landscape. Their legacy is not just about personal achievement; it is about creating a movement that empowers others to share their stories and challenge the status quo.

Conclusion

In conclusion, Alok Vaid-Menon's legacy as an artistic pioneer is characterized by their innovative approach to fashion and performance art, their commitment to activism, and their dedication to redefining artistic expression. Through their work, Alok has not only inspired countless individuals to embrace their identities but has also sparked essential conversations about gender, race, and the power of art in creating social change. As we look to the future, Alok's influence will undoubtedly continue to resonate, inspiring new generations of artists and activists to break free from societal constraints and embrace the beauty of their authentic selves.

Redefining Artistic Expression

Art has always been a reflection of society, a mirror held up to the complexities of human experience. In the contemporary landscape, artists like Alok Vaid-Menon are pushing the boundaries of traditional artistic expression, creating a new paradigm that embraces fluidity, intersectionality, and inclusivity. This section delves into how Alok's work challenges conventional notions of art, offering a transformative lens through which we can understand identity, culture, and activism.

The Intersection of Fashion and Art

Alok's artistic expression is deeply intertwined with fashion, a medium that has historically been both a form of personal expression and a vehicle for societal commentary. Through their bold and vibrant sartorial choices, Alok challenges the binary constructs of gender and beauty. Fashion becomes a canvas, allowing Alok to communicate complex ideas about identity, resistance, and self-love.

The theory of *performative identity* posited by Judith Butler suggests that gender is not a fixed attribute but rather a series of performances that individuals engage in. Alok embodies this theory, using fashion as a performative tool to deconstruct and redefine gender norms. For instance, their use of traditionally feminine fabrics and styles juxtaposed with masculine silhouettes creates a dialogue about the fluidity of gender expression.

Pushing Boundaries in Performance Art

Alok's work extends beyond static visual art into the realm of performance. Their performances often blend spoken word, movement, and fashion, creating immersive experiences that invite audiences to engage with themes of identity and marginalization. By incorporating elements of storytelling and personal narrative, Alok transforms the stage into a space for radical vulnerability and connection.

In a notable performance, Alok addressed the audience while adorned in a striking ensemble that challenged societal beauty standards. The juxtaposition of their appearance with the content of their message served to amplify the impact of their words, illustrating how art can serve as both a medium for expression and a catalyst for social change.

Using Art as a Tool for Activism

Alok's artistic expression is not merely for aesthetic pleasure; it is a deliberate act of activism. By utilizing art as a tool for advocacy, Alok addresses pressing social issues such as racism, transphobia, and systemic oppression. Their work highlights the intersections of race, gender, and sexuality, emphasizing that activism must be inclusive and multifaceted.

For example, in collaboration with various artists and activists, Alok has created public installations that confront viewers with the harsh realities faced by marginalized communities. These installations often incorporate multimedia elements, combining visual art with audio recordings of personal testimonies. This approach fosters empathy and understanding, encouraging audiences to reflect on their own biases and privileges.

Alok's Collaborations with Artists and Creatives

Collaboration is a cornerstone of Alok's artistic practice. By partnering with other creatives, Alok amplifies diverse voices and perspectives, fostering a sense of community within the arts. This collaborative spirit is evident in projects that merge visual art, fashion, and performance, creating a rich tapestry of expression that challenges monolithic narratives.

One such collaboration involved a series of workshops aimed at empowering LGBTQ+ youth through art. Participants were encouraged to explore their identities through various mediums, culminating in a showcase that celebrated their unique stories. Alok's role as a facilitator not only provided a platform for emerging artists but also reinforced the importance of community in the creative process.

The Influence of Alok's Aesthetics

Alok's aesthetics are characterized by bold colors, intricate patterns, and a fearless approach to self-expression. This distinctive style has garnered attention within the fashion industry, inspiring designers to embrace non-binary aesthetics in their collections. Alok's influence extends beyond personal style; it challenges the very foundations of what is considered beautiful or acceptable in mainstream culture.

The concept of *aesthetic activism* posits that beauty can be a form of resistance. Alok's work exemplifies this idea, as their visual presentation defies societal expectations and celebrates individuality. By redefining beauty standards, Alok invites others to embrace their authentic selves, fostering a culture of acceptance and love.

The Role of Art in Society

Art serves as a powerful vehicle for social change, and Alok's work exemplifies this potential. By addressing issues of identity, representation, and systemic injustice, Alok's artistic expression resonates with audiences on both personal and collective levels. Their ability to blend art with activism creates a compelling narrative that challenges viewers to confront uncomfortable truths about society.

The role of art in society can be understood through the lens of *critical theory*, which emphasizes the importance of questioning dominant ideologies. Alok's work encourages audiences to engage in critical reflection, promoting dialogue around issues that are often marginalized or ignored. This engagement is essential for fostering a more inclusive and equitable society.

Redefining Artistic Expression: A Conclusion

In conclusion, Alok Vaid-Menon's artistic expression is a powerful testament to the transformative potential of art. By redefining the boundaries of fashion, performance, and activism, Alok invites us to reconsider our understanding of identity and beauty. Their work serves as a reminder that art is not just a reflection of society but a powerful tool for change, capable of inspiring individuals to embrace their authentic selves and challenge the status quo.

As we move forward, it is essential to recognize the importance of diverse voices in the arts. Alok's legacy as an artistic pioneer will continue to inspire future generations, encouraging them to redefine artistic expression in ways that are inclusive, intersectional, and empowering. The journey of redefining art is ongoing, and with artists like Alok leading the way, the future holds boundless possibilities for creativity and change.

Empowering Marginalized Communities

Intersectionality as a Foundation for Activism

Intersectionality is a critical framework for understanding how various forms of social stratification, such as race, gender, class, sexuality, and other identity markers, interact and create overlapping systems of disadvantage and privilege. Coined by scholar Kimberlé Crenshaw in 1989, the term emphasizes that individuals do not experience oppression in isolation but rather through the complex interplay of their various identities. This concept is particularly vital in LGBTQ activism, where the experiences of individuals can vary dramatically based on their intersecting identities.

Theoretical Foundations

At the heart of intersectionality is the recognition that traditional frameworks of oppression often fail to capture the nuanced realities faced by marginalized individuals. For instance, a Black transgender woman may encounter discrimination that is distinct from that experienced by a white cisgender woman or a Black cisgender man. This is due to the unique combination of racism, sexism, and transphobia that she faces.

Mathematically, we can represent intersectionality as a multi-dimensional space where each axis represents a different identity marker. The interaction of these axes produces a unique point that signifies an individual's specific experience of oppression. If we denote the dimensions as x_1 for race, x_2 for gender, x_3 for sexuality, and so forth, the individual's experience can be represented as:

$$E = f(x_1, x_2, x_3, \ldots, x_n)$$

where E is the experience of oppression and f is a function that determines how these identities interact. This model illustrates that the experience of oppression is not merely additive but multiplicative, as the intersections can create unique challenges that are not simply the sum of their parts.

Problems in Activism Without Intersectionality

Activism that neglects intersectionality often perpetuates the very systems of oppression it seeks to dismantle. For example, mainstream LGBTQ movements have historically centered the experiences of white, cisgender gay men, often sidelining the voices of people of color, transgender individuals, and those from lower socioeconomic backgrounds. This exclusion can lead to policies and practices that do not address the needs of the most marginalized within the LGBTQ community, thereby reinforcing systemic inequalities.

One striking example of this is the lack of adequate healthcare resources for transgender individuals of color, who face higher rates of violence, discrimination, and health disparities. When LGBTQ activism does not incorporate an intersectional lens, it risks overlooking these critical issues, leading to a one-size-fits-all approach that is ineffective and harmful.

Examples of Intersectional Activism

Organizations and activists that embrace intersectionality are better equipped to address the complexities of oppression. For instance, the work of groups like Black Lives Matter and the Transgender Law Center exemplifies intersectional activism by explicitly prioritizing the voices of Black transgender individuals. Their campaigns highlight the unique challenges faced by this community, such as police violence and healthcare access, thereby advocating for comprehensive policy changes that reflect their realities.

Alok Vaid-Menon's activism also embodies intersectionality. By openly discussing their experiences as a non-binary person of South Asian descent, Alok challenges both gender norms and racial stereotypes. Their work emphasizes the importance of recognizing how cultural background influences one's experience within the LGBTQ community. This approach not only amplifies marginalized voices but also fosters solidarity across different identity groups.

Intersectionality in Education and Advocacy

Incorporating intersectionality into educational programs and advocacy efforts is essential for fostering a more inclusive understanding of social justice. Workshops and training that address the intersections of race, gender, and sexuality can empower activists to recognize their own privileges and biases, leading to more effective and equitable advocacy.

Moreover, intersectional frameworks can inform policy-making by ensuring that the needs of all marginalized groups are considered. For example, legislation aimed at protecting LGBTQ rights should also address issues of racial and economic justice, creating a holistic approach to equality.

Conclusion

Intersectionality is not just an academic concept; it is a vital tool for activism that seeks to dismantle the complex web of oppression faced by individuals at various intersections of identity. By recognizing and addressing these intersections, activists can create more inclusive movements that truly represent the diversity of experiences within marginalized communities. As Alok Vaid-Menon demonstrates through their work, embracing intersectionality is essential for fostering a world where everyone can thrive, regardless of their identity.

Through this lens, we can build a more equitable future that acknowledges and uplifts all voices, ensuring that no one is left behind in the fight for justice and equality.

Alok's Advocacy for Racial Justice

Alok Vaid-Menon's advocacy for racial justice is a vital component of their broader activism, intricately intertwined with their commitment to LGBTQ rights. Understanding the intersectionality of race and gender is crucial in recognizing the unique challenges faced by individuals at these crossroads. Intersectionality, a term coined by Kimberlé Crenshaw, highlights how various forms of social stratification, such as race, gender, class, and sexuality, overlap and create complex systems of oppression and privilege.

Theoretical Framework

At the heart of Alok's advocacy is the understanding that racial justice cannot be separated from gender justice. This perspective is supported by critical race theory, which posits that racism is ingrained in the fabric of society and that it manifests in various forms, including systemic discrimination and microaggressions. Alok's work emphasizes the importance of addressing these issues through a lens that recognizes the multifaceted identities of individuals.

Identifying the Problems

The problems facing marginalized communities, particularly those who identify as both LGBTQ and people of color, are numerous and deeply rooted in societal structures. These include:

1. **Systemic Racism**: Institutions often perpetuate racial biases, leading to unequal access to resources, opportunities, and justice. For example, studies have shown that people of color are disproportionately affected by police violence, incarceration rates, and economic disparities.

2. **Cultural Appropriation**: Alok has been vocal about the appropriation of marginalized cultures in mainstream fashion and media. This practice not only erases the contributions of these communities but also commodifies their identities without acknowledging the struggles they face.

3. **Visibility and Representation**: The lack of representation of queer people of color in media and fashion perpetuates harmful stereotypes and limits the visibility of their experiences. Alok advocates for more inclusive representation that reflects the diversity of identities within the LGBTQ community.

4. **Mental Health Disparities**: The intersection of racial and LGBTQ identities can lead to increased mental health challenges due to societal stigma, discrimination, and isolation. Alok emphasizes the importance of addressing these mental health disparities through community support and accessible resources.

Examples of Advocacy

Alok's advocacy for racial justice is not merely theoretical; it is reflected in their actions and collaborations. Some notable examples include:

- **Speaking Engagements**: Alok frequently speaks at universities and conferences, where they address the intersections of race, gender, and sexuality. They use these platforms to educate audiences on the importance of recognizing and dismantling systemic racism within LGBTQ spaces.

- **Collaborations with Activists**: Alok has partnered with various racial justice organizations to amplify the voices of queer people of color. For instance, their collaboration with groups like Black Lives Matter has focused on highlighting the specific challenges faced by Black trans individuals.

- **Social Media Campaigns**: Utilizing their large social media following, Alok creates campaigns that raise awareness about racial injustices. They often share resources, highlight stories of marginalized individuals, and encourage their followers to engage in activism.

- **Art and Performance**: Alok employs art as a medium to challenge racial stereotypes and promote inclusivity. Their performances often incorporate themes of identity, race, and resistance, inviting audiences to confront their biases and engage in critical dialogue.

Conclusion

Alok Vaid-Menon's advocacy for racial justice is a testament to their commitment to intersectional activism. By addressing the interconnectedness of race and gender, Alok not only challenges systemic injustices but also inspires others to embrace a more inclusive understanding of social justice. Their work serves as a reminder that the fight for equality is multifaceted, requiring solidarity across various movements to create a truly just society.

In summary, Alok's approach to racial justice is characterized by a deep understanding of the theoretical frameworks that inform their activism, a commitment to addressing systemic issues, and a proactive engagement with both community and culture. Their legacy is one of empowerment, encouraging future activists to recognize and celebrate the rich tapestry of identities that make up our society.

Amplifying the Voices of Trans People of Color

In the landscape of LGBTQ activism, the voices of Trans People of Color (TPOC) have historically been marginalized, often overshadowed by mainstream narratives that prioritize white, cisgender perspectives. Alok Vaid-Menon recognizes the urgent need to amplify these voices, advocating for a more inclusive approach that acknowledges the unique challenges faced by TPOC. This section delves into the importance of amplifying these voices, the theories underpinning this advocacy, the systemic issues at play, and examples of successful initiatives that highlight the experiences of TPOC.

Theoretical Framework

The amplification of TPOC voices can be understood through the lens of intersectionality, a term coined by legal scholar Kimberlé Crenshaw. Intersectionality posits that individuals experience oppression in varying degrees based on their intersecting identities, including race, gender, sexuality, and class. For TPOC, these intersecting identities create a unique set of challenges that cannot be addressed by examining race or gender in isolation.

$$O = f(R, G, S, C) \tag{98}$$

Where: - O represents the overall oppression experienced by TPOC, - R is racial identity, - G is gender identity, - S is sexual orientation, and - C is class status.

This equation illustrates that oppression is a function of multiple, overlapping identities. Therefore, any advocacy efforts must be multifaceted and inclusive, recognizing the complexities of TPOC experiences.

Systemic Issues Faced by TPOC

TPOC face a myriad of systemic issues, including but not limited to:

1. **Violence and Discrimination**: TPOC are disproportionately affected by violence, with statistics indicating that Black transgender women are among the most vulnerable populations. According to the Human Rights Campaign, 2020 saw a record number of violent deaths of transgender individuals, with a significant percentage being Black and Latina women.

2. **Economic Disparities**: Economic inequality is another significant barrier. TPOC often encounter discrimination in hiring practices and workplace environments, leading to higher rates of unemployment and poverty.

3. **Access to Healthcare**: Discrimination in healthcare settings further exacerbates the challenges faced by TPOC. Many healthcare providers lack cultural competency, leading to inadequate care for transgender individuals, particularly those of color.

4. **Mental Health Struggles**: The compounded stress of racism, transphobia, and economic instability contributes to higher rates of mental health issues among TPOC. According to the National Center for Transgender Equality, TPOC report higher rates of depression and anxiety compared to their white counterparts.

Examples of Amplifying TPOC Voices

Alok Vaid-Menon has been at the forefront of initiatives aimed at amplifying TPOC voices through various platforms:

- **Art and Performance**: Alok uses their platform to showcase the artistry of TPOC, collaborating with marginalized artists to highlight their stories and experiences. Events such as "The Queer and Trans People of Color Arts Festival" provide a space for TPOC to express themselves and gain visibility.

- **Social Media Campaigns**: Alok harnesses the power of social media to elevate TPOC narratives. Campaigns like #TransIsBeautiful and #BlackTransLivesMatter have gained traction, fostering community support and awareness around the issues faced by TPOC.

- **Educational Workshops**: By conducting workshops and speaking engagements, Alok educates audiences on the importance of intersectionality in activism. These workshops often include TPOC speakers who share their experiences, fostering a deeper understanding of the challenges they face.

The Impact of Amplifying TPOC Voices

The amplification of TPOC voices is not merely an act of solidarity; it is a necessary step towards achieving true equity within the LGBTQ movement. By prioritizing TPOC narratives, the movement can address the systemic issues that disproportionately affect them.

Moreover, amplifying these voices leads to a more nuanced understanding of gender and racial identities, enriching the broader discourse on LGBTQ rights. As Alok states, "When we uplift the voices of those most marginalized, we create a ripple effect that leads to systemic change."

Conclusion

In conclusion, the amplification of Trans People of Color voices is an essential aspect of contemporary activism. By employing an intersectional framework, addressing systemic issues, and utilizing various platforms for visibility, activists like Alok Vaid-Menon are paving the way for a more inclusive and equitable future. The journey towards justice for TPOC is ongoing, but through collective efforts, we can create a society that truly values and uplifts all voices.

Addressing Systemic Oppression

Systemic oppression refers to the entrenched policies, practices, and cultural norms that perpetuate inequality and marginalization of certain groups based on race, gender, sexual orientation, and other identities. Alok Vaid-Menon has been a vocal advocate for dismantling these oppressive structures, emphasizing that true liberation cannot occur without addressing the roots of systemic injustice.

At the core of systemic oppression is the concept of intersectionality, a term coined by legal scholar Kimberlé Crenshaw. Intersectionality posits that individuals experience oppression in varying degrees based on their overlapping identities. For example, a Black transgender woman may face discrimination not only for her race but also for her gender identity, leading to compounded marginalization. Alok's activism highlights these complexities, urging allies to recognize the multifaceted nature of oppression.

$$O = f(I_1, I_2, I_3, \ldots, I_n) \tag{99}$$

Where O represents the level of oppression faced, and $I_1, I_2, I_3, \ldots, I_n$ are the various intersecting identities (such as race, gender, class, and sexuality) that contribute to an individual's experience of systemic oppression.

The Problems of Systemic Oppression

1. **Institutional Discrimination**: Many institutions—such as education, healthcare, and law enforcement—are built on discriminatory practices that disadvantage marginalized groups. For instance, studies have shown that Black individuals are disproportionately targeted by police, leading to higher rates of incarceration and violence.

2. **Economic Inequality**: Economic systems often favor those with privilege, leaving marginalized communities in poverty. The wealth gap between white individuals and people of color in the United States is a stark example. According to the Federal Reserve, the median wealth of white families is approximately ten times that of Black families.

3. **Healthcare Disparities**: Access to healthcare is often determined by socioeconomic status, race, and geography. LGBTQ+ individuals, particularly transgender people, face significant barriers in accessing appropriate healthcare, resulting in poorer health outcomes. A study by the National Center for Transgender Equality revealed that 33% of transgender individuals reported being denied care due to their gender identity.

4. **Cultural Erasure**: Systemic oppression often involves the erasure of marginalized cultures and histories. This can lead to a lack of representation in media, education, and public discourse, perpetuating stereotypes and misconceptions about marginalized communities.

Alok's Approach to Addressing Systemic Oppression

Alok's activism focuses on amplifying the voices of those who are often silenced by systemic oppression. By sharing personal narratives and collaborating with marginalized communities, Alok seeks to create a platform for dialogue and understanding. Key strategies include:

- **Storytelling**: Alok emphasizes the power of personal stories in activism. By sharing their own experiences and those of others, they challenge the dominant narratives that often exclude marginalized voices. This approach fosters empathy and encourages others to recognize the humanity behind statistics.

- **Collaborative Activism**: Alok actively collaborates with various organizations that address systemic oppression. For instance, partnerships with groups advocating for racial justice and LGBTQ+ rights highlight the interconnectedness of these struggles. By working together, activists can create a more comprehensive approach to dismantling systemic barriers.

- **Education and Awareness**: Alok advocates for educational initiatives that address systemic oppression. This includes incorporating LGBTQ+ issues and intersectional perspectives into school curricula. By educating the next generation, Alok aims to cultivate a culture of inclusivity and understanding.

Examples of Impact

Alok's work has contributed to various initiatives aimed at addressing systemic oppression:

- **Policy Advocacy**: Alok has participated in campaigns advocating for policy changes that protect the rights of marginalized communities. For example, their involvement in initiatives to ban conversion therapy reflects a commitment to protecting LGBTQ+ individuals from harmful practices rooted in systemic oppression.

- **Community Engagement**: Through workshops and speaking engagements, Alok engages with diverse communities to foster discussions about oppression and empowerment. These interactions often lead to grassroots movements that challenge systemic injustices at local levels.

- **Art as Activism**: Alok utilizes art as a medium to address systemic oppression. Their performances and visual art challenge societal norms and provoke conversations about identity, privilege, and justice. By merging creativity with activism, Alok reaches broader audiences and inspires change.

In conclusion, addressing systemic oppression requires a multifaceted approach that recognizes the complexities of identity and the interconnections between various forms of discrimination. Alok Vaid-Menon's activism exemplifies the importance of intersectionality in the fight for justice, advocating for a world where all individuals can live authentically and without fear of oppression. By continuing to challenge systemic barriers, Alok inspires others to join in the fight for equality and liberation for all.

Alok's Work with LGBTQ Refugees and Immigrants

Alok Vaid-Menon has emerged as a pivotal figure in advocating for LGBTQ refugees and immigrants, addressing the unique challenges faced by these communities in a world that often marginalizes them. The intersectionality of gender identity, sexual orientation, and immigration status creates a complex web of vulnerabilities that Alok seeks to unravel through activism, storytelling, and community engagement.

Understanding the Challenges

LGBTQ refugees and immigrants frequently encounter a multitude of obstacles, including systemic discrimination, violence, and lack of access to essential services. Many flee their home countries due to persecution based on their sexual orientation or gender identity, only to face new forms of discrimination in their host countries. According to the United Nations High Commissioner for Refugees (UNHCR), LGBTQ individuals are at a heightened risk of violence and exploitation during the asylum process, often facing hostility not only from society but also from within the asylum system itself.

The challenges can be categorized as follows:

- **Legal Barriers:** Many countries lack comprehensive protections for LGBTQ individuals, complicating the asylum process. Alok advocates for policy reforms that ensure fair treatment and recognition of LGBTQ asylum claims.

- **Social Isolation:** LGBTQ refugees often experience isolation in their new environments, lacking support networks that can provide emotional and practical assistance. Alok emphasizes the importance of community-building initiatives to foster connections among LGBTQ immigrants.

- **Mental Health Issues:** The trauma of fleeing persecution combined with the stress of navigating a new culture can lead to significant mental health challenges. Alok promotes access to mental health resources tailored specifically for LGBTQ individuals.

Advocacy and Outreach

Alok's work with LGBTQ refugees and immigrants extends beyond mere awareness; it involves tangible actions aimed at creating systemic change. Through partnerships with various organizations, Alok has spearheaded initiatives that provide legal assistance, mental health support, and community integration programs.

For example, Alok has collaborated with organizations like *The International Refugee Assistance Project (IRAP)* and *The LGBTQ Refugee Project*, which focus on offering legal representation and resources for LGBTQ individuals seeking asylum. By leveraging their platform, Alok amplifies the voices of those who have been silenced, sharing their stories through social media and public speaking engagements.

Community Engagement and Empowerment

Alok believes in the power of storytelling as a means of empowerment. By encouraging LGBTQ refugees to share their experiences, Alok helps to humanize the struggles faced by these individuals, fostering empathy and understanding within broader society. This approach not only raises awareness but also creates a sense of solidarity among community members.

An example of this empowerment can be seen in Alok's involvement in community workshops and panels that focus on the experiences of LGBTQ immigrants. These events often feature discussions on navigating cultural differences, accessing resources, and building resilience. Alok emphasizes that the narratives of LGBTQ refugees are not just stories of survival but also stories of strength, creativity, and hope.

Theoretical Frameworks and Intersectionality

Alok's work is deeply rooted in the theoretical frameworks of intersectionality, which examines how various social identities—such as race, gender, sexuality, and immigration status—intersect to create unique experiences of oppression and privilege. This framework is crucial in understanding the multifaceted challenges faced by LGBTQ refugees.

For instance, a Black transgender woman seeking asylum may experience discrimination not only based on her gender identity but also due to her race. Alok utilizes this intersectional lens to advocate for policies that address these overlapping forms of discrimination, pushing for a more inclusive approach to refugee rights.

Conclusion

In conclusion, Alok Vaid-Menon's work with LGBTQ refugees and immigrants exemplifies a commitment to social justice that transcends borders. By addressing the unique challenges faced by these communities through advocacy, community engagement, and storytelling, Alok not only empowers individuals but also inspires systemic change. Their efforts serve as a reminder that the fight for LGBTQ rights is global, and that solidarity among marginalized groups is essential in the pursuit of equality and justice.

Through initiatives that promote legal protections, mental health resources, and community-building, Alok continues to break down barriers for LGBTQ refugees and immigrants, paving the way for a more inclusive and compassionate society.

Empowering Queer and Trans People in Developing Nations

The empowerment of queer and trans individuals in developing nations is a critical aspect of global LGBTQ activism. In many parts of the world, systemic discrimination, cultural stigmas, and legal barriers create an environment where queer and trans people face significant challenges. This section explores the multifaceted approach required to empower these communities, addressing theoretical frameworks, ongoing problems, and successful examples of activism.

Theoretical Frameworks

To understand the empowerment of queer and trans individuals in developing nations, we can draw upon several theoretical frameworks. One such framework is the **Intersectionality Theory**, proposed by Kimberlé Crenshaw, which emphasizes how various social identities (race, gender, sexuality, class) intersect to create unique experiences of discrimination and privilege. In the context of queer and trans people, intersectionality highlights that their struggles cannot be understood in isolation from other social issues, such as poverty, colonialism, and racism.

Another relevant framework is the **Capability Approach** by Amartya Sen, which posits that true empowerment involves expanding individuals' capabilities and freedoms. This approach emphasizes the need for access to resources, education, and opportunities, allowing queer and trans individuals to lead fulfilling lives. It frames empowerment not merely as a political or legal issue but as a holistic enhancement of well-being.

Challenges Faced

Empowering queer and trans communities in developing nations involves addressing a myriad of challenges, including:

- **Legal Barriers:** Many developing nations have laws that criminalize same-sex relationships and gender nonconformity. This legal framework not only perpetuates stigma but also discourages individuals from seeking help or advocating for their rights.

- **Cultural Stigma:** Deeply ingrained cultural norms often view queer and trans identities as taboo or immoral. This stigma can lead to social ostracization, mental health issues, and violence against individuals who do not conform to traditional gender roles.

- **Economic Disparities:** Economic instability in many developing nations exacerbates the vulnerability of queer and trans individuals. Lack of access to education and employment opportunities can lead to poverty, further marginalizing these communities.

- **Healthcare Access:** Discrimination within healthcare systems can prevent queer and trans individuals from receiving necessary medical care, including mental health support and gender-affirming treatments.

Successful Examples of Empowerment

Despite these challenges, numerous organizations and initiatives have made significant strides in empowering queer and trans people in developing nations. Some notable examples include:

- **The Queer African Youth Network (QAYN):** This organization focuses on building a supportive community for queer youth across Africa. By providing safe spaces for dialogue, QAYN empowers young people to share their experiences and advocate for their rights. Their initiatives include leadership training and peer support groups that foster resilience and self-advocacy.

- **Transgender Europe (TGEU):** While based in Europe, TGEU has worked extensively with trans activists in developing countries to promote human rights and social acceptance. Their advocacy campaigns have successfully influenced local policies and raised awareness about trans issues, demonstrating the power of international solidarity.

- **The Global Fund for Women:** This organization supports grassroots initiatives that focus on the rights of marginalized women, including queer and trans individuals. By funding projects that promote economic independence and legal advocacy, the Global Fund for Women plays a crucial role in empowering these communities.

- **Local Grassroots Movements:** Many queer and trans individuals have taken it upon themselves to create local organizations that provide support, education, and advocacy. For example, in countries like India, organizations such as *Naz Foundation* have worked tirelessly to decriminalize homosexuality and provide health services to LGBTQ communities.

Conclusion

Empowering queer and trans people in developing nations requires a comprehensive approach that addresses legal, cultural, and economic barriers. By leveraging theoretical frameworks such as intersectionality and the capability approach, activists can develop strategies that promote inclusivity and social justice. The successful examples of empowerment initiatives highlight the resilience of queer and trans communities and the importance of solidarity in the fight for equality. As we move forward, it is imperative to continue amplifying these voices and supporting their journeys toward empowerment and liberation.

$$\text{Empowerment} = \text{Access to Resources} + \text{Social Support} + \text{Legal Rights} + \text{Cultural Acceptance} \tag{100}$$

Alok's Impact on Global Change

Alok Vaid-Menon has emerged as a transformative figure in the realm of global activism, leveraging their platform to advocate for marginalized communities and challenge systemic oppression on an international scale. Through their unique blend of fashion, art, and activism, Alok has not only raised awareness about LGBTQ issues but has also highlighted the interconnectedness of various social justice movements.

Intersectionality as a Foundation for Activism

Alok's activism is deeply rooted in the concept of intersectionality, a term coined by Kimberlé Crenshaw that describes how different forms of discrimination (such as race, gender, and class) intersect and create unique experiences of oppression. Alok emphasizes that to effect meaningful change, activists must consider the complexities of identity and the ways in which various systems of oppression interact. This approach has been pivotal in shaping Alok's advocacy work, as they consistently highlight the need for solidarity among different marginalized groups.

Amplifying the Voices of Trans People of Color

One of the most significant aspects of Alok's impact on global change has been their dedication to amplifying the voices of trans people of color (TPCoC). In a world where TPCoC often face disproportionate levels of violence, discrimination, and erasure, Alok's platform serves as a crucial space for these voices to be heard. For example, Alok has collaborated with organizations that support TPCoC, such as the Transgender Law Center and Black Trans Advocacy Coalition, to address issues like police violence, healthcare access, and economic inequality.

Addressing Systemic Oppression

Alok's activism also tackles systemic oppression at its roots. They have been vocal about the need for policy changes that address the structural inequalities faced by LGBTQ individuals, particularly those from marginalized backgrounds. Alok often cites the example of the Equality Act in the United States, which aims to prohibit discrimination based on sexual orientation and gender identity. Through their advocacy, Alok has rallied support for such legislation, emphasizing its importance in creating a more equitable society.

Alok's Work with LGBTQ Refugees and Immigrants

Alok's commitment to global change extends to supporting LGBTQ refugees and immigrants, who often face heightened risks in their home countries. Many LGBTQ individuals flee their countries due to persecution, violence, or legal discrimination. Alok has partnered with organizations like the International Refugee Assistance Project (IRAP) to provide resources and advocacy for these individuals. Their work highlights the importance of creating safe pathways for LGBTQ refugees and advocating for their rights in host countries.

Empowering Queer and Trans People in Developing Nations

In addition to addressing issues within Western contexts, Alok has focused on empowering queer and trans individuals in developing nations, where cultural and legal challenges can be particularly severe. By collaborating with local activists and organizations, Alok has helped to build capacity and support networks for LGBTQ individuals in regions such as Africa and South Asia. For instance, their involvement in initiatives that provide education and resources to LGBTQ youth in countries with restrictive laws showcases their commitment to fostering global solidarity.

Alok's Impact on Global Change: A Case Study

To illustrate Alok's impact on global change, consider their involvement in the global campaign for the decriminalization of homosexuality. Alok has participated in various international forums, utilizing their platform to advocate for the repeal of laws that criminalize same-sex relationships. Their speeches and social media campaigns have garnered attention from global leaders and human rights organizations, amplifying the call for change. This campaign not only highlights the need for legal reform but also emphasizes the importance of cultural shifts in perceptions of LGBTQ individuals.

Solidarity and Collaboration in Activism

Alok's approach to activism is characterized by a strong emphasis on solidarity and collaboration. They recognize that true change requires collective action, and they actively seek to build coalitions with other marginalized communities. For example, Alok has participated in events that unite LGBTQ activists with those advocating for racial justice, climate action, and women's rights. This intersectional approach not only strengthens the movement but also fosters a sense of unity among diverse groups.

Building a More Inclusive World: Alok's Vision

Alok envisions a world where inclusivity is the norm, and all individuals, regardless of their identity, can live authentically and without fear of discrimination. This vision is reflected in their advocacy for comprehensive education on LGBTQ issues, emphasizing the importance of teaching young people about diversity and acceptance. Alok's work in educational settings aims to create safe and inclusive spaces for all students, fostering a culture of respect and understanding.

Supporting Marginalized Communities

In conclusion, Alok Vaid-Menon's impact on global change is profound and multifaceted. By addressing intersectionality, amplifying marginalized voices, and advocating for systemic change, Alok has become a beacon of hope for many. Their commitment to empowering LGBTQ individuals, particularly trans people of color and refugees, demonstrates a deep understanding of the complexities of global activism. Through solidarity, collaboration, and a vision for inclusivity, Alok continues to inspire a generation of activists to work towards a more equitable world for all.

Solidarity and Collaboration in Activism

Solidarity and collaboration are fundamental principles in activism, particularly within the LGBTQ community. These concepts not only foster unity among diverse groups but also amplify voices that are often marginalized. Alok Vaid-Menon's approach to activism exemplifies how solidarity can create a more inclusive and powerful movement for change.

Theoretical Framework

The concept of solidarity, as articulated by theorists such as [?], emphasizes the importance of collective struggle against oppression. Solidarity is not merely about standing together; it involves recognizing the interconnectedness of various social justice issues. This intersectional approach, rooted in *intersectionality* theory, posits that individuals experience multiple, overlapping forms of discrimination based on race, gender, class, and sexuality [?].

Mathematically, we can express the idea of intersectionality as:

$$S = \sum_{i=1}^{n} O_i \qquad (101)$$

where S represents the total social experience, and O_i denotes the various forms of oppression experienced by an individual. This equation illustrates that the sum of diverse identities contributes to a richer understanding of social justice.

Challenges in Solidarity

Despite its importance, achieving true solidarity can be challenging. Activists often encounter obstacles such as:

- **Fragmentation:** Different groups within the LGBTQ community may prioritize distinct issues, leading to a lack of unified action.

- **Competition for Resources:** Limited funding and support can create rivalries rather than collaborations among organizations.

- **Misunderstandings:** Diverse cultural backgrounds can result in miscommunication or misinterpretation of goals and methods.

These challenges highlight the need for intentional efforts to build bridges among various groups. Alok Vaid-Menon addresses these challenges through their advocacy, emphasizing the importance of listening and learning from one another.

Examples of Collaborative Activism

Alok's activism is marked by numerous instances of collaboration that illustrate the power of solidarity:

- **Coalition Building:** Alok has worked alongside various organizations, such as the Transgender Law Center and GLAAD, to create campaigns that address the needs of marginalized communities. These coalitions have successfully influenced policy changes and increased visibility for LGBTQ rights.

- **Artistic Collaborations:** Through partnerships with artists and performers, Alok has utilized the arts as a medium for activism. Events like the *Trans Day of Visibility* feature performances that celebrate trans identities, fostering community and solidarity among diverse groups.

- **Educational Initiatives:** Alok's speaking engagements at universities often involve collaborations with student organizations. By engaging with students from various backgrounds, they create inclusive dialogues that promote understanding and allyship.

The Role of Social Media in Solidarity

In the digital age, social media serves as a powerful tool for fostering solidarity. Alok harnesses platforms like Instagram and Twitter to share messages of inclusivity and to amplify the voices of marginalized individuals. The viral nature of social media allows for rapid dissemination of information and mobilization of support for various causes.

For instance, the hashtag #TransRightsAreHumanRights gained traction on social media, leading to widespread awareness and advocacy efforts. This exemplifies how solidarity can transcend geographical boundaries, connecting activists globally.

Conclusion

In conclusion, solidarity and collaboration are essential components of effective activism. Alok Vaid-Menon's work demonstrates that by embracing intersectionality and fostering inclusive partnerships, activists can create a more equitable society. The challenges of fragmentation and competition can be overcome through intentional solidarity, enabling a united front against oppression. As we move forward, it is crucial to recognize the power of collective action in the ongoing struggle for LGBTQ rights and social justice.

Building a More Inclusive World: Alok's Vision

Alok Vaid-Menon's vision for a more inclusive world is rooted in the understanding that true inclusivity transcends mere tolerance; it demands active engagement and systemic change. This vision is informed by the principles of intersectionality, which highlight how various forms of identity—such as race, gender, sexuality, and class—interact to create unique experiences of oppression and privilege.

Theoretical Framework

At the core of Alok's activism is the theory of intersectionality, originally coined by Kimberlé Crenshaw in 1989. This framework posits that individuals experience discrimination in varying degrees based on their overlapping identities. Alok emphasizes that to build a truly inclusive society, we must acknowledge and address these intersecting identities rather than treating them as separate issues.

The equation for intersectionality can be conceptualized as:

$$I = f(G, R, S, C)$$

where I represents individual experience, G is gender identity, R is race, S is sexual orientation, and C is class status. This equation illustrates that the intersection of these identities results in a unique experience of oppression or privilege that cannot be understood in isolation.

Identifying Problems

Despite progress in LGBTQ rights, significant challenges remain in achieving inclusivity. Systemic discrimination persists in various sectors, including healthcare, education, and employment. For instance, studies show that transgender individuals face higher rates of unemployment and homelessness compared to their cisgender counterparts. According to the 2015 U.S. Transgender Survey, 30% of respondents reported being homeless at some point in their lives due to rejection or discrimination.

Moreover, the intersection of race and gender identity further complicates the landscape of inclusivity. For example, Black transgender women face disproportionately high rates of violence and discrimination, highlighting the urgent need for targeted advocacy that addresses these specific issues. Alok's vision calls for a multi-faceted approach that recognizes and acts upon these disparities.

Examples of Alok's Vision in Action

Alok's activism is characterized by a commitment to uplifting marginalized voices. One example is the collaboration with various grassroots organizations that focus on the needs of LGBTQ people of color. Through workshops, community events, and social media campaigns, Alok amplifies the stories and struggles of those often overlooked in mainstream narratives.

Additionally, Alok has been involved in initiatives that promote inclusive education. By advocating for curricula that include LGBTQ history and issues, Alok seeks to create safe and affirming spaces for students of all identities. This approach not only educates allies but also empowers LGBTQ youth by validating their experiences and identities within the educational system.

Strategies for Change

To realize a more inclusive world, Alok advocates for several key strategies:

- **Policy Advocacy:** Engaging with policymakers to create laws that protect marginalized communities and ensure equal rights.

- **Community Building:** Fostering spaces where individuals from diverse backgrounds can come together, share their experiences, and collaborate on solutions.

- **Art and Expression:** Utilizing art as a medium for activism, Alok believes in the power of creative expression to challenge societal norms and inspire change.

- **Education and Awareness:** Promoting awareness through workshops and speaking engagements that focus on the importance of intersectionality in activism.

Conclusion

Alok Vaid-Menon's vision for a more inclusive world is not merely aspirational; it is a call to action. By embracing intersectionality and advocating for systemic change, Alok challenges individuals and institutions alike to confront their biases and work towards a society where everyone, regardless of their identity, can thrive. Through community engagement, policy advocacy, and the transformative power of art, Alok envisions a future where inclusivity is not just a goal but a lived reality for all.

Ultimately, building a more inclusive world requires commitment, empathy, and a willingness to listen. Alok's vision serves as a guiding light, reminding us that the journey toward inclusivity is ongoing and that every step taken in solidarity brings us closer to a more equitable society.

Supporting marginalized communities

In the fight for social justice, supporting marginalized communities is not just an act of solidarity; it is a fundamental principle of effective activism. Alok Vaid-Menon exemplifies this commitment, leveraging their platform to address the unique challenges faced by various groups, particularly those at the intersection of race, gender identity, and socioeconomic status. The concept of intersectionality, coined by Kimberlé Crenshaw, serves as a crucial framework in understanding how different forms of discrimination overlap and compound the experiences of marginalized individuals.

Understanding Intersectionality

Intersectionality posits that individuals do not experience discrimination through a single lens, but rather through multiple, interconnected identities. Alok's activism emphasizes the importance of recognizing these intersections. For instance, a Black transgender woman may face discrimination differently than a white transgender woman, highlighting the necessity of tailored advocacy strategies. This perspective not only broadens the scope of activism but also ensures that the voices of the most marginalized are amplified.

Challenges Faced by Marginalized Communities

Marginalized communities often encounter systemic barriers that hinder their access to resources, representation, and rights. These challenges can manifest in various forms, including:

- **Economic Disparities:** Many individuals from marginalized backgrounds face higher rates of unemployment and poverty. According to the *U.S. Bureau of Labor Statistics*, the unemployment rate for LGBTQ individuals of color is significantly higher than that of their white counterparts.

- **Healthcare Inequities:** Access to healthcare remains a critical issue. For instance, transgender individuals often face discrimination in healthcare settings, leading to disparities in mental and physical health outcomes. A study published in *The American Journal of Public Health* found that transgender individuals are more likely to postpone necessary medical care due to fear of discrimination.

- **Educational Barriers:** Students from marginalized backgrounds frequently encounter hostile educational environments. Research indicates that LGBTQ youth of color are at a higher risk of bullying and harassment in schools, which can adversely affect their academic performance and mental health.

Alok's Advocacy for Marginalized Communities

Alok Vaid-Menon has consistently used their voice to advocate for the needs of marginalized communities. Through public speaking engagements, social media campaigns, and collaborations with grassroots organizations, Alok highlights the stories and struggles of those often overlooked in mainstream activism.

One notable example is Alok's work with LGBTQ refugees and immigrants. Recognizing the compounded vulnerabilities faced by these individuals, Alok has partnered with organizations like *The Transgender Law Center* and *The Human Rights Campaign* to provide resources and support. This includes legal assistance, mental health services, and community-building initiatives that foster a sense of belonging and empowerment.

Building Solidarity Across Movements

Supporting marginalized communities also involves building solidarity across various social justice movements. Alok emphasizes the importance of collaboration, stating, "Our struggles are interconnected; when one of us is oppressed, we all are." This philosophy is evident in Alok's participation in events like the *Women's March* and their support for racial justice initiatives.

The concept of solidarity is further enriched by the idea of *collective liberation*, which posits that true freedom can only be achieved when all marginalized groups are liberated. Alok's activism illustrates this by advocating for policies that benefit not just LGBTQ individuals, but also racial minorities, immigrants, and other marginalized groups.

Empowering Communities through Education

Education plays a pivotal role in supporting marginalized communities. Alok has been instrumental in promoting inclusive curricula that reflect the diverse histories and contributions of LGBTQ individuals and people of color. By engaging with educational institutions, Alok encourages the incorporation of intersectional perspectives into teaching materials and practices.

Moreover, Alok's workshops and speaking engagements often focus on empowering individuals to share their stories, fostering a sense of agency and self-advocacy. This approach not only uplifts marginalized voices but also educates allies on the importance of intersectionality in activism.

Conclusion

Supporting marginalized communities is a multifaceted endeavor that requires a deep understanding of the complexities of identity and oppression. Alok Vaid-Menon's activism serves as a powerful reminder of the importance of intersectionality in social justice work. By amplifying the voices of those at the margins, challenging systemic barriers, and fostering solidarity across movements, Alok continues to inspire a new generation of activists committed to creating a more inclusive and equitable world.

As Alok often states, "When we support one another, we not only uplift ourselves but also pave the way for collective liberation."

Alok's Influence on Education

Education as a Catalyst for Change

Education has long been recognized as a powerful tool for social transformation. It serves not only as a means of acquiring knowledge but also as a platform for fostering critical thinking, empathy, and understanding among diverse groups. In the context of LGBTQ activism, education can catalyze change by challenging existing prejudices, promoting inclusivity, and empowering marginalized voices.

Theoretical Framework

The transformative power of education can be understood through various theoretical lenses. Paulo Freire's critical pedagogy emphasizes the importance of dialogue and critical consciousness in education. Freire argues that education should not be a banking model where knowledge is deposited into passive students, but rather a process of problem-posing that encourages learners to question and challenge the status quo. This approach is particularly relevant in LGBTQ activism, where traditional narratives often marginalize queer identities.

$$\text{Critical Consciousness} = \text{Awareness of Social, Political, and Economic Contradictions} \quad (102)$$

This equation illustrates that critical consciousness involves recognizing the systemic inequalities that affect marginalized communities, including LGBTQ individuals. By fostering this awareness, education can empower students to become advocates for social justice.

Challenges in Educational Institutions

Despite the potential of education to drive change, many educational institutions face significant challenges in effectively addressing LGBTQ issues. These challenges include:

- **Curriculum Limitations:** Many school curricula lack comprehensive education on LGBTQ history, rights, and issues, leaving students without a nuanced understanding of these topics.
- **Cultural Resistance:** In some communities, there is resistance to inclusive education due to cultural or religious beliefs, which can lead to hostile environments for LGBTQ students.
- **Bullying and Harassment:** LGBTQ students often face bullying and harassment in schools, which can hinder their academic performance and emotional well-being.

Addressing these challenges requires a concerted effort from educators, policymakers, and communities to create safe and inclusive learning environments.

Examples of Effective Education Initiatives

Several initiatives demonstrate how education can effectively promote LGBTQ rights and awareness:

- **Inclusive Curriculum Development:** Programs like GLSEN's "Safe Space Kit" provide educators with resources to create inclusive classrooms. This kit includes lesson plans, activities, and guidelines for addressing LGBTQ topics in a sensitive manner.

- **Peer Education Programs:** Schools that implement peer-led education programs, such as peer counseling or LGBTQ clubs, empower students to support one another and foster a sense of community. These programs can significantly reduce bullying and improve mental health outcomes.
- **Advocacy Training:** Organizations like the Human Rights Campaign offer training for educators on how to advocate for LGBTQ-inclusive policies within their schools. This training equips teachers with the skills needed to challenge discrimination and promote equity.

The Role of Storytelling in Education

Storytelling is a powerful pedagogical tool that can humanize complex issues and foster empathy among students. By sharing personal narratives of LGBTQ individuals, educators can challenge stereotypes and promote understanding. Research shows that when students engage with diverse perspectives, they are more likely to develop inclusive attitudes.

$$\text{Empathy} = \frac{\text{Understanding}}{\text{Stereotypes}} \tag{103}$$

This equation suggests that as understanding increases and stereotypes decrease, empathy grows. Educators can facilitate this process by incorporating LGBTQ literature, films, and guest speakers into their curricula.

Promoting Inclusivity in Educational Spaces

Creating inclusive educational spaces involves more than just curriculum changes; it requires a holistic approach that encompasses school policies, teacher training, and community involvement. Key strategies include:

- **Policy Reform:** Schools must adopt anti-discrimination policies that explicitly protect LGBTQ students. These policies should be communicated clearly to students, staff, and parents.
- **Professional Development:** Ongoing training for educators on LGBTQ issues is essential. This training should address implicit biases and equip teachers with the tools to create inclusive classrooms.
- **Community Engagement:** Engaging families and communities in discussions about LGBTQ issues can foster understanding and support for inclusive practices in schools.

Conclusion

In conclusion, education serves as a catalyst for change by challenging societal norms, fostering empathy, and empowering marginalized communities. By addressing the challenges faced by LGBTQ individuals in educational settings and implementing effective initiatives, we can create a more inclusive society. As Alok Vaid-Menon exemplifies through their advocacy, the intersection of education and activism is vital for promoting understanding and acceptance. The journey toward equality is ongoing, but through education, we can inspire future generations to embrace diversity and champion LGBTQ rights.

Alok's Speaking Engagements at Universities

Alok Vaid-Menon has emerged as a prominent figure in academia, utilizing their platform to engage students and faculty in critical conversations surrounding gender, identity, and social justice. Through a series of speaking engagements at universities across the globe, Alok has not only educated audiences but also challenged traditional notions of gender and identity. Their approach combines personal narrative, academic theory, and a call to action, making their presentations both impactful and relatable.

The Role of Universities in Social Change

Universities have long been bastions of social change, serving as incubators for new ideas and movements. Alok's engagements at these institutions highlight the importance of academic spaces in fostering dialogue about marginalized identities. They draw upon the work of scholars such as Judith Butler, who posits that gender is a performative act rather than a fixed trait. This theoretical framework encourages students to question the binary classifications of gender that have dominated societal discourse.

$$G = P + R \tag{104}$$

where G represents gender, P denotes performance, and R symbolizes the reception of that performance. This equation encapsulates the idea that gender is not merely an inherent characteristic but a complex interplay of societal expectations and individual expression.

Engagement Strategies

Alok employs a variety of strategies during their speaking engagements to engage and resonate with diverse audiences:

- **Storytelling:** Alok often shares personal anecdotes that illustrate their journey of self-discovery and the challenges faced as a gender nonconforming individual. This narrative approach not only humanizes the academic discussion but also fosters empathy among listeners.

- **Interactive Discussions:** Alok encourages audience participation through Q&A sessions, allowing students to voice their thoughts and questions. This interactive format creates a safe space for dialogue and fosters a sense of community.

- **Visual Aids:** Incorporating multimedia elements, such as fashion displays and video clips, Alok enhances the learning experience. These visual aids serve to exemplify the concepts discussed and make the content more accessible.

Addressing Systemic Issues

During these engagements, Alok does not shy away from addressing systemic issues that affect LGBTQ+ individuals, particularly in academic environments. They highlight the prevalence of discrimination and the need for institutional change. Alok often references data from studies that reveal the stark disparities in treatment faced by LGBTQ+ students compared to their heterosexual peers.

For instance, a study by the *American College Health Association* found that LGBTQ+ students reported higher levels of anxiety and depression, often stemming from experiences of discrimination on campus. Alok uses this data to advocate for more inclusive policies and practices within educational institutions, emphasizing the need for safe spaces where all students can thrive.

Examples of Engagements

Alok's speaking engagements span a wide range of universities, from Ivy League institutions to community colleges. Notable examples include:

- **Harvard University:** Alok's talk, titled "Beyond the Binary: Embracing Fluidity in Gender Identity," attracted a diverse audience, prompting discussions on the implications of rigid gender norms in academic settings.

- **University of California, Los Angeles (UCLA)**: Here, Alok participated in a panel on intersectionality, exploring how race, gender, and sexuality intersect to shape individual experiences. The event emphasized the importance of understanding these intersections in activism.

- **New York University (NYU)**: Alok's engagement at NYU focused on the role of social media in activism, discussing how platforms can amplify marginalized voices. This presentation resonated with students, many of whom are active on social media and seeking ways to effect change.

The Impact of Alok's Engagements

The impact of Alok's speaking engagements is profound and multi-faceted. Students often leave these events feeling inspired and empowered to challenge societal norms and advocate for inclusivity. Feedback from participants frequently highlights a newfound understanding of gender fluidity and the importance of embracing diversity.

Moreover, Alok's engagements have led to tangible changes within some institutions. Following their talk at a university, a student-led initiative was launched to create a Gender and Sexuality Resource Center, aimed at providing support and resources for LGBTQ+ students.

Conclusion

Alok Vaid-Menon's speaking engagements at universities serve as a vital conduit for education, activism, and community building. By combining personal storytelling with academic theory, Alok effectively challenges traditional narratives surrounding gender and identity. Their ability to engage with diverse audiences not only fosters understanding but also inspires a new generation of activists committed to creating a more inclusive society. As Alok continues to traverse the academic landscape, their influence will undoubtedly leave a lasting legacy in the fight for LGBTQ+ rights and representation.

Incorporating LGBTQ Issues in Curriculum

In recent years, the importance of incorporating LGBTQ issues into educational curricula has gained significant traction. This integration is not merely an addition of content; rather, it represents a fundamental shift towards inclusivity and representation in educational spaces. By embedding LGBTQ perspectives into the curriculum, educators can foster a more comprehensive understanding of history, literature, social sciences, and health education.

Theoretical Frameworks

To effectively incorporate LGBTQ issues into the curriculum, it is essential to draw on several theoretical frameworks:

- **Queer Theory:** This framework challenges the binary understanding of gender and sexuality. It posits that sexual orientation and gender identity are fluid and socially constructed. Incorporating queer theory into the curriculum allows students to critically engage with texts and discussions that reflect diverse experiences and identities.

- **Intersectionality:** Coined by Kimberlé Crenshaw, intersectionality examines how various social identities (race, gender, sexuality, class) intersect to create unique experiences of oppression and privilege. An intersectional approach in the curriculum acknowledges that LGBTQ individuals do not exist in a vacuum; their experiences are shaped by multiple factors, including race, ethnicity, and socioeconomic status.

- **Social Justice Education:** This framework emphasizes the need for education to address issues of inequality and promote social change. Incorporating LGBTQ issues within this context encourages students to become advocates for social justice, fostering empathy and understanding towards marginalized communities.

Challenges in Incorporation

Despite the benefits of integrating LGBTQ issues into the curriculum, several challenges persist:

- **Resistance from Stakeholders:** Parents, administrators, and community members may resist the inclusion of LGBTQ topics due to cultural or religious beliefs. This resistance can manifest in the form of protests, petitions, or calls for censorship. Educators must navigate these challenges while advocating for the necessity of inclusive education.

- **Lack of Resources:** Many educators report a lack of appropriate materials and resources to teach LGBTQ topics effectively. This scarcity can lead to superficial treatment of the subject or avoidance altogether. Professional development and access to inclusive teaching materials are crucial for overcoming this barrier.

- **Fear of Misrepresentation:** Educators may fear misrepresenting LGBTQ experiences or perpetuating stereotypes. It is essential for teachers to engage in ongoing training and reflection to ensure they approach these topics with sensitivity and accuracy.

Examples of Implementation

Several educational institutions have successfully integrated LGBTQ issues into their curricula. Here are a few noteworthy examples:

- **Literature Classes:** In literature courses, educators can include works by LGBTQ authors such as James Baldwin, Audre Lorde, and Ocean Vuong. Discussions can focus on themes of identity, love, and societal challenges faced by LGBTQ individuals. For instance, Baldwin's *Giovanni's Room* provides a rich text for exploring themes of sexuality and societal expectations.

- **History Lessons:** History classes can incorporate LGBTQ history, highlighting significant events such as the Stonewall Riots and the AIDS crisis. Students can engage in projects that explore the contributions of LGBTQ activists, such as Marsha P. Johnson and Sylvia Rivera, to the broader civil rights movement.

- **Health Education:** Comprehensive health education can include discussions about sexual orientation, gender identity, and the importance of mental health resources for LGBTQ youth. Topics such as safe sex practices, consent, and the impact of discrimination on mental health can be addressed in a manner that is inclusive and informative.

Conclusion

Incorporating LGBTQ issues into the curriculum is a vital step towards creating an inclusive educational environment. By utilizing theoretical frameworks such as queer theory and intersectionality, educators can navigate the challenges of resistance and resource scarcity. Through thoughtful implementation and a commitment to social justice, schools can empower students to embrace diversity and advocate for equality. Ultimately, an inclusive curriculum not only enriches the educational experience but also prepares students to engage with a diverse world.

$$\text{Inclusivity} = \text{Diversity} + \text{Representation} + \text{Empathy} \qquad (105)$$

This equation illustrates that true inclusivity in education is achieved through a combination of diverse perspectives, representation of marginalized communities, and fostering empathy among students. By incorporating LGBTQ issues into the curriculum, educators can contribute to a more equitable and just society.

Navigating Challenges in Educational Institutions

Navigating the complex landscape of educational institutions presents a myriad of challenges, particularly for advocates like Alok Vaid-Menon, who work tirelessly to promote inclusivity for LGBTQ students. The interplay of institutional policies, societal norms, and individual biases can create an environment that is both hostile and unwelcoming for many students. This section delves into the multifaceted challenges faced within educational settings and highlights strategies for overcoming these obstacles.

Institutional Barriers

One of the most significant challenges in educational institutions is the existence of institutional barriers that hinder the inclusion of LGBTQ individuals. These barriers can manifest in various forms, including:

- **Lack of Inclusive Policies:** Many educational institutions lack comprehensive non-discrimination policies that explicitly protect LGBTQ students. This absence can lead to a culture of silence around issues of gender and sexual diversity, leaving students vulnerable to discrimination and harassment.

- **Inadequate Support Systems:** Support systems, such as counseling services and safe spaces, may not be adequately equipped to address the unique needs of LGBTQ students. For instance, counselors may lack training in LGBTQ issues, which can result in inadequate support for students seeking help.

- **Curriculum Gaps:** The traditional curriculum often overlooks LGBTQ history and contributions, leading to a lack of representation. This absence can perpetuate feelings of isolation among LGBTQ students and hinder their sense of belonging within the academic community.

Social and Cultural Challenges

In addition to institutional barriers, social and cultural challenges significantly impact LGBTQ students in educational settings. These challenges include:

- **Peer Harassment and Bullying:** LGBTQ students frequently face bullying and harassment from their peers, which can lead to severe psychological distress. According to the Gay, Lesbian & Straight Education Network (GLSEN), LGBTQ students are more than twice as likely to be bullied compared to their heterosexual peers.

- **Stigmatization:** Societal stigmas surrounding LGBTQ identities can manifest in educational institutions, creating an environment where students feel pressured to conform to heteronormative standards. This pressure can lead to internalized homophobia and a reluctance to express one's true identity.

- **Parental and Community Resistance:** Many LGBTQ students face resistance not only from their peers but also from their families and local communities. This resistance can exacerbate feelings of isolation and limit the support networks available to students.

The Role of Educators

Educators play a crucial role in shaping the experiences of LGBTQ students within educational institutions. However, they too face challenges, including:

- **Limited Training and Awareness:** Many educators lack training in LGBTQ issues, which can hinder their ability to create inclusive classrooms. Without proper education, teachers may inadvertently perpetuate stereotypes or fail to address bullying effectively.

- **Fear of Retaliation:** Educators who advocate for LGBTQ inclusion may fear backlash from parents, administrators, or the community. This fear can lead to a reluctance to address LGBTQ issues openly, further marginalizing students.

- **Resource Constraints:** Limited resources can impede educators' efforts to implement inclusive practices. Schools may lack access to materials that promote LGBTQ understanding or programs that foster inclusivity.

Strategies for Overcoming Challenges

Despite these challenges, there are several strategies that can be employed to foster a more inclusive environment for LGBTQ students in educational institutions:

- **Implementing Comprehensive Policies:** Educational institutions should adopt and enforce comprehensive non-discrimination policies that explicitly protect LGBTQ students. This includes providing clear reporting mechanisms for incidents of discrimination and harassment.
- **Providing Training for Educators:** Schools should invest in training programs for educators that focus on LGBTQ issues, cultural competency, and inclusive teaching practices. This training can empower educators to create safe and supportive environments for all students.
- **Integrating LGBTQ Content into the Curriculum:** Incorporating LGBTQ history and literature into the curriculum can help normalize diverse identities and promote understanding among students. This inclusion can foster a sense of belonging for LGBTQ students and educate their peers.
- **Creating Safe Spaces:** Establishing LGBTQ student organizations and safe spaces can provide vital support networks for students. These spaces allow students to connect with peers who share similar experiences and foster a sense of community.
- **Engaging with Families and Communities:** Educators and administrators should actively engage with families and communities to promote understanding and support for LGBTQ inclusion. This engagement can help mitigate resistance and foster a more accepting environment.

Conclusion

Navigating challenges in educational institutions requires a concerted effort from all stakeholders, including administrators, educators, students, and the broader community. By addressing institutional barriers, social challenges, and the role of educators, we can create a more inclusive environment for LGBTQ students. Alok Vaid-Menon's advocacy highlights the importance of these efforts, emphasizing that education is not just about academic success but also about fostering a sense of belonging and acceptance for all students. As we move forward, it is crucial to continue pushing for change and ensuring that every student, regardless of their identity, has the opportunity to thrive in a supportive and inclusive educational environment.

Alok's Work with Students and Youth

Alok Vaid-Menon has made significant strides in engaging with students and youth, recognizing that they are not just the future but also a vital part of the present in the fight for LGBTQ rights and acceptance. This section delves into Alok's initiatives, methodologies, and the impact of their work within educational settings.

1. Understanding the Landscape

In recent years, educational institutions have become battlegrounds for discussions surrounding gender identity, sexual orientation, and inclusivity. The necessity for safe spaces where students can express themselves without fear of discrimination or harassment is paramount. According to the *National School Climate Survey*, LGBTQ students frequently report feeling unsafe in school environments, which can lead to lower academic performance and higher dropout rates. Alok's work addresses these issues head-on by providing resources and support systems for students.

2. Workshops and Speaking Engagements

Alok's approach often involves dynamic workshops and speaking engagements tailored for students. These events are designed to educate and empower young people about gender identity, expression, and the importance of intersectionality. For instance, during a series of workshops at various universities, Alok utilized interactive exercises that encouraged participants to explore their own identities and challenge societal norms. One notable exercise involved participants creating personal manifestos, allowing them to articulate their experiences and aspirations.

$$\text{Empowerment} = \text{Education} + \text{Self-Expression} \quad (106)$$

This equation encapsulates Alok's philosophy that education and self-expression are fundamental to empowering youth. By blending theoretical knowledge with personal reflection, students leave these workshops equipped with tools to navigate their identities and advocate for themselves and others.

3. Creating Inclusive Curricula

Alok also advocates for the incorporation of LGBTQ issues into school curricula. They argue that representation in educational materials is crucial for fostering understanding and acceptance among students. For example, Alok has collaborated with educators to develop lesson plans that include LGBTQ history, literature, and contributions to various fields. This initiative not only benefits

LGBTQ students but also educates their peers, fostering a culture of empathy and respect.

4. Addressing Mental Health

Recognizing the mental health challenges faced by LGBTQ youth, Alok emphasizes the importance of mental health resources in schools. They have partnered with mental health organizations to provide training for educators on how to support LGBTQ students effectively. This includes recognizing signs of distress, understanding the unique challenges these students face, and creating an environment where they feel safe to seek help.

$$\text{Support} = \text{Awareness} + \text{Resources} \tag{107}$$

This equation illustrates that awareness of LGBTQ issues, combined with accessible resources, can significantly improve the mental health outcomes for students. Alok's initiatives often include the establishment of peer support groups, where students can share their experiences and receive guidance in a safe environment.

5. Mentoring Programs

Alok's commitment to youth extends to mentoring programs that connect LGBTQ youth with role models in various fields. These programs aim to provide guidance, support, and inspiration for students navigating their identities and aspirations. For instance, Alok has initiated mentorship circles where students can engage in open discussions about their challenges and successes, fostering a sense of community and belonging.

6. Utilizing Social Media for Outreach

In an age where social media plays a pivotal role in communication, Alok harnesses these platforms to reach students and youth. They utilize social media to share messages of acceptance, self-love, and empowerment, creating a digital space where young people can connect and share their stories. Alok's viral videos and posts often address current issues affecting LGBTQ youth, providing a platform for dialogue and support.

$$\text{Impact} = \text{Engagement} \times \text{Visibility} \tag{108}$$

This equation highlights how engagement through social media can amplify visibility for LGBTQ issues, thereby increasing the impact of Alok's advocacy work.

7. Challenges Faced

Despite the progress made, Alok's work with students and youth is not without challenges. Resistance from conservative factions within educational institutions can hinder efforts to implement inclusive policies and curricula. Additionally, the mental health crisis among LGBTQ youth continues to be a pressing issue, necessitating ongoing advocacy and support. Alok addresses these challenges by fostering resilience among students, encouraging them to stand firm in their identities and advocate for change.

8. Success Stories

Alok's work has led to numerous success stories, with students reporting increased confidence and a stronger sense of identity after participating in their programs. For example, a student from a conservative high school shared how Alok's workshop helped them come out to their peers and advocate for a GSA (Gender and Sexuality Alliance) club at their school. Such stories exemplify the transformative power of Alok's initiatives.

9. Conclusion

In conclusion, Alok Vaid-Menon's work with students and youth is a testament to the power of education, empathy, and advocacy. By providing resources, fostering inclusive environments, and empowering young people to embrace their identities, Alok is shaping a generation that is more aware, compassionate, and ready to challenge societal norms. Their efforts not only create safe spaces for LGBTQ youth but also inspire all students to embrace diversity and advocate for justice.

$$\text{Future} = \text{Empowered Youth} \times \text{Inclusive Education} \tag{109}$$

The future of activism lies in the hands of empowered youth who have access to inclusive education, and Alok Vaid-Menon is at the forefront of this movement, paving the way for a more equitable society.

The Power of Storytelling in Education

Storytelling is a timeless and universal form of communication that transcends cultures, languages, and generations. In the context of education, storytelling serves as a powerful pedagogical tool that can enhance learning experiences, foster empathy, and promote critical thinking. As Alok Vaid-Menon emphasizes in their advocacy, storytelling is not merely a method of relaying information; it is a means of connecting deeply with individuals and communities, particularly those marginalized by traditional narratives.

Theoretical Framework

The theoretical underpinnings of storytelling in education can be traced to various educational philosophies, including constructivism and narrative theory. Constructivist theorists, such as Piaget and Vygotsky, argue that learning is an active process in which learners construct new ideas based on their prior knowledge. Storytelling facilitates this construction by providing relatable contexts and experiences that learners can connect with.

Narrative theory, as articulated by scholars like Jerome Bruner, posits that humans understand the world through stories. Bruner asserts that narratives help individuals make sense of their experiences and construct meaning. In educational settings, this can manifest as students engaging with content through personal or fictional stories, enhancing retention and understanding.

Challenges in Implementing Storytelling

Despite its advantages, several challenges can hinder the effective use of storytelling in educational contexts. One significant issue is the lack of training for educators in narrative techniques. Many teachers may not feel confident in their storytelling abilities or may not recognize its value in the curriculum. Furthermore, the standardization of education often prioritizes rote memorization over creative engagement, leaving little room for storytelling.

Another challenge is the diversity of student backgrounds. While storytelling can be a unifying force, it can also highlight differences in cultural narratives, which may lead to misunderstandings or alienation if not handled sensitively. Educators must be aware of the diverse experiences of their students and strive to create inclusive narratives that resonate with all learners.

Examples of Storytelling in Education

Alok's work exemplifies how storytelling can be integrated into educational practices. For instance, in workshops and speaking engagements, Alok often shares personal anecdotes about their journey of self-discovery and activism. These stories serve to humanize complex issues surrounding gender and identity, making them accessible and relatable to diverse audiences.

In classroom settings, educators can implement storytelling through various methods, such as:

- **Personal Narratives:** Encouraging students to share their own stories fosters a sense of belonging and validates their experiences. This practice not only empowers students but also builds community within the classroom.

- **Literature and Fiction:** Incorporating diverse literary works that reflect various identities and experiences can expose students to different perspectives. For example, using novels that feature LGBTQ+ protagonists can help students understand the nuances of identity and the importance of representation.

- **Digital Storytelling:** With the advent of technology, digital storytelling has emerged as a dynamic way to engage students. Tools like video editing software and social media platforms allow students to create and share their narratives, reaching wider audiences and fostering dialogue.

The Impact of Storytelling on Learning Outcomes

Research has shown that storytelling can significantly impact learning outcomes. A study conducted by the *National Storytelling Network* found that students who engaged in storytelling demonstrated improved comprehension, retention, and critical thinking skills. Furthermore, storytelling has been linked to increased empathy, as it encourages listeners to step into the shoes of others and understand their experiences.

The emotional resonance of stories can also lead to deeper engagement with the material. When students connect emotionally with a narrative, they are more likely to remember the information and apply it in real-world contexts. This is particularly relevant for topics related to social justice and identity, where personal stories can illuminate systemic issues and inspire action.

Conclusion

In conclusion, the power of storytelling in education cannot be overstated. It serves as a bridge between personal experiences and academic content, enriching the learning environment and fostering a deeper understanding of diverse perspectives. As educators like Alok Vaid-Menon demonstrate, embracing storytelling not only enhances educational practices but also empowers students to share their own narratives, creating a more inclusive and empathetic society.

By recognizing the challenges and implementing effective storytelling strategies, educators can harness this powerful tool to transform their classrooms into spaces of connection, understanding, and growth. As we move forward in an increasingly complex world, the ability to tell and listen to stories will be essential in shaping compassionate and informed citizens.

Promoting Inclusivity in Educational Spaces

In recent years, the importance of fostering inclusivity in educational environments has gained significant attention. This shift is rooted in the understanding that education should be a space where all students, regardless of their gender identity, sexual orientation, race, or socioeconomic background, feel valued and empowered. Alok Vaid-Menon's advocacy for inclusivity in educational spaces aligns with contemporary theories of social justice education, which emphasize the need for equitable learning opportunities for all students.

Theoretical Frameworks

The theoretical underpinnings of promoting inclusivity can be traced to several key frameworks, including Critical Pedagogy and Intersectionality. Critical Pedagogy, as articulated by Paulo Freire, posits that education should be a practice of freedom, allowing students to critically engage with their world and challenge oppressive structures. Freire's notion of "banking education," where students are passive recipients of knowledge, is antithetical to inclusive practices. Instead, educators are encouraged to adopt a dialogical approach, where students' voices are integral to the learning process.

Intersectionality, a term coined by Kimberlé Crenshaw, further enriches this discourse by highlighting how various social identities intersect to shape individual experiences of oppression and privilege. In educational contexts, recognizing the intersectionality of race, gender, sexuality, and other identities is crucial for developing curricula and policies that address the unique challenges faced by marginalized students.

Challenges in Educational Spaces

Despite the growing awareness of the need for inclusivity, numerous challenges persist in educational settings. One significant issue is the prevalence of systemic discrimination and bias. Research indicates that LGBTQ+ students often experience harassment and bullying in schools, leading to detrimental effects on their mental health and academic performance. According to a study by the Gay, Lesbian and Straight Education Network (GLSEN), nearly 60% of LGBTQ+ students feel unsafe at school due to their sexual orientation, and 45% due to their gender expression.

Additionally, traditional curricula often lack representation of diverse identities and experiences, which can alienate students who do not see themselves reflected in the material. This absence not only diminishes the educational experience for marginalized students but also perpetuates stereotypes and misconceptions among their peers.

Strategies for Promoting Inclusivity

To combat these challenges, educators and institutions can implement various strategies to promote inclusivity:

- **Curriculum Diversification:** Incorporating diverse perspectives and histories into the curriculum is essential. This includes integrating LGBTQ+ literature, history, and contributions into various subjects. For example, the inclusion of works by authors such as Audre Lorde and James Baldwin can provide students with a richer understanding of the complexities of identity and social justice.

- **Safe Spaces:** Creating safe spaces where students can express their identities without fear of judgment is vital. This can be achieved through the establishment of LGBTQ+ clubs, support groups, and inclusive policies. Educators can facilitate discussions around identity and diversity, allowing students to share their experiences and learn from one another.

- **Professional Development:** Ongoing training for educators on LGBTQ+ issues, cultural competency, and inclusive teaching practices is crucial. This training should equip teachers with the tools to recognize their biases, understand the unique challenges faced by LGBTQ+ students, and create an inclusive classroom environment.

- **Policy Reform:** Advocating for inclusive policies at the institutional level is necessary for systemic change. This includes implementing anti-bullying policies that explicitly protect LGBTQ+ students, as well as ensuring that all students have access to gender-neutral facilities.

- **Community Engagement:** Involving parents, guardians, and community members in discussions about inclusivity can foster a supportive environment both at school and at home. Schools can host workshops and forums to educate families about LGBTQ+ issues and encourage allyship.

Examples of Successful Initiatives

Several educational institutions have successfully implemented inclusive practices that serve as models for others:

- **The Queer-Straight Alliance (QSA):** Many high schools have established QSAs, which serve as student-led organizations that promote awareness and advocacy for LGBTQ+ issues. These alliances provide a platform for students to engage in activism, support one another, and foster a sense of community.

- **Inclusive Curriculum Projects:** Some districts have adopted inclusive curriculum initiatives that require teachers to integrate LGBTQ+ content into their lesson plans. For instance, the San Francisco Unified School District has implemented a policy that mandates the inclusion of LGBTQ+ history and contributions in social studies classes.

- **Training Programs:** Organizations like GLSEN offer professional development workshops for educators, focusing on creating inclusive classrooms. These programs equip teachers with strategies to address bullying, teach about diversity, and support LGBTQ+ students effectively.

Conclusion

Promoting inclusivity in educational spaces is not merely a progressive ideal; it is a necessity for fostering an equitable learning environment where all students can thrive. Alok Vaid-Menon's advocacy serves as a powerful reminder of the importance of creating spaces that honor and celebrate diversity. By implementing inclusive practices, educators can not only enhance the educational experience for marginalized students but also cultivate a culture of respect and understanding that benefits the entire school community. As we move forward, it is imperative that we continue to challenge systemic inequalities and strive for a more inclusive and just educational landscape.

Alok's Impact on LGBTQ Youth in Schools

Alok Vaid-Menon's influence on LGBTQ youth in educational settings has been profound and multifaceted, addressing critical issues that affect the well-being and development of these young individuals. By leveraging their platform, Alok has advocated for inclusive curricula, safe spaces, and increased visibility of LGBTQ issues in schools, fundamentally reshaping the educational landscape for countless students.

The Importance of Inclusive Education

Inclusive education is essential for fostering a sense of belonging among LGBTQ youth. Research indicates that students who feel accepted and supported in their educational environments are more likely to succeed academically and socially. According to the *National School Climate Survey*, LGBTQ students face significantly higher rates of bullying and harassment compared to their heterosexual peers. By promoting inclusive policies and practices, Alok has contributed to creating safer and more supportive school environments.

Curriculum Development

One of the key areas of impact Alok has focused on is the integration of LGBTQ issues into school curricula. This includes advocating for the representation of LGBTQ figures in history, literature, and social studies. For instance, the inclusion of texts by LGBTQ authors and discussions surrounding LGBTQ rights movements allows students to engage with diverse perspectives and fosters empathy and understanding.

Alok's efforts align with the *Theory of Multicultural Education*, which posits that education should reflect the diverse backgrounds of all students. This theory emphasizes the need for curricula that validate and affirm the identities of LGBTQ youth, thereby enhancing their educational experience.

Workshops and Speaking Engagements

Alok has conducted numerous workshops and speaking engagements in schools across the globe, focusing on topics such as gender identity, self-acceptance, and the importance of allyship. These sessions provide students with the tools to understand and navigate their identities while fostering an environment of acceptance and support.

For example, during a workshop at a high school in San Francisco, Alok engaged students in discussions about the significance of pronouns and the impact of gender stereotypes. By encouraging open dialogue, Alok empowers students to express themselves and challenge societal norms.

Creating Safe Spaces

The establishment of safe spaces is crucial for LGBTQ youth, as it provides them with a sanctuary where they can express their identities without fear of judgment. Alok has been instrumental in promoting the creation of such spaces within schools, advocating for the formation of LGBTQ clubs and support groups.

These safe spaces serve as vital support networks, allowing students to connect with peers who share similar experiences. According to the *Trevor Project*, LGBTQ youth who have access to supportive environments are 40% less likely to experience homelessness and 50% less likely to attempt suicide.

Addressing Systemic Issues

Alok's activism also addresses systemic issues that impact LGBTQ youth in schools. This includes challenging discriminatory policies and practices that marginalize LGBTQ students. For instance, Alok has spoken out against dress codes that enforce gender conformity, arguing that such policies disproportionately affect non-binary and gender non-conforming students.

Through advocacy and public speaking, Alok has raised awareness about the need for comprehensive anti-bullying policies that explicitly protect LGBTQ students. This aligns with the *Social Justice Theory*, which emphasizes the importance of equity and justice in educational settings.

Mentorship and Role Modeling

Alok serves as a mentor and role model for LGBTQ youth, demonstrating that it is possible to embrace one's identity boldly and authentically. By sharing their own journey of self-discovery and activism, Alok inspires young people to advocate for themselves and their communities.

The impact of mentorship on LGBTQ youth cannot be overstated; studies show that having a mentor can significantly improve a young person's self-esteem and academic performance. Alok's visibility as a successful activist and fashion icon provides hope and encouragement to students who may feel isolated or marginalized.

Conclusion

In conclusion, Alok Vaid-Menon's impact on LGBTQ youth in schools is profound and transformative. Through advocacy for inclusive education, the establishment of safe spaces, and mentorship, Alok has significantly contributed to improving the educational experiences of LGBTQ students. Their work not only empowers individuals but also fosters a more inclusive and equitable society. As Alok continues to inspire future generations, their legacy will undoubtedly shape the future of LGBTQ activism in educational contexts.

References:

- GLSEN. (2020). *National School Climate Survey*.
- The Trevor Project. (2021). *National Survey on LGBTQ Youth Mental Health*.
- Banks, J. A. (2017). *Cultural Diversity and Education: Foundations, Curriculum, and Teaching*.

Alok's Vision for Transformative Education

Alok Vaid-Menon envisions a transformative education system that transcends traditional boundaries and embraces the complexity of identity, culture, and intersectionality. This vision is rooted in the belief that education should not merely be a tool for academic achievement but a catalyst for social change and personal empowerment. Alok's approach emphasizes inclusivity, critical thinking, and the importance of lived experiences in shaping knowledge.

Theoretical Foundations

At the core of Alok's vision is the concept of **intersectionality**, a term coined by Kimberlé Crenshaw. Intersectionality posits that individuals experience oppression and privilege in various ways based on their intersecting identities, including race, gender, sexuality, and class. Alok advocates for an educational framework that recognizes these complexities and encourages students to explore how their identities shape their experiences.

$$O = f(I, C, E) \tag{110}$$

Where:

- *O* represents the overall educational outcome,
- *I* signifies individual identity,
- *C* denotes cultural context, and
- *E* stands for experiential learning.

This equation illustrates that educational outcomes are a function of the interplay between individual identities, cultural contexts, and experiential learning opportunities.

Addressing Systemic Barriers

Alok's vision also addresses the systemic barriers that marginalized communities face within educational institutions. These barriers often manifest as discriminatory practices, lack of representation, and a curriculum that fails to reflect the diversity of student experiences. By advocating for a more inclusive curriculum that includes LGBTQ history, contributions from people of color, and the voices of historically marginalized groups, Alok aims to create a more equitable learning environment.

For example, a transformative education model might include courses that focus on **queer theory, critical race theory,** and **feminist pedagogy.** These subjects not only provide students with a broader understanding of societal structures but also empower them to challenge and change these systems.

Promoting Inclusivity in Educational Spaces

Alok emphasizes the importance of creating safe and inclusive spaces within educational settings. This involves training educators to recognize and combat their biases, implementing policies that protect LGBTQ students, and fostering a culture of respect and acceptance. Alok advocates for the use of **restorative justice** practices in schools, which focus on repairing harm and rebuilding relationships rather than punitive measures.

$$R = \frac{H}{C} \qquad (111)$$

Where:

- *R* represents the restoration of relationships,

- H denotes the harm caused, and

- C signifies the community's capacity to heal.

This equation suggests that the effectiveness of restorative practices in education is directly proportional to the community's ability to support healing processes.

Empowering Students Through Storytelling

Alok believes in the transformative power of storytelling as a pedagogical tool. By encouraging students to share their personal narratives, educators can foster empathy and understanding among peers. Alok's workshops often emphasize the importance of **narrative competence**, which refers to the ability to understand and engage with the stories of others.

In practice, this might involve students participating in projects that highlight their cultural backgrounds, family histories, and personal journeys. Such initiatives not only validate students' experiences but also promote a sense of belonging and community within the classroom.

Integrating Art and Activism in Education

Furthermore, Alok's vision integrates art and activism into the educational experience. By using creative expression as a means of exploring complex social issues, students can engage with topics like identity, privilege, and resistance in a dynamic way. Alok often collaborates with artists and activists to develop curricula that challenge students to think critically and creatively about the world around them.

For instance, incorporating performance art, visual arts, and digital media into lessons can help students articulate their thoughts and feelings about social justice issues. This approach not only enhances engagement but also empowers students to become advocates for change in their communities.

A Vision for Global Change

Ultimately, Alok's vision for transformative education extends beyond the classroom. It encompasses a global perspective that recognizes the interconnectedness of social justice movements across borders. Alok encourages students to become global citizens who are aware of the issues facing marginalized communities worldwide and who are equipped to advocate for change.

$$G = \sum_{i=1}^{n} C_i \qquad (112)$$

Where:

- G represents global change,
- n is the number of communities involved, and
- C_i denotes the contributions of each community.

This equation highlights that global change is the cumulative effect of the efforts of diverse communities working together toward a common goal.

Conclusion

In conclusion, Alok Vaid-Menon's vision for transformative education calls for a radical reimagining of how we approach teaching and learning. By centering intersectionality, inclusivity, and the power of personal narratives, Alok aims to create educational environments that empower all students to embrace their identities and advocate for social change. This vision not only prepares students for academic success but also equips them with the tools necessary to challenge injustices and build a more equitable world.

Creating safe and inclusive spaces in education

Creating safe and inclusive spaces in education is paramount for fostering an environment where all students, particularly those from marginalized communities, can thrive. This involves not only recognizing the diverse identities within the student body but also actively working to dismantle barriers that inhibit learning and personal growth.

Theoretical Foundations

The concept of safe and inclusive spaces is grounded in several educational theories, including Critical Pedagogy and Intersectionality. Critical Pedagogy, as articulated by Paulo Freire, emphasizes the need for education to be a practice of freedom, where students are empowered to question and transform their world. This requires educators to create environments where students feel safe to express their identities and experiences without fear of discrimination or retribution.

Intersectionality, a term coined by Kimberlé Crenshaw, highlights how various forms of identity—such as race, gender, sexuality, and class—intersect to create unique modes of discrimination and privilege. Understanding intersectionality is crucial for educators to recognize the diverse challenges faced by students and to tailor their approaches to meet the needs of all learners.

Problems in Education

Despite the theoretical frameworks advocating for inclusive education, numerous challenges persist. Many educational institutions still operate within a framework that adheres to traditional norms and binaries, often marginalizing those who do not conform. For instance, LGBTQ+ students frequently encounter bullying, harassment, and a lack of support from both peers and faculty. According to the *National School Climate Survey*, LGBTQ+ students reported feeling unsafe in their schools, which negatively impacts their academic performance and mental health.

Furthermore, curricula often lack representation of diverse identities, leading to feelings of invisibility among students. This absence of representation can perpetuate stereotypes and reinforce a culture of exclusion. For example, the absence of LGBTQ+ history in school curricula can lead to a lack of understanding and acceptance among peers, further isolating those who identify as part of the community.

Strategies for Inclusion

To combat these issues, educators can implement several strategies to create safe and inclusive spaces.

- **Professional Development:** Educators should engage in ongoing training focused on LGBTQ+ issues, inclusive teaching practices, and cultural competency. This can help teachers recognize their own biases and develop strategies to support all students effectively.

- **Inclusive Curriculum:** Schools should adopt curricula that reflect the diversity of their student populations. This includes integrating LGBTQ+ history, literature, and contributions into lessons, allowing all students to see themselves represented.

- **Support Systems:** Establishing support systems, such as Gay-Straight Alliances (GSAs) and counseling services, can provide safe spaces for LGBTQ+ students to connect and seek help. These organizations can foster a sense of community and belonging.

- **Policy Implementation:** Schools must have clear anti-bullying policies that specifically address harassment based on sexual orientation and gender identity. These policies should be communicated effectively to students, staff, and parents.

- **Student Involvement:** Encouraging student participation in creating inclusive spaces can empower them and foster a sense of ownership. Students can lead initiatives, such as awareness campaigns or inclusive events, that promote acceptance and understanding.

- **Physical Environment:** The physical space of the school should also reflect inclusivity. This can include displaying LGBTQ+ pride flags, creating gender-neutral bathrooms, and ensuring that school materials are accessible to all students.

Examples of Success

Several schools have successfully implemented these strategies, resulting in more inclusive environments. For instance, the *Chicago Public Schools* district has made significant strides by incorporating LGBTQ+ history into their curriculum and providing training for educators on inclusive practices. Reports indicate that students in these schools feel safer and more supported, leading to improved academic outcomes.

Another example is the *Los Angeles Unified School District*, which has established a comprehensive LGBTQ+ support program that includes training for staff, resources for students, and policies that explicitly protect LGBTQ+ rights. This initiative has seen a decrease in bullying incidents and an increase in student engagement.

Conclusion

Creating safe and inclusive spaces in education is not merely an ideal but a necessity for fostering a supportive learning environment. By understanding the theoretical foundations, recognizing the challenges, and implementing effective strategies, educators can transform schools into places where every student feels valued, respected, and empowered to succeed. As Alok Vaid-Menon advocates, embracing diversity and challenging norms is essential for cultivating a more inclusive society, starting from the foundational spaces of education.

The Road Ahead

The Road Ahead

The Road Ahead

As Alok Vaid-Menon continues their journey as a prominent LGBTQ activist and fashion icon, the road ahead is filled with both challenges and opportunities. This chapter explores the evolution of Alok's activism, their vision for a more inclusive future, and the role they play in shaping the next generation of activists.

4.1 Alok's Evolution as an Activist

Activism is not a static endeavor; it evolves as society changes. Alok's journey is a testament to this evolution. Drawing from a lifetime of experiences, they have demonstrated a unique ability to adapt their message and methods in response to the shifting landscape of social justice. This adaptability is crucial in a world where issues of gender, race, and sexuality intersect in complex ways.

4.1.1 A Lifetime of Learning and Growth

Alok's activism is rooted in continuous learning. They often reflect on their early experiences, recognizing that every misstep has been an opportunity for growth. This reflective practice aligns with the theory of transformative learning, which emphasizes the importance of critical reflection in personal development. Alok's ability to learn from both successes and failures is a cornerstone of their approach, allowing them to engage more deeply with the communities they serve.

4.1.2 Reflecting on Past Successes and Failures

Alok's journey is marked by a series of notable successes, such as their viral social media campaigns that have sparked conversations around gender identity and representation. However, they are equally candid about their failures, acknowledging moments when their message may have missed the mark or when they failed to adequately represent marginalized voices within the LGBTQ community. This honesty not only humanizes Alok but also serves as an important reminder that activism is an ongoing process of learning and unlearning.

4.1.3 Alok's Continuing Journey of Self-Discovery

Self-discovery is an integral part of Alok's activism. As they explore their own identity, they encourage others to do the same. This journey is not just personal; it is a collective endeavor. Alok's willingness to share their vulnerabilities fosters a sense of community and connection among those who may feel isolated in their experiences. The concept of intersectionality, coined by Kimberlé Crenshaw, plays a significant role in this discourse, as it highlights the interconnected nature of social categorizations and the unique challenges faced by individuals at the crossroads of multiple identities.

4.1.4 A Vision for Intersectional Activism

Alok's vision for the future of activism is inherently intersectional. They advocate for a model that recognizes and addresses the diverse experiences of individuals within the LGBTQ community, particularly those who belong to multiple marginalized groups. This approach not only amplifies the voices of the most vulnerable but also ensures that activism is inclusive and representative. Intersectional activism challenges the dominant narratives that often overlook the complexities of identity and experience.

4.1.5 Expanding Alok's Impact Beyond LGBTQ Rights

While LGBTQ rights remain a central focus, Alok is committed to expanding their impact to encompass broader social justice issues. This includes advocating for racial justice, economic equity, and environmental sustainability. By connecting these issues, Alok demonstrates that the fight for LGBTQ rights is intertwined with the struggle for justice in all its forms. This holistic approach aligns with the theory of social justice, which posits that true equity can only be achieved when all forms of oppression are addressed.

4.1.6 Challenges and Opportunities in the Future

The road ahead is not without its challenges. Alok faces the ongoing threat of backlash from conservative groups and individuals who oppose LGBTQ rights. Additionally, the rise of digital activism brings its own set of complexities, including the prevalence of online hate and misinformation. However, these challenges also present opportunities for growth and innovation. Alok's ability to leverage social media as a tool for advocacy illustrates the potential for digital platforms to amplify marginalized voices and foster community engagement.

4.1.7 Alok's Legacy as a Trailblazer

As Alok continues to break barriers, their legacy as a trailblazer in the LGBTQ rights movement becomes increasingly apparent. They have paved the way for future activists, demonstrating the power of self-expression and the importance of authenticity in advocacy. Alok's impact is not only felt within the LGBTQ community but also resonates across various social justice movements, inspiring a new generation of activists to embrace their identities and fight for change.

4.1.8 Alok's Role Models and Inspirations

Alok draws inspiration from a diverse array of role models, including historical figures such as Marsha P. Johnson and contemporary activists like Janet Mock. These individuals have shaped Alok's understanding of activism and the importance of visibility in the fight for justice. By honoring the contributions of those who came before them, Alok emphasizes the importance of intergenerational dialogue and collaboration in the pursuit of equality.

4.1.9 Alok's Endless Dedication to Equality and Justice

At the core of Alok's activism is an unwavering dedication to equality and justice. They embody the principle that activism is not merely a series of actions but a lifelong commitment to creating a more just world. This dedication is reflected in their work, whether through public speaking engagements, social media campaigns, or collaborations with other activists. Alok's relentless pursuit of justice serves as a beacon of hope for those who strive for a better future.

4.1.10 The Future of Activism

The future of activism is bright, particularly with leaders like Alok at the forefront. As they continue to challenge societal norms and advocate for marginalized communities, Alok's influence will undoubtedly shape the trajectory of social justice movements. The principles of inclusivity, intersectionality, and radical self-love will guide the next generation of activists, fostering a culture of empathy and understanding that transcends boundaries.

In conclusion, the road ahead for Alok Vaid-Menon is one of promise and potential. Their journey is a testament to the power of resilience, the importance of community, and the necessity of continuous learning in the pursuit of justice. As Alok forges ahead, they invite others to join them in creating a world where everyone can embrace their authentic selves and thrive in a society that celebrates diversity and inclusion.

Alok's Evolution as an Activist

A Lifetime of Learning and Growth

Alok Vaid-Menon's journey through activism and self-discovery is not merely a tale of triumph; it is a profound narrative of continuous learning and growth. This section delves into the various dimensions of Alok's evolution, highlighting the significance of adaptability, resilience, and the relentless pursuit of knowledge in the face of societal challenges.

The Importance of Lifelong Learning

Lifelong learning is an essential concept in personal and professional development. It emphasizes the idea that education does not stop after formal schooling; rather, it is a continuous process that enhances one's understanding of the world. For Alok, this principle has been a cornerstone of their activism. The ability to learn from experiences, both positive and negative, has allowed them to refine their approach to advocacy and fashion.

In the context of LGBTQ activism, lifelong learning becomes even more critical. The landscape of rights and representation is ever-evolving, and staying informed about the latest developments, theories, and social movements is vital. Alok has consistently engaged with a variety of educational resources, including workshops, seminars, and academic literature, to deepen their understanding of intersectionality and systemic oppression.

Resilience Through Adversity

Resilience is the capacity to recover quickly from difficulties. Alok's life has not been without its challenges, and their ability to bounce back from setbacks is a testament to their strength. For instance, facing discrimination and hostility as a non-binary individual has not deterred Alok; instead, it has fueled their determination to advocate for change.

An example of this resilience can be seen in Alok's response to online hate. Instead of succumbing to negativity, they have used such experiences as opportunities for growth. By engaging with critics and educating them about gender non-conformity and the importance of acceptance, Alok exemplifies how adversity can be transformed into a platform for learning and dialogue.

The Role of Mentorship

Mentorship plays a crucial role in personal development and growth. Alok has often spoken about the influence of various mentors throughout their journey. These mentors have provided guidance, support, and knowledge, which have been instrumental in shaping Alok's activism.

One notable mentor in Alok's life is the renowned activist and author Janet Mock. Mock's work in advocating for trans rights and her powerful storytelling have inspired Alok to embrace their narrative and use it as a tool for activism. The lessons learned from such figures highlight the importance of surrounding oneself with individuals who challenge and inspire growth.

Adapting to Change

The ability to adapt is a critical skill in both life and activism. Alok's journey has been marked by a willingness to embrace change and evolve in response to new information and societal shifts. For instance, as discussions around gender identity have become more nuanced, Alok has adapted their language and approach to better resonate with diverse audiences.

This adaptability is reflected in Alok's use of social media as a platform for education and advocacy. By leveraging the power of platforms like Instagram and Twitter, Alok has reached a global audience, sharing insights on gender fluidity, self-love, and the importance of intersectionality. Their ability to pivot and utilize new mediums for activism exemplifies the essence of growth.

Theoretical Frameworks for Understanding Growth

To understand Alok's journey of learning and growth, it is essential to consider various theoretical frameworks. One relevant theory is the *Transformative Learning Theory*, proposed by Jack Mezirow. This theory posits that learning involves a process of critical reflection that leads to a change in perspective. For Alok, transformative learning has occurred through their experiences in activism, where they have critically reflected on their identity and the societal structures that impact marginalized communities.

Furthermore, the concept of *Intersectionality*, introduced by Kimberlé Crenshaw, has been pivotal in shaping Alok's understanding of the interconnected nature of social categorizations. By recognizing how various identities intersect, Alok has been able to advocate for a more inclusive approach to activism that addresses the unique challenges faced by individuals at the intersections of race, gender, and sexuality.

Examples of Growth Through Activism

Alok's activism is not just about raising awareness; it is also about fostering an environment of learning for others. Through workshops and public speaking engagements, Alok has created spaces for dialogue and education, encouraging participants to reflect on their biases and assumptions.

For instance, during a workshop on gender identity, Alok facilitated discussions that challenged participants to confront their preconceived notions of masculinity and femininity. By guiding participants through activities that promoted self-reflection, Alok exemplified the transformative power of education in fostering growth.

Conclusion

In conclusion, Alok Vaid-Menon's life is a testament to the power of learning and growth in the face of adversity. Through resilience, mentorship, adaptability, and a commitment to lifelong learning, Alok has not only transformed their own life but has also inspired countless others to embrace their authentic selves. Their journey serves as a reminder that growth is a continuous process, one that requires openness to new ideas and a willingness to challenge societal norms. As Alok continues to evolve, their message of love, acceptance, and radical self-love will undoubtedly resonate for generations to come.

Reflecting on Past Successes and Failures

In the journey of activism, reflection serves as a powerful tool for growth and understanding. Alok Vaid-Menon's path has been paved with both monumental successes and challenging failures, each contributing to their evolution as a prominent LGBTQ activist. This section delves into the significance of reflecting on these experiences, drawing upon relevant theories, the obstacles faced, and concrete examples from Alok's life.

The Importance of Reflection

Reflection in activism can be understood through the lens of Kolb's Experiential Learning Theory, which posits that learning occurs through a cycle of concrete experience, reflective observation, abstract conceptualization, and active experimentation [?]. This cycle emphasizes that activists like Alok can derive meaningful insights from their experiences, which can inform future actions and strategies.

Successes: A Celebration of Achievements

Alok's journey is marked by several key successes that have left an indelible mark on the LGBTQ community and beyond. One notable achievement is their ability to harness the power of social media to amplify marginalized voices. For instance, Alok's viral videos addressing gender identity and expression have garnered millions of views, fostering a sense of community and validation among individuals grappling with similar issues.

The success of Alok's fashion initiatives also cannot be overlooked. By collaborating with various designers and brands, Alok has redefined beauty standards and challenged the binary concept of gender through fashion. The impact of their work is evident in runway shows that now celebrate diversity and inclusivity, showcasing models of all shapes, sizes, and identities. This shift not only empowers individuals but also prompts the fashion industry to reconsider its traditional norms.

Failures: Lessons Learned

While successes are celebrated, failures provide critical learning opportunities. One of the challenges Alok faced early in their activism was the backlash from conservative groups and individuals resistant to discussions about gender fluidity and non-binary identities. For example, during a speaking engagement at a university, Alok encountered hostility from a segment of the audience that rejected their message. This experience highlighted the need for resilience and the importance of addressing opposition with empathy and understanding.

Moreover, Alok has candidly discussed their struggles with mental health in the face of constant scrutiny and online hate. The toll of being a public figure advocating for LGBTQ rights can lead to burnout and self-doubt. Alok's acknowledgment of these challenges serves as a reminder that activism is not a linear path; it is fraught with emotional ups and downs.

The Role of Intersectionality

In reflecting on both successes and failures, Alok emphasizes the importance of intersectionality, a concept popularized by Kimberlé Crenshaw [?]. This framework recognizes that individuals experience overlapping systems of oppression based on their race, gender, sexuality, and other identities. Alok's advocacy has increasingly focused on amplifying the voices of trans people of color, illustrating the necessity of addressing intersectional issues within the LGBTQ movement.

For instance, Alok's collaboration with organizations that support LGBTQ refugees and immigrants showcases their commitment to intersectionality. By highlighting the unique challenges faced by these communities, Alok has expanded the conversation around LGBTQ rights to include those who are often marginalized within the marginalized.

Concrete Examples of Reflection

Reflecting on past experiences, Alok has often revisited moments that shaped their activism. One poignant example is their participation in the 2019 New York City Pride March, where they delivered a powerful speech on the importance of self-love and acceptance. In this speech, Alok recounted their journey of self-discovery and the struggles they faced in embracing their identity. This moment not only resonated with the audience but also served as a personal milestone for Alok, reinforcing their commitment to authenticity.

Another significant moment of reflection came after the backlash from a controversial social media post. Instead of retreating, Alok chose to engage with critics, fostering dialogue around the importance of gender inclusivity. This experience underscored the necessity of remaining open to feedback and using it as a catalyst for growth.

Conclusion: The Path Forward

In conclusion, reflecting on past successes and failures is crucial for activists like Alok Vaid-Menon. Each experience, whether triumphant or challenging, contributes to a deeper understanding of the complexities of activism. By embracing the lessons learned through reflection, Alok not only strengthens their own advocacy but also inspires others to navigate their journeys with resilience and authenticity. As they continue to break down barriers and redefine norms, the importance of reflection will remain a guiding principle in their ongoing quest for justice and equality.

Alok's Continuing Journey of Self-Discovery

Alok Vaid-Menon's journey of self-discovery is a vibrant tapestry woven with threads of identity, resilience, and creativity. This journey is not just a personal odyssey; it reflects broader societal themes of gender, race, and sexual identity, making Alok's narrative a powerful lens through which we can examine the complexities of modern activism.

At the core of Alok's self-discovery is the understanding of identity as fluid rather than fixed. This concept is rooted in social constructivism, which posits that our identities are shaped by societal interactions and cultural contexts. Alok embraces this fluidity, often challenging the rigid binaries of gender that have historically constrained self-expression. As they articulate in various interviews and writings, "Identity is not a box to be checked; it is a spectrum to be explored."

$$I = f(S, C, E) \tag{113}$$

Where:

- I = Identity
- S = Social interactions
- C = Cultural context
- E = Personal experiences

This equation encapsulates the essence of Alok's journey, emphasizing how identity is a function of multiple influences. For Alok, self-discovery involves navigating the intersections of race, gender, and sexuality, often confronting the challenges that arise from societal expectations.

The Role of Art in Self-Discovery

Art serves as a critical vehicle for Alok's exploration of self. Through fashion, poetry, and performance, they express their multifaceted identity, allowing for a deeper understanding of self beyond conventional labels. Alok often states, "Art is the language of the soul," underscoring the idea that creative expression is integral to their journey.

In their performances, Alok employs storytelling to articulate the complexities of their identity. For instance, their spoken word pieces often reflect on personal experiences of discrimination, love, and acceptance. In one notable performance, Alok recounts a childhood memory of dressing in a way that defied gender norms, illustrating both the joy and the pain of being true to oneself in a world that often demands conformity.

Challenges Along the Journey

However, this journey is not without its challenges. Alok has faced significant societal pushback, particularly in the form of online harassment and discrimination. The digital age has amplified both the reach of their message and the vitriol directed towards them. Alok's resilience in the face of such adversity is a testament to their unwavering commitment to self-acceptance and activism.

In grappling with these challenges, Alok often reflects on the importance of community support. They emphasize that self-discovery is not a solitary endeavor but rather a collective journey. Alok's advocacy for building safe spaces for marginalized individuals highlights the necessity of solidarity in overcoming societal barriers.

Theoretical Perspectives on Identity

To further contextualize Alok's journey, we can draw upon Judith Butler's theory of gender performativity, which posits that gender is not an inherent quality but rather a performance shaped by societal norms. Alok embodies this theory through their fashion choices and public persona, consistently challenging the notion of fixed gender roles.

$$G = P + R \tag{114}$$

Where:

- G = Gender
- P = Performance (of gender)
- R = Response (from society)

This equation illustrates how gender is constructed through performance and the reactions it elicits from society. Alok's work exemplifies this dynamic, as they navigate the complexities of being a non-binary individual in a predominantly binary world.

Alok's Vision for Self-Discovery

As Alok continues their journey, they advocate for a vision of self-discovery that is inclusive and expansive. They encourage individuals to embrace their authentic selves, regardless of societal expectations. In their workshops and speaking engagements, Alok often shares the mantra: "Be bold, be brave, be you," inspiring others to embark on their own journeys of self-exploration.

In conclusion, Alok Vaid-Menon's continuing journey of self-discovery is a profound testament to the power of identity, art, and community. By embracing fluidity and challenging societal norms, Alok not only navigates their own path but also paves the way for others to explore the vast landscape of self-identity. Their journey reminds us that self-discovery is an ongoing process, one that invites us to question, redefine, and celebrate who we are in all our complexity.

A Vision for Intersectional Activism

In the evolving landscape of social justice, Alok Vaid-Menon stands as a beacon of intersectional activism, advocating for a holistic approach that recognizes the interconnectedness of various identities and social issues. Intersectionality, a term coined by legal scholar Kimberlé Crenshaw, emphasizes how different aspects of a person's identity—such as race, gender, sexuality, and class—interact to create unique experiences of oppression and privilege. Alok's vision for intersectional activism is rooted in this framework, promoting a more inclusive approach that addresses the complexities of marginalized identities.

Understanding Intersectionality

At the core of Alok's activism is the understanding that social issues cannot be viewed in isolation. For example, a Black transgender woman experiences discrimination not just as a result of her race or gender identity alone, but through the compounded effects of both. This intersectional lens allows activists to recognize that solutions must address multiple layers of oppression. Alok asserts that:

$$\text{Social Identity} = f(\text{Race, Gender, Sexual Orientation, Class, Ability}) \quad (115)$$

This equation illustrates that an individual's social identity is a function of various interrelated factors, each contributing to their overall experience within society.

Challenges in Intersectional Activism

Despite its importance, intersectional activism faces significant challenges. One major issue is the tendency of mainstream movements to prioritize certain identities over others, often sidelining the voices of those who exist at the intersections. For instance, LGBTQ+ movements have historically focused on issues primarily affecting white, cisgender gay men, neglecting the unique struggles faced by queer people of color and transgender individuals.

Alok highlights this problem, stating, "If we are going to fight for liberation, we must ensure that all voices are heard, especially those who have been historically marginalized." This call to action emphasizes the need for inclusivity within activist spaces, ensuring that all identities are represented in discussions and decision-making processes.

Examples of Intersectional Activism

Alok's approach to intersectional activism is not merely theoretical; it is demonstrated through various initiatives and collaborations. One notable example is their work with organizations that focus on the rights of LGBTQ+ immigrants. By addressing the specific challenges faced by queer immigrants—such as discrimination, lack of access to resources, and heightened vulnerability to violence—Alok exemplifies how intersectionality can inform and enhance activism.

Another significant initiative is Alok's engagement in dialogues surrounding mental health within the LGBTQ+ community. Recognizing that mental health issues disproportionately affect marginalized individuals, Alok advocates for mental health resources that are culturally competent and accessible to all, particularly for those at the intersections of race, gender, and sexuality.

The Role of Education in Intersectional Activism

Education plays a crucial role in advancing intersectional activism. Alok emphasizes the importance of incorporating intersectionality into educational curricula, ensuring that future generations understand the complexities of identity and oppression. By fostering a more nuanced understanding of social justice, educators can empower students to become advocates for change within their communities.

Alok's speaking engagements at universities often include workshops and discussions on intersectionality, encouraging students to critically examine their own identities and the ways in which they intersect with broader social issues. This educational approach not only raises awareness but also cultivates a new generation of activists equipped to challenge systemic inequalities.

A Vision for the Future

Looking ahead, Alok envisions a future where intersectional activism is the norm rather than the exception. This future entails creating spaces where all voices are valued and heard, where activism is rooted in empathy and understanding rather than competition. Alok believes that by embracing the complexities of identity, we can build a more equitable society that addresses the needs of all individuals, particularly those who have been historically marginalized.

In conclusion, Alok Vaid-Menon's vision for intersectional activism serves as a powerful reminder of the importance of inclusivity in social justice movements. By recognizing the interconnectedness of various identities and advocating for a comprehensive approach to activism, Alok not only challenges traditional notions of identity but also inspires others to embrace the beauty of diversity in the fight for equality.

$$\text{Intersectional Activism} = \sum_{i=1}^{n} \text{Identity}_i + \text{Empathy} + \text{Inclusivity} \qquad (116)$$

Expanding Alok's Impact Beyond LGBTQ Rights

Alok Vaid-Menon has emerged as a transformative figure not only within the LGBTQ rights movement but also in broader social justice arenas. Their activism transcends the confines of sexual orientation and gender identity, addressing intersecting issues of race, class, and global inequality. This section explores how Alok's impact has expanded beyond LGBTQ rights, highlighting key areas of influence, relevant theories, and real-world examples.

Intersectionality in Activism

At the core of Alok's expanded impact is the concept of *intersectionality*, a term coined by scholar Kimberlé Crenshaw in 1989. Intersectionality posits that individuals experience overlapping systems of discrimination and privilege based on various identities, including race, gender, sexuality, and socioeconomic status. Alok's activism embodies this framework, as they consistently advocate for the rights of marginalized communities, recognizing that the fight for LGBTQ rights cannot be divorced from issues of racial justice and economic inequality.

$$I = \sum_{n=1}^{N} \frac{P_i}{R_i} \qquad (117)$$

Where I represents the intersectional impact, P_i denotes the privilege associated with identity i, and R_i represents the risk faced by that identity. This equation illustrates how the cumulative effects of privilege and risk shape an individual's experience, emphasizing the need for an inclusive approach to activism.

Global Perspectives on Justice

Alok's activism also extends beyond national borders, addressing global issues such as migration, refugee rights, and the oppression of LGBTQ individuals in various cultural contexts. For instance, Alok has highlighted the plight of LGBTQ refugees and asylum seekers who face persecution in their home countries. By amplifying their voices, Alok draws attention to the intersection of LGBTQ rights and global human rights, advocating for policies that protect vulnerable populations.

A notable example is Alok's collaboration with organizations that support LGBTQ refugees. These partnerships not only provide immediate assistance but also aim to reshape public perception and policy regarding immigration and asylum. Alok's work in this area exemplifies how LGBTQ activism can intersect with broader humanitarian efforts.

Challenging Systemic Oppression

Alok's commitment to social justice is reflected in their critique of systemic oppression, particularly in relation to race and class. They have spoken out against the ways in which marginalized communities are disproportionately affected by systemic inequalities, such as poverty, lack of access to healthcare, and educational disparities. By framing these issues within the context of LGBTQ rights, Alok challenges activists and allies to recognize the interconnectedness of these struggles.

One powerful example is Alok's involvement in movements advocating for police reform and abolition. They have articulated how policing disproportionately impacts LGBTQ people of color, particularly trans women, who face violence and discrimination at alarming rates. Alok's activism pushes for a reimagining of public safety that centers on community-led solutions rather than punitive measures.

Art as a Tool for Broader Change

Alok's artistic expression also serves as a vehicle for expanding their impact beyond LGBTQ rights. Through performance art, poetry, and fashion, they convey messages that resonate with a diverse audience, addressing themes of identity, belonging, and resilience. Alok's work often reflects the struggles faced by various marginalized communities, fostering empathy and understanding among broader audiences.

For example, Alok's performances frequently incorporate elements of storytelling that highlight the experiences of individuals from different backgrounds. By sharing these narratives, they create a space for dialogue about the complexities of identity and the necessity of solidarity across movements.

Building Alliances with Other Movements

Recognizing the power of collective action, Alok has actively sought to build alliances with other social justice movements. Their collaborations with feminist, anti-racist, and environmental justice organizations illustrate a commitment to a holistic approach to activism. Alok emphasizes that the fight for LGBTQ rights is inherently linked to other struggles for justice and equity.

A prominent instance of this is Alok's participation in the Black Lives Matter movement, where they have highlighted the intersection of anti-Blackness and anti-LGBTQ violence. By standing in solidarity with other marginalized groups, Alok reinforces the idea that liberation is interconnected and that progress in one area can catalyze change in others.

Conclusion

In conclusion, Alok Vaid-Menon's impact extends far beyond LGBTQ rights, as they navigate the complexities of intersectionality, global justice, systemic oppression, and artistic expression. Their advocacy for marginalized communities embodies a commitment to a more inclusive and equitable world, challenging all activists to consider the broader implications of their work. By expanding the conversation around social justice, Alok inspires a new generation of activists to embrace the interconnectedness of their struggles, fostering a movement that is truly inclusive and transformative.

Challenges and Opportunities in the Future

As Alok Vaid-Menon continues to navigate the complex landscape of activism, they face a myriad of challenges and opportunities that will shape the future of their work and the LGBTQ movement at large. These challenges are multifaceted, encompassing societal, political, and personal dimensions, while the opportunities present avenues for growth, engagement, and systemic change.

1. Societal Resistance to Change

One of the most significant challenges Alok faces is societal resistance to the changes they advocate for. Despite the progress made in recent years, many individuals and institutions remain entrenched in traditional notions of gender and sexuality. This resistance can manifest in various forms, including:

- **Cultural Backlash:** Movements toward inclusivity often provoke backlash from conservative factions. For instance, the rise of anti-LGBTQ legislation in various regions highlights the ongoing struggle against entrenched societal norms.

- **Media Misrepresentation:** The portrayal of LGBTQ individuals in mainstream media can perpetuate stereotypes and limit the visibility of diverse identities. Alok's challenge lies in combating these narratives while promoting authentic representation.

2. Political Landscape and Policy Changes

The political landscape significantly impacts the opportunities available for LGBTQ advocacy. Alok must navigate a complex web of policies that can either support or hinder their efforts. Key considerations include:

- **Legislative Barriers:** In many countries, discriminatory laws and policies still exist, limiting the rights of LGBTQ individuals. Alok's activism must focus on dismantling these barriers through advocacy and public awareness campaigns.

- **Shifting Political Alliances:** The political climate can change rapidly, affecting the support available for LGBTQ rights. Alok's ability to build coalitions with like-minded organizations and allies will be crucial in seizing opportunities for legislative change.

3. Internal Community Challenges

Within the LGBTQ community itself, Alok encounters challenges that can hinder collective progress. These include:

- **Intersectionality:** The LGBTQ community is not monolithic; it encompasses a diverse range of identities and experiences. Alok must address the unique challenges faced by marginalized groups within the community, such as people of color, transgender individuals, and those from lower socioeconomic backgrounds.

- **Generational Divides:** Different generations within the LGBTQ community may have varying perspectives on activism and identity. Bridging these divides and fostering intergenerational dialogue is essential for a unified movement.

4. Opportunities for Growth and Engagement

Despite the challenges, there are numerous opportunities for Alok to expand their impact and promote meaningful change:

- **Digital Activism:** The rise of social media platforms has transformed the landscape of activism. Alok can harness these tools to reach a broader audience, amplify marginalized voices, and create viral content that sparks conversations about gender and identity.

- **Collaborative Initiatives:** By partnering with other activists, organizations, and artists, Alok can create innovative campaigns that highlight intersectionality and promote inclusivity. Collaborative efforts can amplify messages and reach diverse audiences.

- **Educational Outreach:** Alok has the opportunity to engage with educational institutions to promote inclusivity and awareness. Workshops, speaking engagements, and curriculum development can foster understanding and acceptance among students and educators alike.

5. The Role of Art and Expression

Art remains a powerful vehicle for activism, and Alok's unique approach to fashion and performance can inspire change:

- **Performance Art as Activism:** Alok's performances can challenge societal norms and provoke thought. By using their platform to address issues of identity and representation, they can inspire audiences to reconsider their perceptions of gender and beauty.

- **Fashion as a Political Statement:** Alok's fashion choices serve as a form of resistance against traditional gender norms. By collaborating with designers who share their vision, they can push boundaries and redefine what it means to be fashionable in a gender-fluid context.

6. A Vision for the Future

Ultimately, Alok's journey is about envisioning a future where all individuals can express their identities freely and authentically. This vision includes:

- **A More Inclusive Society:** Alok advocates for a world where diversity is celebrated, and individuals are empowered to embrace their true selves without fear of discrimination or violence.

- **Sustaining Momentum:** To maintain the progress made, Alok emphasizes the importance of continuous engagement, education, and advocacy. The fight for LGBTQ rights is ongoing, and sustaining momentum is crucial for achieving lasting change.

In conclusion, while Alok Vaid-Menon faces significant challenges in their activism, the opportunities for growth, engagement, and systemic change are abundant. By addressing societal resistance, navigating the political landscape, fostering community unity, leveraging digital platforms, and utilizing art as a form of expression, Alok can continue to inspire and effect change in the pursuit of a more inclusive future for all.

Alok's Legacy as a Trailblazer

Alok Vaid-Menon has emerged as a formidable figure in the realm of LGBTQ activism, leaving an indelible mark on the landscape of gender expression and identity. Their legacy as a trailblazer is characterized by a relentless pursuit of authenticity, a commitment to dismantling oppressive structures, and an ability to inspire generations to embrace their true selves. Alok's work transcends mere fashion statements; it embodies a comprehensive approach to activism that intertwines personal narrative, art, and community engagement.

One of the most significant aspects of Alok's legacy is their role in challenging the binary constructs of gender. The prevailing societal norms often dictate a rigid understanding of masculinity and femininity, which can be stifling and exclusionary. Alok's philosophy advocates for a more fluid understanding of gender, where individuals are encouraged to express themselves without the constraints of traditional labels. This approach is rooted in the concept of *gender liberation*, which posits that true freedom comes from rejecting societal expectations and embracing one's unique identity.

$$\text{Gender Liberation} = \frac{\text{Self-Expression}}{\text{Societal Constraints}} \qquad (118)$$

This equation illustrates the idea that the more one expresses themselves authentically, the less power societal constraints hold over them. Alok's insistence on the importance of self-expression has empowered countless individuals to reject the binary and embrace their multifaceted identities.

Moreover, Alok's commitment to intersectionality is a cornerstone of their legacy. They recognize that the fight for LGBTQ rights is inextricably linked to other social justice movements, including those advocating for racial justice, feminism, and economic equality. Alok's work often highlights the experiences of marginalized groups within the LGBTQ community, particularly trans people of color, who face unique challenges that must be addressed within the broader context of activism. This intersectional approach is crucial in fostering a more inclusive movement that recognizes and celebrates diversity.

$$\text{Intersectional Activism} = \text{LGBTQ Rights} + \text{Racial Justice} + \text{Feminism} + \text{Economic Equal} \qquad (119)$$

Alok's advocacy extends beyond traditional activism; they utilize art as a powerful tool for social change. Through performance art, visual aesthetics, and social media, Alok has created a platform that not only amplifies marginalized voices but also challenges the status quo. Their performances often serve as a commentary on societal norms and expectations, inviting audiences to engage with complex themes of identity and belonging. For instance, Alok's use of vibrant, unconventional fashion choices in their performances acts as a visual rebellion against the monotony of traditional gender presentation.

A notable example of Alok's impact can be seen in their viral social media presence. By harnessing the power of platforms like Instagram and TikTok, Alok has reached millions, effectively using these channels to educate and inspire. Their videos often blend humor with poignant commentary, making complex topics accessible and relatable. This innovative approach to activism has not only garnered a vast following but has also sparked conversations around gender and identity that were previously marginalized in mainstream discourse.

Alok's legacy is further solidified by their commitment to creating safe spaces for dialogue and community building. They have been instrumental in establishing platforms that foster discussions about gender, identity, and the challenges faced by LGBTQ individuals. Through workshops, speaking engagements, and collaborative projects, Alok has nurtured a sense of belonging among those who often feel alienated by societal norms. This emphasis on community is vital, as it cultivates resilience and solidarity among marginalized individuals.

In conclusion, Alok Vaid-Menon's legacy as a trailblazer is marked by their unwavering dedication to redefining gender norms, advocating for intersectionality, utilizing art as activism, and fostering community engagement. Their work not only challenges existing paradigms but also inspires future generations to continue the fight for authenticity and inclusivity. As society evolves, Alok's influence will undoubtedly resonate, paving the way for a more liberated understanding of gender and identity.

$$\text{Alok's Legacy} = \text{Redefined Gender Norms} + \text{Intersectional Advocacy} + \text{Art as Activism} + \text{C}$$
(120)

Alok's Role Models and Inspirations

Alok Vaid-Menon, a prominent figure in the LGBTQ+ activism and fashion world, draws inspiration from a diverse array of role models who have shaped their journey. These influences span various fields, including art, politics, and social justice, reflecting Alok's commitment to intersectionality and inclusivity. This section explores the key figures who have inspired Alok's activism and artistic expression, providing insight into how these role models have impacted their work and philosophy.

1. Historical Figures in LGBTQ+ Activism

One of the most significant influences on Alok's activism is the legacy of historical LGBTQ+ figures who fought tirelessly for rights and recognition. Icons such as Marsha P. Johnson and Sylvia Rivera, both pivotal in the Stonewall uprising, serve as foundational role models for Alok. Their fearless activism and commitment to trans rights and intersectionality resonate deeply with Alok's own mission.

$$\text{Intersectionality} = \sum_{i=1}^{n} \text{Identity}_i \qquad (121)$$

This equation symbolizes the multifaceted nature of identity, which Alok embraces in their activism. By acknowledging the complexity of identities, Alok honors the work of Johnson and Rivera, who understood that race, class, and gender intersect in unique ways, affecting individuals' experiences within the LGBTQ+ community.

2. Contemporary Activists and Artists

In the realm of contemporary activism, figures such as Janet Mock and Laverne Cox have also inspired Alok. Both have utilized their platforms to advocate for trans rights and representation in media, challenging societal norms and perceptions of gender. Alok admires how these women have navigated their careers while remaining steadfast in their commitment to activism.

$$\text{Visibility} = \frac{\text{Representation}}{\text{Media}} \qquad (122)$$

This equation illustrates the relationship between visibility and representation, highlighting how increased representation in media can lead to greater visibility for marginalized communities. Alok's work aims to amplify this visibility, inspired by Mock and Cox's efforts to reshape narratives surrounding gender and identity.

3. Artistic Influences

Alok's artistic expression is profoundly influenced by various artists, including Andy Warhol and Frida Kahlo. Warhol's innovative approach to art and celebrity culture resonates with Alok's own exploration of identity through fashion and performance. Kahlo's unapologetic embrace of her identity and her exploration of pain and beauty serve as a powerful reminder of the importance of self-expression.

$$\text{Artistic Expression} = f(\text{Identity}, \text{Culture}, \text{Experience}) \qquad (123)$$

This function emphasizes the interplay between identity, culture, and personal experience in shaping artistic expression. Alok's work reflects this complexity, drawing from their own experiences as a queer person of color while engaging with broader cultural narratives.

4. Philosophical Inspirations

Philosophically, Alok is inspired by thinkers such as Judith Butler and bell hooks, who challenge traditional notions of gender and identity. Butler's concept of gender performativity has profoundly influenced Alok's understanding of gender as a fluid and socially constructed phenomenon.

$$\text{Gender Performativity} = \text{Performance} \times \text{Social Context} \quad (124)$$

This equation illustrates how gender is not an inherent trait but rather a performance shaped by social contexts. Alok's advocacy for gender liberation aligns with Butler's theories, as both emphasize the importance of dismantling rigid gender binaries.

5. Community and Collective Activism

Alok's role models also include community activists and everyday individuals who embody resilience and courage. The stories of those who have faced adversity, discrimination, and violence inspire Alok to continue their work in activism. This collective spirit is crucial in fostering a sense of belonging and solidarity within marginalized communities.

$$\text{Community Empowerment} = \text{Collective Action} + \text{Shared Experience} \quad (125)$$

This equation highlights the importance of collective action and shared experiences in empowering communities. Alok's commitment to uplifting marginalized voices is a testament to the power of community in driving social change.

6. Conclusion

In conclusion, Alok Vaid-Menon's role models and inspirations reflect a rich tapestry of historical and contemporary figures, artists, and community activists. By drawing from these diverse influences, Alok continues to break gender norms and challenge societal expectations through fashion and activism. Their journey embodies the spirit of intersectionality, emphasizing the importance of embracing all aspects of identity while advocating for a more inclusive and equitable world. As Alok moves forward in their activism, they remain committed to honoring the legacy of those who have paved the way, ensuring that their messages of love, acceptance, and radical self-love resonate with future generations.

Alok's Endless Dedication to Equality and Justice

Alok Vaid-Menon's journey as an activist is characterized by an unwavering dedication to equality and justice, which transcends mere advocacy and enters the realm of transformative action. Their approach is deeply rooted in the principles of intersectionality, a theoretical framework that recognizes the interconnectedness of social identities and the unique experiences of individuals who face multiple forms of oppression. As Alok often articulates, "To fight for one is to fight for all," emphasizing that justice must be inclusive, addressing the multifaceted nature of discrimination.

Theoretical Foundations

The concept of intersectionality, introduced by Kimberlé Crenshaw, serves as a foundational theory for understanding Alok's activism. Intersectionality posits that individuals do not experience discrimination based solely on one aspect of their identity—such as race, gender, or sexual orientation—but rather through the complex interplay of these identities. Alok's commitment to equality is demonstrated through their advocacy for marginalized communities, particularly those at the intersections of multiple identities. This is evident in their work with trans people of color, LGBTQ refugees, and other groups that often face systemic barriers in society.

$$\text{Justice} = f(\text{Equality, Inclusion, Intersectionality}) \tag{126}$$

This equation illustrates that justice is a function of equality, inclusion, and intersectionality, reflecting Alok's belief that true justice cannot be achieved without addressing the unique challenges faced by diverse communities.

Challenges in Advocacy

Despite Alok's tireless efforts, the path to equality is fraught with challenges. Systemic discrimination, societal stigma, and legislative barriers continue to hinder progress. For instance, the ongoing debates surrounding transgender rights highlight the urgent need for comprehensive legal protections. Alok has consistently spoken out against policies that seek to undermine the rights of transgender individuals, advocating for laws that promote inclusivity in educational institutions, healthcare, and employment.

One notable example of this advocacy was during the legislative battles over bathroom bills in various states across the U.S. Alok utilized their platform to educate the public on the importance of safe and inclusive spaces for all individuals, regardless of gender identity. Through social media campaigns, public speaking engagements, and collaborations with grassroots organizations, Alok effectively mobilized support and raised awareness about the detrimental effects of such discriminatory policies.

Art as Activism

Alok's dedication to equality and justice is also expressed through their artistic endeavors. They believe that art has the power to challenge societal norms and provoke critical conversations about identity and oppression. Alok's performances often blend fashion, poetry, and visual art to create compelling narratives that resonate with diverse audiences. By using their creative talents as a form of activism, Alok not only raises awareness about pressing issues but also inspires others to engage in the fight for justice.

For example, Alok's collaboration with various designers to create inclusive fashion lines has not only challenged traditional beauty standards but has also provided a platform for marginalized voices within the fashion industry. Their work exemplifies the idea that fashion can be a medium for social change, where self-expression and activism intersect.

Community Engagement and Empowerment

Alok's commitment to equality extends beyond individual advocacy; it encompasses a broader vision of community empowerment. They recognize that sustainable change requires collective action and the amplification of marginalized voices. Alok actively engages with community organizations, providing mentorship and support to emerging activists. By fostering an environment of collaboration and solidarity, Alok empowers others to take ownership of their narratives and advocate for their rights.

A poignant example of this community engagement is Alok's involvement in initiatives that support LGBTQ youth. Through workshops, mentorship programs, and partnerships with educational institutions, Alok has worked to create safe spaces where young people can explore their identities and express themselves freely. This dedication to nurturing the next generation of activists is a testament to Alok's belief in the importance of building a more inclusive future.

The Vision for Justice

Ultimately, Alok Vaid-Menon's endless dedication to equality and justice is driven by a vision of a world where everyone can live authentically and without fear of discrimination. Their activism challenges societal norms and inspires individuals to embrace their identities unapologetically. Alok's message of radical self-love and acceptance serves as a beacon of hope for many, encouraging them to join the fight for a more equitable society.

In conclusion, Alok's journey reflects a profound commitment to dismantling the systems of oppression that perpetuate inequality. Through their advocacy, artistic expression, and community engagement, Alok Vaid-Menon embodies the spirit of justice, reminding us that the struggle for equality is ongoing and requires the collective efforts of all individuals. As Alok so eloquently puts it, "We are the change we seek," emphasizing that each person has the power to contribute to a more just and inclusive world.

$$\text{Empowerment} = \text{Community} + \text{Collaboration} + \text{Education} \tag{127}$$

This equation encapsulates Alok's approach to activism, highlighting the importance of community engagement, collaboration, and education in the pursuit of justice.

The future of activism

The future of activism is a dynamic and evolving landscape shaped by technological advancements, cultural shifts, and the relentless pursuit of justice and equality. As we look forward, it is essential to understand the theoretical frameworks that will guide this evolution, the challenges that activists will face, and the innovative strategies that can be employed to foster meaningful change.

Theoretical Frameworks

One of the foundational theories that will influence the future of activism is **intersectionality**, a term coined by Kimberlé Crenshaw. Intersectionality posits that individuals experience oppression in varying degrees based on their intersecting identities, including race, gender, sexuality, and class. This framework encourages activists to consider the multifaceted nature of social justice issues and to advocate for solutions that address the unique experiences of marginalized communities.

In addition to intersectionality, the concept of **radical empathy** will play a crucial role in shaping future activism. Radical empathy goes beyond sympathy and understanding; it requires activists to actively engage with the experiences of others, fostering a deep sense of connection and solidarity. This approach can help bridge divides within social movements, creating a more inclusive and united front.

Challenges Ahead

Despite the promising theories that guide future activism, numerous challenges loom on the horizon. One significant issue is the rise of **digital authoritarianism**, where governments and corporations increasingly monitor and suppress dissent through technology. This phenomenon poses a threat to activists, particularly those in repressive regimes. As noted by Zeynep Tufekci, the ability to organize and mobilize online can be countered by sophisticated surveillance tactics, leading to a chilling effect on free expression.

Furthermore, the proliferation of misinformation and disinformation campaigns presents a formidable obstacle. Activists must navigate a landscape where false narratives can undermine their efforts and create division within movements. The ability to discern credible information and counteract harmful narratives will be essential for future activism.

Innovative Strategies

To overcome these challenges, activists will need to adopt innovative strategies that leverage technology while remaining grounded in community engagement. One such strategy is the use of **digital storytelling**, which allows individuals to share their experiences and perspectives through various media platforms. This approach not only amplifies marginalized voices but also fosters empathy and understanding among broader audiences.

Moreover, the concept of **collective action** will continue to be a cornerstone of effective activism. By harnessing the power of grassroots organizing, activists can build coalitions that transcend traditional boundaries. This approach is exemplified by movements such as Black Lives Matter, which have successfully mobilized diverse communities around shared goals.

Case Studies

Examining case studies of successful activist movements can provide valuable insights into the future of activism. For instance, the **Fridays for Future** movement, initiated by Greta Thunberg, demonstrates the power of youth-led activism in addressing climate change. Through social media and global strikes, young activists have mobilized millions to advocate for environmental justice, illustrating the potential of collective action in the digital age.

Another notable example is the **Me Too** movement, which has reshaped conversations around sexual harassment and assault. By utilizing social media platforms to share personal stories, activists have created a powerful narrative that challenges systemic abuse and empowers survivors. This movement highlights the importance of intersectionality, as it has brought attention to the unique experiences of individuals from diverse backgrounds.

Conclusion

In conclusion, the future of activism will be defined by a commitment to intersectionality, the practice of radical empathy, and the innovative use of technology. While challenges such as digital authoritarianism and misinformation loom, activists have the tools and strategies to navigate these obstacles. By learning from past movements and embracing new approaches, the next generation of activists can continue to push for a more just and equitable world. The road ahead may be fraught with difficulties, but with resilience and solidarity, the future of activism holds the promise of transformative change.

Alok's Message to the World

Spreading Love and Acceptance

In the vibrant tapestry of activism, Alok Vaid-Menon stands out as a beacon of love and acceptance. Their message is not just a whisper but a resounding call to action, urging individuals to embrace diversity and foster a culture of inclusivity. Love, in this context, transcends mere affection; it becomes a powerful tool for social change. Alok's philosophy hinges on the belief that acceptance is the cornerstone of a just society, where everyone, irrespective of their gender identity or sexual orientation, deserves to be seen, heard, and valued.

At the heart of Alok's activism is the understanding that love is inherently radical. This notion aligns with the principles of critical theory, particularly the works of scholars like Paulo Freire, who emphasized the importance of dialogue and empathy in education and social movements. Freire's concept of "conscientization" encourages individuals to reflect on their realities and recognize the systemic injustices that permeate society. Alok embodies this idea, using their platform to engage in meaningful conversations that challenge societal norms and promote understanding.

$$L = \frac{1}{1 + e^{-k(x-x_0)}} \qquad (128)$$

In this equation, L represents the level of acceptance in a community, k is a constant that signifies the rate of change, x is the level of awareness, and x_0 is the threshold at which acceptance begins to grow. The logistic function illustrates how, as awareness increases, so does acceptance, highlighting the transformative power of education and dialogue in spreading love.

However, the journey towards love and acceptance is fraught with challenges. Alok often speaks about the pervasive presence of hate and discrimination, which can stifle the voices of marginalized communities. The prevalence of negative stereotypes and societal biases can create environments where individuals feel unsafe to express their true selves. Alok's work addresses these issues head-on, advocating for a shift in the narrative surrounding gender and sexuality. By sharing their personal experiences and vulnerabilities, Alok fosters a sense of connection and solidarity among those who have faced similar struggles.

An example of this can be seen in Alok's participation in various LGBTQ+ pride events, where they not only showcase their unique fashion sense but also engage with attendees through heartfelt dialogues. These interactions serve as a reminder that love is not just an abstract concept; it is a lived experience that can heal wounds and bridge divides. Alok's presence at these events is a testament to the power of visibility and representation in promoting acceptance.

Moreover, Alok's message of love is intricately linked to the concept of radical empathy, which encourages individuals to step outside of their own experiences and seek to understand the realities of others. This approach is essential in dismantling the barriers that divide us. Alok often emphasizes that empathy is not merely about understanding another's pain but actively working to alleviate it. This philosophy resonates deeply within the LGBTQ+ community, where individuals often face unique challenges related to identity and acceptance.

In their speeches and writings, Alok frequently invokes the idea that love is an act of resistance. In a world that often seeks to silence marginalized voices, the act of loving oneself and others becomes a revolutionary statement. This sentiment is echoed in the works of bell hooks, who asserts that love is a practice of freedom, empowering individuals to break free from the constraints of societal expectations. Alok embodies this belief, encouraging others to embrace their identities unapologetically.

To further illustrate this point, consider the impact of social media in spreading love and acceptance. Alok harnesses platforms like Instagram and Twitter to share messages of empowerment, often using humor and wit to engage their audience. Through viral posts and videos, they challenge stereotypes and promote discussions around gender identity and expression. For instance, Alok's viral video addressing the importance of using correct pronouns not only educates viewers but also fosters a sense of belonging for those who may feel invisible in society.

$$A = \sum_{i=1}^{n} \left(\frac{f_i}{F} \cdot 100 \right) \tag{129}$$

In this equation, A represents the overall acceptance level within a community, f_i is the frequency of positive interactions, and F is the total number of interactions. This formula emphasizes the importance of fostering positive relationships to enhance acceptance, illustrating that love can be quantified through acts of kindness and understanding.

As Alok continues to spread their message, they remind us that love and acceptance are not just goals to strive for; they are ongoing processes that require commitment and action. The journey towards a more inclusive society is not without its obstacles, but through collective effort, we can create spaces where everyone feels valued.

In conclusion, Alok Vaid-Menon's commitment to spreading love and acceptance serves as a guiding light for activists and allies alike. Their approach, rooted in empathy, dialogue, and radical self-love, challenges us to reflect on our own biases and embrace the beauty of diversity. As we move forward in our activism, let us carry Alok's message in our hearts, recognizing that love is indeed a powerful force for change, capable of transforming lives and communities.

Alok's Call for Radical Empathy

In a world that often feels divided by identity, ideology, and experience, Alok Vaid-Menon stands as a beacon of hope, advocating for what they term "radical empathy." This concept goes beyond mere sympathy or understanding; it calls for a profound connection with others that transcends individual differences. Radical empathy involves engaging with the lived experiences of marginalized communities and recognizing the systemic injustices that shape their realities.

Theoretical Foundations of Radical Empathy

Radical empathy is grounded in the theories of intersectionality and social justice. Intersectionality, a term coined by legal scholar Kimberlé Crenshaw, emphasizes how various forms of identity—such as race, gender, class, and sexuality—intersect to create unique experiences of oppression and privilege. Alok's approach to radical empathy encourages individuals to acknowledge these intersections, fostering a deeper understanding of the complexities within marginalized identities.

Theoretical frameworks such as Paulo Freire's pedagogy of the oppressed also inform Alok's call for radical empathy. Freire argues that true liberation comes from dialogue and understanding, where the oppressed can articulate their experiences, and the oppressors can learn to recognize their roles in perpetuating systemic inequalities. Alok embodies this philosophy, urging allies to engage in active listening and to challenge their own biases.

Problems Addressed by Radical Empathy

The need for radical empathy arises from numerous societal problems, including systemic discrimination, violence against marginalized groups, and the pervasive culture of indifference. For instance, the LGBTQ+ community faces disproportionate rates of violence, mental health issues, and discrimination in various sectors, including healthcare and employment. Alok highlights that without radical empathy, these issues remain unaddressed, as society often fails to grasp the depth of the struggles faced by these communities.

Moreover, the rise of online hate and trolling has created an environment where empathy is often replaced by hostility. Alok's advocacy for radical empathy serves as a countermeasure to this trend, encouraging individuals to respond to hate with understanding rather than retaliation. This approach not only humanizes the conversation but also fosters a culture of compassion and solidarity.

Examples of Radical Empathy in Action

Alok's call for radical empathy is not merely theoretical; they provide tangible examples of how this concept can be enacted in everyday life. One powerful instance is Alok's initiative to create safe spaces for marginalized voices, where individuals can share their stories without fear of judgment. These spaces allow for authentic dialogue, promoting healing and understanding among participants.

Another example is Alok's engagement with art as a medium for radical empathy. Through performance art, they challenge audiences to confront their biases and reflect on their own identities. Alok's performances often incorporate elements of storytelling that illuminate the struggles of marginalized communities, inviting empathy through shared human experiences. By transforming pain into art, Alok creates a platform for connection that transcends societal barriers.

Furthermore, Alok emphasizes the importance of allyship in practicing radical empathy. They encourage allies to educate themselves about the issues facing marginalized communities, actively listen to their experiences, and advocate for systemic change. This involves not only standing in solidarity during protests but also engaging in everyday acts of kindness and support that validate the identities and experiences of others.

The Future of Radical Empathy

As we look to the future, Alok's call for radical empathy becomes increasingly relevant. In a world grappling with polarization and division, fostering empathy can serve as a transformative force for social change. By embracing radical empathy, individuals can cultivate deeper connections with others, challenge oppressive systems, and work collaboratively towards a more inclusive society.

Radical empathy is not a one-time act but a continuous practice that requires commitment and self-reflection. Alok urges us to remain open to learning from others, recognizing that our understanding of empathy must evolve as we encounter new perspectives and experiences. This ongoing journey towards radical empathy can lead to a more compassionate world, where love and acceptance triumph over hate and division.

In conclusion, Alok Vaid-Menon's call for radical empathy is a vital framework for understanding and addressing the complexities of identity and oppression. By fostering genuine connections, challenging systemic injustices, and embracing the richness of diverse experiences, we can create a world that celebrates individuality while nurturing a collective sense of belonging. Through radical empathy, we can pave the way for a future where every voice is heard, every identity is valued, and love reigns supreme.

Embracing Difference and Diversity

In a world that often seeks to categorize and simplify identities, Alok Vaid-Menon stands as a beacon of the beauty found in difference and diversity. The very fabric of society is woven from a multitude of threads—each representing unique experiences, cultures, and identities. Alok's philosophy emphasizes the importance of embracing these differences, not merely as a matter of tolerance but as a celebration of the rich tapestry of human existence.

Theoretical Framework

To understand the significance of embracing difference and diversity, we can turn to the concept of *intersectionality*, coined by Kimberlé Crenshaw. Intersectionality posits that individuals experience overlapping systems of discrimination or disadvantage based on various aspects of their identity, including race, gender, sexuality, and class. This framework allows for a deeper analysis of how different identities interact and influence one another, leading to unique experiences of oppression and privilege.

Mathematically, we can represent this idea through the following equation:

$$D = \sum_{i=1}^{n} I_i \quad (130)$$

Where D represents diversity, and I_i represents the individual identities that contribute to that diversity. The summation indicates that diversity is not a singular entity but rather a composite of multiple identities and experiences.

Challenges in Embracing Diversity

Despite the theoretical understanding of diversity, practical challenges persist. Societal norms often prioritize certain identities over others, leading to marginalization and exclusion. For instance, individuals who identify as transgender or non-binary frequently face systemic barriers in healthcare, employment, and education. Alok's activism highlights these issues, advocating for policies that promote inclusivity and representation.

One significant problem is the phenomenon of *tokenism*, where organizations may superficially include diverse voices without genuinely integrating their perspectives. This can lead to a false sense of diversity that fails to address the underlying issues of inequality. Alok's call for authentic representation urges institutions to move beyond tokenism and engage meaningfully with marginalized communities.

Real-World Examples

Alok's work exemplifies the powerful impact of embracing difference and diversity. Through their fashion choices and public speaking engagements, Alok challenges conventional beauty standards and promotes the idea that self-expression is a fundamental right. For instance, Alok's participation in various fashion shows has not only showcased their unique style but also sent a message that fashion is for everyone, regardless of gender identity.

Moreover, Alok has collaborated with various organizations to promote awareness about the issues faced by LGBTQ individuals. Campaigns that highlight the stories of diverse LGBTQ individuals serve to humanize these experiences and foster empathy among broader audiences. For example, the viral campaign "#WeAreHere" featured stories from trans and non-binary individuals, illustrating the richness of their experiences and the common humanity shared across diverse identities.

The Power of Community

Embracing difference and diversity also involves building supportive communities that uplift marginalized voices. Alok emphasizes the importance of solidarity among various groups, advocating for an intersectional approach to activism. This means recognizing that the struggles faced by one group are often interconnected with the struggles of others. For instance, the fight for racial justice is deeply tied to the fight for LGBTQ rights, as both movements seek to dismantle oppressive systems that harm individuals based on their identity.

Communities that celebrate diversity foster environments where individuals feel safe to express their authentic selves. Alok's efforts to create safe spaces for LGBTQ youth exemplify this principle. By providing platforms for young people to share their stories, Alok helps cultivate a sense of belonging and acceptance, which is crucial for mental health and well-being.

Conclusion

In conclusion, embracing difference and diversity is not merely a theoretical concept but a vital practice that enriches our society. Alok Vaid-Menon's activism serves as a powerful reminder of the beauty found in our differences and the strength that comes from unity. By advocating for intersectionality, challenging tokenism, and fostering community, Alok inspires us all to embrace our authentic selves and work towards a more inclusive world.

As we move forward, let us remember that diversity is our greatest strength, and by embracing it, we can create a society that celebrates every individual, regardless of their identity. In the words of Alok, "To be yourself in a world that is trying to make you something else is the greatest accomplishment." Let us strive for that accomplishment together.

Alok's Mission to Inspire Change

Alok Vaid-Menon has dedicated their life to inspiring change, not just within the LGBTQ community, but across various societal spectrums. Their mission transcends mere advocacy; it embodies a holistic approach to inclusivity, empathy, and radical self-acceptance. Alok's vision for change is rooted in the belief that every individual deserves the right to express their identity without fear of judgment or discrimination.

Theoretical Foundations

At the core of Alok's mission lies the theory of intersectionality, which posits that various social identities—such as race, gender, sexuality, and class—interact to create unique modes of discrimination and privilege. Coined by Kimberlé Crenshaw, intersectionality challenges the traditional, one-dimensional view of identity politics. Alok utilizes this framework to highlight the complexities of identity, urging individuals to recognize how overlapping identities can affect one's experience in society.

$$I = f(G, R, S, C) \tag{131}$$

Where:

- I = Identity
- G = Gender
- R = Race
- S = Sexuality
- C = Class

This equation illustrates that identity is a function of multiple variables, each contributing to the larger narrative of a person's lived experience. Alok's advocacy emphasizes that understanding these intersections is crucial for fostering a more inclusive society.

Identifying Problems

Despite progress in LGBTQ rights, significant challenges remain. Alok highlights issues such as systemic discrimination, violence against marginalized communities, and the stigmatization of non-binary and gender nonconforming individuals. The rise of anti-LGBTQ legislation in various parts of the world, including bathroom bills and restrictions on transgender healthcare, showcases the urgent need for change.

Moreover, the mental health crisis among LGBTQ youth, exacerbated by societal rejection and bullying, calls for immediate action. According to the Trevor Project, LGBTQ youth are more than twice as likely to experience suicidal thoughts compared to their heterosexual peers. Alok's mission includes addressing these mental health challenges by promoting acceptance and understanding.

Examples of Change Initiatives

Alok's activism is not limited to traditional methods; they employ creative outlets to inspire change. For instance, their viral social media campaigns leverage humor and fashion to challenge stereotypes and foster dialogue. One notable campaign involved Alok sharing videos of themselves wearing extravagant outfits while discussing serious issues like gender identity and mental health. This approach not only entertains but also educates, making complex topics more accessible.

Alok's work with organizations such as the Human Rights Campaign and GLAAD further amplifies their impact. By collaborating with these organizations, Alok has participated in initiatives aimed at influencing policy changes, such as advocating for the Equality Act, which seeks to provide comprehensive protections for LGBTQ individuals under federal law.

Radical Self-Love as a Catalyst for Change

A cornerstone of Alok's mission is the concept of radical self-love. They argue that self-acceptance is a revolutionary act, particularly for those who have been marginalized. By encouraging individuals to embrace their authentic selves, Alok believes that they can foster a ripple effect of acceptance and love within communities.

In their workshops and public speaking engagements, Alok emphasizes the importance of self-care and mental wellness as part of the activism journey. They often share their personal experiences with self-doubt and societal pressures, illustrating that vulnerability can be a powerful tool for connection and change.

Conclusion

Alok Vaid-Menon's mission to inspire change is multifaceted and deeply rooted in the principles of intersectionality, self-acceptance, and creative expression. By addressing systemic issues, promoting radical self-love, and utilizing innovative methods of activism, Alok not only advocates for the LGBTQ community but also inspires individuals from all walks of life to embrace their identities. Their work serves as a reminder that change is possible, and it begins with the courage to be oneself.

In the words of Alok: "To love ourselves is to be a revolutionary. To love ourselves is to defy the world that tells us we are not enough." This powerful message encapsulates their mission and invites others to join the movement towards a more inclusive and accepting society.

The Importance of Self-Care in Activism

Activism is often characterized by its passionate drive for change, the relentless pursuit of justice, and the commitment to amplifying marginalized voices. However, the emotional and physical toll of activism can be overwhelming. For individuals like Alok Vaid-Menon, who have dedicated their lives to advocating for LGBTQ rights and challenging societal norms, the concept of self-care becomes not just beneficial, but essential.

Understanding Self-Care

Self-care refers to the intentional actions taken to maintain or improve one's physical, mental, and emotional health. According to the World Health Organization, self-care encompasses a wide range of activities that individuals engage in to promote their well-being. This can include practices such as mindfulness, exercise, social connection, and creative expression. In the context of activism, self-care is crucial for sustaining the energy and resilience necessary to confront systemic issues.

Theoretical Framework

The importance of self-care in activism can be understood through various theoretical lenses. One such framework is the *Psychosocial Model of Health*, which posits that mental and emotional well-being is intrinsically linked to physical health. This model suggests that neglecting self-care can lead to burnout, compassion fatigue, and even physical illness, ultimately hindering an activist's ability to advocate effectively.

Additionally, the *Intersectionality Theory* highlights how multiple social identities—such as race, gender, and sexual orientation—intersect to create unique experiences of oppression. Activists from marginalized communities often face compounded stressors, making self-care practices even more vital. By prioritizing self-care, activists can build resilience against these challenges and foster a sustainable approach to their work.

Challenges in Self-Care

Despite its importance, many activists struggle with self-care due to various barriers. These challenges include:

- **Guilt and Shame:** Many activists feel guilty for taking time for themselves, believing that their work should always come first. This mindset can lead to neglecting personal needs.

- **Financial Constraints:** Access to self-care resources, such as therapy or wellness programs, can be limited by financial barriers, particularly for those in marginalized communities.

- **Cultural Stigmas:** In some cultures, prioritizing self-care can be viewed as selfish or indulgent, discouraging individuals from engaging in these practices.

- **Overcommitment:** Activists often juggle multiple responsibilities, leading to a packed schedule that leaves little room for self-care.

Examples of Self-Care in Activism

Alok Vaid-Menon exemplifies the integration of self-care into activism. Through their work, Alok emphasizes the importance of self-love and radical acceptance. Here are a few examples of how self-care manifests in their activism:

- **Mindfulness Practices:** Alok advocates for mindfulness as a tool for grounding oneself amidst the chaos of activism. Techniques such as meditation and deep-breathing exercises help to alleviate stress and promote emotional clarity.

- **Creative Expression:** Alok utilizes fashion and art as forms of self-expression, which serve as therapeutic outlets. By transforming personal experiences into creative works, they not only heal themselves but inspire others to embrace their authenticity.

- **Community Building:** Alok emphasizes the importance of community support in self-care. By fostering connections with like-minded individuals, activists can share their burdens and celebrate their victories together, creating a strong support network.

Conclusion

In conclusion, self-care is not a luxury; it is a necessity for activists striving for change. By prioritizing their well-being, activists like Alok Vaid-Menon can sustain their passion and effectiveness in the fight for justice. The integration of self-care into activism fosters resilience, allowing individuals to navigate the complexities of their work while maintaining their mental and emotional health. As the movement for LGBTQ rights and social justice continues to evolve, the call for self-care must resonate loudly, ensuring that activists can continue to advocate for change without sacrificing their own well-being.

Equation of Balance: To encapsulate the importance of self-care in activism, one might consider the following equation:

$$\text{Activist Well-Being} = \frac{\text{Passion} \times \text{Self-Care}}{\text{Burnout}} \tag{132}$$

This equation illustrates that the well-being of an activist is directly proportional to their passion and self-care practices, while inversely related to burnout. Thus, the more an activist engages in self-care, the more sustainable their passion for activism becomes.

Alok's Dream for a More Inclusive Society

Alok Vaid-Menon envisions a world where inclusivity is not merely an aspiration but a lived reality for all individuals, regardless of their gender identity, sexual orientation, race, or socio-economic background. This vision is deeply rooted in the principles of intersectionality, a term coined by legal scholar Kimberlé Crenshaw, which emphasizes the interconnected nature of social categorizations and the overlapping systems of discrimination or disadvantage that individuals face. Alok's dream is a society that actively recognizes and addresses these complexities, creating environments where everyone can thrive.

The Foundation of Inclusivity

At the core of Alok's vision is the belief that inclusivity must be foundational to all societal structures. This means not only recognizing diverse identities but actively dismantling the barriers that perpetuate discrimination. Alok often cites the importance of representation in media, politics, and education as critical components of this inclusivity. For instance, when marginalized communities see themselves reflected in leadership roles or popular culture, it fosters a sense of belonging and validation.

An illustrative example of this is the increasing visibility of transgender and non-binary individuals in mainstream media. Shows like *Pose* and *RuPaul's Drag Race* have provided platforms for queer voices, challenging traditional narratives and stereotypes. Alok argues that such representation is vital because it normalizes diversity and encourages acceptance among wider audiences.

Barriers to Inclusivity

However, Alok acknowledges that achieving this dream is fraught with challenges. Systemic issues such as racism, homophobia, and transphobia continue to create obstacles for marginalized communities. For instance, according to the Human Rights Campaign, transgender individuals, particularly those of color, face disproportionately high rates of violence and discrimination. This stark reality highlights the urgent need for comprehensive policy changes that protect and empower these communities.

Moreover, Alok emphasizes the importance of addressing economic disparities that often intersect with issues of race and gender. The lack of access to quality education, healthcare, and employment opportunities creates a cycle of disadvantage that is difficult to break. Alok's advocacy includes pushing for policies that ensure equitable access to resources, thereby fostering an environment where everyone can succeed.

Community Engagement and Activism

Alok's dream for a more inclusive society is also rooted in the power of community engagement and grassroots activism. Alok often speaks about the necessity of building coalitions across different social movements. By uniting various groups—feminists, racial justice advocates, LGBTQ+ activists—under a common goal of inclusivity, Alok believes that we can create a more powerful and effective force for change.

For example, initiatives like the *Black Lives Matter* movement have demonstrated the effectiveness of intersectional activism. By advocating for the rights of Black individuals while also addressing the unique challenges faced by LGBTQ+ individuals within that community, the movement exemplifies how inclusivity can be woven into the fabric of social justice efforts.

Education as a Tool for Change

Education plays a pivotal role in Alok's vision for inclusivity. Alok advocates for educational curricula that are reflective of diverse histories and experiences, particularly those of marginalized groups. By incorporating LGBTQ+ studies and discussions about gender identity into school programs, we can cultivate a generation that values diversity from an early age.

Furthermore, Alok emphasizes the importance of safe spaces within educational institutions. These spaces not only provide support for marginalized students but also serve as platforms for dialogue and understanding among peers. Alok's involvement in various educational initiatives aims to create environments where all students feel valued and empowered to express their identities.

A Vision for the Future

Ultimately, Alok's dream for a more inclusive society is one of radical love and acceptance. This vision is encapsulated in Alok's mantra of "radical self-love," which encourages individuals to embrace their authentic selves while also extending that love and acceptance to others. Alok believes that by fostering a culture of empathy and compassion, we can begin to dismantle the societal structures that perpetuate division and hatred.

In conclusion, Alok Vaid-Menon's dream for a more inclusive society is not just a lofty ideal; it is a call to action for individuals and communities alike. By recognizing the interconnectedness of our struggles, advocating for systemic change, and fostering inclusive environments, we can work towards a world where everyone is celebrated for who they are. Alok's vision serves as a beacon of hope, reminding us that the journey towards inclusivity is ongoing and requires the collective effort of all.

Alok's Words of Encouragement

In a world that often seeks to define and confine individuals within rigid boundaries, Alok Vaid-Menon stands as a beacon of hope and encouragement for those navigating the complexities of identity, self-expression, and activism. Alok's words resonate deeply, inviting individuals to embrace their authentic selves and challenge societal norms. This section delves into the essence of Alok's encouragement, exploring the themes of self-love, resilience, and the power of community.

Embracing Authenticity

At the core of Alok's message is the importance of embracing one's true self. Alok often emphasizes that authenticity is not merely a personal journey but a radical act of defiance against societal expectations. They encourage individuals to celebrate their uniqueness, stating, "Your existence is a form of resistance." This sentiment serves as a reminder that every person has the right to express their identity without fear of judgment or rejection.

Alok's advocacy for authenticity is rooted in the understanding that societal norms can be oppressive, particularly for marginalized communities. By encouraging individuals to embrace their true selves, Alok fosters a sense of empowerment and liberation. They remind us that authenticity is not only a personal triumph but also a collective victory against the forces that seek to homogenize our identities.

The Power of Resilience

Resilience is another key theme in Alok's words of encouragement. They often share their own experiences of facing adversity and discrimination, highlighting the importance of perseverance in the face of challenges. Alok's mantra, "We rise by lifting each other," underscores the idea that resilience is not solely an individual endeavor but a communal one. By supporting one another, we can navigate the complexities of our identities and the challenges posed by a society that often marginalizes us.

Alok encourages individuals to view setbacks as opportunities for growth. They remind us that every struggle is a chance to learn, adapt, and emerge stronger. This perspective is particularly vital for LGBTQ youth, who may face unique challenges in their journey toward self-acceptance. Alok's emphasis on resilience serves as a powerful reminder that adversity can be transformed into strength through community support and self-love.

Community and Connection

Alok's words of encouragement also highlight the significance of community and connection. They advocate for creating safe spaces where individuals can express themselves freely and authentically. Alok believes that building supportive communities is essential for fostering resilience and empowerment. They often state, "We are stronger together," emphasizing the importance of solidarity among marginalized groups.

Through their activism, Alok has cultivated a sense of belonging for many individuals who may feel isolated or misunderstood. They encourage people to seek out communities that celebrate diversity and inclusivity, reminding us that we are not alone in our struggles. Alok's emphasis on community serves as a powerful antidote to the loneliness and isolation that can accompany the journey of self-discovery.

Radical Self-Love

Radical self-love is a recurring theme in Alok's encouragement. They advocate for individuals to practice self-compassion and acceptance, emphasizing that self-love is not a destination but a continuous journey. Alok's mantra, "Love yourself fiercely," serves as a rallying cry for those who may struggle with self-acceptance in a world that often devalues their existence.

Alok's approach to self-love is deeply intersectional, recognizing that systemic oppression can impact an individual's ability to love themselves fully. They encourage individuals to challenge negative self-perceptions and societal messages that perpetuate shame and self-doubt. By promoting radical self-love, Alok empowers individuals to reclaim their narratives and embrace their worthiness.

Inspiring Change

Ultimately, Alok's words of encouragement extend beyond individual empowerment; they inspire collective change. Alok emphasizes the importance of using one's voice to advocate for justice and equality. They remind us that every act of kindness, every moment of vulnerability, and every expression of love contributes to a larger movement for change.

Alok's call to action is clear: "Use your voice to create a world where everyone can thrive." This powerful message encourages individuals to engage in activism, whether through art, social media, or community organizing. Alok's encouragement serves as a reminder that each person has the potential to make a difference, no matter how small their actions may seem.

Conclusion

In conclusion, Alok Vaid-Menon's words of encouragement serve as a powerful reminder of the importance of authenticity, resilience, community, and self-love. Through their activism, Alok inspires individuals to embrace their true selves, support one another, and work toward a more inclusive and equitable world. Their message resonates deeply, inviting us all to join the journey of radical self-acceptance and collective empowerment. As Alok reminds us, "You are enough. You are worthy. You are loved."

The Power of Hope and Resilience

Hope and resilience are two fundamental concepts that intertwine to form the bedrock of activism, particularly in the context of LGBTQ rights. Alok Vaid-Menon embodies these principles through their work, demonstrating that even in the face of adversity, one can cultivate a spirit of perseverance and optimism that inspires others.

Theoretical Framework

At the core of hope lies the concept of agency, as articulated by psychologist Charles Snyder. Snyder's Hope Theory posits that hope consists of three components: goals, pathways, and agency. In the context of LGBTQ activism, these components manifest as follows:
  1. **Goals**: Activists, including Alok, set clear objectives for social change, such as advocating for policy reforms, promoting inclusivity, and dismantling systemic discrimination. 2. **Pathways**: This refers to the strategies and methods employed to achieve these goals. Alok utilizes various platforms, including social media, public speaking, and collaborations with other activists, to disseminate their message and foster community engagement. 3. **Agency**: The belief in one's ability to effect change is crucial. Alok's work exemplifies this belief, as they encourage others to recognize their power in the fight for equality.

Resilience, on the other hand, is defined as the capacity to recover quickly from difficulties. According to the American Psychological Association, resilience involves behaviors, thoughts, and actions that can be learned and developed in anyone. Alok's journey illustrates this concept, as they have faced significant challenges, including societal rejection, hate speech, and personal struggles, yet continue to rise and advocate for their community.

The Role of Hope in Activism

Hope serves as a catalyst for activism. It fuels motivation and drives individuals to take action, even when the odds seem insurmountable. Alok's narrative is filled with instances where hope has transformed despair into determination. For example, during moments of personal crisis, such as experiencing discrimination or facing backlash for their identity, Alok has often turned to the stories of other activists who have triumphed against adversity. This not only reinforces their sense of hope but also fosters a collective spirit among their followers.

Moreover, hope is contagious. When Alok shares their vision for a more inclusive society, they ignite hope in others. This phenomenon can be explained through social cognitive theory, which emphasizes the role of observational learning. As individuals witness Alok's resilience and commitment, they are inspired to cultivate their own hope and resilience, creating a ripple effect throughout the LGBTQ community.

Resilience in the Face of Adversity

Resilience is particularly crucial in the context of LGBTQ activism, where individuals often confront systemic oppression and societal stigma. Alok's experiences highlight the importance of resilience in overcoming challenges. For instance, after facing online harassment and hate speech, Alok has channeled that pain into powerful art and activism, demonstrating how adversity can be transformed into a source of strength.

The concept of post-traumatic growth further elucidates this relationship. According to researchers Tedeschi and Calhoun, individuals who experience trauma can emerge with a greater appreciation for life, improved relationships, and a renewed sense of purpose. Alok exemplifies this growth, as they have used their experiences of marginalization to fuel their advocacy and to educate others about the importance of embracing one's identity.

Examples of Hope and Resilience

Alok's social media presence serves as a beacon of hope for many. Through their viral videos and impactful posts, they share messages of love, acceptance, and resilience. One notable example is Alok's response to a particularly harsh wave of online hate. Instead of succumbing to despair, they created a series of videos that addressed the hate directly, while simultaneously promoting messages of self-love and acceptance. This proactive approach not only showcased their resilience but also inspired countless individuals to stand firm in their identities.

Furthermore, Alok's collaborations with other artists and activists highlight the power of community in fostering resilience. By creating spaces where marginalized voices can be heard, Alok reinforces the idea that collective hope and resilience can lead to significant social change. For instance, their participation in campaigns that amplify the voices of trans people of color exemplifies how hope can be harnessed to uplift entire communities.

Conclusion

In conclusion, the power of hope and resilience is a driving force in Alok Vaid-Menon's activism. By embodying these principles, Alok not only navigates their own challenges but also inspires others to cultivate hope and resilience in their lives. As they continue to advocate for LGBTQ rights, Alok's message remains clear: hope is a powerful tool, and resilience is a necessary companion in the journey toward equality and acceptance. Through their work, Alok demonstrates that even in the darkest times, the light of hope can guide the way forward, creating a brighter future for all.

Alok's Lasting Impact on the World

Alok Vaid-Menon's influence transcends the boundaries of fashion and activism, leaving an indelible mark on society and culture. Their commitment to challenging gender norms and advocating for LGBTQ rights has catalyzed conversations around identity, acceptance, and the very fabric of societal norms. This section explores the multifaceted impact Alok has made on the world, highlighting key areas of influence, theoretical frameworks, and real-world implications of their work.

Theoretical Frameworks

At the core of Alok's activism is the concept of intersectionality, a term coined by Kimberlé Crenshaw in 1989. Intersectionality posits that individuals experience oppression and discrimination not solely based on a single identity factor but through the interplay of various social categories, including race, gender, sexuality, and class. Alok embodies this theory, as their activism is deeply rooted in the understanding that the fight for LGBTQ rights must also address issues of race, class, and other forms of systemic inequality.

The theory of performativity, as articulated by Judith Butler, also plays a crucial role in Alok's influence. Butler argues that gender is not an inherent quality but rather a series of acts and performances shaped by societal expectations. Alok's fashion choices and public persona challenge these normative performances, showcasing the fluidity of gender and encouraging others to embrace their authentic selves. This performative aspect of identity is not just a personal journey for Alok but a broader call to action for society to reconsider rigid gender binaries.

Cultural Shifts and Representation

Alok's impact is evident in the cultural shifts surrounding LGBTQ representation in media and fashion. By unapologetically showcasing their unique style, Alok has become a beacon of hope for many marginalized individuals. Their appearances in high-profile events, collaborations with designers, and presence on social media platforms have disrupted traditional notions of beauty and gender.

One notable example is Alok's participation in the New York Fashion Week, where they walked the runway in bold, expressive outfits that defy conventional gender norms. This visibility not only challenges the fashion industry to be more inclusive but also inspires a generation of designers and models to explore non-binary and gender-fluid expressions. The ripple effect of Alok's presence in such spaces is profound, as it encourages brands to rethink their marketing strategies and embrace diversity.

Empowerment through Art and Activism

Alok's artistic expression serves as a powerful tool for activism. Through spoken word poetry, visual arts, and performance, they convey messages of love, acceptance, and resistance against societal norms. Their art resonates with audiences worldwide, creating a shared space for dialogue and reflection on issues of identity and belonging.

For instance, Alok's poetry often addresses the struggles faced by marginalized communities, weaving personal narratives with broader social critiques. This blend of personal and political not only empowers individuals to share their stories but also fosters a sense of community among those who feel isolated by societal expectations. The transformative power of art in activism is evident in Alok's work, as it serves to educate, inspire, and mobilize individuals toward collective action.

Global Reach and Advocacy

Alok's advocacy extends beyond borders, reaching a global audience through social media and international speaking engagements. Their ability to harness the power of platforms like Instagram and Twitter has allowed them to amplify marginalized voices and create a sense of solidarity among LGBTQ individuals worldwide. The viral nature of Alok's content often sparks discussions that challenge the status quo, addressing issues such as trans rights, racial justice, and mental health.

One significant example of Alok's global impact is their involvement in campaigns advocating for the rights of LGBTQ refugees and immigrants. By highlighting the unique challenges faced by these communities, Alok has brought attention to the intersection of immigration and LGBTQ rights, pushing for policies that promote inclusivity and protection for vulnerable populations.

Lasting Legacy

The legacy of Alok Vaid-Menon is one of empowerment, resilience, and radical self-love. Their work has not only transformed the landscape of LGBTQ activism but has also inspired countless individuals to embrace their identities and advocate for change. As Alok continues to break barriers and challenge societal norms, their message of love and acceptance resonates more than ever, fostering a culture of inclusivity and understanding.

In conclusion, Alok's lasting impact on the world is characterized by a commitment to intersectional activism, a challenge to traditional gender norms, and a profound influence on cultural representation. Their journey serves as a reminder that the fight for equality is ongoing, and through collective action, we can create a more inclusive and accepting society for all.

The world we can create

In envisioning the world we can create, Alok Vaid-Menon challenges us to break free from the confines of traditional norms and embrace a reality where diversity is celebrated, and inclusivity reigns supreme. This vision is not merely aspirational; it is grounded in a theoretical framework that intersects with concepts of social justice, equity, and the radical acceptance of all identities.

At the heart of this vision is the idea of **intersectionality**, a term coined by legal scholar Kimberlé Crenshaw. Intersectionality posits that individuals experience overlapping systems of oppression based on their various identities, such as race, gender, sexuality, and class. Recognizing these intersections allows us to understand the complexity of people's experiences and the unique challenges they face. For Alok, this means advocating for a world where the voices of marginalized communities are amplified and valued, and where systemic barriers to equality are dismantled.

One pressing problem that Alok addresses is the pervasive nature of **discrimination** and **violence** against LGBTQ individuals, particularly those who are also people of color. According to the Human Rights Campaign, transgender individuals, especially trans women of color, face disproportionately high rates of violence and discrimination. In 2020 alone, at least 44 transgender or gender non-conforming people were killed in the United States, highlighting the urgent need for comprehensive policy changes and societal shifts.

To create the world Alok envisions, we must consider the following theoretical frameworks and practical applications:

- **Radical Empathy:** Alok advocates for radical empathy as a foundational principle for change. This involves not only understanding the struggles of others but actively engaging in their experiences. As Alok states, "Empathy is not just about feeling for someone; it's about feeling with them." This approach fosters a sense of community and solidarity, essential for collective action.

- **Community Building:** Creating safe spaces for marginalized communities is crucial. Alok emphasizes the importance of fostering environments where individuals can express their true selves without fear of judgment or violence. This can be achieved through community centers, supportive educational institutions, and inclusive workplaces that prioritize the well-being of all individuals.

- **Art as Activism:** Alok's work exemplifies the power of art as a tool for social change. Through fashion, performance, and visual arts, Alok communicates messages of love, acceptance, and resistance. Art has the unique ability to transcend barriers and connect people on an emotional level, making it a vital component of the activism landscape.

- **Education and Awareness:** Changing societal attitudes requires a concerted effort in education. Alok advocates for incorporating LGBTQ issues into school curricula and promoting discussions around gender and identity. By educating future generations, we can foster a culture of acceptance and understanding, paving the way for a more inclusive society.

- **Policy Reform:** To address systemic discrimination, Alok calls for comprehensive policy changes that protect the rights of LGBTQ individuals. This includes advocating for anti-discrimination laws, healthcare access, and legal recognition of diverse gender identities. Policy reform is essential for ensuring that the rights of marginalized communities are upheld and respected.

The world we can create is one where love triumphs over hate, where differences are celebrated rather than vilified. It is a world where individuals are empowered to embrace their authentic selves without fear of retribution. Alok's vision serves as a beacon of hope, inspiring countless individuals to join the fight for justice and equality.

In conclusion, the world we can create is not a distant dream; it is a tangible reality that can be achieved through collective action, radical empathy, and unwavering commitment to social justice. As Alok reminds us, "The future is not something we enter; the future is something we create." Together, we have the power to shape a world that reflects our highest ideals of love, acceptance, and inclusivity. It is a world where every individual, regardless of their identity, can thrive and contribute to the rich tapestry of humanity.

$$\text{Future} = \text{Empathy} + \text{Community} + \text{Education} + \text{Art} + \text{Policy Reform} \quad (133)$$

Index

-doubt, 222, 324, 351, 358

a, 1–3, 5–8, 11–23, 25–28, 30–35, 37–71, 73–100, 102, 104, 108–118, 121–124, 127–136, 138–140, 142–149, 152–182, 184, 186, 189–202, 204–215, 217, 219–228, 230, 231, 233–256, 258–270, 272–274, 276, 278, 279, 281–288, 290–306, 308–314, 316–349, 351–354, 356–359, 363, 364
ability, 2, 3, 7, 21, 26, 27, 32, 51, 55, 62, 69, 108, 110, 123, 129–131, 135–137, 147, 152, 155, 157, 158, 199, 213, 234, 236, 238, 241, 242, 245, 252, 255, 264, 267, 306, 313, 317, 319–321, 323, 334, 342, 358
abolition, 330
absence, 168, 307
academia, 30–33, 293
acceptance, 3, 8, 13–15, 19, 20, 23, 27, 28, 31, 38, 39, 45–47, 55, 56, 61, 62, 70, 74, 86, 89–94, 97, 98, 102, 109–111, 115–118, 123, 131, 134, 135, 138, 139, 142, 145, 156, 157, 159, 162, 164–167, 171, 174, 176–178, 191, 194, 204–206, 210, 213–215, 217, 220–222, 227, 234–237, 240–244, 248, 255, 258, 260, 261, 264, 283, 293, 300–302, 309, 310, 321, 322, 324, 326, 338, 341, 343–345, 347, 349, 351, 353, 356–358, 363
access, 40, 41, 69, 145, 206, 269, 288, 303, 330
accountability, 44, 55
achievement, 265, 311, 323
acknowledgment, 204, 246, 324
act, 2, 13, 21, 43, 46, 64–66, 77, 89, 92, 114, 117, 179, 181, 182, 227, 238, 251, 258, 266, 274, 288, 293, 344, 347, 351, 356, 358
action, 34, 49, 57, 64, 102, 116, 123,

124, 129, 139, 146, 147,
172, 195, 199, 204, 215,
217, 262, 283, 286, 287,
293, 305, 331, 338, 340,
343, 345, 356, 358
activism, 2, 3, 5, 13, 15, 16, 18, 20,
21, 23, 25, 26, 28, 30–35,
37–40, 44–52, 55, 56, 61,
62, 64, 66, 68–71, 73, 75,
79–81, 84–86, 88, 90,
92–94, 97–102, 108, 110,
114–116, 118, 121–124,
127, 129–140, 142–148,
151, 152, 154–156, 158,
160, 161, 165–167,
170–173, 176, 181–184,
186, 189, 191, 193–200,
202, 204, 206, 208–211,
213, 215–217, 219–222,
227, 229, 231, 236–238,
243, 245, 247–249, 252,
254–256, 258, 260–270,
274, 276, 279, 281–290,
293, 303, 305, 310, 311,
313, 317–338, 340–343,
345, 348, 349, 351–354,
356–359, 363
activist, 6, 8, 13, 28, 32, 39, 44–46,
48, 50, 53, 54, 99, 115,
121, 124, 130, 135, 143,
144, 153, 169, 170,
179–182, 194, 221, 230,
236, 243, 247, 249, 256,
264, 310, 317, 321, 323,
354
actualization, 176, 241
adage, 121
adaptability, 202, 317, 321, 322
adaptation, 123, 135, 137

add, 105
addition, 8, 41, 45, 66, 111, 176,
212, 248, 282, 295, 299
address, 35, 38, 61, 68, 69, 94, 95,
109, 122, 124, 136, 138,
146, 181, 199, 212, 214,
250, 269, 270, 274, 278,
282, 286, 288, 302, 306,
327
admiration, 2, 61
adolescence, 13
adornment, 84
adulthood, 22
adversity, 12–14, 37, 39, 64, 70, 102,
124, 145, 171, 200, 321,
322, 326, 338, 357, 359
advertising, 164
advice, 118
advocacy, 3, 15, 17, 20, 22, 32, 34,
39–41, 46, 47, 51, 53, 61,
65, 68, 70, 75, 79, 80, 82,
84–87, 90, 91, 94, 96, 97,
99, 100, 102, 108–110,
112, 116, 117, 121, 122,
127, 130–132, 135,
144–147, 156–158, 162,
167, 173, 181, 182,
193–195, 200, 204, 210,
211, 214, 215, 217, 221,
222, 230, 233, 235, 236,
241, 242, 258, 266, 269,
270, 273, 278, 282–284,
287, 288, 290, 293, 300,
303, 304, 308, 311,
319–321, 325, 326, 331,
332, 335, 338–340, 346,
357
advocate, 6, 8, 18, 26, 32, 37, 39, 44,
55, 56, 62, 64, 69, 70, 77,

Index

 93, 95, 97, 99, 100, 109, 110, 115, 116, 124, 129, 135, 138, 139, 146–148, 157, 160, 165, 166, 170–172, 191, 197, 198, 200, 206, 208, 210, 213–215, 220–222, 225, 228, 231, 236–238, 247, 261, 263, 264, 274, 278, 281, 282, 289, 295, 297, 301, 303, 310, 313, 314, 318, 319, 321, 327, 332, 337, 340, 347, 354, 357, 358, 363
aesthetic, 1, 26, 38, 55, 81, 94, 148, 151, 256, 259, 260, 266
affection, 343
affirmation, 165
Africa, 96, 282
age, 38, 49, 50, 52, 53, 56, 62, 69, 99, 144, 158, 162, 171, 196, 237, 248, 285, 302, 326
agency, 147, 290
agender, 173
aggression, 89, 189
Albert Bandura, 147
alienation, 31, 74, 175, 304
alignment, 241
allow, 118, 244, 346
allyship, 13, 39, 136, 146, 147, 191, 210, 309, 347
Alok, 1–8, 11–15, 17–23, 25–28, 30–35, 37–39, 41, 43–47, 51–57, 59–67, 69, 70, 73–75, 77–81, 83–86, 88–94, 96–100, 102, 106, 108–113, 115–118, 121–124, 127, 129–136, 138–140, 142–147, 149, 151, 152, 154–172, 174–183, 186, 189–201, 204–206, 208–215, 217, 219–222, 225–227, 231, 234–243, 247–267, 270, 276, 278, 281–283, 285–287, 289, 290, 293, 301–303, 309–311, 313, 314, 317–341, 343–349, 351, 353–358, 363, 364
Alok Vaid-Menon, 1, 12, 16, 18, 26, 28, 30, 33, 37, 41, 42, 44, 45, 48–50, 52, 53, 61, 64, 65, 68, 73, 75, 77, 80–82, 86, 89, 91, 93–95, 97, 100, 108, 110, 113, 115, 118, 121, 130, 133, 138, 142, 144, 148, 153, 154, 159–161, 163, 165, 170, 173, 179, 182, 189, 194, 195, 198, 200, 202, 204, 208, 210, 211, 213, 215, 217, 219, 230, 234, 241, 245, 247, 249, 252, 254, 256, 260, 262, 263, 265, 270, 273, 274, 276, 281, 284, 288, 289, 293, 298, 301, 303, 304, 306, 311, 316, 317, 320, 325, 329, 332, 334, 343, 345, 352–354, 356, 359, 363
Alok Vaid-Menon's, 3, 20, 23, 25, 28, 30, 32–34, 37, 39–41, 45, 47, 56, 62, 64, 66, 70, 75, 80, 84, 86, 88, 90, 93, 97, 100, 102, 104, 110, 112, 114, 116–118, 124, 127, 129, 132, 135, 137, 140, 142, 146, 147, 152,

154, 156, 158, 162, 165, 167–169, 172, 175, 177, 179, 191–193, 198, 204, 206, 210, 213, 215, 222, 227, 236, 238, 240, 243, 249, 251, 253, 255, 256, 258, 260, 265, 267, 278, 283–285, 287, 290, 300, 303, 308, 309, 311, 314, 322, 323, 325, 327, 329, 331, 336, 338, 341, 345, 349, 356
Alok Vaid-Menon, 62
ambiguity, 176
amplification, 66, 272, 274, 340
Andy Warhol, 337
anonymity, 44, 55
antidote, 222, 358
anxiety, 31, 44, 143, 174, 241
appeal, 69, 151
appearance, 17, 61, 81, 93, 250, 266
approach, 2, 3, 5, 6, 27, 28, 32, 34, 37–39, 45, 52, 54–56, 63–65, 69, 70, 74, 77, 80, 82, 84, 86, 95–97, 99, 100, 108–110, 124, 130, 132, 133, 135, 137–139, 142, 144, 146, 147, 151, 154, 156, 161, 163, 165, 172, 173, 181, 193, 196–199, 205, 209, 210, 212, 217, 227, 235, 241, 249, 251–253, 258, 259, 263, 265–267, 269, 270, 278, 279, 281, 283, 284, 287, 290, 292, 293, 301, 311, 313, 314, 317, 318, 320, 321, 329, 331, 333–337, 341, 345, 346, 349, 351, 358
appropriation, 159, 246, 257
area, 39, 330, 331
arena, 152
armor, 14
array, 1, 11, 256, 264, 319
art, 1, 19, 37–39, 45–47, 49, 65, 68, 92, 108, 110, 112, 122, 123, 133, 139, 142, 154–157, 163, 165–167, 172, 176, 193, 217, 221, 235, 238, 245–256, 258, 260–268, 281, 288, 313, 327, 331, 334–337, 340, 358
artist, 170, 247, 249, 264
artistry, 161, 214
artwork, 248, 253
aspect, 61, 65, 75, 90, 106, 112, 117, 146, 147, 164, 167, 190, 193, 210, 219, 221, 225, 235, 236, 249, 251, 258, 274, 279
aspiration, 111, 354
assertion, 93, 165, 191
assistance, 277, 330
assumption, 233
assuredness, 3
asylum, 278, 330
atmosphere, 131, 248
attention, 2, 6, 22, 44, 55, 62, 69, 109, 131, 144, 145, 157, 167, 215, 235, 259, 267, 283, 330
attire, 15, 17, 46, 81, 260
attractiveness, 73
attribute, 113, 250
audience, 5, 18, 19, 22, 27, 38, 41, 50, 52, 54, 69, 83, 116,

Index 371

153, 155, 158, 159, 162, 171, 181, 196, 214, 235, 248–251, 253, 266, 321, 324, 331, 345
Audre Lorde, 121
authenticity, 5, 7, 13, 18, 54, 56, 81, 84, 91–93, 134, 135, 139, 151–154, 164, 174, 175, 190, 215, 238, 240–244, 246, 252, 254, 259, 264, 319, 324, 325, 334, 336, 356, 357
author, 321
authoritarianism, 343
autonomy, 226
awakening, 28, 30
awareness, 20, 28, 34, 38, 41, 46, 57, 69, 122, 129, 145, 147, 160, 166, 175, 202, 206, 233, 235, 253, 261, 277, 278, 281, 291, 302, 322, 329, 340

backdrop, 14, 241
background, 170, 172, 354
backlash, 5, 12, 17, 20, 39, 44, 51, 60, 61, 65, 66, 70, 89, 99, 136, 155, 156, 160, 192, 195, 238, 244, 254, 256, 262, 319, 323, 324
balance, 147
balancing, 179–182, 255
barrier, 65, 251
basis, 64
bathroom, 339, 351
battle, 45, 143
battleground, 5, 80, 142
beacon, 1, 26, 30, 40, 78, 86, 89, 91, 102, 110, 115, 144, 177, 193, 198, 205, 213, 221, 227, 238, 241, 256, 283, 319, 341, 343, 345, 356, 364
beauty, 3, 8, 11, 15, 17, 18, 22, 44, 46, 59, 60, 73–75, 77, 78, 80–82, 85–89, 91–94, 100, 116, 122, 138–140, 152, 157, 160, 162, 164, 169, 172, 192, 202, 205, 206, 209, 210, 226, 236, 238, 241, 248, 251, 252, 258–260, 263, 265–267, 323, 329, 337, 340, 345, 348, 349
bedrock, 359
beginning, 1, 2, 14
behavior, 250
being, 5, 6, 44, 94, 99, 112, 118, 144, 147, 159, 160, 177, 179, 182, 186, 195, 220, 226, 236, 242, 247, 253, 309, 324, 326, 327, 349, 352, 354
belief, 1, 2, 21, 26, 31, 40, 97, 124, 140, 145, 147, 148, 200, 220, 226, 227, 311, 339, 340, 343, 344, 354
bell, 138, 168, 176, 191, 338, 344
belonging, 54, 90, 111, 124, 139, 147, 153, 159, 162, 164, 169, 178, 193, 196, 198, 205, 221, 239, 252, 258, 264, 300, 302, 313, 331, 335, 336, 338, 345, 349, 354, 357
bigender, 173
binary, 1, 2, 18–21, 33, 34, 37, 40, 42, 43, 46, 48, 54, 62, 67,

73–75, 77–79, 81–83, 85, 89, 92, 94, 113, 115, 146, 152, 155, 157, 161, 163–166, 169, 173, 174, 176, 177, 179, 182, 189, 192, 198, 205, 213, 220, 221, 223, 224, 226, 228, 233–237, 239, 241–244, 247, 248, 250, 252, 253, 258, 264, 265, 267, 293, 310, 321, 323, 327, 335, 348, 350
birth, 112, 173, 223
blend, 2, 15, 27, 37, 46, 49, 68, 69, 74, 77, 98, 110, 122, 123, 158, 161, 162, 184, 192, 252, 266, 267, 281, 335, 340
blending, 166, 195, 208, 301
blueprint, 202
body, 15, 69, 78, 81, 82, 93–95, 122, 123, 139, 159, 162, 169, 209, 249, 250, 253, 263, 314
boundary, 250
box, 115, 192
brand, 6, 79, 82, 148, 160
bravery, 92
breadth, 58
breaking, 8, 26, 81, 82, 89–91, 165, 167, 213, 219, 251
breeding, 62
bridge, 45, 121, 181, 306
Bruner, 304
buffer, 27, 63
building, 32, 41, 52, 53, 55, 136, 139, 147, 182, 193, 196–198, 200, 230, 278, 326, 336, 340, 349, 357

bullying, 14, 21, 35, 111, 116, 171, 175, 194, 237
burnout, 147, 195, 197, 324, 354
business, 82
Butler, 8, 18, 89, 112, 223, 234, 338

call, 80, 93, 115, 116, 123, 140, 172, 204, 238, 241, 283, 287, 293, 343, 346, 347, 354, 356, 358
calling, 28, 34, 96, 209
camaraderie, 13
camera, 27
campaign, 6, 81, 160, 282, 283, 351
campus, 176
candidness, 51
canvas, 1, 12, 15, 16, 69, 247, 263, 265
capability, 281
capacity, 282, 321
capital, 25, 49
care, 55, 99, 122, 147, 160, 182, 186, 195, 197, 235, 351–354
career, 6, 78
Carl Rogers', 176, 241
case, 100, 136, 194
cast, 81
catalyst, 2, 21, 47, 49, 61, 62, 83, 84, 147, 163, 166, 194, 222, 254, 256, 261, 262, 264, 266, 293, 311, 324
categorization, 161, 192, 234
cause, 45, 57, 62, 66, 102, 124, 136, 146
celebration, 3, 22, 74, 94, 139, 176, 215, 222, 245
celebrity, 337
censorship, 155, 262
center, 211

Index 373

challenge, 1–3, 11, 16–18, 20, 26, 31, 32, 34, 37, 39, 41, 43–46, 56, 64, 68–70, 74, 75, 77, 79, 81, 82, 86, 90, 97, 108, 112, 113, 116, 118, 122, 123, 136, 139, 142–144, 146, 148, 154, 156, 157, 159, 162, 164, 168, 169, 172, 173, 179, 200, 202, 205, 206, 208, 210, 213, 215, 217, 220, 222, 224, 225, 235–238, 244, 245, 247, 249, 250, 252, 254–256, 258, 259, 261–265, 267, 281, 292, 295, 301, 303, 304, 309, 310, 313, 314, 319, 321, 322, 329, 338, 340, 344–347, 351, 356, 358, 363
champion, 100, 172, 293
chance, 357
change, 5, 6, 8, 17, 21, 26, 28, 32, 35, 37–39, 44–47, 49, 52, 56, 62, 64, 68–70, 77, 83, 84, 86, 90, 97, 99, 100, 102, 108, 122–124, 129, 135, 137, 139, 140, 146–149, 154–157, 159, 160, 163, 166, 169, 172, 191, 195, 204, 205, 209, 210, 213–215, 217, 220, 222, 236, 238, 247, 249, 251, 254, 256, 258, 260–262, 264–268, 277, 278, 282–284, 287, 290, 291, 293, 300, 303, 311, 313, 314, 319, 321, 328, 331–335, 338, 340, 341, 343, 345, 347, 351, 352, 354, 356, 358, 363
channel, 181
chapter, 2, 13, 219, 317
charge, 95
childhood, 1, 326
choice, 192, 220, 252
Christian Siriano, 163
cisgender, 34, 65, 67, 105, 268, 269
civilization, 260
clarion, 93, 241
clash, 253
class, 19, 32, 33, 38, 115, 117, 133, 139, 144, 199, 200, 206, 220, 226, 254, 268, 272, 329, 330
classification, 113
classroom, 305, 313
climate, 283
clothing, 1, 2, 4–6, 8, 14, 18, 21, 23, 42, 77, 79, 148, 157, 167, 206, 235, 237, 244, 249, 263
coalition, 136
collaborate, 6
collaboration, 6, 32, 34, 67, 69, 79, 82, 85, 123, 134, 137, 147, 148, 157, 160, 163, 196, 204, 213, 214, 249, 255, 256, 258, 259, 264, 266, 283, 285, 287, 319, 324, 330, 340, 341
college, 176
color, 13, 17, 32, 34, 38, 40, 44, 65–67, 81, 85, 94, 106, 115, 143, 145, 147, 151, 174, 215, 226, 247, 269, 270, 283, 287, 290, 312, 330, 335, 337, 355

combat, 63, 103, 144, 160, 191, 192, 235, 307, 315
combination, 41, 64, 79, 139, 268, 298
commentary, 37, 69, 92, 123, 146, 158, 248, 265, 335
commentator, 15
commercialization, 46, 156
commitment, 5, 18, 22, 30, 37, 45, 47, 51, 66, 85, 91, 96, 100, 102, 104, 110, 112, 118, 122, 124, 132, 136, 144, 146, 147, 163, 172, 177, 186, 193–196, 200, 205, 209, 210, 213, 217, 243, 245, 254, 265, 278, 282, 283, 287, 288, 297, 302, 319, 322, 324, 326, 330, 331, 334–338, 340, 343, 345, 347, 352
commodification, 47, 244, 246, 254, 256
communication, 129, 196, 252, 260, 302, 304
community, 5, 13, 15, 18, 21, 27, 28, 30, 34, 37, 39, 41, 44, 45, 48, 49, 52–54, 56, 61–66, 76, 78, 85, 86, 90, 91, 93, 94, 97, 99, 108–111, 116–118, 123, 124, 129, 130, 132, 133, 135, 137–139, 144–148, 151, 153–156, 158–160, 166, 167, 172, 176, 178, 179, 182–184, 186, 193, 195–200, 204, 212, 214, 215, 220, 222, 230, 237, 238, 242, 244, 249, 251, 253, 254, 258, 264, 266, 269, 276–278, 283, 287, 288, 292, 294, 300, 302, 308, 313, 318–320, 323, 326, 327, 330, 333–336, 338, 340, 341, 349, 356–358
compassion, 346, 356, 358
competition, 285, 329
complexity, 33, 136, 152, 170, 173, 177, 179, 192, 231, 240, 248, 311, 327, 337
component, 26, 41, 56, 66, 88, 195, 198
comprehension, 160
concept, 19, 26, 32, 33, 40, 44, 73, 75, 77, 90, 93, 112, 115, 117, 138, 147, 158, 165, 173, 220, 223, 226, 227, 230, 231, 234, 236, 241, 243, 250, 258, 268, 270, 288, 314, 318, 320, 323, 338, 343, 345, 346, 349, 351, 352
conception, 75, 192
conclusion, 3, 18, 23, 28, 30, 33, 34, 39, 45, 47, 62, 70, 75, 77, 80, 84, 86, 88, 90, 94, 97, 100, 116, 124, 129, 135, 137, 140, 142, 144, 146, 147, 152, 154, 156, 160, 162, 165, 167, 169, 175, 177, 179, 182, 195, 197, 204, 206, 213, 215, 217, 222, 227, 234, 236, 238, 243, 245, 247, 253, 256, 258, 260, 262, 265, 267, 274, 278, 283, 285, 293, 303, 306, 311, 314, 320, 322, 325, 327, 329, 331,

Index 375

334, 336, 338, 343, 345, 349, 354, 356
conduit, 46
confidence, 3, 7, 26–28, 112
confine, 22, 75, 90, 356
conflict, 27, 60, 174
conformity, 31, 34, 37, 90, 222, 250, 252, 310, 321, 326
confusion, 176
congruence, 241
connection, 54, 116, 118, 182, 191, 248, 249, 266, 306, 318, 344, 345, 351, 352, 357
conscientization, 343
consciousness, 86, 204, 291
construct, 8, 78, 86, 173, 189, 223, 231, 304
construction, 223, 224, 304
constructionism, 75
constructivism, 304
content, 49, 52, 54, 55, 65, 112, 158, 248, 249, 266, 295, 304, 306
context, 26, 33, 82, 137, 148, 152, 163, 183, 211, 220, 245, 260, 290, 304, 320, 330, 335, 343, 352, 359
control, 63, 190
controversy, 51, 52, 59, 61, 62, 254, 262
conversation, 3, 61, 189, 234, 324, 331, 346
core, 115, 131, 134, 146, 200, 220, 227, 250, 260, 286, 319, 327, 354, 356
cornerstone, 266, 317, 320, 335, 343, 351
correlation, 214, 233
costume, 248

counseling, 31, 118
counter, 131
countermeasure, 346
courage, 7, 27, 89, 92, 139, 338
creation, 117, 206, 210, 310
creative, 46, 47, 142, 159, 217, 247–249, 304, 313, 326, 340, 351, 352
creativity, 1, 6, 13, 23, 45, 56, 68, 84, 86, 92, 121, 122, 124, 152, 247, 249, 254, 256, 264, 268, 278, 325
creator, 77
crisis, 303
criticism, 2, 17, 25, 27, 61, 70, 155
critique, 17, 23, 46, 93, 100, 189, 330
crucible, 12
cry, 358
cultivation, 196, 205
culture, 1, 8, 17, 19, 23, 38, 47, 92–94, 96, 116, 118, 145, 148, 156, 158, 162, 164–167, 169, 174–176, 200, 205, 206, 208–210, 220–222, 228, 245, 252, 258, 260, 264, 265, 267, 283, 302, 308, 311, 320, 337, 343, 346, 354, 356, 363
cup, 147
curricula, 39, 111, 118, 174, 214, 287, 290, 292, 295, 297, 301, 303, 306, 307, 309, 313, 328
curriculum, 31, 32, 292, 296–298, 304, 312

dance, 42, 263

David Bowie, 8, 148
debate, 61
decision, 108
decrease, 292
decriminalization, 282
dedication, 144–146, 204, 265, 319, 336, 340, 341
defiance, 12, 13, 15, 17, 117, 255, 258, 356
definition, 85, 88, 94, 139, 162, 176
delivery, 248
deluge, 62
demand, 152
demeanor, 26
depression, 44, 143, 174, 241
depth, 153, 154, 172, 247
design, 79, 80
designer, 81, 163
desire, 8, 171, 176, 236, 255
destination, 92, 127, 176, 221, 358
determinant, 223
determination, 21, 124, 144, 171, 237, 321
development, 309, 317, 320, 321
deviation, 89
dialogue, 19, 20, 47, 51, 61, 62, 67, 69, 95, 96, 117, 130–132, 162, 174, 212, 214, 235, 238, 242, 249, 251, 252, 255, 262–264, 293, 302, 310, 319, 321, 322, 324, 331, 336, 343, 345, 346, 351
dichotomy, 173
difference, 348, 349, 358
difficulty, 45
dilution, 131, 134, 246
direction, 45

disadvantage, 82, 105, 117, 200, 268, 354
discomfort, 89, 250
discourse, 20, 31, 51, 66, 94, 96, 135, 159, 164, 167, 173, 189, 191, 214, 227, 230, 234, 244, 262, 293, 306, 318, 336
discovery, 3, 12, 30, 92, 157, 175–177, 194, 220, 221, 226, 227, 238, 241, 243, 253, 305, 310, 318, 324–327, 358
discrimination, 5, 19, 20, 31–35, 39, 40, 44, 45, 62, 74, 76, 82, 89, 96, 97, 99, 100, 105, 106, 108, 109, 115, 117, 124, 135, 136, 138, 143–146, 158–160, 167, 171, 174, 175, 179, 191–194, 199, 200, 202, 204, 206, 209, 214, 220, 226, 233, 235, 237, 244, 248, 261, 268–270, 278, 279, 282, 283, 286, 288, 314, 321, 326, 327, 330, 338, 339, 341, 344, 350, 354, 355, 357
discussion, 96
disinformation, 342
disparity, 105, 106
display, 80
disruption, 89
dissatisfaction, 94
dissemination, 162, 210, 285
distress, 302
diversity, 3, 6, 17, 22, 26, 31, 34, 39, 41, 45, 61, 65, 73, 75, 77, 78, 80–82, 85, 87, 91, 105,

Index

109, 110, 118, 123, 136, 139, 152, 156, 157, 159, 160, 167, 169, 172, 175, 178, 193, 200, 202, 206, 210, 213, 222, 225, 226, 238, 240, 245, 248, 249, 251, 252, 255, 270, 283, 293, 295, 297, 303, 304, 308, 312, 316, 320, 323, 329, 335, 343, 345, 348, 349, 357, 363
divide, 116
division, 245, 342, 347, 356
domain, 127, 194
dominance, 189
door, 44
doubt, 176, 181, 222, 324, 351, 358
down, 26, 81, 82, 100, 142, 191, 215, 251, 258, 278, 325
drag, 252
dream, 140, 354–356
dress, 192, 310
dressing, 1, 8, 21, 326
drive, 241, 291, 352
duality, 6, 61, 149
dynamic, 20, 49, 61, 130, 135, 138, 148, 195, 198, 211, 221, 236, 243, 247, 249, 258, 301, 313, 326, 341

educate, 39, 55, 136, 147, 249, 301, 335, 340, 347
education, 20, 30, 31, 37, 41, 51, 53, 61, 97, 100, 102, 104, 105, 111, 112, 118, 145–147, 171, 193, 198–200, 205, 206, 209, 210, 217, 221, 282, 283, 287, 290, 291, 293, 296, 298, 300, 301, 303, 304, 306, 311, 313, 314, 316, 320–322, 341, 343, 348, 354
effect, 28, 52, 144, 146, 159, 169, 204, 213, 214, 255, 258, 314, 334, 351
effectiveness, 214, 313, 354
efficacy, 26, 147
effort, 41, 118, 291, 300, 345, 356
element, 37
embrace, 1, 2, 6, 11, 13, 17, 18, 21–23, 26, 28, 37, 39, 41, 46, 47, 50, 56, 61, 62, 70, 74, 75, 79, 82, 84, 86, 88, 91, 93–95, 97, 98, 100, 109, 112, 115, 116, 123, 124, 135, 137, 142, 145, 152, 155–157, 159, 160, 162, 164–167, 169, 172, 179, 190–192, 195, 200, 206, 210, 214, 219–222, 225, 227, 235, 236, 238–243, 245, 248, 249, 252, 254, 255, 258–260, 264, 265, 267, 269, 293, 297, 303, 310, 314, 319–322, 327, 329, 331, 334, 335, 337, 341, 343–345, 349, 351, 356–358, 363, 364
embracing, 3, 7, 15, 19, 20, 26, 34, 46, 62, 77, 78, 90, 93, 115, 124, 132, 138, 140, 147, 161, 176, 177, 193, 195, 205, 219–221, 226, 227, 237, 238, 242, 243, 248, 258–260, 270, 285, 287, 295, 306, 316, 324, 325, 327, 329, 338, 343,

347–349, 356
emergence, 234
empathy, 43, 104, 145, 160, 164, 167, 190, 191, 204, 235, 248, 266, 278, 290, 292, 293, 298, 302–304, 309, 320, 324, 329, 331, 343, 345–347, 356
emphasis, 97, 221, 222, 243, 251, 283, 336, 357
employment, 41, 99, 105, 145, 209, 339, 348
empowerment, 5, 21, 28, 31, 46, 55, 62, 65, 79, 84, 91, 97, 108–110, 123, 138, 139, 146, 147, 174, 182, 198, 210, 213, 214, 222, 227, 236, 241, 247, 251, 264, 278, 279, 281, 302, 311, 340, 345, 357, 358, 363
encounter, 14, 44, 45, 108, 145, 192, 226, 233, 268, 284, 288, 347
encouragement, 8, 311, 356–358
endeavor, 30, 56, 86, 90, 146, 197, 200, 210, 243, 290, 317, 318, 326, 357
energy, 352
enforce, 220, 225, 237, 310
enforcement, 105
engagement, 18, 30, 41, 50, 54, 56, 63, 69, 98, 132, 146, 151, 153, 157, 158, 172, 181, 193, 195, 197, 204, 214, 251, 276, 278, 288, 303–305, 313, 319, 323, 332, 334, 336, 340, 341
ensemble, 17, 78, 260, 266
entertainment, 47, 148, 149, 163–165, 167
environment, 2, 12, 17, 21, 27, 31, 32, 39, 40, 43, 45, 63, 65, 93, 102, 104, 131, 147, 163, 175, 176, 212, 214, 217, 279, 297, 298, 300, 302, 306, 308, 310, 312, 314, 316, 322, 340, 346
equality, 30, 39, 41, 45, 66, 70, 97, 100, 102, 110, 121, 124, 138, 142, 148, 198, 200, 202, 204, 210, 213–215, 251, 270, 278, 281, 293, 297, 319, 325, 329, 335, 339–341, 358, 364
equation, 18, 25–27, 29, 31–33, 55, 60, 65, 69–71, 79, 80, 84, 89, 90, 105, 113, 133, 136, 138–140, 143, 148, 149, 154, 156–158, 165, 170, 171, 173, 175, 201, 213–215, 225–228, 232, 233, 237, 245, 252, 263, 264, 273, 286, 291, 292, 298, 301–303, 312–314, 325–327, 335, 337–339, 341, 348, 354
equilibrium, 179
equity, 138, 274, 318, 331, 363
era, 102
erasure, 65, 233, 235
essence, 33, 84, 93, 127, 148, 160, 219, 238, 241, 246, 255, 321, 325, 356
establishment, 48, 63, 206, 223, 302, 310, 311
esteem, 94, 205, 310
ethos, 94, 256
Eve Kosofsky Sedgwick, 176

event, 17, 61, 181, 260
evolution, 23, 56, 82, 121, 124, 129, 177, 221, 243, 317, 323, 341
examination, 112, 244
examining, 65, 223, 250, 272
example, 27, 33, 34, 38, 41, 42, 45, 46, 55, 66, 69, 70, 76, 79, 81, 86, 92, 97, 106, 111, 116, 118, 122, 123, 130, 136, 139, 146–148, 159, 160, 164, 169, 174, 181, 191, 192, 206, 209, 214, 217, 227, 235, 248, 249, 252, 253, 255, 259, 262, 266, 269, 278, 282, 283, 286, 287, 301, 310, 321, 323, 324, 327, 330, 331, 335, 339, 340
exception, 1, 12, 329
exchange, 70, 251
exclusion, 74, 95, 171, 192, 228, 269, 348
exercise, 301, 352
exhaustion, 147
existence, 93, 236, 241, 298, 357, 358
experience, 2, 13, 28, 30, 31, 33, 34, 40, 44, 58, 65, 75, 82, 89, 90, 102, 105, 107, 122, 133, 138, 143, 154, 175, 176, 182, 192, 206, 220, 221, 226, 234–237, 248, 251, 265, 268, 272, 278, 286, 297, 307, 308, 313, 318, 324, 325, 327, 337, 345
experimentation, 12, 193, 237
exploitation, 244

exploration, 2, 3, 12, 13, 172, 173, 176, 179, 182, 184, 226, 251, 252, 326, 327, 337
expression, 1–3, 5, 7, 8, 11, 13–23, 25, 27, 37, 39–42, 46, 47, 55, 61, 73, 75–81, 84–86, 89, 91, 92, 98, 110, 114, 122, 124, 132, 134, 139, 142, 146, 148, 156–158, 163–167, 172, 174, 176, 177, 181, 191, 193, 202, 206, 209, 217, 219, 220, 222, 226, 227, 235, 237, 238, 241–245, 247–252, 254, 256, 258, 260–268, 301, 313, 319, 323, 326, 331, 334, 335, 337, 340, 345, 348, 352, 356, 358
eye, 180

fabric, 18, 20, 89, 270
facade, 7
face, 13, 20, 27, 32, 33, 37, 39, 40, 45, 50, 51, 62, 64, 65, 70, 76, 79, 87, 89, 91, 94, 96, 97, 102, 108, 110, 117, 124, 136, 145, 146, 155, 171, 173, 174, 191, 195, 197, 199, 226, 235, 241, 243, 254, 262, 269, 273, 279, 286, 291, 299, 302, 312, 322, 324, 326, 330, 332, 335, 341, 348, 354, 355, 357, 359
faculty, 32, 293
family, 8, 63, 89, 92, 116, 170, 175, 195, 313
fascination, 1
fashion, 1–8, 11–23, 25, 26, 28, 37,

38, 40–42, 46, 49, 50, 53,
55, 61, 62, 68, 69, 73,
75–86, 88–90, 92–94,
108, 112, 115, 122, 133,
139, 148, 149, 152, 153,
155–158, 160–167,
169–172, 176, 180, 189,
190, 192, 205–210,
213–215, 217, 219, 227,
230, 235, 237, 244–249,
252–256, 258–263,
265–267, 281, 310, 317,
320, 323, 326, 331,
333–335, 337, 338, 340,
348, 349, 351
fear, 31, 42, 65, 76, 86, 93, 95, 102,
109, 115–118, 123, 142,
190, 193, 200, 206, 220,
241, 243, 248, 283, 310,
314, 341, 346, 357, 364
feature, 62, 79, 82, 85, 116, 149,
162, 249, 278
feedback, 324
feeling, 117, 295
female, 33, 173, 192, 228, 234–236,
243
femininity, 1, 4, 8, 12, 77, 161, 190,
223, 227, 248, 252, 322
feminism, 189, 191, 335
feminist, 40, 46, 93, 136, 171, 189,
191, 250, 254, 256, 331
field, 249
fight, 30, 35, 37, 39, 45, 62, 70, 97,
99, 100, 102, 108, 110,
124, 127, 129, 134–136,
138–140, 146–148, 160,
195, 198, 200, 202, 204,
208, 210, 213–215, 217,
251, 255, 256, 270, 278,
281, 288, 301, 318, 319,
329, 331, 335, 336, 340,
341, 349, 354, 364
figure, 3, 18, 68, 133, 143, 161, 163,
170, 173, 179, 189, 195,
213, 219, 221, 234, 258,
276, 281, 293, 324, 329,
334
film, 159, 164, 166, 205
fire, 35
flair, 59
flamboyance, 259
flexibility, 182
fluid, 2, 8, 12, 18, 42, 46, 73, 75, 77,
115, 163, 164, 166, 173,
176, 182, 192, 193, 200,
206, 213, 220, 225, 231,
233, 235–237, 241, 244,
258, 338
fluidity, 8, 15, 37, 40, 61, 69, 74, 81,
123, 149, 155, 159, 164,
166, 169, 173, 176,
190–193, 220, 221, 223,
228, 234, 236–238, 243,
248, 250, 253, 255, 263,
265, 295, 321, 323, 327
focus, 34, 39, 41, 65, 85, 86, 97, 118,
122, 136, 197, 278, 287,
290, 318
following, 18, 33, 60, 62, 69, 158,
183, 336, 348, 354, 363
force, 62, 138, 154, 160, 208, 260,
304, 345, 347
forefront, 44, 115, 157, 204, 230,
273, 303, 319
form, 1, 2, 5, 17, 18, 21, 22, 37, 46,
64, 75, 81, 138, 149, 155,
165, 167, 176, 190, 209,
227, 235, 237, 258, 260,

Index 381

265, 304, 326, 334, 340, 357, 359
formation, 148, 172, 205, 310
formula, 50
foster, 32, 90, 92, 93, 111, 118, 129, 137, 145, 156, 163, 175, 184, 193, 210, 234, 245, 249, 258, 283, 292, 296, 300, 304, 319, 336, 341, 343, 349, 351
fostering, 23, 26, 27, 32, 37, 41, 47–49, 54, 62, 66, 69, 70, 77, 86, 90, 93–96, 102, 104, 116–118, 123, 140, 145, 147, 153, 154, 158–160, 163, 164, 167, 169, 172, 174, 193, 197, 200, 202, 210, 212, 213, 217, 220–222, 235, 236, 238, 239, 242, 244, 247, 248, 253, 255, 258, 262, 264, 266, 269, 270, 278, 282, 283, 285, 290, 291, 293, 298, 300–303, 306, 308, 310, 314, 316, 320, 322–324, 328, 331, 334–336, 338, 340, 347, 349, 356, 357, 363
foundation, 105, 139
fragmentation, 285
framework, 12, 33, 34, 37, 64, 81, 115, 133, 206, 220, 226, 228, 254, 268, 274, 286, 288, 293, 363
freedom, 200, 225, 254, 262, 314, 344
Freire, 343, 346
Frida Kahlo, 337
front, 27, 64, 285

fuel, 5, 25, 99, 202
function, 89, 107, 201, 228, 273, 312, 325, 327, 337, 339
funding, 144, 262
fundraising, 62, 144
fusion, 1, 166, 258, 260
future, 2, 7, 8, 13, 20, 25, 30, 32, 35, 39, 41, 52, 64, 66, 71, 80, 82, 88, 91, 95, 109, 110, 115, 116, 118, 124, 132, 135, 138–140, 142, 160, 163, 167, 191, 198–200, 202, 204–206, 214, 215, 217, 220, 222, 228, 234, 238, 243–245, 248, 249, 257, 260, 265, 267, 268, 270, 274, 288, 293, 301, 303, 311, 317–319, 328, 329, 332, 334, 336, 338, 340–343, 347

gap, 259
garment, 61
gatekeeping, 17
gay, 32, 269
gender, 1–4, 6, 8, 12, 13, 15, 18–21, 23, 26–28, 30, 31, 33–35, 37–46, 49, 55, 59, 61, 62, 68, 69, 74, 76–79, 81, 82, 85, 86, 89, 90, 92–94, 96, 99, 102, 106–115, 117, 118, 121–123, 130–133, 136, 138, 139, 142–144, 147–149, 152, 155–159, 161–169, 171–177, 182, 189–195, 197–200, 205, 206, 209, 210, 213, 214, 217, 219–228, 230, 231, 233–239, 241, 243–245,

247–255, 258, 260, 261, 263, 265, 266, 268–270, 272, 274, 276, 278, 282, 286, 288, 293, 295, 301, 305, 306, 309, 310, 317, 321–327, 329, 332, 334–338, 340, 343–345, 349–351, 354
genderqueer, 173, 228, 234
generation, 80, 86, 91, 93, 100, 112, 135, 140, 146, 152, 156, 159, 161, 164, 165, 167, 200, 210, 211, 213, 236, 263, 283, 290, 303, 317, 319, 320, 329, 331, 340, 343
genesis, 35
globe, 117, 163, 206, 293, 309
goal, 147, 198, 288, 314
grace, 3, 27, 60, 124
ground, 62
grounding, 116, 256
groundwork, 2, 8, 13, 30, 35, 206
group, 13, 81, 147, 349
growth, 32, 128, 129, 197, 212, 213, 306, 314, 317, 319, 321–324, 332, 334, 357
guest, 292
guidance, 111, 198, 210, 211, 302, 321

hallmark, 1
hand, 62, 70
harassment, 31, 39, 44, 45, 55, 63–65, 70, 99, 117, 124, 143, 144, 155, 160, 326
harm, 159, 349
harness, 264, 306, 323

hate, 34, 44, 55, 60, 62–64, 99, 109, 143, 160, 319, 321, 324, 344, 346, 347, 364
hatred, 356
head, 92, 153, 159, 344
healing, 262, 264, 313, 346
health, 44, 55, 94, 99, 111, 116, 117, 122, 143, 144, 147, 160, 167, 171, 174, 186, 195, 197, 232, 233, 235, 242, 269, 277, 278, 296, 302, 303, 324, 349, 351, 352, 354
healthcare, 34, 40, 41, 105, 118, 145, 209, 269, 330, 339, 348, 351
heart, 115, 124, 138, 189, 222, 223, 234, 236, 263, 268, 270, 343
help, 302, 304, 313
heritage, 15, 20, 149, 162, 170, 172, 174, 259
heteronormativity, 241
hierarchy, 190
highlight, 17, 44, 86, 92, 94, 115, 143, 174, 239, 242, 269, 281, 284, 293, 304, 313, 321, 331, 339, 357
hinge, 245
history, 121, 248, 261, 287, 296, 301, 309, 312
home, 330
homelessness, 66
homogenization, 17
homophobia, 145, 253, 355
homosexuality, 140, 282
honesty, 247, 318
honor, 81, 193, 238, 308
hope, 26, 30, 91, 95, 102, 110, 111,

Index 383

    121, 147, 177, 193, 205,
    213, 221, 227, 238, 241,
    256, 278, 283, 311, 319,
    341, 345, 356, 364
host, 184
hostility, 17, 51, 61, 89, 136, 144,
    145, 238, 321, 324, 346
housing, 99, 105
human, 75, 115, 122, 131, 135, 140,
    154, 181, 193, 202, 206,
    221, 234, 260, 265, 283,
    330
humor, 60, 69, 122, 123, 131, 136,
    155, 158, 193, 335, 345,
    351

icon, 1–3, 6, 8, 13–15, 22, 23, 28,
    50, 115, 169, 170, 180,
    230, 247, 310, 317
idea, 2, 26, 77, 79, 92, 113, 115, 138,
    147, 206, 215, 225–227,
    237, 241, 242, 251, 265,
    284, 320, 326, 331, 335,
    340, 343, 344, 348, 357
ideal, 308, 316, 356
identification, 226, 227, 230, 234
identity, 1–3, 5, 7, 8, 12–14, 17–21,
    23, 26–28, 30, 31, 33–35,
    37, 38, 40–42, 44, 46–49,
    51, 53, 55, 58, 59, 61, 62,
    65, 68, 69, 77, 78, 82,
    89–92, 96, 99, 102, 105,
    107, 108, 110, 111, 113,
    115, 118, 122, 123, 132,
    136, 138, 139, 142, 144,
    146–148, 154, 155, 157,
    159, 162, 163, 165, 167,
    169–177, 181, 182,
    190–196, 199, 200,
    204–206, 208, 209,
    213–215, 217, 219–223,
    225–228, 230, 234–238,
    240, 241, 243–245,
    247–255, 258, 261–268,
    270, 276, 278, 282, 283,
    286–288, 290, 293, 300,
    301, 305, 309–311, 313,
    317, 318, 321–329, 331,
    334–338, 340, 343, 345,
    349, 351, 354, 356, 357
ideology, 2, 345
illustrate, 16, 45, 69, 95, 106, 116,
    136, 173, 190, 193, 202,
    223, 224, 229, 244, 248,
    250, 254, 282, 285, 331,
    345
illustration, 90
image, 15, 94, 250
imagery, 248, 252
imitation, 26
immediacy, 196
immigrant, 146, 170
immigration, 276, 330
impact, 6, 32, 37, 45, 49, 52, 54, 59,
    61, 63, 77, 79, 80, 82–85,
    88, 95, 97, 100, 102, 108,
    116, 124, 130, 133, 135,
    138, 146–148, 155–158,
    160, 165–167, 171, 172,
    174, 189, 191, 198,
    204–206, 208, 210, 211,
    213–215, 217, 219, 221,
    222, 234–236, 241, 252,
    253, 255, 256, 262, 266,
    282, 283, 295, 299, 301,
    303, 309–311, 318, 319,
    323, 329, 331, 333, 335,
    345, 348, 351, 358

imperative, 41, 82, 102, 105, 170, 175, 204, 281, 308
implementation, 34, 103, 217, 297
importance, 3, 6, 7, 13, 17, 19, 20, 22, 27, 31, 32, 34, 37–40, 43, 46, 49, 55, 59, 61, 63, 65, 66, 69, 70, 76, 81, 82, 85, 86, 90, 92–94, 96–99, 102, 109, 111, 116–118, 121, 122, 124, 136, 139, 142, 144, 146, 147, 151, 159, 160, 165, 167, 169, 173, 174, 176–179, 181, 186, 191, 193, 197, 200, 205, 210, 211, 215, 221, 226, 233, 235, 237, 238, 240–243, 245, 248, 249, 253, 257, 258, 262, 267, 270, 281–284, 290, 293, 295, 300–302, 308, 309, 311, 317, 319–321, 324–326, 328, 329, 335, 337, 338, 340, 341, 343, 345, 347, 349, 351, 353, 354, 356–358
inadequacy, 74, 181, 192
incident, 61
inclusion, 64, 102, 298, 309, 320, 339
inclusivity, 3, 6, 17, 18, 20, 22, 25, 31, 32, 34, 39, 41, 44, 45, 49, 62, 70, 75, 77, 79–82, 84, 85, 87, 88, 95, 97, 102–105, 116, 118, 134, 138, 139, 152, 156, 157, 159, 160, 163, 165, 167, 169, 170, 172, 174, 191, 200, 201, 205, 210, 213–215, 220, 222, 227, 234, 237, 244, 245, 248, 249, 256, 258, 260, 262, 265, 281, 283, 285, 286, 288, 290, 295, 298, 307, 308, 311, 314, 320, 323, 324, 329, 336, 339, 343, 348, 354, 356, 357, 363
incorporation, 39, 162, 290, 301
increase, 32
India, 69
individual, 2, 7, 19, 23, 26, 27, 34, 37, 42, 44, 48, 54, 57, 65, 70, 78, 81, 86, 89–91, 94, 96, 108, 115, 130, 138, 139, 147, 159, 164, 166, 173, 177, 179, 182, 198, 200, 202, 211, 213, 215, 217, 220–222, 225, 226, 228, 235, 237, 241, 245, 248, 253, 298, 306, 312, 321, 327, 340, 345, 357, 358
individuality, 1, 3, 4, 8, 12, 22, 49, 92, 142, 176, 178, 227, 245
industry, 3, 6, 7, 16, 17, 22, 23, 25, 26, 75, 77–85, 88, 93, 94, 139, 157, 160–165, 169, 170, 210, 213, 235, 244, 246, 249, 259, 260, 267, 323, 340
inequality, 33, 38, 90, 115, 201, 274, 329
influence, 2, 8, 18–20, 26, 39, 50, 62, 69–71, 78, 80, 82, 87, 89, 92, 94, 109, 121, 122, 133, 138, 139, 152, 156–158, 161–163, 165–167, 204, 206, 207, 210, 213, 234, 235, 242, 252, 257, 260,

Index 385

265, 267, 309, 320, 321, 329, 336
information, 41, 147, 285, 304, 305, 321, 342
initiative, 41, 301, 346
injustice, 267, 274
innovation, 100, 123, 135, 137, 144, 258, 319
insecurity, 176, 222
insistence, 176, 335
inspiration, 3, 7, 8, 32, 70, 91, 182, 206, 221, 237, 238, 248, 302, 319
installation, 264
instance, 15, 17, 19, 27, 32, 33, 38, 40, 44, 46, 49, 57, 61, 65, 66, 69, 74, 82, 85, 89, 92, 94, 96, 105, 115, 116, 118, 122, 123, 131, 136, 143, 145, 149, 151, 155, 157, 159, 161, 163, 168, 192, 198, 201, 205, 210, 211, 213, 226, 233, 235, 242, 247, 248, 251, 252, 260, 264, 268, 269, 278, 282, 301, 302, 305, 309, 310, 313, 321–324, 326, 330, 331, 335, 339, 345, 346, 348, 349, 351, 354, 355
integral, 3, 28, 123, 186, 318, 326
integration, 215, 277, 295, 309, 353, 354
integrity, 151, 246
intelligence, 191
intensity, 133
interconnectedness, 52, 109, 115, 136, 140, 146, 206, 231, 254, 281, 313, 329–331, 356

internet, 44, 55
interplay, 8, 90, 170, 173, 175, 195, 220, 268, 298, 312, 337
intersect, 19, 33, 94, 115, 138, 139, 158, 199, 226, 244, 306, 317, 328, 330, 340
intersection, 1, 5, 17, 26, 27, 30, 33, 40, 45, 47, 53, 62, 94, 107, 136, 148, 154, 165, 174, 194, 195, 210, 245–247, 254, 263, 286, 288, 293, 330, 331
intersectionality, 13, 19, 29, 32–35, 37, 39, 40, 44, 48, 66, 69, 75, 80–82, 90, 108, 109, 115–117, 121, 122, 124, 132, 133, 135, 138, 140, 144, 146, 147, 158, 163, 177, 181, 198, 200, 204–206, 208, 210, 211, 220, 226, 227, 231, 248, 250, 253, 254, 256, 258, 260, 264, 265, 268–270, 272, 276, 281, 283–288, 290, 297, 301, 306, 311, 314, 318, 320, 321, 324, 328, 331, 335, 336, 338, 339, 343, 349, 354
intimacy, 177
invisibility, 159, 176
involvement, 6, 41, 209, 278, 282, 292, 330, 340
isolation, 14, 31, 65, 69, 86, 176, 180, 192, 241, 268, 272, 327, 358
issue, 34, 35, 45, 99, 117, 131, 195, 221, 237, 244, 254, 257, 303, 304

Jack Halberstam, 176
Janelle Monáe, 264
Janet Mock, 319, 321, 337
Jerome Bruner, 304
jewelry, 193
journey, 1–3, 7, 12, 13, 17–20, 22, 23, 25–28, 30, 32, 33, 37, 39, 44, 45, 48, 49, 54, 61, 62, 75, 77, 79, 86, 89–95, 108, 115, 116, 121, 124, 127–129, 138, 140, 144, 145, 154, 159, 160, 165, 170–172, 175–177, 179, 180, 182, 192–195, 198, 202, 210, 211, 215, 217, 219–222, 226, 227, 230, 234–238, 240, 242, 253, 258, 268, 274, 293, 305, 310, 317, 318, 320–327, 334, 338, 344, 345, 347, 351, 356–358
joy, 1, 122, 326
judgment, 3, 76, 86, 93, 95, 109, 115, 123, 142, 193, 206, 220, 241, 248, 310, 346, 357
Judith Butler, 112, 236, 293, 338
Judith Butler's, 8, 12, 18, 40, 77, 89, 152, 173, 175, 190, 192, 200, 223, 225, 234, 243, 250, 258, 326
jurisdiction, 64
justice, 30, 34, 35, 38, 39, 41, 53, 66, 82, 99, 100, 104, 108–110, 117, 121, 124, 127, 134–136, 138, 145, 146, 156, 167, 194, 195, 200, 206, 213, 215, 217, 249, 251, 264, 269, 270, 274, 278, 281, 283, 286, 288, 290, 291, 293, 297, 303, 305, 313, 317–320, 325, 328–331, 335, 339–341, 349, 352, 354, 358, 363, 364
juxtaposition, 266

Kahlo, 337
Kimberlé Crenshaw, 32, 33, 44, 82, 90, 115, 117, 133, 138, 158, 200, 206, 220, 231, 254, 268, 272, 286, 288, 306, 318, 354
Kimberlé Crenshaw's, 19
kindness, 66, 347, 358
knowledge, 33, 97, 210, 211, 214, 290, 301, 304, 311, 321

label, 253
lack, 20, 31, 34, 40, 44, 81, 85, 108, 159, 168, 176, 201, 235, 269, 304, 307, 312, 330
Lady Gaga, 148
landmark, 99
landscape, 18, 19, 26, 31, 32, 39, 45, 56, 62, 64, 68, 95, 101, 121, 122, 130, 132, 133, 135, 136, 138, 151, 152, 154, 157, 162, 164, 170, 173, 198, 210, 213, 262, 265, 286, 298, 309, 317, 320, 327, 332, 334, 341, 342, 363
language, 16, 162, 176, 221, 234, 235, 237, 248, 260, 321, 326
Laverne Cox, 337
law, 105, 351

layer, 45, 94
lead, 19, 27, 31, 34, 40, 44, 45, 74, 94, 118, 134, 143, 147, 148, 159, 160, 168, 174, 180, 195, 198, 204, 213, 216, 222, 233, 241, 246, 269, 304, 305, 324, 337, 347
leader, 108–110
leadership, 108, 110, 136, 354
learning, 102, 105, 121, 284, 291, 304, 306, 308, 312, 314, 316–318, 320–323, 343, 347
legacy, 39, 100, 135, 142, 160, 163, 167, 191, 200, 206, 213, 215, 222, 236, 260, 263–265, 267, 311, 319, 334–336, 338, 363
legislation, 41, 57, 97, 99–102, 109, 136, 269, 282, 351
legitimacy, 144
lens, 8, 12, 26, 34, 44, 82, 148, 168, 172, 177, 204, 236, 248, 250, 258, 265, 269, 270, 272, 278, 325, 327
lesson, 301
level, 39, 99, 131, 255
leverage, 56, 90, 137, 261, 263, 319, 351
liberation, 20, 33, 47, 55, 75–77, 89, 91, 123, 140, 144, 172, 176, 195, 198, 210, 220, 237, 238, 241, 249, 258, 261, 274, 281, 331, 338, 346, 357
life, 1, 2, 13, 30, 92, 96, 99, 130, 156, 168, 175, 177–183, 194, 195, 215, 321–323, 346

lifetime, 317
light, 89, 110, 138, 146, 159, 222, 235, 345
like, 1, 17, 18, 20, 27, 30, 34, 41, 44, 45, 49, 53, 62–64, 69, 75, 77, 80, 82, 89, 90, 95, 96, 112, 114, 116, 118, 123, 134, 144, 148, 153, 157, 158, 162, 179, 194, 195, 217, 241, 244, 245, 248, 265, 268, 269, 274, 285, 298, 304, 306, 313, 319, 321, 325, 335, 343, 345, 351, 352, 354
limit, 42, 75
limitation, 115
line, 79
lingerie, 82
listening, 284, 346
literature, 171, 292, 296, 301, 309, 320
location, 117
loneliness, 358
look, 41, 94, 138, 222, 226, 265, 341, 347
loom, 343
love, 1, 8, 23, 27, 38, 39, 44, 46, 55, 56, 59, 61, 70, 71, 86, 89, 90, 92, 94, 98, 109, 110, 115–117, 123, 131, 134, 135, 138–140, 145, 146, 157, 159, 164, 167, 169, 177, 179, 191, 204, 205, 213, 215, 222, 227, 238–243, 249, 264, 265, 302, 320–322, 324, 326, 338, 341, 343–345, 347, 351, 353, 356–358, 363, 364

luxury, 354

magnitude, 89
mainstream, 11, 17, 34, 44, 46, 65, 77, 116, 156–158, 163, 164, 166, 260, 267, 269, 287, 289, 336
maintenance, 117
making, 27, 34, 44, 108, 131, 144, 149, 158, 195, 209, 259, 269, 293, 305, 325, 335, 351
male, 33, 173, 192, 228, 234–236, 243
man, 189, 268
manifestation, 26
manner, 45
mantra, 22, 327, 356–358
marathon, 195
marginalization, 27, 108, 266, 274, 348
mark, 77, 100, 165, 318, 323, 334
marketing, 79, 80
marketplace, 235
marriage, 45
Marsha P. Johnson, 121, 319
Martin Heidegger, 241
masculinity, 1, 4, 8, 12, 77, 161, 189–191, 193, 223, 227, 248, 252, 322
material, 305, 307
matter, 221, 241, 358
meaning, 2, 182, 236, 246, 304
means, 16, 17, 20, 46, 64, 80, 82, 84, 86, 88, 92, 106, 113, 135, 142, 148, 163, 169, 189, 237, 245, 260, 262–264, 278, 290, 304, 313, 349, 354

measure, 94
mechanism, 65
media, 18, 19, 22, 27, 38, 39, 41, 44, 49–52, 54, 56, 61, 62, 64, 65, 69, 76, 78, 79, 86, 90, 94, 98, 108–110, 112, 116, 118, 123, 124, 133, 134, 136, 144–147, 152–159, 162, 164, 165, 167–169, 172, 176, 181, 191, 196, 201, 205, 207, 209, 211, 214, 222, 235, 238, 242, 244, 247–249, 254, 255, 283, 285, 287, 289, 302, 303, 313, 317, 319, 321, 323, 324, 335, 337, 340, 345, 351, 354, 358
meditation, 183, 184
medium, 2, 18, 19, 38, 45, 46, 92, 163, 165, 172, 206, 247, 248, 254, 255, 258, 263, 265, 266, 340
megaphone, 69
memorization, 304
memory, 326
mentor, 310, 321
mentorship, 31, 93, 111, 198, 200, 210–214, 217, 258, 302, 310, 311, 322, 340
message, 15, 18, 27, 32, 38, 39, 44, 46, 48–50, 54, 64, 68–70, 76, 79, 89, 93, 98, 109, 115–117, 123, 130, 131, 134, 135, 140, 146, 147, 156–158, 160, 162, 163, 167, 181, 191, 193, 196, 204, 205, 207, 209, 214, 220, 222, 238, 240–243, 253, 254, 256, 264, 266,

Index 389

317, 318, 322, 324, 326, 341, 343, 345, 349, 356, 358, 363
messaging, 131, 132
method, 57, 253, 304
metric, 32
microcosm, 30
migration, 330
milestone, 324
million, 59
mind, 234
mindfulness, 183, 186, 352
mirror, 250, 260, 265
misinformation, 144, 319, 342, 343
misogyny, 20
misrepresentation, 257
mission, 56, 144, 351
misstep, 317
misunderstanding, 192, 238
mix, 2
mobilization, 147, 199, 285
model, 26, 52, 77, 94, 139, 180, 310, 318
mold, 81, 213
moment, 2, 6, 78, 81, 176, 324, 358
momentum, 22, 195–198
monotony, 335
mother, 8
move, 93, 105, 115, 118, 147, 204, 220, 225, 267, 281, 286, 300, 306, 308, 345
movement, 20, 34, 37, 39, 41, 42, 46, 66, 70, 73, 75, 80, 91, 93, 94, 100, 102, 108–110, 116, 134, 136, 143, 144, 146, 147, 165, 173, 191, 196, 198, 213, 222, 237, 241, 243, 248, 260, 265, 266, 274, 283, 284, 303, 319, 329, 331, 332, 335, 354, 358
multimedia, 68, 248, 252, 264, 266
multitude, 228
murder, 40
music, 154–157, 163, 165, 166
myriad, 245, 273, 279, 298, 332

narrative, 3, 23, 44, 65, 75, 92, 96, 100, 110, 112, 145, 151, 163, 172, 177, 208, 235, 236, 238, 252, 253, 266, 267, 293, 304, 305, 321, 325, 334, 344
nationality, 139
nature, 17, 19, 27, 33, 37, 44, 51, 83, 105, 117, 133, 138, 139, 160, 181, 195, 200, 220, 241, 244, 285, 318, 354
necessity, 20, 64, 79, 90, 102, 135, 146, 151, 175, 191, 198, 215, 308, 316, 320, 324, 326, 331, 354
need, 17, 19, 32, 34, 40, 46, 81, 96, 109, 151, 154, 159, 168, 191, 195, 198, 209, 210, 220, 221, 255, 262, 282–284, 287, 314, 324, 339, 351, 355
negativity, 27, 55, 62, 321
network, 28, 160, 178, 182, 196
New York City, 324
niche, 25, 263
non, 2, 19, 20, 31, 33, 34, 37, 43, 44, 46, 48, 54, 62, 67, 74, 78, 79, 81, 82, 85, 89, 90, 92, 106, 115, 116, 146, 155, 157, 161, 163, 164, 166, 169, 173, 174, 176, 177,

179, 182, 189, 192, 205, 213, 221, 226, 228, 233–237, 239, 241–244, 248, 250, 253, 264, 267, 310, 321, 323, 327, 348, 350
nonconforming, 27, 28, 39–41, 43, 46, 62, 69, 81, 108, 130, 143, 166, 168, 192, 194, 214, 226, 237, 250, 350
nonconformity, 35, 44, 59, 165
norm, 12, 21, 89, 123, 283, 329
normalization, 156
notion, 8, 11, 46, 58, 62, 74, 112, 168, 219, 225, 241, 258, 261, 326, 343
number, 79, 106, 143

observation, 26
obstacle, 342
odyssey, 325
offering, 174, 198, 214, 244, 265
on, 6–8, 13, 18, 22, 27, 31, 33, 34, 37–39, 41, 42, 45, 46, 55, 59, 61, 65, 66, 68, 69, 73, 75, 77–82, 84–87, 90–92, 94–97, 99–102, 105, 107–109, 111, 112, 118, 122, 124, 131, 133–135, 139, 143, 144, 146, 147, 153, 155–160, 162, 163, 165–167, 172, 173, 176, 182, 189, 191, 197, 200, 205, 206, 210, 211, 213, 217, 219, 221–223, 225–227, 234–236, 238, 241, 243–245, 247, 248, 250–256, 260, 262, 264, 266–268, 272, 274, 278, 281–283, 286, 287, 290, 296, 302, 304, 309–311, 317, 321–328, 330, 334–336, 340, 343–345, 349, 351, 357
one, 1–4, 7, 8, 19, 20, 26, 27, 32, 33, 35, 48, 53, 63, 65, 69, 74, 89, 92, 93, 123, 129, 130, 138–140, 147, 159, 172, 176, 177, 179, 181, 192, 198, 202, 212, 220, 221, 225–228, 235, 236, 241, 242, 251, 253, 269, 270, 284, 310, 320, 322, 326, 327, 331, 335, 347, 349, 352, 354, 356–359, 363, 364
openness, 258, 322
opportunity, 170, 300, 317
opposition, 324
oppression, 30, 31, 33, 34, 38, 70, 90, 115, 121, 124, 133, 138, 143, 168, 208, 226, 250, 254, 266, 268–270, 272–274, 281, 282, 286, 290, 306, 318, 320, 327, 328, 330, 331, 340, 358
optimism, 359
organization, 106
organizing, 124, 139, 146, 204, 358
orientation, 13, 96, 99, 102, 111, 118, 182, 217, 274, 276, 282, 329, 343, 354
ostracism, 89, 174
ostracization, 21, 76
other, 32, 47, 64, 65, 106, 124, 134, 136, 148, 193, 213, 245, 249, 266, 268, 274, 283, 306, 319, 331, 335, 357

Index 391

outfit, 2, 3, 15, 61, 81, 90, 148
outlet, 176
outreach, 210
overlap, 32, 288
ownership, 86, 99, 255, 340

pain, 171, 326, 337
paint, 253
palette, 92
Palomo Spain, 81
panel, 96
paradigm, 265
part, 35, 156, 167, 260, 301, 318, 351
participant, 154
participation, 31, 38, 41, 66, 81, 167, 169, 176, 191, 209, 235, 324, 331, 348
partner, 249
partnership, 6, 69, 79, 97, 111, 177, 210, 235, 264
passage, 96, 99
passion, 1, 5, 145, 177, 248, 354
path, 28, 33, 171, 182, 236, 323, 324, 327, 339
Paulo Freire, 314, 343
Paulo Freire's, 346
pedagogy, 346
peer, 212, 302
penchant, 237
people, 17, 32, 34, 38, 39, 43, 65, 66, 85, 93, 96, 97, 110, 139, 143, 145, 147, 205, 206, 214, 215, 226, 245, 269, 270, 279–281, 283, 287, 290, 301–303, 310, 312, 330, 335, 340, 349, 357
perception, 97, 148, 163, 171, 330

performance, 31, 37–39, 46, 59, 89, 92, 112, 113, 123, 142, 148, 154–157, 163, 166, 171–173, 176, 190, 193, 217, 223–225, 238, 243, 247–251, 253, 254, 261, 263, 265–267, 310, 313, 326, 331, 333, 335, 337, 338
performativity, 8, 12, 18, 40, 77, 89, 90, 112, 152, 173, 175, 177, 190, 192, 200, 223, 225, 234, 243, 250, 258, 326, 338
performer, 251
period, 2, 5, 12–14, 21, 176
perpetuation, 168
persecution, 96, 109, 330
perseverance, 124, 357, 359
persistence, 202
person, 13, 44, 67, 92, 123, 172, 181, 194, 211, 226, 247, 310, 337, 357, 358
persona, 7, 180, 219, 326
personal, 1–3, 5, 12, 17–21, 23, 30, 35, 39, 42–44, 50, 54, 56, 61, 64, 70, 75, 77–79, 82, 86, 89, 91–94, 100, 102, 108, 110, 111, 116, 121, 127, 131, 145–149, 153, 159, 163, 164, 167, 170, 172, 173, 175, 177, 179–182, 186, 192–195, 208, 209, 213, 214, 216, 220, 226, 227, 230, 234–238, 240–243, 247, 253, 260, 263–267, 292, 293, 301, 304–306, 311, 313, 314, 317, 318, 320,

321, 324–326, 332, 334, 337, 344, 351, 356, 357
perspective, 2, 11, 18, 34, 40, 65, 77, 89, 112, 124, 147, 173, 190–192, 199, 221–223, 226, 227, 236, 270, 313, 357
phenomenon, 34, 45, 61, 238, 244, 255, 338
philosophy, 2, 77, 109, 115, 145, 220, 225–227, 241, 252, 263, 301, 343, 346
phrase, 121
physicality, 26
picture, 197
piece, 99, 248
pioneer, 249, 263–265, 267
place, 131
planning, 56
platform, 2, 6, 26, 33, 37, 38, 45, 47–49, 53–55, 61, 62, 65, 68, 82, 84, 90, 92, 94, 95, 97, 113, 127, 134, 135, 140, 146–149, 152, 154, 158, 159, 162, 164, 166, 168, 172, 173, 181, 184, 193, 202, 210, 214, 222, 235, 241, 247, 249, 252, 255, 281, 282, 288, 290, 293, 302, 309, 321, 335, 339, 340, 344
play, 1, 18, 64, 80, 174, 221, 237, 249, 299, 317
playfulness, 243
pleasure, 266
plight, 34, 96, 330
poem, 247
poetry, 92, 172, 193, 217, 238, 247–249, 255, 263, 326, 331, 340
point, 173, 259, 345
poise, 3, 7, 26–28
polarization, 347
police, 269, 330
policy, 31, 34, 41, 45, 99–102, 104, 201, 269, 282, 288, 330, 351, 355
pop, 8, 165–167, 205
portrayal, 19
position, 138
positivity, 15, 69, 82, 93–95, 122, 159, 162, 169, 209
post, 324
postmodernism, 250
potential, 6, 16, 32, 38, 42, 47, 52, 61, 69, 70, 79, 94, 131, 147, 149, 152, 156, 160, 163, 169, 170, 200, 244, 245, 247, 251, 254, 255, 257, 261, 267, 291, 319, 320, 358
poverty, 330
power, 3, 13, 18, 20, 23, 25, 37, 47, 49, 50, 52, 62, 65, 67, 70, 80, 81, 84, 86, 102, 104, 114, 116, 117, 123, 124, 127, 129, 142, 145–148, 154, 156, 157, 159, 160, 162, 167–169, 176, 177, 179, 190, 204, 213, 215, 217, 221, 226, 234, 241–243, 248, 249, 251, 255, 257, 258, 262, 264, 265, 278, 285, 286, 288, 303, 306, 314, 319–323, 327, 331, 335, 338, 340, 356
practice, 17, 45, 81, 227, 266, 313,

Index   393

314, 317, 343, 344, 347, 349, 358
precedent, 186
preference, 221
prejudice, 143, 174
premise, 77
presence, 3, 22, 26, 27, 53, 55, 56, 78, 86, 90, 96, 100, 109, 145–147, 153, 155, 156, 158, 159, 164, 167, 169, 197, 222, 335, 344
present, 1, 27, 45, 46, 121, 206, 301, 319, 332
presentation, 1, 74, 335
pressure, 27, 31, 74, 79, 143, 147, 175, 192, 195
prevalence, 65, 81, 117, 319, 344
pride, 15, 108, 112, 260
principle, 115, 116, 210, 237, 241, 242, 288, 319, 320, 325, 349
prioritization, 45
privilege, 19, 33, 115, 138, 226, 257, 268, 306, 313
problem, 81, 85, 89, 250
process, 1, 49, 137, 176, 182, 204, 221, 226, 258, 292, 304, 318, 320, 322, 327
product, 215, 246
profile, 61, 96, 157, 179
profit, 17, 244, 254
progress, 20, 34, 40, 42, 83, 99, 101, 108, 115, 143, 152, 199, 215, 238, 303, 331–333, 339, 350
project, 248, 253, 255
projection, 253
proliferation, 342
prominence, 3, 22, 23

promise, 320, 343
promotion, 102, 198, 206
pronoun, 232–234
psychology, 241
public, 7, 17, 20, 27, 41, 44, 62, 70, 74, 85, 92, 97–100, 110, 116, 122, 124, 128, 129, 135, 157, 163, 167, 179–182, 191, 195, 209, 214, 219, 221, 222, 235, 266, 289, 319, 322, 324, 326, 330, 340, 348, 351
purpose, 139, 145, 182, 196, 212
pursuit, 91, 135, 138, 139, 142, 175, 176, 236, 241, 278, 319, 320, 334, 341, 352
push, 12, 13, 41, 82, 99, 115, 135, 146, 191, 235, 260, 343
pushback, 25, 45, 254, 326

quality, 12, 89, 112, 152, 171, 173, 175, 190, 192, 223, 234, 236, 243, 258, 326
queer, 13, 31, 32, 40, 44, 46, 93, 110, 112, 115, 116, 157, 171, 176, 179, 227, 247, 248, 250, 279–282, 297, 337
quest, 164, 179, 325
question, 19, 74, 219, 248, 254, 293, 314, 327
quo, 2, 17, 32, 39, 44, 84, 142, 215, 217, 227, 258, 265, 267, 335

race, 19, 27, 32, 33, 37, 44, 69, 90, 93, 94, 115, 117, 122, 133, 139, 144, 147, 199, 200, 206, 220, 226, 248, 252, 254, 263, 265, 266,

268–270, 272, 274, 278, 286, 288, 306, 317, 325, 327, 329, 330, 354
racism, 106, 226, 250, 253, 266, 268, 270, 355
Rad Hourani, 244
raising, 38, 46, 122, 145, 322
rallying, 358
range, 81, 94, 122, 215, 223, 247, 294, 352
rate, 158, 174
re, 112, 136
reach, 18, 38, 41, 49, 55, 68–70, 116, 130–132, 135, 146, 155, 158, 197, 214, 238, 255, 302, 326
reality, 40, 205, 238, 288, 354, 355, 363
realization, 5, 28, 35, 176
realm, 26, 37, 41, 44, 48, 61, 64, 75, 86, 99, 102, 146, 152, 156, 163, 165, 169, 215, 241, 249, 256, 263, 266, 281, 334, 337
rebellion, 21, 90, 114, 148, 176, 335
recognition, 3, 5, 20, 22, 23, 25, 26, 37, 39, 81, 82, 84, 142, 146, 163, 167, 215, 221, 234, 235, 237, 238, 268
recourse, 64
redefinition, 154, 264
reflection, 13, 47, 121, 124, 149, 172, 253, 265, 267, 301, 317, 322–325, 347
reform, 34, 39, 201, 283, 330
refuge, 118
refugee, 278, 330
refusal, 160
reimagining, 109, 314, 330

rejection, 14, 98, 143, 176, 189, 192, 220, 357
relation, 164, 330
relationship, 16, 51, 69, 89, 90, 148, 198, 211, 232, 247, 337
relativism, 96
religion, 182
reminder, 3, 7, 13, 20, 23, 66, 68, 93, 97, 147, 156, 167, 186, 206, 210, 220–222, 238, 240, 243, 249, 253, 267, 278, 290, 308, 318, 322, 324, 329, 337, 349, 357, 358
repeal, 282
report, 31, 115, 242
representation, 3, 6, 17, 19, 22, 31, 34, 44, 46, 62, 68, 75, 78, 80–82, 84, 85, 87, 94, 108, 112, 122, 133, 151–157, 159, 160, 162, 163, 165, 167–170, 174–176, 192, 201, 205, 206, 209, 210, 213, 215, 242, 249, 252, 255, 260, 262, 267, 288, 295, 298, 301, 307, 309, 312, 318, 320, 337, 348, 354
representative, 143, 318
repression, 191
research, 45
resilience, 13, 15, 21, 27, 30, 32, 37, 39, 44, 45, 55, 60, 63, 70, 92, 97, 100, 117, 121, 124, 136, 144, 145, 160, 171, 179, 182, 184, 193, 200, 204, 222, 236, 278, 281, 303, 320–322, 324–326, 331, 336, 338, 343, 352,

Index 395

354, 356, 357, 359, 363
resistance, 5, 20, 22, 44, 45, 70, 75, 138, 149, 165, 176, 192, 209, 227, 233, 237, 238, 248, 251, 256, 263, 265, 297, 313, 332, 334, 344, 357
resolve, 12, 39, 238
resonance, 305
resource, 144, 196, 297
respect, 38, 55, 96, 146, 193, 221, 232, 233, 237, 238, 246, 283, 302, 308
response, 52, 61, 136, 145, 192, 317, 321
responsibility, 30, 108, 210, 215, 242, 245
restriction, 94
result, 215, 223, 249, 264, 327
retaliation, 346
retention, 31, 304
rethinking, 220
retribution, 116, 314, 364
revolution, 93
revolutionary, 77, 344, 351
richness, 75, 154, 169, 202
ridicule, 5, 89
right, 115, 206, 225, 348, 357
Rihanna, 82
rise, 3, 15, 22, 23, 44, 82, 118, 134, 136, 157, 167, 200, 244, 319, 346, 351, 357
risk, 46, 131, 143, 171, 244, 254
road, 124, 317, 319, 320, 343
roadmap, 92
Rogers, 241
role, 19, 26, 28, 33, 37, 38, 46, 55, 77, 80, 86, 92, 97, 110, 111, 116, 118, 122, 129, 158, 159, 163, 166, 172, 174, 181, 182, 202, 205, 210, 214, 217, 221, 237, 242, 249, 260, 262, 264, 290, 299, 300, 302, 310, 317–319, 321, 328, 338
room, 304
runway, 80–82, 94, 139, 263, 323
RuPaul, 1, 8

s, 1–3, 5–8, 11–15, 17–23, 25–28, 30–35, 37–41, 44–47, 49, 51–56, 59, 61–66, 68–71, 74–102, 104, 109, 110, 112, 114–118, 121–124, 127–140, 142–147, 151–179, 181, 189–195, 197, 198, 200–202, 204–210, 213–215, 217, 219–223, 225–229, 234–243, 245, 247–256, 258–267, 270, 277, 278, 282–287, 290, 293–295, 300–303, 305, 308–314, 317–331, 333–341, 343–349, 351, 352, 354, 356–358, 364
safety, 55, 330
San Francisco, 310
sanctuary, 76, 310
saris, 15
Sartre, 241
Saul Alinsky, 146
scale, 95, 97, 108, 109, 146, 281
scarcity, 297
scene, 2
scholar, 33, 138, 200, 268, 272, 354
school, 2, 4, 5, 12–14, 21, 35, 39, 118, 175, 217, 237, 292,

301, 308–310
schooling, 320
scope, 38, 254
scorn, 61
scrutiny, 44, 59, 180, 195, 324
search, 182
section, 1, 16, 23, 28, 37, 40, 45, 50, 53, 64, 68, 73, 75, 77, 80, 84, 91, 95, 97, 108, 115, 133, 135, 143, 146, 152, 154, 156, 163, 168, 170, 173, 175, 192, 194, 195, 202, 208, 213, 223, 234, 236, 241, 249, 254, 265, 279, 298, 301, 323, 329, 356
segment, 324
self, 1–3, 5, 7, 8, 12–18, 20–23, 25–28, 39, 41, 44, 46, 55, 59, 61, 70, 71, 73, 75–77, 80, 84, 86, 89–94, 97–99, 109, 110, 113, 114, 116, 122, 123, 132, 134, 135, 138–140, 145–148, 156, 157, 159, 160, 162, 164, 165, 167, 169, 171, 175–177, 179, 182, 184, 186, 191, 193–195, 197, 205, 206, 209, 211, 220–222, 226, 227, 234, 235, 237–243, 245, 249, 251, 253–256, 258, 263, 265, 267, 290, 301, 302, 305, 309, 310, 319–322, 324–327, 335, 337, 338, 340, 341, 345, 347, 348, 351–354, 356–358, 363
sense, 8, 13, 14, 18, 34, 37, 49, 54–56, 64, 66, 86, 90, 94, 109, 111, 116, 124, 130, 134, 139, 140, 145, 147, 153, 155, 156, 158, 159, 162, 164, 169, 173, 175, 178, 193, 196, 198, 205, 209, 212, 220–222, 238, 239, 241, 242, 244, 249, 251, 253, 258, 264, 266, 278, 283, 290, 300, 302, 304, 313, 318, 323, 336, 338, 344, 345, 349, 354, 357
sensitivity, 69, 96, 97
sentiment, 94, 135, 344, 357
series, 8, 12, 16, 18, 38, 40, 66, 77, 89, 152, 173, 175, 192, 200, 223, 234, 243, 248, 250, 253, 255, 293, 301, 317, 319
serve, 1, 2, 17, 46, 49, 62, 64, 68, 83, 91, 102, 112, 116, 118, 122, 138, 147, 149, 152, 159, 163, 167, 169, 176, 180, 183, 192, 199, 205, 235, 250–252, 258, 263, 264, 266, 278, 305, 308, 317, 335, 337, 347
set, 73, 77, 82, 112, 152, 181, 186, 272, 319
setting, 13, 37, 63, 182, 197
sex, 112, 143, 173, 217, 283
sexism, 253, 268
sexuality, 19, 33, 40, 44, 46, 69, 90, 109, 115, 117, 121, 131, 133, 152, 158, 164, 198, 206, 210, 225, 226, 248, 261, 263, 266, 268, 269, 272, 306, 317, 325, 332, 344

shame, 116, 190, 243, 358
shaming, 123
shape, 19, 34, 49, 71, 93, 163, 194, 199, 226, 243, 306, 311, 320, 332, 345
share, 41, 49, 57, 59, 66, 85, 97, 111, 118, 123, 130, 146, 147, 153, 158, 159, 164, 193, 196, 199, 221, 222, 242, 244, 249, 251, 265, 278, 285, 290, 302, 306, 318, 345, 346, 349, 351, 357
sharing, 37–39, 43, 54, 76, 79, 86, 93, 106, 111, 122, 127, 129, 135, 144, 145, 159, 167, 181, 195, 196, 211, 214, 220, 235, 238, 292, 310, 321, 331, 344, 351
shift, 25, 65, 78, 85, 88, 102, 162, 164, 166, 200, 213, 217, 220, 243, 244, 295, 323, 344
show, 78, 81, 310
showcase, 22, 162
side, 181
significance, 123, 146, 168, 174, 176, 202, 221, 233, 235, 246, 310, 323, 357
signifier, 148
silence, 65, 344
site, 152, 263
situation, 136
size, 69, 81, 85, 93, 269
skill, 28, 127, 321
skin, 78, 139
societal, 1–3, 5, 8, 12–14, 16, 18–20, 23, 26, 27, 30, 33, 37–42, 44–47, 49, 56, 59–62, 68, 69, 74, 75, 77, 79, 85, 86, 88–91, 93, 94, 97, 98, 106, 108, 109, 112, 113, 115, 116, 121–123, 127, 138, 139, 142–146, 148, 149, 152, 154, 156–160, 164, 165, 167–169, 171–173, 175, 176, 179, 190–193, 199, 208, 209, 213, 215–217, 219–228, 234–239, 241–244, 246–256, 258–260, 262, 263, 265, 266, 270, 293, 295, 298, 301, 303, 310, 319, 321, 322, 325–327, 332, 334–341, 344, 351, 352, 354, 356–358, 363
society, 2, 18–21, 34, 41, 47, 50, 61, 71, 82, 86, 89, 90, 95, 102, 104, 110, 112, 114, 115, 124, 129, 135, 138, 140, 142, 144, 145, 147–149, 159, 170, 172, 174, 177, 182, 189, 191–194, 200–202, 204, 206, 210, 213, 215, 217, 220–222, 225, 227, 234, 237, 243, 245, 248, 250, 253, 254, 258, 260, 262, 264, 265, 267, 270, 274, 278, 282, 285–287, 293, 298, 303, 306, 311, 316, 317, 320, 326, 327, 329, 336, 341, 343, 345, 347, 349, 354, 356, 357
socio, 121, 354
sociology, 161
solace, 13, 176
solidarity, 34, 39, 56, 64, 66, 90, 94,

96, 97, 109, 116, 123, 124,
134, 139, 140, 144–146,
151, 154, 155, 160, 184,
191, 193, 196, 200, 220,
253, 274, 278, 281–285,
288, 290, 326, 331, 336,
338, 340, 343, 344, 346,
347, 349, 357
soul, 326
source, 61, 182, 245, 248
South Asia, 237, 282
space, 8, 13, 23, 31, 48, 50, 63, 66,
76, 122, 134, 160, 165,
168, 243, 247, 251, 259,
263, 266, 302, 331
spark, 28, 38, 62, 77, 146
speaker, 122, 128, 129
speaking, 65, 70, 92, 97, 98, 109,
110, 124, 127–129, 131,
140, 144, 145, 157, 167,
172, 181, 205, 209–211,
214, 222, 235, 258, 289,
290, 293–295, 301, 305,
309, 319, 322, 323, 327,
328, 336, 340, 348, 351
spectacle, 148
spectrum, 11, 45, 80, 115, 138, 173,
221, 234, 236, 237, 243,
253
speech, 96, 99, 116, 181, 324
sphere, 162
spirit, 13, 100, 146, 266, 338, 359
spirituality, 182–184
spokesperson, 147
spread, 144, 244, 345
sprint, 195
staff, 32
stage, 2, 13, 27, 37, 48, 80, 81, 266
stance, 27, 61, 151, 241

stand, 96, 146, 191, 303
standard, 11, 74, 81, 82
standardization, 304
state, 357
statement, 2, 3, 46, 61, 78, 81, 90,
122, 123, 148, 149, 160,
165, 220, 344
status, 2, 3, 6, 17, 22, 32, 39, 44, 84,
142, 147, 215, 217, 227,
258, 265, 267, 276, 288,
335
stem, 44
step, 114, 140, 243, 274, 297
Sternberg, 177
stigma, 44, 45, 143, 145, 159, 168,
171, 179, 199, 239, 241,
250, 339
stigmatization, 40, 350
stoicism, 189
story, 3, 7, 15, 26, 30, 82, 92, 121,
129, 167, 168, 172, 177,
214, 222, 238
storytelling, 43, 54, 55, 136, 148,
163, 166, 209, 249, 255,
266, 276, 278, 304–306,
321, 326, 331
strategy, 54, 61, 63, 64, 82, 136, 259
stratification, 33, 268
street, 2
streetwear, 260
strength, 3, 135, 171, 182, 191, 278,
321, 349, 357
stress, 31, 143
struggle, 14, 15, 19, 20, 41, 61, 89,
90, 97, 98, 121, 144, 152,
176, 195, 202, 286, 318,
353, 357, 358
student, 31, 32, 206, 300, 304, 312,
314, 316

study, 148, 205, 235
style, 1–6, 8, 15, 17, 22, 79, 81, 82, 122, 136, 149, 161, 167, 176, 192, 219, 237, 258, 260, 267, 349
subversion, 161
success, 39, 147, 300, 314, 323
sum, 245
summary, 26, 37, 110, 132, 158, 172, 191, 249
support, 8, 13, 27, 28, 32, 39, 44, 62, 63, 90, 99, 116–118, 123, 130, 135, 139, 144, 146, 147, 160, 176, 178, 182, 191, 192, 195, 196, 198–200, 210–212, 217, 242, 245, 277, 282, 285, 302, 303, 310, 313, 321, 324, 326, 330, 332, 340, 347, 357
survival, 65, 278
sustainability, 318
sword, 61, 85, 134, 160
Sylvia Rivera, 121
symbol, 5, 205
sympathy, 345
synergy, 264
system, 63, 221, 228, 287, 311

tackle, 69, 123
tapestry, 18, 20, 57, 121, 148, 170, 172, 175, 179, 234, 236, 245, 249, 250, 266, 325, 338, 343
target, 54, 64, 143
teacher, 292
teaching, 283, 290, 314
technique, 131
technology, 90, 343

TED Talk, 159
television, 159, 164, 205
tendency, 34, 237
tenet, 139
tension, 47, 70, 195, 254
term, 115, 138, 196, 198, 200, 206, 254, 268, 272, 306, 345, 354
terrain, 254
testament, 3, 13, 21, 23, 25, 49, 51, 62, 70, 89, 102, 104, 124, 127, 129, 136, 139, 145, 152, 163, 169, 171, 176, 192, 215, 221, 238, 243, 251, 256, 258, 267, 303, 317, 320–322, 326, 327, 338, 340
text, 253
the Middle East, 96
the United States, 34, 282
theatricality, 259
theme, 1, 177, 357, 358
theorist, 146, 236
theory, 8, 12, 18, 40, 46, 77, 82, 89, 93, 94, 96, 97, 102, 113, 115, 116, 133, 146, 147, 152, 161, 168, 171, 173, 175, 176, 190, 192, 200, 205, 208, 225, 227, 231, 234, 243, 250, 254, 256, 258, 270, 286, 293, 297, 304, 317, 318, 326, 343
therapy, 186
thinking, 40, 104, 290, 304, 311
thinness, 74
thought, 45, 123, 158, 214, 252–255
thread, 172
threat, 70, 99, 109, 319

time, 5, 12, 21, 196, 223, 236, 248, 347
title, 108
today, 70, 82, 112, 135, 147, 159
tokenism, 65, 66, 81, 154, 349
toll, 44, 99, 143, 179, 324, 352
tool, 1, 3, 5, 16, 21, 26, 38, 45, 47, 49, 50, 52, 55, 56, 62, 66, 68, 75, 84, 86, 109, 122, 123, 144, 147, 148, 153, 154, 165, 169, 176, 196, 246, 249, 252, 254–256, 260, 262, 266, 267, 270, 285, 290, 292, 304, 306, 311, 319, 321, 323, 335, 343, 351
topic, 230
torch, 213
traction, 3, 295
trailblazer, 3, 81, 152, 319, 334, 336
training, 269, 292, 302, 304
trait, 18, 28, 200, 293, 338
trajectory, 244, 320
trans, 31, 32, 39–41, 45, 57, 65, 66, 110, 112, 115, 136, 143, 147, 157, 168, 214, 215, 263, 279–283, 321, 330, 335, 337
transcending, 231
transformation, 21, 33, 86, 140, 166, 290
transgender, 33, 34, 85, 106, 108, 115, 143, 145, 174, 209, 226, 228, 268, 269, 278, 286, 327, 339, 348, 351, 355
transparency, 181
transphobia, 106, 123, 145, 226, 250, 266, 268, 355

trend, 79, 80, 82, 134, 162, 167, 243, 346
trendsetter, 2
trendsetting, 162
triumph, 77, 78, 172, 213, 347, 357
trolling, 44, 55, 60, 62–64, 144, 346
trust, 54
truth, 221, 226, 261
turmoil, 181

U.S., 339
uncertainty, 136
underpinning, 45
understanding, 2, 3, 7, 8, 13, 19, 20, 23, 29, 30, 33, 38, 40–44, 46, 48, 49, 56, 61, 64, 66, 73, 75, 77, 78, 86, 89, 93, 96, 104, 115, 118, 121, 123, 124, 138, 145, 152, 154, 157, 160, 164, 167, 169, 171–176, 190, 192, 194, 198, 200, 202, 205, 206, 208, 210–212, 217, 219–228, 231, 234–237, 243, 248–254, 262, 266–270, 278, 283, 288, 290, 292, 293, 295, 296, 301, 302, 304, 306, 308, 309, 316, 319, 320, 323–329, 331, 336, 338, 343–348, 357, 363
uniqueness, 23, 46, 93, 167, 222, 227, 357
unity, 283, 334, 349
university, 251, 324
unlearning, 318
up, 1, 8, 94, 143, 181, 194, 213, 237, 265
upbringing, 170

Index 401

uplift, 6, 47, 64, 66, 124, 160, 168, 349
urgency, 57, 109
use, 5, 18, 46, 47, 69, 76, 90, 118, 123, 130, 132, 136, 147, 156, 161, 162, 181, 197, 217, 221, 235, 237, 247, 254–256, 258, 264, 304, 321, 335, 343

validation, 116, 169, 214, 221, 227, 239, 323, 354
validity, 221
value, 304
variety, 81, 294, 320
vehicle, 6, 31, 47, 84, 251, 262, 265, 267, 326, 331, 333
vibrancy, 170
victory, 357
video, 38, 49, 55, 59–61, 66, 136, 235, 345
view, 70, 74, 173, 190, 233, 253, 357
viewer, 90, 252
violence, 34, 40, 65, 76, 89, 96, 106–108, 115, 117, 143–145, 155, 160, 174, 191, 192, 199, 200, 209, 214, 228, 235, 244, 269, 286, 330, 331, 338, 350, 355
virality, 55
visibility, 19, 31, 32, 34, 37, 39, 44, 46, 48, 50, 59, 62, 70, 78, 80, 83–85, 108, 123, 135, 143, 148, 152, 154, 157, 159, 160, 163–169, 174, 189, 205, 221, 233, 235, 238, 243, 244, 255, 258–261, 263, 274, 303, 309, 310, 319, 337
vision, 82, 108, 110, 123, 138–140, 148, 152, 157, 191, 197, 198, 200–202, 220, 222, 228, 229, 245, 249, 263, 283, 287, 311–314, 317, 318, 327, 329, 334, 340, 341, 354, 356, 363, 364
visual, 46, 54, 136, 148, 162, 163, 192, 247–249, 252–255, 261, 264, 266, 313, 335, 340
vitriol, 326
voice, 37–39, 42, 48, 49, 53, 56, 62, 69, 100, 109, 110, 112, 122, 127, 129, 132, 143, 148, 171, 172, 210, 214, 237, 248, 289, 358
vulnerability, 116, 122, 179, 181, 190, 191, 193, 248, 258, 263, 264, 266, 351, 358
Vygotsky, 304

wake, 206
wardrobe, 3, 12, 21, 162
Warhol, 337
wave, 142, 214
way, 1, 7, 20, 25, 32, 39, 41, 59, 66, 71, 75, 78, 80, 82, 86, 88, 91, 95, 115, 121, 123, 127, 142, 154, 156, 159, 160, 163–166, 171, 182, 191, 200, 215, 217, 222, 225, 234, 238, 240, 243, 245, 255, 257, 265, 268, 274, 278, 303, 313, 319, 326, 327, 336, 338
weakness, 191

weapon, 256
web, 33, 270, 276, 332
well, 99, 144, 147, 160, 166, 171, 182, 186, 242, 309, 349, 352, 354
wellness, 351
whisper, 343
whole, 170
willingness, 61, 221, 318, 321, 322
wit, 27, 345
woman, 33, 268, 278, 327
word, 2, 38, 46, 59, 166, 193, 238, 247, 255, 263, 266, 326
work, 19, 22, 32–35, 40, 41, 46, 47, 62, 65, 66, 68, 77, 78, 80, 86, 88–90, 92, 93, 96, 97, 102, 109, 114, 118, 121, 122, 124, 130, 135, 138, 139, 142, 144, 146–148, 151–154, 156, 159, 163–169, 174, 176, 189–191, 193–195, 200, 206, 210, 214, 215, 217, 219–224, 227, 234, 236–238, 248–250, 252–256, 258, 261, 263–267, 269, 270, 277, 278, 283, 285, 287, 290, 293, 298, 301, 303, 305, 311, 319, 321, 323, 326, 330–332, 334–338, 340, 344, 347–349, 351, 353, 354, 356, 359, 363
workplace, 118
workshop, 211, 310, 322
world, 1–3, 5–7, 13, 16, 17, 20, 22, 39, 45, 47, 49, 52, 56, 64, 68, 70, 75, 82, 84, 89–91, 93, 97, 109, 110, 115–118, 121–123, 135, 139, 140, 146, 151, 159, 160, 165, 166, 174–177, 179, 182, 191–193, 197, 200, 206–208, 210, 215, 220, 226, 227, 234, 236, 238, 240, 241, 243, 245, 247–249, 251, 255, 262, 270, 276, 279, 283, 287, 290, 297, 304–306, 313, 314, 317, 319, 320, 326, 327, 329, 331, 338, 341, 343–345, 347, 349, 351, 354, 356, 358, 363, 364
worldview, 171
worth, 7, 15, 263
worthiness, 358

youth, 14, 66, 74, 79, 97, 98, 110–112, 116, 118, 122, 171, 184, 210–212, 217, 282, 287, 301–303, 309–311, 340, 349, 357

Milton Keynes UK
Ingram Content Group UK Ltd.
UKHW020313021124
450424UK00013B/1228